IMPORTANT

HERE IS YOUR REGISTRATION CODE TO ACCESS PREMIUM CONTENT AND MCGRAW-HILL ONLINE RESOURCES

For key premium online resources you need THIS CODE to gain access. Once the code is entered, you will be able to use the web resources for the length of your course.

Access is provided only if you have purchased a new book.

If the registration code is missing from this book, the registration screen on our website, and within your WebCT or Blackboard course will tell you how to obtain your new code. Your registration code can be used only once to establish access. It is not transferable

XFH3-KEQH-43EJ

REGISTRATION CODE

To gain access to these online resources

1. **USE** your web browser to go to: www.mhhe.com/nelson
2. **CLICK** on "First Time User"
3. **ENTER** the Registration Code printed on the tear-off bookmark on the right
4. After you have entered your registration code, click on "Register"
5. **FOLLOW** the instructions to setup your personal UserID and Password
6. **WRITE** your UserID and Password down for future reference. Keep it in a safe place.

If your course is using WebCT or Blackboard, you'll be able to use this code to access the McGraw-Hill content within your instructor's online course.

To gain access to the McGraw-Hill content in your instructor's WebCT or Blackboard course simply log into the course with the user ID and Password provided by your instructor. Enter the registration code exactly as it appears to the right when prompted by the system. You will only need to use this code the first time you click on McGraw-Hill content.

These instructions are specifically for student access. Instructors are not required to register via the above instructions.

Thank you, and welcome to your McGraw-Hill Online Resources.

978-0-07-321112-1
0-07-321112-5 t/a
Nelson
Public Communication, 1/e

Public Speaking
A Guide for the Engaged Communicator

Public Speaking
A Guide for the Engaged Communicator

Paul E. Nelson
North Dakota State University

Scott Titsworth
Ohio University

Judy C. Pearson
North Dakota State University

Boston   Burr Ridge, IL   Dubuque, IA   Madison, WI   New York   San Francisco   St. Louis
Bangkok   Bogotá   Caracas   Kuala Lumpur   Lisbon   London   Madrid   Mexico City
Milan   Montreal   New Delhi   Santiago   Seoul   Singapore   Sydney   Taipei   Toronto

PUBLIC SPEAKING: A GUIDE FOR THE ENGAGED COMMUNICATOR
Published by McGraw-Hill, a business unit of The McGraw-Hill Companies, Inc., 1221 Avenue of the Americas, New York, NY, 10020. Copyright © 2007 by The McGraw-Hill Companies, Inc. All rights reserved. No part of this publication may be reproduced or distributed in any form or by any means, or stored in a database or retrieval system, without the prior written consent of The McGraw-Hill Companies, Inc., including, but not limited to, in any network or other electronic storage or transmission, or broadcast for distance learning.
Some ancillaries, including electronic and print components, may not be available to customers outside the United States.

This book is printed on acid-free paper.

2 3 4 5 6 7 8 9 0 VNH/VNH 0 9 8 7 6

ISBN-13: 978-0-07-311258-9 (student edition)
ISBN-10: 0-07-311258-5 (student edition)
ISBN-13: 978-0-07-311262-6 (annotated instructor's edition)
ISBN-10: 0-07-311262-3 (annotated instructor's edition)

Editor in Chief: *Emily Barrosse*
Publisher: *Phillip A. Butcher*
Executive Editor: *Nanette Giles*
Sponsoring Editor: *Suzanne Earth*
Senior Marketing Manager: *Leslie Oberhuber*
Director of Development: *Rhona Robbin*
Senior Developmental Editor: *Jennie Katsaros*
Managing Editor: *Jean Dal Porto*
Senior Project Manager: *Becky Komro*
Lead Designer: *Gino Cieslik*
Text and Cover Designer: *Ellen Pettengell*
Art Editor: *Emma C. Ghiselli*

Photo Research Coordinator: *Natalia C. Peschiera*
Photo Researcher: *PoYee Oster*
Cover Photos: Bottom left: @ *Dr. Yorgos Nikas/Photo Researchers, Inc.*; all other photos: *Getty Images*
Senior Media Project Manager: *Nancy Garcia*
Production Supervisor: *Janean A. Utley*
Permissions Editor: *Julie Brown*
Composition: *10/12 New Baskerville by GTS-Los Angeles, CA Campus*
Printing: *45# Pub Matte, Von Hoffmann Corporation*

Credits: The credits section for this book begins on page C–1 and is considered an extension of the copyright page.

Library of Congress Cataloging-in-Publication Data

Public Speaking: A Guide for the Engaged Communicator
Nelson, Paul E. (Paul Edward), 1941–
  /Paul E. Nelson, Scott Titsworth, Judy C. Pearson.–Annotated
  instructor's ed.
    p. cm.
  Includes bibliographical references and index
    ISBN-13: 978-0-07-311258-9 (SE softcover: alk. paper)
    ISBN-10: 0-07-311258-5 (SE softcover: alk. paper)
    ISBN-13: 978-0-07-311262-6 (AIE softcover: alk. paper)
    ISBN-10: 0-07-311262-3 (AIE softcover: alk. paper)
  1. Public speaking. I. Titsworth, Scott. II. Pearson, Judy C. III. Title.
PN4129.15.N46 2007
808.5'1–dc22

2005049230

The Internet addresses listed in the text were accurate at the time of publication. The inclusion of a Web site does not indicate an endorsement by the authors of McGraw-Hill, and McGraw-Hill does not guarantee the accuracy of the information presented at these sites.

www.mhhe.com

brief contents

BRIEF CONTENTS

Preface   xiii

Acknowledgments   xxiv

Four Key Features   xxvi

PART ONE Preparing Your Presentations

CHAPTER **1** Getting Started   2

CHAPTER **2** Preparing Your First Presentation   24

CHAPTER **3** Selecting a Topic and Purpose   44

CHAPTER **4** Analyzing the Audience   64

PART TWO Selecting and Arranging Content

CHAPTER **5** Finding Information and Supporting Your Ideas   90

CHAPTER **6** Organizing and Outlining Your Presentation   116

CHAPTER **7** Delivering Speeches   140

CHAPTER **8** Choosing Your Words   162

CHAPTER **9** Visual Resources and Presentation Technology   182

PART THREE Types of Presentations

CHAPTER **10** Presenting to Inform   202

CHAPTER **11** Presenting Persuasive Messages   226

CHAPTER **12** Working and Presenting as a Group   250

APPENDIX **A** Speaking on Special Occasions   A

Glossary   G–1

Credits   C–1

Index   I–1

contents

Preface xiii

Acknowledgments xxiv

Four Key Features xxvi

PART ONE Preparing Your Presentations

CHAPTER ONE
Getting Started 2

Speaking Excites 4
  What's the Worst-Case Scenario? 5

Why Study Public Speaking? 6
  Democracy 6
  Life Skills 6
  Work and Career 6

Do People Really Speak Anymore? 7

What Is the Presentation Process? 8
  What Are the Seven Components of the Communication Process? 8

Why Is Public Speaking a Unique Form of Communication? 12

What Topics Should You Talk About? 13

What Should You Avoid in a Presentation? 14

Becoming an Effective Speaker 15

How to Reduce Your Fear of Presenting 18
  Understanding Communication Apprehension 18
  Reducing Anxiety 18

Resources for Review and Discussion 22

Summary 22

Key Terms 23

References 23

Application Exercises 23

CHAPTER TWO
Preparing Your First Presentation 24

Foundations of Public Communication 26
  The Roots of Rhetoric: The Five Canons 27

Tips for Preparing Your First Presentation 35
  Tips for Planning Your Presentation 35

Common Types of First Presentations 37
  Impromptu Presentations 37
  Presenting Yourself 38
  Presenting a Classmate 38
  Demonstration Presentations 39

Sample Speech for Review and Analysis 40

Resources for Review and Discussion 42

Summary 42

Key Terms 42

References 43

Application Exercises 43

CHAPTER THREE
Selecting a Topic and Purpose 44

Searching for a Topic 46
  Individual Brainstorming 47
  Categorical Brainstorming 47
  Conducting a Personal Inventory 48
  Current Topic Identification 49
  Internet Searching 49

vii

viii   Contents

Selecting a Topic   51

Evaluating Topics   52
   Appropriate for You   52
   Appropriate for the Audience   53
   Appropriate for the Occasion   53

Purposes of Speeches   54
   General Purposes   54
   Specific Purposes   57
   Thesis Statement   58

From Topic Selection to Thesis Statement: A
Three-Step Process   59

Resources for Review and Discussion   61

Summary   61

Key Terms   61

Application Exercises   61

CHAPTER **FOUR**

Analyzing the Audience   64

Audience Analysis   66
   Conventional Wisdom   67
   Demographics   68

Methods of Audience Analysis   76
   Observation   76
   Informants   77

Interviews   77
Questionnaires   77

Analysis of the Situation   79
   Size of Audience   79
   The Environment   79
   Occasion   80
   Time   80
   Importance   81

The Uniqueness of the Classroom
Audience   81

Adapting to Your Audience   82

Listening and Public Speaking   84
   The Importance of Listening   84
   Becoming a Better Listener   84

Ethics and the Audience   87

Next Steps in Audience Analysis   87

Resources for Review and Discussion   88

Summary   88

Key Terms   88

References   88

Application Exercises   89

PART **TWO**   Selecting and Arranging Content

CHAPTER **FIVE**

Finding Information and Supporting Your Ideas   90

Why You'll Benefit from Research   92

Finding Sources of Information   93
   Personal Experience   93
   Interviews with Others   94
   Library Resources   96
   The Internet   98
   Other Resources on the Web   102

Evaluating and Using Sources of Information   104
   Criteria for Evaluating Sources   104
   Citing Sources of Information Correctly   105

Identifying Appropriate Supporting Materials   106
   Examples   107
   Surveys   108
   Testimony   109
   Numbers and Statistics   110

Analogies   110
Definitions   111

The Ethical Use of Supporting Material   111

Resources for Review and Discussion   113

Summary   113

Key Terms   113

References   114

Application Exercises   114

CHAPTER **SIX**

Organizing and Outlining Your Presentation   116

Why Organize?   118

How to Organize the Body of the Presentation   118
   Emphasize Main Points   118
   Determine the Order of the Main Points   120
   Incorporate Supporting Materials   127

What Holds the Presentation Together? 127

Principles of Outlining 128

Subordination 129
Division 129
Parallelism 129

Types of Outlines 130

The Preparation Outline 130
The Formal Sentence Outline 131
The Key Word Outline 133

How Do You Introduce Your Presentation? 134

Gaining and Maintaining Favorable Attention 134
Relating the Topic to the Audience 135
Relating the Topic to the Presenter 135
Previewing the Message 135

What Are the Functions of a Conclusion? 136

Tips for Concluding 136

Resources for Review and Discussion 138

Summary 138

Key Terms 138

References 139

Application Exercises 139

CHAPTER **SEVEN**

Delivering Speeches 140

What Is Effective Delivery? 142

What Are the Four Modes of Delivery? 143

Extemporaneous Mode 143
Memorized Mode 144
Manuscript Mode 145
Impromptu Mode 146

How Can You Use Your Voice Effectively? 148

Adjust Your Rate to Content, Audience, and Situation 148
Use Pause for Effect 149
Use Duration for Attention 149
Use Rhythm to Establish Tempo 150
Use Pitch for Expression 150
Use Volume for Emphasis 151
Use Enunciation for Clarity 151
Use Fluency for Fluidity 152

How Can You Use Your Body to Communicate Effectively? 152

Use Eye Contact to Hold Audience Attention 153
Use Facial Expression to Communicate 154
Use Gestures to Reinforce Message 154
Use Bodily Movement for Purpose 155
Wear Appropriate Attire 156

Question-and-Answer Sessions 157

How Can You Improve Your Delivery? 158

Resources for Review and Discussion 159

Summary 159

Key Terms 159

References 159

Application Exercises 160

CHAPTER **EIGHT**

Choosing Your Words 162

Word Power 164

Language Is Symbolic 164
Language Is Powerful 165
Words Organize and Classify 165
Words Shape Thought 166

Levels of Abstraction 167

Denotative and Connotative Words 168

Descriptive and Evaluative Language 168

Comparison and Contrast 169

Literal and Figurative Language 169

Written and Spoken Language 169

Using Language Respectfully 170

Use Inclusive Language 170
Use Approved Names 171
Stereotypes and Differences 171

What Words Should You Use? 172

Use Words That Simplify 172
Use Substitutions and Definitions 173
Use Synonyms and Antonyms 173
Reveal the Origin of the Word 173
Use Words That Evoke Images 174
Use Correct Grammar 174
Use Repetition 175
Alluring Alliteration 175

Using Words Ethically 176

Exaggeration and Oversimplification 176
Language and Perspective Taking 176

Tips for Using Language in Presentations 177

Last Thoughts on Language 178

Resources for Review and Discussion 179

Summary 179

Key Terms 179

References 180

Application Exercises 180

Contents

CHAPTER NINE
Visual Resources and Presentation Technology   182

How You Can Benefit from Using Sensory Aids   184

Types of Visual Aids and Other Sensory Resources   185

Electronic and Multimedia Resources   185
Other Visual and Sensory Resources   194

Tips on Using Visual and Sensory Aids   197

Remember Your Purpose   199

Resources for Review and Discussion   200

Summary   200

Key Terms   200

References   200

Application Exercises   201

PART THREE   Types of Presentations

CHAPTER TEN
Presenting to Inform   202

Principles of Informative Presentations   204

Relate the Presenter to the Topic   205
Relate the Topic to the Audience   205

How to Identify the Purpose of Your Informative Presentations   206

Create Information Hunger   207
Help the Audience Understand the Information   208
Help the Audience Remember the Information   209
Help the Audience Apply the Information   211

Principles of Learning   212

Build on the Known   212
Use Humor and Wit   212
Use Sensory Aids   214
Organize to Optimize Learning   214
Reward Your Listeners   215

Skills for the Informative Presenter   216

Defining in an Informative Presentation   216
Describing in an Informative Presentation   216
Explaining in an Informative Presentation   217
Demonstrating in an Informative Presentation   217

Ethics and Informative Presentations   218

An Example of an Informative Presentation   219

Resources for Review and Discussion   223

Summary   223

Key Terms   223

References   223

Application Exercises   224

CHAPTER ELEVEN
Presenting Persuasive Messages   226

The Role of Persuasion in Public Discourse   228

You as Target of and Sender of Persuasion   228
What Are Persuasive Presentations?   229

Types of Persuasive Presentations   230

What Communication Research Says about Persuasion?   231

What Should You Know about Your Audience?   231
How Can You Create an Effective Message?   232

Fact, Value, and Policy in Persuasive Presentations   233

Organizing Your Persuasive Presentation   234

Introducing the Persuasive Presentation   234
Concluding the Persuasive Presentation   234
Choosing Patterns of Organization for Persuasive Presentations   235

Persuasive Strategies   236

Consistency Persuades   236
Small, Gradual Changes Persuade   236
Benefits Persuade   236
Need Fulfillment Persuades   237

Critical Thinking through Reasoning   238

Using Inductive Reasoning   238
Using Deductive Reasoning   239
Using Hard Evidence in Reasoning   239
Using Soft Evidence in Reasoning   239
Using Reasoning from Cause   240
Using Reasoning from Sign   240
Using Reasoning from Generalization   240

Contents   **xi**

Avoid Fallacies   241

Ethics and Persuasive Speaking   242

An Example of a Persuasive Presentation   243

Resources for Review and Discussion   247

Summary   247

Key Terms   247

References   248

Application Exercises   248

CHAPTER **TWELVE**
Working and Presenting as a Group   250

How Are Small Groups and Public Communication Connected?   252

What Are Small Groups?   252

Why Are Small Groups Used for Presentations?   253

Key Skills for Effective Group Presentations   255

Key Skills for Effective Group Communication   256

Group Leadership Skills   256

Group Interaction Skills   258

Improving Your Group Communication Skills   260

Group Problem Solving   261

Wording the Discussion Question   262

Discussing Criteria   263

Identifying Alternatives   264

Evaluating Alternatives   264

Types of Group Presentations   265

Symposia   265

Panels   269

Debates   270

Evaluating Group Productivity   271

Resources for Review and Discussion   274

Summary   274

Key Terms   274

References   275

Application Exercises   275

APPENDIX **A**
Speaking on Special Occasions   A

Unique Characteristics of Special Occasion Presentations   A–2

Purpose   A–2

Style   A–2

Organization   A–3

Formality   A–3

Types of Special Occasion Presentations   A–4

Presentations to Welcome   A–4

Presentations to Pay Tribute   A–4

Presentations to Introduce   A–5

Presentations to Nominate   A–5

Presentations to Dedicate   A–6

Presentations to Commemorate   A–6

Presentations to Entertain   A–7

How to Prepare Special Occasion Presentations   A–7

Sample Special Occasion Presentation   A–8

Resources for Review and Discussion   A–10

Summary   A–10

Key Terms   A–10

Application Exercises   A–10

Glossary   G

Credits   C–1

Index   I–1

preface

PREFACE

Public Speaking: A Guide for the Engaged Communicator is designed for the beginning speaker. The primary goal of the book is to efficiently guide you toward becoming an effective, confident communicator in public situations. As you read the chapters, you will learn how to:

- Find a topic that is appropriate for your assignment and audience
- Discover and select information that is relevant to your topic
- Adapt your ideas to a specific audience
- Organize your ideas for greater understanding
- Deliver your ideas well
- Evaluate presentations, including your own, and suggest improvements
- Approach your work ethically

Public Speaking: A Guide for the Engaged Communicator also was written so that you will see speaking in public as a critical component of democratic societies and healthy communities. Throughout this book, the authors integrate student-oriented examples of presentations that concern the themes listed below. You will see in the text that we refer to these themes as VITAL, because of their immediate and daily relevance to our homes, communities, cultures, and world.

- Environment
- Education
- Health
- Democracy
- Ethics
- Diversity
- Technology

Through these seven vital themes, we strive to convey a hopeful tone and positive outlook, intended to reflect the actual contributions that students and their schools are now making to their communities in the form of course-related service learning and other types of civic engagement. Campus Compact, a national coalition of more than 950 U.S. university presidents representing more than 5 million students, reports that in 2004, 30% of the students on its member campuses participated in community service, spending an average of 4 hours per week on service-related activities. The organization estimates that the value of this service to local communities was $4.45 billion during the 32-week school year in 2003 and 2004. You have heard the clichés and stereotypes about "young people today" being self-centered, unmotivated, and interested only in computer games, instant

xiii

messaging, and celebrities. Based on studies by Campus Compact and UCLA's Higher Education Research Institute, these biases are far from reality.

We surmise from the statistics and from activities in our own campus communities that students today should have plenty to talk about in their public speaking courses. By using vital themes in the numerous student-oriented examples throughout the text, we have made a deliberate, concerted effort to represent public speaking as a crucial component of service and civic engagement and as a practical conduit for progress, collaboration, and personal happiness.

Whether or not you attend a school that incorporates civic engagement and service learning into its curricular and extracurricular programs, we hope that the examples in this book will inspire you to think about issues you truly care about and to look at the concerns of your own local community when considering your speech assignments.

At the end of the school term, many students in public speaking courses reflect on how much they have grown through the course. We can only imagine what happens to those students taking the course while simultaneously engaging in the community by working as volunteers, taking a course with service learning credit, or just spending a little time to explore what is happening in their towns. That they are truly making the world a better place is the only thought that comes to our minds! Martin Luther King Jr. once famously said, "Everybody can be great because everybody can serve."

We finally hope that both students and instructors will appreciate the brevity of this text. We know you are busy with heavy courseloads, volunteer work, family life, and full- and part-time employment, not to mention all that speech preparation! In these 12 chapters, we wanted to provide the basics with plenty of examples that would resonate with your lives. Good luck, and please tell us what you think of our effort.

Speech Is Free.

Make It Matter.

Paul Nelson
Scott Titsworth
Judy Pearson

Preface   **xv**

Chapter 1: Getting Started

Chapter-by-Chapter

- Positions public speaking as an exciting and positive experience.
- Unique section "What's the Worst-Case Scenario?" creatively addresses concerns of the first-time public speaker.
- Explains how the course can improve students' lives.
- Portrays public speaking as a critical component of democracy at the local community level.
- Clearly demonstrates the seven components of the communication process.
- Describes the unique characteristics of public presentations.
- Encourages students to choose appropriate, vital topics.
- Advises students about what to avoid when presenting.
- Prepares students for their first speech.
- Stresses the importance of ethics in public speaking.
- Links students to view the "Relating a Speech to the Listeners' Self-Interest" on the Student CD-ROM.

"The seven components of the public speaking process are especially well-written, using language that students will find accessible."   *Jean Perry, Glendale Community College, California*

"I really like the conversational tone of this chapter. It speaks directly to students and presents a positive, upfront discussion of fear."   *Gayle Pesavento, John A. Logan College*

"My favorite section of the chapter is "What's the Worst-Case Scenario?" In my experience no textbook has so creatively laid out what students really worry about. I talk about this in class, and it was great to see it published."   *Victoria Leonard, College of the Canyons*

"It is interesting that you start right away with introducing ethics and integrating it throughout the text, rather than treating it as a separate chapter. This is a much better approach."   *Mark Chase, Slippery Rock University*

Chapter 2: Preparing Your First Presentation

- Introduces readers to the classical roots of public communication by using the Five Canons of Rhetoric as a practical framework for preparing the first presentation.
- Emphasizes substance in relation to delivery.
- Introduces foundational concepts addressed in subsequent chapters.
- Shows students how to develop a clearly identifiable introduction, body, and conclusion for their first presentations.
- Provides practical tips for planning and preparing impromptu presentations, speeches of introduction, and demonstration presentations.
- Analyzes a sample speech of introduction.
- Links students to view the following videos on the Student CD-ROM: "Using an Analogy" and "How to Play the Drums."

"The table of the Rhetorical Canons provides an easily digestible method of under-standing the skills necessary for effective speaking. I especially appreciate the use of concept mapping—a technique students will relate to and successfully co-create. It also provides concrete and constructive examples of creative language and narrative. Excellent hints for preparing a first presentation without overwhelming students." Jean Perry, Glendale Community College, California

"Generally, my least favorite chapter in a public speaking text is the introduction to the first presentation. Having said that, I find this chapter to be a true exception. You have provided abundant and clear examples to which students will certainly be able to relate."   Thomas Stewart, Slippery Rock University

"The first thing I notice about Chapter Two is how unthreatening it makes the first presentation seem."   Sandra Pensoneau, Wayne State University

Chapter 3: Selecting a Topic and Purpose

- Helps students select important topics quickly and efficiently.
- Presents five methods for searching for a topic and integrates nearly 100 contemporary examples while doing so.
- Emphasizes appropriateness of topic according to the speaker, audience, and occasion, and provides brief, practical guidelines for achieving topic appropriateness.
- Teaches about specific purpose and thesis statements according to three main types of speeches: informative, persuasive, and special occasion. Integrates nearly 80 examples, all written to resonate with students.
- Unique Table 3.2 takes students from topic to purpose to thesis statement for three types of presentations.
- Prompts students to view the video clip "Conveying the Central Idea" on the Student CD-ROM.

"'Selecting a Topic' presents useful information that students can return to and locate with ease."   Scott Douglass, Chattanooga State Technical College

"I like the importance that this chapter places on the selection of significant and audi-ence relevant topics. An excellent chapter! Practical suggestions and good examples make the chapter useful and clear."   George Ziegelmueller, Wayne State University

"As I read this chapter, I got a lot of ideas for how to approach the material in my own classes, and found the end-of-chapter section to have helpful in-class and home-work exercises."   Dayle C. Hardy-Short, Northern Arizona University

"The specific purpose examples are very well done. You provide consistency in form while dealing with a diversity of topics."   Thomas Stewart, Slippery Rock University

Chapter 4: Analyzing the Audience

- Begins with a precise definition of audience analysis and by asking the stu-dent to identify audiences they may face during their lifetime.
- Offers unique considerations of audience, including conventional wisdom and worldview.

Preface **xvii**

- Portrays the uniqueness of the classroom audience with practical "implications" for the speaker to consider.
- Explains how to adapt your presentation to your audience.
- Demonstrates engagement with the audience and audience adaptation through a practical discussion of active listening.
- Numerous examples support both the conceptual and practical aspects of this chapter.

"I like the fact that there is just one chapter devoted to this topic. I think the examples are easy to understand and represent situations that the students will be able to identify." Karen Otto, Florida Community College, Jacksonville

"I appreciate the emphasis on diversity throughout the examples, exercises, and explanations of the topics." Kathleen Clark, University of Akron

"Perhaps one of the most useful and comprehensive discussions of audience analysis that I've read in a public speaking text." Jonathan Amsbary, University of Alabama

Chapter 5: Finding Information and Supporting Your Ideas

- Presents a detailed explanation of how effective research skills can improve all aspects of a presentation, ranging from more creative introductions to more confident delivery.
- Discusses how personal experience, interviews, library resources, and the Internet can be used to locate supporting materials during the invention process.
- Provides a practical set of key criteria for evaluating sources. Special attention is devoted to the evaluation of Internet sources.
- Teaches readers how to cite sources in both written format and orally during a presentation.
- Illustrates how to effectively use examples, surveys, testimonials, statistics, analogies, and definitions as supporting material during a presentation.
- Identifies three ethical principles to guide the selection and use of supporting material. Students are introduced to the topic of plagiarism as an ethical consideration.
- Links to the following videos on the Student CD-ROM: "Using an Example," "Using an Analogy," "Using Testimony," "Using Statistics," and "Supporting Stem Cell Research."

"An excellent and timely introduction to research on the Web and to the distinction between searching the Web and dealing with databases at the university library." Kathleen Clark, University of Akron

"The examples in this chapter are especially relevant to common student attitudes about information gathering." Charla Windley, University of Idaho

Chapter 6: Organizing and Outlining Your Presentation

- Reveals why organization is important to the speaker and to the audience.
- Demonstrates how to shape your presentation into a few main points.

- Offers examples of time-sequence, spatial relations, cause-effect, topical sequence, problem-solution, and Monroe's Motivated Sequence patterns of organization.
- Links organizational patterns to speech purposes.
- Explains how to use supporting material, transitions, signposts, internal previews, and internal reviews.
- Explains the principles of subordination, division, and parallelism in outlining.
- Shows examples of a preparation outline, a key word outline, and a formal sentence outline.
- Focuses on the functions of the introduction, the body, and the conclusion.
- Links students to the following videos on the Student CD-ROM: "Relating a Story," "Citing a Quotation," "Arousing Curiosity," "Providing an Illustration," and "Relating the Presentation to the Listener's Self Interest."

"Unlike books that just teach to make students learn, this book gets students thinking on their own. Thinking about what they know, how they can teach, and how to have organized thoughts. The ideas in this chapter about organization can be applied to more areas of a student's education than just public speaking." Angela Lynn Blais, University of Minnesota, Duluth

"Most texts typically go through the 'how' of organizing with minimal support. I particularly like the way this text gives the 'how' AND the 'why' of organizing a presentation. The explanations for each step and the examples of each technique or approach show the reader why each is important and how it will help them be more effective, successful communicators." Dudley Turner, University of Akron

Chapter 7: Delivering Speeches

- Explains and compares the different modes of delivery—extemporaneous, memorized, manuscript, and impromptu, with an emphasis on the extemporaneous mode.
- Reveals how to use voice and body, the nonverbal aspects of delivery: pitch, rate, pause, projection, enunciation, pronunciation, and articulation.
- Emphasizes fluency and vocal variety and offers a list of practical guidelines for improving vocal aspects of delivery.
- Provides advice on bodily aspects of delivery: gestures, facial expression, eye contact, and purposeful movement.
- Offers guidelines for appropriate attire.
- Concludes with practical steps for improving delivery.
- Links students to the following videos on the Student CD-ROM: "Citing a Quotation" and "I'll Take the Cow Over the Chemicals."

"The definition of delivery 'that does not call attention to itself' sets the tone for a useful discussion and explanation of the essential components of effective delivery. This helps inexperienced speakers get out of the performance mode right from the beginning." Charla Windley, University of Idaho

"I found the discussion question asking whether content is more important than aspects of delivery to be thought-provoking for students."   Karen Otto, Florida Community College, Jacksonville

"I appreciated the discussion of diversity. Eye contact is culturally based, and many texts make suggestions about eye contact without taking culture into account." Victoria Leonard, College of the Canyons

"The section on clarity, articulation, pronunciation, and fluency is superior. The book also has valuable suggestions on appropriate attire."   Donald Reuter, North Carolina State University, Raleigh

Chapter 8: Choosing Your Words

- Explains the symbolic nature of words, the power of language, and how to use words to organize, classify, and shape thought.
- Demonstrates that language can be relatively concrete or abstract, denotative or connotative, descriptive or evaluative, literal or figurative.
- Shows similarities and differences between written and spoken language and between reading and listening.
- Offers guidelines for avoiding problems with words and using inclusive, respectful language.
- Discusses a selection of word categories to use: words that simplify or define, words that are similar or different, words with a history, and words that evoke images.
- Encourages correct grammar, repetition, and alliteration while avoiding oversimplification and exaggeration.
- Concludes with practical tips for using language in presentations.
- Links students to the following videos on the Student CD-ROM: "Making a Contrast," "Using a Vivid Image," and "Using an Example."

"The section on using words ethically is outstanding."   James Duncan, Ivy Tech Community College, Indianapolis

"I have never seen a better explanation of using language effectively."   Carole Madere, Southeastern Louisiana University

"This is my favorite chapter. It is chock full of interesting and valuable information." Rachel Santine, Hutchinson Community College

"This chapter is exceptionally well written and practical. The examples are really fresh, strong, and accessible to students."   Rebecca Roberts, University of Wyoming

"I love this chapter . . . I found it to be entertaining and clever, diverse and representative of most language skills."   Diona Wilson, Brigham Young University

Chapter 9: Visual Resources and Presentation Technology

- Uses the concept of dual coding to illustrate the importance of using visual and other sensory aids to supplement the verbal presentation of a message.

- Explains how text slides, tables, charts, flowcharts, pictures, and video can be used to create effective sensory resources for a presentation.
- Refers to studies related to visual preferences among co-cultures.
- Recommends key things to emphasize or avoid when using PowerPoint during a presentation.
- Explains how unique visual and sensory aids like self-demonstrations, objects, models, audio/video, handouts, slides, and transparencies can be used.
- Provides several tips for using any type of sensory aid, including the ethical use of sensory aids, the need for practice, the careful selection and/or creation of such aids, and the need to be audience-centered.
- Links students to the following videos on the Student CD-ROM: "How to Play the Drums" and "Presenting a PowerPoint Build."

"I very much appreciate that the authors do not go on and on about creating Power-Point slides, but give the information relevant for their content, and useful to some-one who has a basic understanding of PowerPoint." Sandra Pensoneau, Wayne State University

"This chapter gives a great explanation of how to incorporate PowerPoint into a pre-sentation. My current text does not accomplish that effectively." Karen Otto, Florida Community College, Jacksonville

"Very good information about being audience-centered when using sensory aids." James Duncan, Ivy Tech Community College, Indianapolis

"This chapter is everything I want a chapter on presentation aids to be. The authors did an excellent job of choosing how much of the technology to explain. It is enough to give us possibilities and parameters and not so much to become outdated in a year. Sending students to their campus media resources is an excellent approach to this problem. Your chapter . . . with its essential topics and appropriate approach to tech-nology is a very pleasant, positive surprise." Charla Windley, University of Idaho

"This chapter takes a very practical approach, considering that some students have never used PowerPoint or related technology, while some students are extremely adept." Marc Skinner, University of Idaho

Chapter 10: Presenting to Inform

- Introduces informative speaking using two basic principles—to relate the presenter to the topic and to relate the topic to the audience.
- Explains the four purposes of informative presentations.
- Explores how learning styles relate to informative presentations.
- Illustrates how you should organize your informative presentations to opti-mize learning.
- Offers four basic skills for informative speaking: defining, describing, explaining, and demonstrating.
- Explores the ethical scenarios you should consider when speaking to inform.
- Provides a brief, practical "Checklist for the Informative Presentation."
- Concludes with a sample annotated informative presentation (presented as a transcription of an actual student speech).

- Links students to the following videos on the Student CD-ROM: "Mad Cow Disease," "Relating a Story," "Citing a Quotation," "Arousing Curiosity," and "Competitive Sports."

"I especially like the principles of learning. Our current text does not address the area of learning styles and I like this coverage in this text." Lisa Orick, Albuquerque Technical Vocational Institute Community College

"The two principles of informative speaking is a new approach I've not seen. I think it is an effective way to convey the audience adaptation challenges of informative speaking." Karrin Vasby Anderson, Colorado State University

"The strength of this chapter is the way the key ideas on speaking are reiterated in the frame of informative speaking; this reinforces the students' understanding of the larger frame of reference, rather than looking at the chapters as discrete units." Margaret Finucane, John Carroll University

"I love the term 'information hunger'." Cory Tomasson, Illinois Valley Community College

"This is a great chapter. The information showing defining, describing, explaining, and demonstrating will help students think more broadly about their presentations." Dudley Turner, University of Akron

Chapter 11: Presenting Persuasive Messages

- Relates persuasion to messages sent and received in everyday life.
- Presents three types of persuasive presentations: to inspire, to convince, and to actuate.
- Examines what social science research reveals about the audience and the message in persuasive presentations.
- Explains questions of fact, value, and policy in persuasive presentations.
- Reviews organization patterns related to persuasive presentation, including introductions and conclusions.
- Offers three basic persuasive strategies of persuasion: small, gradual change; benefits; and need fulfillment.
- Examines critical thinking, including seven types of reasoning.
- Portrays fallacies as errors in reasoning that weaken an argument and that breach ethical persuasive speaking.
- Offers practical guidelines for ethical persuasive presentations.
- Provides a brief, practical "Checklist for the Informative Presentation."
- Concludes with a sample annotated persuasive presentation (presented as a transcription of an actual student speech).
- Links students to the following videos on the Student CD-ROM: "Motorcycle Club," "Relating a Speech to the Listener's Self-Interest," "Stem Cell Research," "Using Inductive Reasoning," "Using Deductive Reasoning," "Using Statistics," "Appealing to Motivations," "Using an Analogy," "I'll Take the Cow Over the Chemicals," and "Sharks: The Misunderstood Monster."

"I think that treating persuasion in one chapter is excellent; too often public speaking texts belabor the topic in two chapters." Margaret Finucane, John Carroll University

"I enjoyed the way the chapter was introduced, and found it effective that the authors lay out how persuasion is used in everyday life. They also provide a clear contrast between informative presentations and persuasive presentations." Victoria Leonard, College of the Canyons

"One of the main strengths of the chapter for me is the use of examples. They're quick, relevant, and easily understandable. With so many factors to consider in persuasive messages, and so many parts that could be included, the examples are particularly helpful in navigating one's way through the parts and principles of persuasive presentations." Sandra Pensoneau, Wayne State University

"Throughout this text, the mix of academic and professional examples has pleased me, and this chapter excels in this regard. The extended description and analysis of the goals of persuasive messages is especially valuable, and often something ignored by other texts." Thomas Stewart, Slippery Rock University

"The example persuasive presentation, with the various parts marked, is quite nice. I think an important point about these examples (including the one in the previous chapter) is that they aren't exemplars; that is, they have both positive aspects and aspects that could use polishing. This gives instructors and readers much food for thought and many points of discussion." Sandra Pensoneau, Wayne State University

"I like the way "What You Should Know about Your Audience?" and "How Can You Create an Effective Message?" build on everything the student will have learned to this point. This chapter and the persuasive speech assignment truly are a capstone experience that pulls everything they've learned together." Kathleen Clark, University of Akron

Chapter 12: Working and Presenting as a Group

- Explains the basics of small groups: what they are and why they are used for presentations.
- Offers unique, practical guidelines for effective group presentations.
- Offers key, practical skills for effective group communication, including leadership and interaction.
- Frames groups as systematic problem solvers.
- Reviews three types of group presentations: symposia, panels, and debates.
- Chapter figures include useful models for coordinating symposia, panels, and debates, as well as practical forms for reporting group progress and evaluating group members.

"There is not one aspect of this chapter I would change. The definitions are clear, and the examples are excellent." Victoria Leonard, College of the Canyons

"Your chapter provides a comprehensive yet concise introduction to group communication, demonstrating its importance and ties to individual presentations. I particularly appreciate the review of common group presentation formats—something not often done well in other textbooks." Thomas Stewart, Slippery Rock University

"The different kinds of symposia are quite interesting. It prompts me to think of interesting assignments students could create, and I think students would be able to read this chapter and be informed about presenting effectively as a group. Students will find the figures showing ways to organize formats for presentations to be very helpful models." Kathleen Clark, University of Akron

Preface   xxiii

Appendix A: Speaking on Special Occasions

- Explains how special occasion speaking differs from other types of presentations from the perspectives of purpose, style, organization, and formality.
- Describes basic attributes of seven types of special occasion presentations: to welcome, pay tribute, introduce, nominate, dedicate, commemorate, and entertain.
- Unique worksheet offers a practical format for preparing any special occasion presentation.
- Concludes with a sample, annotated special occasion presentation: a speech to pay tribute.
- Links students to the following video on the Student CD-ROM: "Motorcycle Club."

acknowledgments

ACKNOWLEDGMENTS

Public Speaking: A Guide for the Engaged Communicator was a team effort guided by our publisher Phil Butcher, brilliantly conceptualized by executive editor Nanette Giles, and managed almost daily by senior development editor Jennie Katsaros. To the editing, design, and production group at McGraw-Hill, we offer our deepest gratitude. We understand that getting a first edition from manuscript to the warehouse is a long, arduous journey, and recognize the following people who guided us so well and with such patience along the route: senior project manager Becky Komro, managing editor Jean Dal Porto, production assistant Margaret Leslie, lead designer Gino Cieslik, art editor Emma Ghiselli, photo research coordinator Natalia Peschiera, production supervisor Janean Utley and, finally, Linda Toy, vice president of editing, design, and production. We appreciate the expertise of senior media project manager Nancy Garcia, who developed the fabulous Online Learning Center and Student CD-ROM for this text specifically. Finally, we are grateful to have Leslie Oberhuber as our senior marketing manager. We know she will bring *Public Speaking* to the market with much creativity, industry, and wisdom.

Over 60 communication colleagues across the country read and shaped this text—from the first draft to the first set of page proofs. We hope you will recognize your contributions as you review the text, because we regarded all your suggestions and questions quite seriously. Some of the reviewers prefer not to be named on these pages, but we want to make sure they know we are as impressed with their dedication, intelligence, and integrity as with that of the instructors we list outright below. Thank you all.

Jonathan Amsbary,
University of Alabama, Birmingham

Karrin Vasby Anderson,
Colorado State University

Angela Blais,
University of Minnesota, Duluth

Nanci Burk,
Glendale Community College, Arizona

Mark E. Chase,
Slippery Rock University

Terence L. Chmielewski,
University of Wisconsin, Eau Claire

Kathleen Clark,
University of Akron

Terry Cole,
Appalachian State University

Genevieve Dardeau,
University of South Alabama

William Davidson,
University of Wisconsin, Stevens Point

Scott Douglass,
Chattanooga State Technical College

James C. Duncan,
Ivy Tech Community College, Indianapolis

Margaret Finucane,
John Carroll University

Margarita Gangotena,
Blinn College

Myra Grinner,
Sinclair Community College

Virginia Gregg,
Minnesota State University, Moorhead

Acknowledgments

Keith Groff,
Franklin University

Laurie Haleta,
South Dakota State University

Dayle Hardy-Short,
Northern Arizona University

Carla Harrell,
Old Dominion University

Mark Hickson,
University of Alabama, Birmingham

David Hoffman,
Ancilla College and Goshen College

William M. Keith,
University of Wisconsin, Milwaukee

Nancy Legge,
Idaho State University

Victoria Leonard,
College of the Canyons

Carole Madere,
Southeast Louisiana University

Charla Markham Shaw,
University of Texas, Arlington

Eric Marlow,
Southeast Louisiana University

Rozilyn Miller,
University of Central Oklahoma

Rebecca Lea Mikesell,
University of Scranton

Lisa Orick,
Albuquerque TVI CC

Karen Otto,
Florida Community College,
Jacksonville

A. David Payne,
University of South Florida, Tampa

Sandra Pensoneau,
Wayne State University

Jean Perry,
Glendale Community College,
California

Gayle Pesavento,
John A. Logan College

Donald Reuter,
North Carolina State University,
Raleigh

Don Rice,
Concordia College

Rebecca Roberts,
University of Wyoming, Laramie

Clayton Redding,
Blinn College

Beth Lynne Ritter-Guth,
Lehigh Carbon Community College

Paul Rodriguez,
Hinds Community College, Raymond

Rachel Santine,
Hutchinson Community College

Marc Skinner,
University of Idaho

Alison Stafford,
Hinds Community College, Raymond

Thomas Stewart,
Slippery Rock University

Cory Tomasson,
Illinois Valley Community College

Dudley Turner,
University of Akron

Michelle Violanti,
University of Tennessee, Knoxville

Diona Wilson,
Brigham Young University

Gerald Wilson,
University of South Alabama

Nancy Wheeler,
South Dakota State University

Charla Windley,
University of Idaho

George Ziegelmueller,
Wayne State University

Kent Zimmerman,
Sinclair Community College

Speech Is Free. Make It Matter.

Freedom of speech and public speaking are critical components of a healthy democracy. Nelson, Titsworth, and Pearson promote this declaration by using examples that reflect vital personal, social, and political themes and that portray campus communities as highly productive local democracies where these themes are played out every day. By drawing on real issues and initiatives taking place in communities across the United States, *Public Speaking: A Guide for the Engaged Communicator* consistently demonstrates that public communication is directly related to what people care about, what people want, and what people do. We think this approach will help you quickly perceive the important role of public speaking, and we hope it will guide you to use public speaking effectively when you engage in your communities.

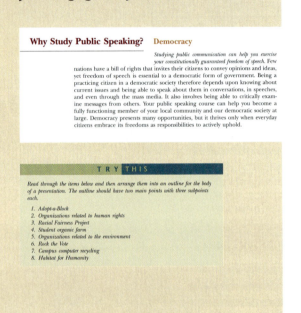

"This text draws on examples which reflect the lives of students and young adults. It integrates many of their interests into the course, helping them see that the public speaking course is more than a speed bump along the way to their degrees."

James Duncan, Ivy Technical Community College, Indianapolis

Practice Exercises Are Interesting and Relevant

Try This

TRY THIS

Use Yahoo! to find information about an issue relevant to your community. Be careful—not all Web sites come from credible or reliable sources. What did you learn from this exercise that could be used to narrow speech topics for your classroom speeches?

TRY THIS

Given your own world view or perspective because of who you are, you should try to think of individuals or groups that your own words tend to treat less than fairly. For example, how do you refer to a person in a wheelchair, a refugee or immigrant, or individuals from a culture other than your own? For more, go to the Wikipedia Web site, http://en.wikipedia.com/wiki/political_correctness.

E-Note

E-Note

PRACTICING FOR IMPROMPTU PRESENTATIONS

The *Architects of Peace* project celebrates 70 women and men from around the world who devoted their lives to community activism and issues of social justice. Using the various suggestions within this section of the textbook, select a person profiled on the *Architects of Peace* Web site (**http://scu.edu/ethics/architects**) and prepare either a short impromptu speech or speech of introduction for that person.

End-of-Chapter Application Exercises

m. To inform my audience about the steps to earning the Eagle Scout Award.
n. A passion for cooking.

2. Divide a piece of paper into four columns. Write one of the following general topics at the top of each of the four columns.
   a. Job experiences I have had.
   b. Places I have traveled.
   c. City, state, or area I am from.
   d. People who make me angry.
   e. Happy experiences I have had.
   f. Unusual experiences I have had.
   g. Personal experiences I have had with crime.
   h. My involvement in marriage, divorce, or other family matters.
   i. My experiences with members of other groups—the old, the young, ethnic groups.
   j. The effect of the drug culture on my life.
   k. My relationship to local, state, or federal government.
   l. My background in painting, music, sculpture, theater, dance, or other fine arts.
   m. My feelings about grades, a college education, sororities and fraternities, college requirements, student government, or alternatives to a college education.
   n. My reactions to current radio, television, or film practices, policies, or programming.
   o. Recent Supreme Court decisions that affect me.
   p. My personal and career goals.

Now, write down specific topics under each of the four general topic areas you chose. Spend no more than five minutes on this exercise brainstorming. Next, underline one topic in each of the four columns that is particularly interesting to you. From these four topics, select the one about which you have the most information or the best access to information. Can you adapt the topic to your specific audience?

Tables and Figures

TABLE 3.2 FROM TOPIC TO PURPOSE TO THESIS STATEMENT

	INFORMATIVE PRESENTATION	PERSUASIVE PRESENTATION	SPECIAL OCCASION PRESENTATION
STEP ONE TOPIC	Wetlands ecology	The ethics of publicly held companies	An anniversary tribute
STEP TWO PURPOSE	To increase the audience's knowledge of wetland ecology	To convince the audience that publicly held businesses have community responsibility	To honor the couple on their tenth anniversary
STEP THREE THESIS STATEMENT	Puerto Rico's Caribbean National Forest is a national treasure.	U.S. businesses need to restore trust with the public.	Congratulations to Ann and Mark on a decade of love and happiness.

A Checklist for the Informative Speech

____ 1. Have you created a desire for information?
____ 2. Have you related the topic to your audience, its modes of learning, and learning styles?
____ 3. Have you revealed your relationship to the topic?
____ 4. Have you used wit and humor when appropriate?
____ 5. Have you helped your audience understand your information?
____ 6. Have you helped your audience remember your information?
____ 7. Can the audience apply the information?
____ 8. Have you built new information on old information?
____ 9. Have you used presentational aids or demonstration when needed?
____ 10. Have you organized your message effectively and presented information ethically?

Figure 10.2

Chapter Structure Is Clear and Consistent

Learning Objectives open each chapter with a clear indication of what will be covered.

What will you learn?
When you have read and thought about this chapter, you will be able to:
1. Explain why a speaker should analyze the audience.
2. Determine how audience characteristics affect your presentation.
3. Identify some of the demographic features of the audience that you should consider in your audience analysis.

A simple, direct learning framework makes what you will be reading, doing, and thinking about in each chapter clear and consistent.

Application Exercises give you a chance to apply what you have studied to interesting exercises that focus on fundamental chapter concepts.

APPLICATION EXERCISES

Go to the self-quizzes on the *Public Speaking* CD-ROM and the Online Learning Center at www.mhhe.com/nelson to test your knowledge of the chapter concepts.

1. Translate the abstract terms in the column on the left into more concrete terms in the blanks on the right.
   a. A recent article
   b. An ethnic neighborhood
   c. A good professor
   d. A big profit
   e. A distant land
   f. A tough course
   g. A tall building
   h. He departed rapidly
   i. She dresses poorly
   j. They are religious

Narrative offers clear headings and key terms presented in boldface and defined in italics.

Audience Analysis What is audience analysis? **Audience analysis** is *discovering as much as possible about an audience for the purpose of improving communication with them.* Audience analysis occurs before, during, and after a presentation. Why should a speaker analyze an audience? Think of public speaking as another version of the kind of speaking you do every day. Nearly always, when you meet a stranger, you size up that person before you disclose your message. Similarly, public speaking requires that you meet and know the members of your audience so you are able to create a message for them. Public speaking is not talking to oneself in front of a group; instead, it is effective message transmission from one person to many people in a setting in which speaker and audience influence each other.

Let us consider the wide variety of audiences you might face in your lifetime:

Your classmatesA political group
Fellow workersA board of directors

The end-of-chapter **Summary** mirrors the flow of the chapter and uses language that is consistent with the headings, narrative, and key terms and definitions.

SUMMARY
In this chapter you have learned the following:
▶ Why a speaker should analyze the audience.
▶ How audience characteristics affect a presentation.
▶ The demographic features of an audience include
  • Gender
  • Age
  • Ethnicity
  • Economic status
  • Occupation
  • Education
• The time
• The importance of the situation
▶ The classroom audience is unique and useful to you.
▶ Audience adaptation is the goal of audience analysis.
▶ Speakers need to apply ethical principles to their audience analysis and adaptation.
▶ The importance of listening
  • Essential to citizenship and civil society
  • Essential to success in your public speaking course

Key Terms present a basic list of every word that is boldfaced and defined in the text. You can study these terms interactively at www.mhhe.com/nelson or by using the Student CD-ROM. There you will find Key Term Flashcards and Crossword Puzzles.

KEY TERMS
Use the *Public Speaking* CD-ROM and the Online Learning Center at www.mhhe.com/nelson to further your understanding of the following terminology.

Audience adaptationConventional wisdomObservation
Audience analysisDegree questionsOpen-ended questions

The Comprehensive Video Series Was Produced Especially for This Text

Public Speaking Videos illustrate various presentation techniques and elements of a speech.

Through these examples you will experience speech making in action, increase your understanding of different kinds of speeches, and develop greater confidence when delivering your own speeches.

Full Speeches

Passionate about Risks (Self-Introduction)
Motorcycle Club (Speech to Pay Tribute)
Cell Phones (Informative: Needs Improvement)
Cell Phones (Informative: Improved Version)
Mad Cow Disease (Informative)
Competitive Sports (Informative)
How to Play the Drums (Demonstration)
Sharks: The Misunderstood Monster (Persuasive: Needs Improvement)
Sharks: The Misunderstood Monster (Persuasive: Improved Version)
Stem Cell Research (Persuasive)
I'll Take the Cow Over the Chemicals (Persuasive)

Video Excerpts

Conveying the Central Idea
Appealing to Motivations
Using an Example
Making a Contrast
Using an Analogy
Using Testimony
Using Statistics
Introductions: Relating a Story
Introductions: Citing a Quotation
Introductions: Arousing Curiosity
Conclusions: Citing a Quotation
Conclusions: Giving an Illustration
Using Internet Graphics
Presenting a PowerPoint "Build"
Using a Vivid Image
Relating a Speech to the Listeners' Self-Interest
Using Deductive Reasoning
Using Inductive Reasoning

Public Speaking
A Guide for the Engaged Communicator

CHAPTER ONE

Congress shall make no law respecting an establishment of religion, or prohibiting the free exercise thereof; or abridging the freedom of speech, or of the press; or the right of the people peaceably to assemble, and to petition the Government for a redress of grievances.

THE FIRST AMENDMENT TO THE U.S. CONSTITUTION

Please use your liberty to promote ours.

AUNG SAN SUU KYI, GENERAL SECRETARY, NATIONAL LEAGUE FOR DEMOCRACY, BURMA

Getting Started

What will you learn?

When you have read and thought about this chapter, you will be able to:

1. Perceive public speaking as an exciting and positive experience.
2. Confront why your fears about public speaking might be exaggerated.
3. Explain how this course could improve your life.
4. Provide examples of how this course can connect you to your community.
5. Demonstrate the components of the communication process.
6. Uncover some of the unique characteristics of public presentations.
7. Distinguish between appropriate and inappropriate topics.
8. Consider vital topics for your presentations.
9. See yourself as an effective speaker.
10. Analyze the definition of communication apprehension.
11. Describe how you can reduce your anxiety about presenting in public.

The purpose of this chapter is to help you face your fears, manage your anxieties, and launch your learning about effective public presentations. It also will remind you of the role public speaking plays in a democratic society at large and will encourage you to view the public speaking course as a way to learn how to be a fully functioning member of your local community. Toward the end of the chapter you will learn unique characteristics of public presentations, tips for effective talks, and techniques for keeping out of trouble with your audience.

Claude Chamberlain was a tough guy who grew up in a neighborhood with more pestilence than pets. He was big and he was strong. A starting fullback in high school, he was now playing varsity football. At 6 feet 5 inches and 250 pounds, Claude was an imposing figure. His tattoos and body ornaments only made him appear more ominous. When Claude approached a crowd, they parted like the Red Sea. Nobody wanted to cross him.

Why then was Claude feeling as if he was ill? Here he was on the first day in his public speaking class. A teacher had just passed out the syllabus and told the class how many speeches they were going to give and when they were going to start. Claude would have rather faced a fearsome foursome on the line than stand up in front of this class of fellow students and talk! For one of the very few times in his life he was feeling an emotion he could barely identify—fear.

Speaking Excites

If you are reading this sentence, you are taking a class in which you—like Claude—are expected to give speeches. Which of the following comes closest to how you feel?

Student 1. I'm eager to get in the spotlight, take center stage, and perform. I'll give a speech that will dazzle my classmates with its brilliance. I am so pleased that I am required to do something that will make me so happy.

Student 2. I'm so scared that I think I'm going to die from fright before I ever get to the front of the room to give a speech.

Yes, these two are extreme cases, and in fact most students face a public speaking class with mixed emotions.

Typically, students who have been active in debate, individual events, theater, and musical performances are more like student one above. Similarly, students who have worked full-time in responsible jobs, are married, have raised kids, or served in the armed forces seem more likely to have confidence. Perhaps they already know more than most people about some subjects, and they are not worried about sharing their experiences.

Think of public speaking as downhill skiing: scary at the outset, exciting while you do it, and satisfying when completed.

The less you have interacted with people, the more likely you are to be worried about public speaking—like Claude and student two above. People who grew up in families, cultures, and communities that value verbal communication may have been encouraged to hone their skills through such activities as debating, acting, volunteering, performing, or working. If you grew up in a family where "silence is golden" or "children are to be seen but not heard," then you may have been discouraged from developing presentation skills.

Almost anything that you do for the first time has an element of risk: the few lines you had to say in front of the class in grade school, the first date, the first kiss, the first job interview, or the first request for a raise. Interestingly, many people who claim to be afraid of public presentations probably like other experiences that scare them—for example, skiing down a steep slope, parachuting from a plane, swimming in riptides, or driving too fast. The authors recently watched an entire boatload of tourists of all ages intentionally jump off a cliff into the sea about 70 feet below, some seriously bruising themselves on splashdown. Look on your public speaking class as an opportunity to give yourself a thrill, just like many other first-time experiences. You will suffer no bruises or head traumas, but you will feel excitement.

What's the Worst-Case Scenario?

One way to face fear is to consider "what is the worst thing that can happen?" Beginning speakers have great imaginations, especially when they fantasize about everything that could go wrong. Let's consider the possibilities:

Will you die? Comedian Jerry Seinfeld had an opening monologue in which he said, "The number two fear people have is death. The number one fear is public speaking. This means if you go to a funeral, you would rather be the person in the coffin than the person delivering the eulogy." The authors of this book have over 90 years of combined teaching experience. We have heard thousands of classroom speeches. So far, not one student has died while speaking. Nor have we ever heard of one who did.

Will you faint? One of the authors used to carry a smelling salts capsule (the kind used to revive people who faint when they give blood), just in case a student fainted while giving a speech. After several thousand student speeches the gauze-wrapped capsule started to get very dirty, but not from ever using it, and the author finally threw the capsule away. None of us has ever seen a student faint.

Will you shake, sweat, look down, and feel your mouth go dry? Probably. Most beginning speakers feel these symptoms of anxiety, but they feel them less as they speak more. Were you as nervous on your third kiss as you were on your first? Well, you will not be as nervous on your third speech as you were on your first.

Will you blush, flush, stammer, and trip over your tongue? You might. You cannot help blushing and flushing. They are natural responses that disappear as you become more comfortable. Sometimes even experienced speakers stammer a bit and mess up on a word. You shouldn't be very concerned even if you do have minor difficulties. Even the pros trip over a word now and then.

Will you forget what you were saying? Could happen. In front of 1,200 students one of the authors used to get 40 feet from the lectern bearing his notes when he would forget what he was trying to explain. He would just ask the class what they thought he was trying to prove, and someone in the front rows always knew. In your presentations, you will likely have note cards of some sort that can help you if you get stuck. If you don't act overly concerned about the lapse, your audience won't be concerned either.

Will you survive the course? Chances are excellent that you will complete the course, learn how to reduce your fears, learn how to focus on the message and the audience, and perhaps even want to speak outside the classroom. The vast majority of public speaking students like the course and understand that it is important—after they have completed it. In fact, our experience is that students often claim they entered the class "dreading" it, but quickly discovered that public speaking was one of their most interesting and enjoyable classes. In the next section, let's address how public speaking will be one of the most useful courses you will take.

TRY THIS

Pair up with a partner and talk with each other about how you feel about taking this course. Probe a bit to find out why the other person likes or dislikes delivering public presentations. Talk for a few minutes about what you might do to increase your comfort level in the course and during the presentations.

Why Study Public Speaking?

Democracy

Studying public communication can help you exercise your constitutionally guaranteed freedom of speech. Few nations have a bill of rights that invites their citizens to convey opinions and ideas, yet freedom of speech is essential to a democratic form of government. Being a practicing citizen in a democratic society therefore depends upon knowing about current issues and being able to speak about them in conversations, in speeches, and even through the mass media. It also involves being able to critically examine messages from others. Your public speaking course can help you become a fully functioning member of your local community and our democratic society at large. Democracy presents many opportunities, but it thrives only when everyday citizens embrace its freedoms as responsibilities to actively uphold.

Life Skills

Studying public speaking can teach you important life skills. It involves learning skills that every person will use at some point in his or her life, such as critical thinking, problem solving, decision making, conflict resolution, team building, and media literacy. Studying communication early in your college career can enhance your success throughout college, too. Consider the centrality of oral communication to all of our classes. You regularly are called on to answer questions in class, to provide reports, to offer explanations, and to make presentations. In addition, your oral and written work depends on your ability to think critically and creatively, to solve problems, and to make decisions. Most likely, you will be engaged in group projects where skills such as team building, conflict resolution, and presenting will be keys to success. These same skills will be essential throughout your life.

Work and Career

Studying public speaking can help you succeed professionally. A look at the job postings in any newspaper will give you an immediate understanding of the importance of improving your knowledge and practice of communication. The following excerpts from classified advertisements in the employment section of the Sunday paper are fairly typical.

- "We need a results-oriented, seasoned professional who is a good communicator and innovator" reads one ad for a home health-care manager.
- Another ad, this one for a marketing analyst, reads, "You should be creative, inquisitive, and a good communicator both in writing and speaking."
- An ad for a computer training specialist calls for "excellent presentation, verbal, and written communication skills, with the ability to interact with all levels within the organization."

Star athletes—like the top people in any endeavor—are often asked to speak. Here, Olympic athlete Jackie Joyner-Kersee speaks in the Old Executive Office Building in Washington, Tuesday, June 17, 1997, during a ceremony to celebrate the 25th anniversary of Title IX, which prohibits sex discrimination in federally assisted education programs.

As a person educated in communication, not only will you acquire the interviewing skills that will positively impact hiring decisions, but you also will have greater access to the most desirable jobs. Personnel managers typically identify effective speaking and listening as the most important reasons for hiring the people they do. Your communication skill-set will continue to be important throughout your career and will always be a factor in upward mobility and successful entrepreneurship.

Do People Really Speak Anymore?

Back in the 1980s, when computers replaced typewriters, experts thought the "electronic office" would eliminate the need for paper and for secretaries. Instead, offices still have secretaries, and workers use more paper than ever before as they download information from Web sites, print electronic messages, and continue to store printouts in filing cabinets. In the 1940s and 1950s, when radio and then television became common and when videoconferencing became possible, experts thought nobody would be interested in paying someone to speak in person when she or he could be projected on a screen and respond interactively with an audience. On the contrary, speakers are even more in demand than before. Universities and colleges have many guest speakers; businesses invite consultants, motivational speakers, successful executives, and salespeople to speak; and every academic and business conference pays speakers to attract people to their conventions. Speaking is very big business.

8   Part One   Preparing Your Presentations

Chances are excellent that you too will have opportunities to speak publicly. Peggy Noonan—speechwriter for President Bush, President Reagan, and a host of business executives—says:

> As more and more businesses become involved in the new media technologies, as we become a nation of fewer widgets and more Web sites, a new premium has been put on the oldest form of communication: the ability to stand and say what you think in front of others.[1]

What if you could hear or see your favorite entertainer (*a*) on radio, (*b*) on TV, (*c*) on a "live" transmission via a large screen, or (*d*) in person? Which would you choose if cost and distance were not an issue? Why do we want to see politicians, athletes, and entertainers in person? We are so overexposed to people on film and video that seeing an important individual in person becomes much more special. More than ever we want to see a flesh-and-blood person talking to us.

What Is the Presentation Process?

Early in the course you need to grasp the big picture of the communication process, with its component parts. Presenting is just one kind of communication context, which can include many others, such as interpersonal communication, group communication, and computer-mediated communication. All of these contexts involve the seven components described below. Just as you are unlikely to understand the particulars of an automobile without understanding how horsepower, pistons, valves, and exhaust contribute to speed, you are unlikely to understand the particulars of public presentations without knowing how the parts interact with each other.

What Are the Seven Components of the Communication Process?

Some basic elements are present in practically all public speaking circumstances:

1. A source, presenter, or speaker who utters the message.
2. A receiver, audience members, or classmates to listen.
3. A message, your words and ideas adapted to that audience.
4. A channel, or means of distributing your words.
5. Feedback, responses from the audience.
6. A situation, the context in which the presentation occurs.
7. Noise—any form of interference with the message.

Let's look more closely at the components of the communication process.

Source

The **source** is *the person who originates the message*. Who the sender is makes a difference in determining who, if anyone, will listen. Consider a person walking down a street in New York City. He or she would hear cell phone conversations, people hailing taxicabs, and vendors selling everything from bagels to baklava. Would you listen to the messages they are sending? Some of the talented singers, dancers, and instrumentalists might attract your attention, but few of the many contenders for your eye and ear would succeed. Sources send messages, but no communication occurs until messages link the source and receiver.

Similarly, in the lecture hall, some professors capture your attention and leave you wishing for more ideas. Occasionally you hear delivery-challenged professors who put you to sleep in spite of their bright ideas. A source is useless without a receiver, and a speaker is useless without an audience.

Receiver

The **receiver,** listener, or audience is *the individual or group that hears, and listens to, the message sent by the source.* All individuals are unique. Receivers are individuals who have inherited certain characteristics and developed others as a result of their families, friends, and education.

The best speakers can "read" an audience; through analysis or intuition they can tell what an audience wants, needs, or responds to. This sort of group empathy allows some speakers to be seen as charismatic: they seem to exhibit what the audience feels. Even a beginning speaker can learn to see the world through the audience's eyes. Nothing helps more in the classroom than to listen carefully to your classmates' speeches, because every speech will reveal as much about the speaker as about the issue being discussed. Few speakers outside the classroom are able to hear each individual in the audience reveal herself or himself through a speech, a unique opportunity to analyze your listeners. The great benefit of speaking is that you get to respond with and to your audience, adapting and supporting your message in a way you cannot do in any other form of communication.

Watch the video clip entitled "Relating a Speech to the Listeners' Self-Interest."

Message

Verbal and nonverbal messages are an integral part of the communication process. What else links the source and the receiver? The **message** is sensed by both the source and the receiver: *the facial expressions seen, the words heard, the visual aids illustrated, and the ideas or meanings conveyed simultaneously between source and receiver.* **Verbal messages** are *the words chosen for the speech.* **Nonverbal messages** are *the movements, gestures, facial expressions, and vocal variations that can reinforce or contradict the words,* such as pitch or tone of voice that can alter the meaning of the words.

Channel

The **channel** is *the means of distributing your words, whether by coaxial cable, fiber optics, microwave, radio, video, or air.* In the public speaking classroom, the channel is first of all the air that carries the sound waves from the mouth of the source to the ear of the receiver. The type of channel might not seem to make very much difference, but messages have decidedly different impacts depending on whether they are heard as a rumor in your ear, observed on network news on TV, or heard from you in the classroom.

Some public speaking students discover the differences among channels when their teacher videotapes their speeches. Watching yourself electronically reproduced is not the same as watching you in a live performance because channels are themselves part of the message. Do you perceive a professor in a classroom the same as you do an instructor of an online course? Probably not. It is the channel that makes a difference. Or, as Marshall McLuhan famously expressed, "The medium is the message."

Feedback

Feedback includes *verbal or nonverbal responses by the audience.* During a public speech, most of the audience feedback is nonverbal: head nodding, smiling, frowning, giving complete attention, fiddling with a watch. All this nonverbal feedback allows the speaker to infer whether the message is being communicated to the listeners.

The question-and-answer session is a good example of verbal feedback in which the audience has an opportunity to seek clarification, to verify speaker positions on issues, and to challenge the speaker's arguments. In any case, feedback, like the thermostat on a furnace or an air conditioner, is the speaker's monitoring device that continuously tells whether the message is working.

Situation

Communication occurs in a context called the **situation**—*the time, place, and occasion in which the message sending and receiving occurs.* The situation can determine what kind of message is appropriate. Only certain kinds of messages and speakers are acceptable at funerals, debates, elementary school meetings, bar mitzvahs, court hearings, and dedications. In the classroom, the situation is a room of a certain size, containing a number of people who fill a specified number of seats. The physical setting can mean that you can talk almost conversationally or that you must shout to be heard.

Noise

Another component of the communication process is **noise,** *interference or obstacles to communication.* Noise can be internal, in which case it can be mental—daydreaming or worry—or physical—headache or illness. Internal noise is unique to the individual. Noise also can be external, in which case it can be auditory (a jackhammer outside the window) or visual (sunlight in your eyes). External noise can affect one or many; it is not unique to the individual.

The **process of communication** is *the dynamic interrelationship of source, receiver, message, channel, feedback, situation, and noise.* In actual, real-life presentations, all of these components function simultaneously and continuously. For example, let's say that you (the source) are trying to convince fellow workers (the receivers) that they should unionize (message). You argue first that the union will result in higher pay (message). The audience appears unimpressed (feedback), so you argue that the union will bring such benefits as better working conditions (message). They doze (feedback). Finally you argue that the workers will get better medical and dental plans for their families, reducing their out-of-pocket health expenses (message). This argument gets attentive looks, some questions, and considerable interest (feedback). The audience has influenced the source and the message through feedback.

The speaker conveys a message through words and action, but the audience gives meaning to that message through its own thought processes. An example is a youthful, local volunteer speaking for MTV's *Rock the Vote*. Audience members who are older may feel outdated by the speaker's looks and gestures and may perceive the message as having little to do with the promotion of basic voter registration.

Audiences interpret messages; they construct messages of their own from the words they hear, and they carry with them their own rendition of the message. The politicians slather their presentations with abstractions that audiences interpret in their own way. The more abstract the language, the greater are the possible interpretations. "I stand for family values," says the politician. The listeners from a variety of different kinds of families can interpret this to mean that the politician is embracing their particular family.

The process of communication is a transaction between source and receivers that includes mutual influence, the interpretation and construction of meaning, and the development of an individualized message that includes how others respond. What is **communication**? *A transaction in which speaker and listener simultaneously send, receive, and interpret messages.* In public speaking, the temptation is to see the action as predominantly one-way communication: the speaker sends words and actions to the audience. However, in many public speaking situations, the audience influences the speaker through continuous feedback, sometimes with words and actions and sometimes almost subconsciously.

To demonstrate the powerful effect of the audience on the speaker, a teacher challenged his class to influence his behavior. One rule was that the moment he knew they were trying to influence him, the game was over. The class had to figure out what they could do to encourage some kind of behavioral change. After 10 weeks, the teacher had not caught the class trying to influence him. They had documented, however, that, when the experiment began, the teacher stroked his chin once or twice each class period. They decided that the teacher would feel rewarded if they paid more attention, asked questions, and showed interest whenever this behavior occurred. Every time the teacher touched his chin, the class subtly rewarded him with their interest, attention, and questions. By the end of the 10-week course, they had the teacher touching his chin over 20 times each class session—and the teacher was totally unaware of this influence.

The point of this anecdote is that audiences influence speakers. In a public rally against gang proliferation and violence, they might do so with the words they yell, the movements and noises they make, or even with the signs they hold. In class, it could be the sight of heads nodding or eyes glazing over. The fact is that speakers influence audiences and audiences influence speakers, and they do so continuously in public speaking situations. See Figure 1.1 for a model of the presentation process.

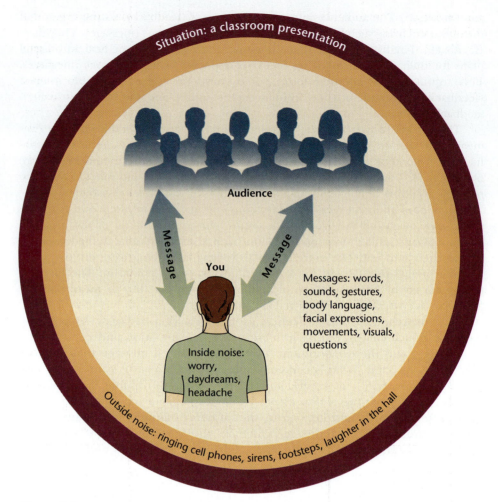

Figure 1.1 The presentation process shows a speaker and an audience simultaneously sending and receiving messages while constructing meaning.

Why Is Public Speaking a Unique Form of Communication?

Public speaking has some unique features that are important for you to know. However, in some ways public speaking is like enhanced conversation. Students, in fact, often are praised for using conversational, everyday language with their classroom audiences. When you meet someone for a friendly conversation, you normally greet (introduction), talk about something (body), and say goodbye (conclusion). Classroom presentations tend to be about serious issues, but so do many conversations. Yet, the language of conversation has fewer rules—you can say just about anything in any manner to a close friend—and conversation has turn-taking, which is usually reserved for the question-and-answer portion of a presentation. And in contrast to everyday conversation, the language of presentations is more carefully chosen to appeal to a larger group. However, both in conversation and in presentations you basically are trying to get some message across to another person. Here are some additional unique features of public presentations, especially classroom speeches.

Time is short. Public speaking presentations typically are short. Ronald Reagan (U.S. President, 1980–1988), who was called "The Great Communicator," once said that no speech should last more than 20 minutes. He meant that 20 minutes is about all an audience can tolerate. Most of your speeches will be considerably shorter.

Simplification is necessary. You cannot say much in five minutes, especially when you consider that the introductory portion of the speech often takes one minute and the conclusion is about half a minute. How much can you say about any subject in the remaining three-and-a-half minutes? Complex topics must be simplified, complicated topics may have to be managed in parts, and deep topics may have to be introduced rather than thoroughly vetted. In his Gettysburg Address in 1863, U.S. President Abraham Lincoln delivered a "deep speech" in about three-and-a-half minutes.

Points are few. Even though bulleted lists are common and most everyone knows "The Top Ten Reasons" format, you need to limit your speech to very few main points—usually two or three. Why? Because people do not remember much. Even if you ask your audience, "What were my three main points?" you will be lucky if they remember one or two. Can you remember a politician's position on global warming, stem cell research, hate crime, or literacy? Probably not. We tend to remember brief declarations such as "No more taxes," "No more war," and "Cheaper gas for all."

Topics are important. You need to have something important to say. A beautifully delivered speech about a trivial topic is still an empty shell, but an important or timely topic can have impact even if the delivery is uninspiring. We listen carefully to messages that are important to us.

What Topics Should You Talk About?

Our concept of freedom of speech—guaranteed by the U.S. Constitution—means that people can talk about almost anything. However, in a public speaking class, some topics work better than others. The following are some practical guidelines to help you think of topics.

Choose vital topics. This book encourages students to select topics on important issues. Among these important topics are:

Democracy

Environment

Technology

Education

Diversity

Ethics

Health

Choose current topics. Audiences prefer speakers who talk about issues that are relevant and timely. They like to be informed about matters that involve them. You could, of course, provide historical context about an important topic, but remember audiences generally care about what is current.

14   Part One   Preparing Your Presentations

Choose topics that improve the audience. You will want to inform the audience about topics that will help them, and to persuade them about topics that will make a positive difference in their lives. You will want to help individuals, improve the community, and serve those who need help.

You can learn to be an effective speaker by choosing vital topics, selecting a current topic, and picking a topic that improves the audience, the community, and/or the country or world.

TRY THIS

With another person in your class make a list of some topics about which you feel competent. Then together size up some of those topics against the features mentioned above. Are they topics you should talk about or topics that invite you to reconsider?

What Should You Avoid in a Presentation?

Communication teachers believe in freedom of speech. We think that U.S. Americans should be allowed to talk about almost anything. All freedoms have limits, however. Although you can talk about almost anything in this country, here are some suggestions for topics and approaches to avoid in the classroom.

Avoid exhausted topics unless you have a new approach. Remember, your speech teacher hears many speeches. Some topics have been talked about so often without making much headway that hearing them again makes the teacher's head throb. What are some examples? Gun control and abortion rights are a couple of culprits.

Avoid illegal items lest you end up suspended or in jail. Most campuses do not allow alcohol, drugs, weapons, or bombs. So do not advocate them, especially by showing them in class. On the other hand, you can argue that something currently illegal ought to be legalized: assisted suicide, medical marijuana laws, treating addictions as a health rather than a legal problem. If you have doubts about the legality or appropriateness of your topic, then you should get your teacher's opinion.

Avoid insulting your audience. Since one of the goals of this course is to teach you how to influence others through public speaking, you need to be careful what you say about others. Ethnic slurs, cultural slights, racial epithets, street lingo, swearing, and attacks on religious beliefs of others may be legal, but they certainly are unwise choices. You can avoid insulting your audience by always approaching them with an attitude of respect.

Avoid getting your speech from the Internet. As any high school student can tell you, the Internet is afloat with thousands of term papers, English compositions, and speeches on practically any subject you can imagine. Some are free, others are for sale. *Using a speech, outline, or manuscript from any source other than you* is called **plagiarism,** an offense punishable by no points, a low grade, suspension, or dismissal from college. Your school likely publishes its policy concerning plagiarism on its Web site. College teachers frequently detect plagiarized speeches. Often they are too good to be true. When a speaker trips over many of the words

E-Note

FINDING VITAL TOPICS ON THE WEB

Most of you would agree that the Web has the potential for generating countless hits when given any one topic to be searched. Here are some starting points for exploring topics that may be relevant to your immediate community and your classroom audience. These URLs represent organizations that connect universities and colleges to opportunities for community service and civic engagement. Try to find your school or community, or at least your state.

www.compact.org (Campus Compact)
www.cns.gov (Corporation for National and Community Service)
www.learnandserve.org (Learn and Serve America)

---

in a speech that is well above his or her language skills, plagiarism is often the problem. Or the speech is so good that the teacher tells the other instructors, several of whom have heard the same great speech in their classrooms for the same assignment. How can you know if your purloined prose might not be delivered in a presentation on the same day as yours? What is the best policy then? Write your own material, and then you do not have to worry. Deliver your own speech. Avoid guilt, remorse, and punishment. Plagiarizing your classroom work will not help you in your career when you are on your own. We will show you how to find and how to cite information from the Internet and elsewhere. You can use other people's ideas—as long as you give them credit.

Becoming an Effective Speaker

You play the most important role in making a presentation. You choose the message, you analyze the listeners, you organize the message, and you deliver the message. A presentation is always a dance, however, in which the speaker (one dance partner) uses a message (the music) to influence the listener (the other dance partner).

The Speaker's Source Credibility

Some students think they must receive a complete makeover before they can be a public speaker. They may see themselves as shy, fearful of audiences, or just cautious in front of a group. They may think they have to look and sound like an entertainer, a famous preacher, or a broadcaster. Actually, the notion of a complete makeover is not possible or desirable. If all speakers looked and sounded alike, then we would grow weary of hearing them speak. If you are not funny now, this course is unlikely to make you humorous. If you are not a live wire now, this course is unlikely to turn you into the Energizer Bunny. And if you lack charisma, this course is unlikely to turn you into the most popular person in the room. If you really concentrate on communicating your message to your audience in a caring and conversational manner, then you will not have to worry about how you look.

The beginning speaker can develop three areas that have been the corner-stones of public speaking for well over two thousand years. The ancients called them ethos, logos, and pathos. We call them source credibility, logical argument, and emotional argument. You need credibility (ethos) to inspire an audience to listen to an emotional story (pathos) that is backed by an argument (logos) for change. We will look most closely in this chapter at you—the source—and how "who you are" and "what you are" affect your influence on an audience. Later, in the chapter on persuasion, we will examine logical and emotional argument.

Benjamin Franklin once said that your reputation is like porcelain or glass: Once broken it is never quite the same again. He was speaking of **source credibility,** *the audience's perception of your effectiveness as a communicator.* Your effectiveness is not based just on presentational or delivery skills but more on what you know and how effectively you communicate your ideas to the audience.

One means of establishing a relationship with your audience is to use **common ground**—*pointing out what features you share with your audience:* "All of us have noticed that our air quality is poor here," "We students need to balance learning with keeping physically healthy," and "What courses should qualify as general edu-cation credits?"

A second means of establishing source credibility is establishing trustworthi-ness. **Trustworthiness** is *the degree to which the audience perceives the presenter as hon-est and honorable.* A student in one author's public speaking class came unprepared. Because the assignment was brief (just the introductory portion of his presenta-tion), he listened carefully to the first five speakers and then confidently jumped to his feet to deliver a two-minute introduction full of facts and figures. After his presentation, classmates inquired about his claim that 4,000 people died from eat-ing junk food during the Super Bowl game. The student admitted that he had made up all the facts and figures while the other students were delivering their presentations. After that, the class never fully trusted him because he lied so obvi-ously in his presentation. Trust is difficult to earn but easy to lose.

A third technique for encouraging your audience to listen to you is to display **competence,** *a thorough familiarity with your topic.* For example, an agriculture major might demonstrate her competence in organic gardening by showing how to com-post, irrigate, and manage pests. You can accomplish the same purpose by pre-senting topics about which you have some expertise beyond most people in your class or topics that you have researched thoroughly.

A fourth feature that encourages your audience to pay attention to you is **dynamism,** *the energy you expend in delivering your message.* Typically audiences are attracted by movement, gestures, facial expression, and voice variety, all delivery characteristics. Think about this comparison. Would you rather watch a presenter who is difficult to hear, rarely looks up from his or her notes, lacks facial expres-sion, speaks in one tone, and never moves or gestures? Or would you rather watch someone who is lively and maybe even a bit dramatic, someone who can whisper and shout, someone who moves, points, and exclaims during the presentation? Listeners tend to respond favorably to presenters whose manner reflects their sin-cerity and conviction about the subject matter.

The good news is that you do not have to be a top performer in all aspects of credibility. You might, for example, be exceedingly strong on trustworthiness but not be particularly dynamic, or you might be highly competent but not have much in common with your listeners. Play to your strengths without feeling that you have to be at the top of every dimension of source credibility.

Here are some ideas for gaining respect from your audience:

1. Talk about something important to you and your audience.

2. Make sure the audience knows why you know about the topic of your talk.

3. Translate your ideas for audience understanding.

4. Organize your ideas for clarity.

5. Speak as if you are having an "enhanced conversation" with people who know and like you.

Figure 1.2 **Tips for gaining respect from your audience.**

Listening

Audience members decide in seconds what they think of a presenter, and what they think of a presenter may determine whether they are merely **hearing** *(receiving sound waves)* or **listening** *(interpreting the sounds as a message)*. Hearing is physiological: You cannot keep from picking up the sounds unless you somehow block the sound from entering your ears. Listening is a psychological process: You need to attend to, think about, and derive meaning from the sounds. For suggestions on listening see Figure 1.3.

You probably listen differently in different situations: passive listening to background music in your car or home and active listening when the sounds demand full attention. Active listening is characterized by posture (forward lean, head cocked for better reception), facial features (eyes alert and on the source of the message), and movement (hand cupped on the ear, hand taking notes). You might be a passive listener when your teacher is giving examples of a concept you already understand, but you are likely to be an active listener when your teacher says the words, "What I am telling you next is on the test." Listening actively in conversation can make you a valued friend, mate, or partner. Listening actively in class is often the difference between the student who earns poor grades and the one who earns good grades. In the public speaking classroom, active listening not only allows you to learn from the content of other speakers, but it invites you to learn what delivery skills are most effective with your audience.

1. **Avoid Distractions.** Sit so the presenter is your main focus, in the front of the room, away from talkative friends, away from distracting sounds and sights.

2. **Actively Engage.** Watch attentively, write down important points and useful observations, not what is not being said, and ask questions for clarification.

3. **Be Thoughtful.** What are the presenter's main points? Were they supported well? Do you agree with the message? Why or why not?

Figure 1.3 **Listening tips.**

Cultural Note

CULTURAL DIFFERENCES IN PRESENTATIONS

Every culture has different ways of presenting. Korean speakers will often say demeaning things about themselves at the outset, the opposite of U.S. Americans with their credibility-building openings. Some Native Americans tend to use more "word pictures" or visual imagery than U.S. Americans of European descent, who tend to be less metaphorical.

How to Reduce Your Fear of Presenting

Effective presenters learn to manage their natural apprehension so that their delivery is not adversely affected. In fact, they often regard "stage fright" positively. Just as athletes feel an adrenaline rush before a big game, and entertainers get "keyed up" before a performance, experienced public speakers know the initial nervousness will pass and likely be transformed to positive energy. Although most of us feel apprehension when presenting in public, we typically get over this natural nervousness quickly. This is not to say that you will never be nervous. The point is that experienced presenters recognize that some nervousness is natural, and they take strategic steps to minimize the possibility that natural nervousness will become so severe that their delivery becomes less conversational. Let's identify these strategies, because nearly everyone experiences some fear when presenting in front of an audience.

Understanding Communication Apprehension

The fear of presenting is called **communication apprehension (CA),** or *an individual's level of fear or anxiety associated with either real or anticipated communication with another person or persons.*[2] Symptoms of CA include sleeplessness, worry, and reluctance before you present, and "interfering, off-task thoughts" while you present.[3] Thinking "off-task thoughts" means losing focus on communicating your message to your audience by concentrating instead on sweaty palms, shaking knees, and "cotton mouth," the feeling that your tongue is swollen and your mouth is as dry as the Sahara. One wit noted that public presenters suffer so often from wet palms and dry mouth that they should stick their hands in their mouth.

What else do we know about CA? Students with high levels of anxiety practically set themselves up for failure.[4] Students high in anxiety exhibit "less audience adaptation, less concern for equipment likely to be available when the speech was presented, less concern about the tools available to aid in preparing the speech, more difficulty in coming up with information for speeches, and greater self-doubts about one's capability as a speaker."[5] On the other hand, CA is not correlated with age, sex, or grade-point average,[6] and students with the highest anxiety in public communication courses "showed the largest improvement in perceived competence."[7]

Reducing Anxiety

What can you do to reduce the anxiety that you are likely to feel before speaking? What thoughts can you think, what actions can you take, and what precautions

Chapter One   Getting Started   19

can you observe to help you shift attention from yourself to your message and your audience? The following six keys to confidence can help you reduce your fear of public speaking.

1. *Act confidently.* Actions often change before attitudes do. You may act as if you like others before you really do. You dress up for a party and as a result, act in a certain way. You decide that you are going to have fun at a social event, and you do.

   You can use the same strategy when you present by thinking of public speaking as acting. You can say to yourself, "I am going to behave in a confident manner when I speak," and then proceed to act confidently even if you are not. This action is not much different from acting cool on the street, playing the role of the intellectual in class, or pretending you are a sports hero in a game. You are simply acting as if you are confident standing in front of the class. Our students suggest the following: Move to the front of the room as if you owned it, and act as if the audience respects you and wants to hear your words.

2. *Know your subject.* Your first presentation should be about something you know already. This early experience should not require very much research. In fact, many communication professors ask you to talk about yourself. Whether you speak about some aspect of yourself or some other topic, you will be a better presenter if you choose a subject that you know something about.

   When LaMarr Doston was assigned to give his first presentation, he could think of nothing about himself that he wanted to share with the class. He was glad that he did not have to do research for the presentation, but he was unhappy that he did not know what to say about himself. After two days of worrying about it, LaMarr was in his office at work when he thought of what he was going to say: "I am LaMarr Doston, the Fast Food King."

   LaMarr had worked for five different fast-food chains over the years. He worked his way from a mop jockey at one place, to counter server at another, to fry cook at a third, to night shift manager at a fourth, and now morning shift manager at the fifth fast-food chain. LaMarr was good at his work, he was promoted frequently, commended often, and recommended highly. He seemed to know every job there was at a fast-food outlet. He was the Fast Food King.

3. *Care about your subject.* Amanda Carroll gave an introductory presentation about being adopted and bi-ethnic. Amanda had one African American biological parent and one European American biological parent. As a baby, she was put up for adoption in a small Ohio town and raised by white parents. Amanda was very perceptive. She knew that people wondered about her origins because of her appearance. She satisfied the audience's curiosity and provided an added dimension by discussing the satisfaction of being chosen as a baby by parents who wanted and loved her.

   If your teacher wants you to speak on a topic other than yourself, you should make sure that you select one that you know and care about. Avoid, in general, politically charged issues, but do select a topic in which you are passionately interested. The more you care about your subject, the more you are going to focus on the message and the audience instead of worrying about yourself.

TABLE 1.1 STATEMENTS OF NEGATIVE AND POSITIVE SELF-ASSESSMENT	
STATEMENTS OF NEGATIVE SELF-ASSESSMENT	STATEMENTS OF POSITIVE SELF-ASSESSMENT
• "I will forget what I am supposed to say."	• "I can prepare well enough to do well on my presentation."
• "I will turn red when I get nervous."	• "Each time I practiced the presentation I felt better about it."
• "My presentation will be boring."	• "People usually respect my opinion on things."
• "I do not know enough about anything to speak on it."	• "I can come up with something to say about anything."

4. *See your classmates as friends.* It is difficult to think of an audience that is more concerned about your success than your classmates in a beginning public speaking course. They worry about you so much that if you should falter, they break into a sweat. They care how you do. See them as friends instead of uncaring strangers, and your perceptions will help you feel confident in front of the classroom. Our own students suggest that you begin talking only when you are ready and that you look at the people in your audience before starting. While speaking, focus on the friendly faces—those who smile, nod, and generally make you feel good about your speech.

5. *See yourself as successful.* If you are an inexperienced presenter, you may need to work at thinking positively about your prospects as a public presenter. You need to think about and then rehearse in your mind how you are going to give your presentation. Some people might call this "worrying," but psychologists call it "mental imaging." Whatever you call this mindfulness, you can use it to help you succeed. Consider the difference between the statements of negative and positive self assessment in Table 1.1. Thinking about your presentation in a positive way will not eliminate all nervousness, but upbeat thinking will keep it from becoming debilitating.

6. *Practice for confidence.* The degree of nervousness you experience is inversely related to your quality and quantity of practice. Indeed, research has demonstrated that that is the case.[8] Our own students recommend having your introduction, main points, and conclusion clear in your head. The more times you practice, the less nervous you will feel. Also, the more closely your practice sessions approximate your actual speaking experience—including an audience, for example—the less nervous you will feel. Although you should not practice your presentation to the point of memorization, you should not overlook the importance of practicing several times over the span of a couple of days.

Make sure that you take every opportunity to stand in front of the class before class begins and as your classmates leave the room. You need to see what the class looks like before you give your speech. Unless you have been a teacher, a business trainer, or have had other opportunities to speak in front of groups, you do not know what an audience looks like from the

Chapter One   Getting Started   21

front of the room. The more you get accustomed to that sight before you give your speech, the more comfortable you will be.

Most universities have classrooms that are empty for some hours during the day or evening. Have some of your friends listen to your presentation as you practice your message in an empty classroom. The experience will be very close to what you will encounter when you actually give your presentation. The practice will make you more confident.

You should be careful not to have unrealistic expectations. Not everyone starts from the same place. People of all ages, cultures, nationalities, and experiences today populate colleges. Some students have been active in the workplace for years. Some have come to college with half a lifetime or more of experience; others have very little experience and may even be uncertain about their command of the English language. Your job in this class is to work on building your confidence, so you can spend a lifetime working on your competence and your effectiveness with audiences in public communication situations. For example, an occasional vocalized pause may not even be noticed if you are involved with the message and the audience and they are focused on your message. Perfection is not really the goal; communicating effectively is the aim of this course.

Resources for Review and Discussion

SUMMARY

In this chapter you have learned the following:

▶ Some people see their public speaking course as a fate worse than death; others see the course as a rare opportunity to perform.
- Nearly everyone gets a rush from standing in front of an audience.
- Nearly always, our fears before speaking turn out to be an exaggeration: nobody dies of heart failure, faints, or falls on the floor.

▶ Why should you study public speaking?
- To exercise your constitutional guarantee of freedom of speech
- To learn life skills
- To succeed professionally

▶ Although we are in the electronic media age, people really do speak to audiences in person, often with hefty speaker fees because audiences like to see live presenters.

▶ The communication process includes seven interactive components: speaker (source), audience (receiver), message, channel, feedback, situation, and noise.

▶ What is different about public speaking?
- Because "time is short," you cannot say much in a single speech.
- Because "simplification is necessary," you have to reduce complex issues, problems, and ideas into small, easy-to-digest parts.
- Because "points are few," you have to select only the most important points, arguments, and ideas for presentation.
- Because "topics are important," you have to carefully select subjects you think will engage your audience.

▶ What should you talk about in your presentations?
- Current topics that interest your audience are a good choice.
- Vital topics that relate to your community will engage you, the speaker, and your audience.

▶ What topics should you avoid?
- Avoid exhausted topics that have been talked about too much—unless you offer a fresh approach.

- Avoid illegal topics that include open use of firearms, illegal drugs, explosives, flammable substances, contaminated blood, etc.
- Avoid insulting topics that disparage ethnic groups, racial groups, religions, or cultural practices.
- Avoid plagiarized speeches that are lifted from the Internet and/or other written or visual sources.

▶ Turning you into an effective presenter.
- Understand the difference between hearing, which is physiological, and listening, which is psychological.
- Establish common ground with individuals in your audience.
- Establish a trusting relationship with your audience.
- Establish that you are competent in the subject matter.
- Demonstrate dynamism or the energetic commitment to the message.

▶ Most speakers experience some anxiety over public communication.

▶ Communication apprehension is an exceptional level of anxiety.
- Symptoms of communication apprehension include sleeplessness, worry, reluctance before you present, and off-task thoughts when you do present.
- Communication apprehension is not correlated with age, sex, or grade point average.

▶ You can reduce anxiety through several behaviors.
- Act confidently.
- Know your subject.
- Care about your subject.
- See your classmates as friends.
- See yourself as successful.
- Practice toward confidence.

KEY TERMS

 Use the *Public Speaking* CD-ROM and the Online Learning Center at www.mhhe.com/nelson to practice your understanding of the following terminology.

Channel	Hearing	Receiver
Common ground	Listening	Situation
Communication	Message	Source
Communication apprehension	Noise	Source credibility
Competence	Nonverbal messages	Trustworthiness
Dynamism	Plagiarism	Verbal messages
Feedback	Process of communication	

REFERENCES

[1] Noonan, Peggy (1998). *Simply speaking.* New York: Regan Books.

[2] McCroskey, J. C. (1997). Oral communication apprehension: A summary of recent theory and research. *Human Communication Research, 4,* 78.

[3] Greene, J. O., Rucker, M. P., Zauss, E. S., & Harris, A. A. (1988). Communication anxiety and the acquisition of message production skill. *Communication Education, 47,* 337–47.

[4] Henningsen, David Dryden, & Miller Henningsen, Mary Lynn. (2004). The effect of individual difference variables on information sharing in decision-making groups. *Human Communication Research, 30.4,* 540–55.

[5] Daly, J. A., Vangelisti, A. L., & Weber, D. J. (1995). Speech anxiety affects how people prepare speeches: A protocol analysis of the preparation processes of speakers. *Communication Monographs, 62,* 394.

[6] Berger, C. R. (2004). Speechlessness: Causal attributions, emotional features, and social consequences. *Journal of Language and Social Psychology, 23,* 147–69. See also Dwyer, K. K. (1998). Communication apprehension and learning style preference: Correlations and implications for teaching. *Communication Education, 49,* 137–50.

[7] MacIntyre, P. D. & MacDonald, J. R. (1998). Public speaking anxiety: Perceived competence and audience congeniality. *Communication Education, 47,* 359–65.

[8] Ayres, Joe. (1996). Speech preparation processes and speech apprehension. *Communication Education, 45,* 228–35. See also Menzel, Kent E., & Carrell, Lori J. (1994). The relationship between preparation and performance in public speaking. *Communication Education, 43,* 17–26.

APPLICATION EXERCISES

 Go to the self-quizzes on the *Public Speaking* CD-ROM and the Online Learning Center at www.mhhe.com/nelson to test your knowledge of the chapter concepts.

1. Talk in groups of 3–5 students for 15 minutes about what you can do to reduce your apprehension about public speaking. Have one person in each group take notes so the groups can share their best ideas with the class after the discussion. The purpose is to allow you to reduce anxiety and to learn some practices to reduce anxiety.
2. Write down as many ideas as you can remember about how to make an effective public presentation. After writing down as many as you remember, you should open the text and add as many more as you can find. The purpose is to mentally reinforce early in the course some of the guidelines for effective presenting.
3. Introduce yourself to your classmates by stating your name and whatever you want them to remember about you. Some ideas: year in school, jobs, armed forces, public service, family, place of origin, travel, languages, talents, special skills, unusual hobbies, different experiences.

CHAPTER TWO

As I look back upon my life, I see that every part of it was a preparation for the next. The most trivial of incidents fits into the larger pattern like a mosaic in a preconceived design.
MARGARET SANGER (1879–1966), NURSE ADVOCATE FOR WOMEN'S HEALTH

Effort is only effort when it begins to hurt.
JOSÉ ORTEGA Y GASSET (1883–1956), SPANISH PHILOSOPHER, ESSAYIST, AND PROFESSOR

Preparing Your First Presentation

What will you learn?

When you have read and thought about this chapter, you will be able to:

1. Enact principles found in the Five Canons of Rhetoric to prepare your first presentation.
2. Prepare presentations with a clearly identifiable introduction, body, and conclusion.
3. Differentiate between clarity and ornamentation as elements of style.
4. Target specific nonverbal behaviors that will increase the effectiveness of your presentation delivery.
5. Develop an impromptu self-introduction, peer introduction, demonstration presentation, or any first presentation assigned by your instructor.

Preparing your first speech can be an exciting and productive challenge. Although most of us have given some sort of speech before—a talk in front of a class in high school, a presentation to a club, or maybe even participation in speech and debate—few of us have had formal instruction in the art and science of effective public communication. This chapter introduces you to foundational concepts that will anchor your learning throughout the course.

Cheri approached her speech class with a mixture of excitement and fear. Speech class certainly seemed more fun than college algebra, but she was a little apprehensive about being graded on speaking in front of other people. As she sat down for the first day of class, she was excited to learn about the course.

"Okay everyone, let's go ahead and get started. My name is Leslie Kuhlman and I am the instructor for the course. I want to begin by telling you how excited I am about teaching this class. I took this class as an undergrad and it was really fun. Before we go through the syllabus, I want to know what questions you have about public communication."

Cheri thought for a second and raised her hand: "Is this going to be like the speeches some of us gave in our high school English class?"

"That's a great question," replied Ms. Kuhlman. "Public speaking and public communication are not necessarily the same things. We think of public speakers as experts, sort of like Olympic athletes who are perfect in their sport. Public communication is not about perfection. I'll try to help you learn to take an idea that's important to you and find ways to talk effectively with a group of people about that idea. I'll try to help you present ideas in a way that people will remember them and maybe even be influenced by them."

Another student raised his hand and asked, "My high school teacher made us memorize our speeches. Are you going to teach us how to do that?"

"Not really. I emphasize a form of speaking called extemporaneous delivery, which allows you to use notes. What you'll work on is using effective notes that allow you to be natural in talking to people—not reading to them."

Cheri became more interested as the teacher went on. In fact, she thought the presentations the teacher had planned for the class sounded like fun.

Foundations of Public Communication

In this story, Cheri's initial excitement and tiny bit of apprehension are representative of the feelings most of us have about "speech class." The idea of giving speeches is fun, or at least more fun than some other types of homework, but there's still some apprehension. Most teachers recognize that students have these conflicting emotions and try to introduce their classes to the process of preparing presentations early in the academic term. That's why this chapter introduces you to the fundamentals of public communication, provides some suggestions for preparing your first presentation, and discusses some of the most common "first speeches" that teachers might assign.

Of course, the first presentation you make in the class will be very different from the last. You will likely improve your delivery after each presentation, and the research and length requirements will probably differ substantially from the beginning of the class to the end. But several elements of your presentation will remain the same. For example, each of your presentations will have an organization, and you will practice the same delivery skills for all presentations. This section introduces you to common steps in preparing for a public presentation; those steps serve as a foundation for subsequent chapters in this book.

The Roots of Rhetoric: The Five Canons

Public communication has a long history. From the time early cave dwellers learned that having a leader enabled them to secure food and safety more effectively, public communication has been central to human activity. Not until the development of democracy in 5th century Greece, however, did public communication serve as a foundation for most social activity—politics, education, and even entertainment. Not surprisingly, then, some of the earliest advice on public communication can be linked to thinkers such as Aristotle and Plato. Cicero, a Roman statesman and scholar, synthesized Greek teachings about public communication into the **Five Canons of Rhetoric,** which describe *the essential skills associated with public dialogue and communication.* Although they are thousands of years old, we find the Five Canons still to be a useful starting point for understanding the process you will go through when preparing your class presentations. Table 2.1 describes each of the Five Canons and suggests the key skills associated with each.

Public presentations are a key component of our democratic system of governance. Presentations are used at all levels of the government, from Congress to local school board meetings.

1. Invention and Public Communication

A common misunderstanding about public communication is that style is more important than substance—how you say your message is more important than what you say. This misunderstanding is a natural by-product of television because we constantly see politicians and other professional speakers talking in carefully edited sound bites. If you attend club meetings, classes, or civic groups, however, you will quickly see that substance is more important because few of us are expert speakers.

The substance of your presentation is directly tied to the **invention** process, which is *the art of finding information.* Invention deals with everything from selecting a topic for your presentation to locating examples, statistics, and other forms of supporting material. From ancient to modern times, speakers have used several approaches to invention.[1] In general, invention attempts to: (1) look at a problem from all sides, (2) ask the right questions, (3) select relevant information, (4) find new ways of talking about old topics, and (5) find new analogies and relationships between things.

Gabriel's teacher asked him to prepare a presentation on a social issue. Because Gabriel's mother works as an emergency management officer for a large county in Texas, Gabriel wanted to present information related to public safety concerns in his community. Gabriel's mother had worked on several recent accidents involving the transportation of hazardous waste, so Gabriel decided to frame his presentation on public safety around those accidents. However, Gabriel knew that his audience might not be interested in hearing a

TABLE 2.1 SKILLS ASSOCIATED WITH THE FIVE CANONS OF RHETORIC

Description of Canon	Key Skills
1. INVENTION *Finding information for your presentation.*	To engage in the invention process you should: • Determine the nature of the presentation. • Determine issues related to your topic. • Look at your topic from all sides to determine various perspectives. • Predict what your audience wants and needs to know. • Conduct research to supplement your personal knowledge.
2. DISPOSITION *Selecting an appropriate arrangement and structure for a presentation.*	To engage in disposition you should: • Prepare an introduction. • Organize main points and supporting material for the body of the presentation. • Develop a conclusion that summarizes the presentation and ends with impact.
3. STYLE *Using clear and ornamental language.*	To effectively use style you should: • Avoid technical language unless necessary. • Define important terms. • Arrange words using patterns appropriate for oral presentation. • Use metaphors, analogy, and creative language to increase artful ornamentation.
4. MEMORY *Being able to recall main ideas and details in your presentation.*	To effectively use memory you should: • Prepare a planning outline of your ideas. • Prepare a shortened presentation outline that will help keep you on track during the presentation. • Engage in extemporaneous delivery to maximize eye contact and conversational delivery.
5. DELIVERY *Using effective verbal and nonverbal behaviors to maximize the effectiveness of your message.*	To engage in effective delivery you should: • Avoid reading your presentation. • Maintain consistent eye contact. • Be natural with your use of gestures, facial expressions, and movement.

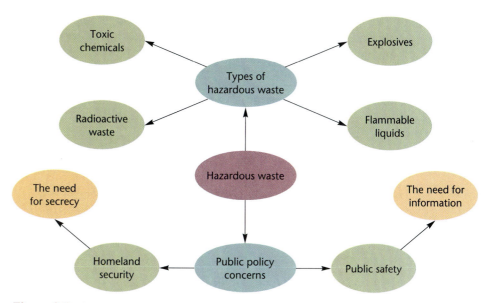

Figure 2.1 Concept map for Gabriel's presentation on hazardous waste.

long list of unknown dangers related to toxic chemicals and flammable liquids. After thinking for a while, Gabriel decided to approach his topic from a different angle by talking about tensions between public safety and homeland security. The main point that Gabriel wanted to make was that the most sensible steps to protect the public—for example, informing local officials when hazardous waste was going to travel through their city—might also arm potential terrorists with dangerous information. By looking at his topic from different sides and asking different types of questions, Gabriel took a seemingly dry topic and made that topic informative for his classmates.

To follow Gabriel's lead and effectively engage in the invention process, we recommend that you ask a series of questions about your topic:

1. *What is the nature of the presentation?* Are you primarily trying to teach, persuade, or entertain your audience? Determine what your audience expects and try to approach the topic in a slightly different way. This approach can effectively capture listeners' attention; however, the use of different "angles" should not obscure your intended objective for the presentation.
2. *What general issues are related to your topic?* By brainstorming with a concept map, you can easily identify various subtopics associated with your overall topic. **Concept maps** are *pictures or diagrams that allow you to visualize main and subordinate ideas related to a more general topic.* Narrowing your focus to one or more of the subtopics can help you effectively select relevant information and find new approaches to talking about your topic. This strategy is precisely the one Gabriel used to talk about hazardous waste. Figure 2.1 provides a concept map related to Gabriel's presentation. In addition to helping you narrow your focus, a concept map can also assist you in identifying points to include in your preparation outline.

30 Part One Preparing Your Presentations

3. *What different angles can you use to elaborate on your topic?* Looking at your topic from all sides will enable you to develop ideas for interesting and novel ways to talk about your topic.
4. *What does your audience need to know and want to know?* Anticipating your audience is a key presentation skill. Taking time to carefully consider your audience is wise because it allows you to adapt your message to their wants and needs.

TRY THIS

Pick your favorite hobby and create a concept map. Place the topic in the center of the concept map and try to complete several branches off of the central topic. Use the diagram provided in Figure 2.1 as an example.

---

2. Disposition (Arrangement) and Public Communication

Disposition refers to *the arrangement and structure of a presentation.* As you will learn in detail later in the course, many presentations have an introduction, body, and conclusion. Let's begin by understanding the function of each part of the presentation.

1. *The introduction.* The purpose of the introduction is to set the stage for the whole presentation by providing a central idea or thesis statement for the presentation and previewing the main ideas to be addressed. Effective introductions find a creative way to introduce the topic—often using a story, example, or audience interaction through questions and answers. Finding ways to establish credibility with your audience is also wise.
2. *The body.* Presentations typically consist of two to four main points or ideas. Selecting two, three, or four main points will enable listeners to more easily follow your presentation and remember key ideas. Carefully consider how to arrange your facts, testimony, and other evidence when outlining the body of the presentation. In particular, you should ensure that all main points have adequate supporting materials. You should start your planning process by arranging the body of your presentation because key elements of the introduction and conclusion are dependent on your main and subordinate points.
3. *The conclusion.* Effective presentations develop endings that not only summarize content, but also end with impact by using, for instance, quotations or stylistic devices such as metaphors and similes. Simply stating "That's it" or "I'm finished now" is not an effective way to end your presentation.

Arrangement and disposition are challenging skills for inexperienced presenters to learn because any topic offers multiple options for arranging ideas and evidence, and no single approach is absolutely correct.[2] In subsequent chapters, we offer sophisticated options for arranging ideas; for now, we recommend that you focus on developing a distinct introduction, clear main points, and a conclusion that brings closure to the presentation by reviewing key ideas.

TRY THIS

Read through the items below and then arrange them into an outline for the body of a presentation. The outline should have two main points with three subpoints each.

1. *Adopt-a-Block*
2. *Organizations related to human rights*
3. *Racial Fairness Project*
4. *Student organic farm*
5. *Organizations related to the environment*
6. *Rock the Vote*
7. *Campus computer recycling*
8. *Habitat for Humanity*

3. Style and Public Communication

Strictly speaking, **style** refers to *the use and ornamentation of language.* Most efforts to define the concept of style have focused on using clear language.[3] Avoid the use of jargon, define technical terms that might be unfamiliar to your audience, and use language and phrases you have in common.[4] Clarity also describes the way you arrange words. Avoid long sentences with multiple clauses so listeners can more easily follow your presentation—however, many short sentences in a row can actually cause confusion because the ideas come across as choppy and disjointed. As a practical matter, use conversational language and avoid preparing an elaborate script, because our style of writing often differs substantially from what listeners expect to hear from an oral presentation.

Using clear language, both in terms of words and arrangement, is an important skill. Yet, rhetorical scholar Ray Keesey notes that "clarity of style is the first consideration but it is ornament that, properly speaking, makes rhetoric art" (p. 52). While clarity refers to the ease with which we interpret langauge, **ornamentation** refers to *the creative and artful use of language.* Using ornamental language is certainly one of the most advanced presentation skills that you can learn. Fortunately, a few strategies can help you begin:

1. *Target certain areas for ornamental language.* When talking about his hobby of studying tornados, Steve used simple stylistic wording to improve clarity and ornamentation. His initial working outline contained this statement for the preview of his presentation:

   Today I will discuss the causes and effects of tornados.

   Steve's wording became much more effective after he edited his preview for style. After editing his initial ideas, Steve changed his preparation outline to read,

   Today I will talk with you about my hobby of studying tornados, one of the most common and most powerful weather phenomena many of us will ever see. First I will twist through the causes of tornados before blowing you away with the destruction they can bring to our communities.

View the CD-ROM video clip titled "Using an Analogy." Consider the effectiveness of this stylistic device.

As you can see, Steve's stylistic approach is much more effective. Adding ornamental language greatly improves Steve's presentation by engaging the audience's imagination.

2. *Use analogies and metaphors.* Analogies and metaphors help you describe something by comparing it to something else. When introducing herself to the class, Cheri used a metaphor to describe her experience of moving to college. "My trip to college is best described as a train wreck because everything that could have gone wrong did go wrong." Such comparisons add vivid description to otherwise common experiences. Accomplished authors make use of stylistic metaphors and analogies to enhance their novels, and presenters can employ similar strategies to captivate audiences.

3. *Use narratives.* As children, we learn to love stories. Many of us cherish memories of hearing our favorite bedtime story, and this love for narrative lasts well into adulthood. Telling stories based on personal experience or other sources of information naturally adds rich description to the issues we examine during presentations. Your own experiences likely confirm this. Your most interesting teachers probably made ample use of stories and examples to enhance their classes. Effective presenters learn quickly that stories and examples bring language to life through vivid descriptions of lived experiences. Consider the story in this speech introduction:

In the summer of 1996, Muhammad Ali, arguably the greatest boxer to enter the ring, stood with trembling hands as he lit the torch signaling the beginning of the summer Olympic Games in Atlanta. Ali's hands shook not because of the emotion of the moment, but because of Parkinson's disease. One year earlier, in Culpepper, Virginia, Christopher Reeve, who is best known for his lead role in "Superman," was flung from his horse and suffered a broken spine near his C1 and C2 vertebrae. Reeve never walked again after that accident. Seven years before Ali's appearance at the Olympic Games, Ronald Reagan, the fortieth president of the United States, left office and all but removed himself from public life due to the progressively debilitating effects of Alzheimer's disease. Although each of these men is very different, both in the way they lived their lives and in the medical problems they faced, each also holds something in common: Their ailments are potentially curable through research using stem cells.

Think about how this approach compares to the simpler approach of just saying "stem cells have the potential to help cure injuries and disease." By using narrative, the speaker not only provides us with important information about the presentation, but the stylistic use of narrative also helps us understand the speaker's humanity.

4. Memory and Public Communication

The **memory** canon assumes that *speakers must have a strong mental awareness of the messages they intend to present.* In ancient Greece (and subsequent civilizations), politicians and other speakers relied on memory as their primary resource for preparing presentations. Of course, until Gutenberg developed the printing press, the mass distribution of knowledge via books was not possible. For that reason, memory was a primary skill in speaking. After the availability of written resources expanded, memory was less important and was often referred to as "the lost canon."

Although we now have numerous resources, including libraries and the Internet, we should not abandon memory as an important presentation skill.[5] Most teachers recommend that students use **extemporaneous delivery,** *a mode of delivery that allows some preparation but does not require the presenter to script out or memorize a presentation.* The presenter can prepare notes to help maintain organization and highlight facts, details, and even quotations used during the presentation. Moreover, because extemporaneous delivery does not require a script or memorization, the presenter is able to react to listeners' feedback and questions more effectively. The "lost canon" of memory is still important because the presenter must remember how to elaborate on points. For instance, Steve's presentation outline for his speech on tornados might state only "Dew points and tornado development." Steve must remember how to explain how dew points can be used to identify potential risk areas for tornado development.

We do not recommend that you attempt to memorize parts of your presentation. Memorization is difficult, time consuming, and rarely effective. We do suggest, however, that you become very familiar with your material and that you strategically use notes to help jog your memory. Taking time to develop a good outline and practicing your speech several times aloud are two of the most effective strategies for ensuring that you will remember what you want to say.

5. Delivery and Public Communication

Delivery includes *the verbal and nonverbal techniques used to present the message.* Professional speakers and politicians are paid thousands of dollars to present speeches, and we have justifiably high expectations for their delivery. The majority of us, however, cannot call upon such skill. We like to use the analogy of baseball. Watching a major league baseball game is enjoyable because the players are able to perform at a very high level—nearly mistake free. Yet, we also think that the intimacy and humanness of a minor league, college, or even Little League baseball game makes the experience every bit as enjoyable as a trip to Wrigley Field in Chicago. We can effectively deliver presentations without approaching the skill of a Malcolm X, Bill Clinton, or Condoleezza Rice. In fact, the most effective presenters learn that being perfect in their delivery is far less important than being yourself.

Although you will learn several techniques for effective delivery later in the course, for now we suggest that you begin working on a couple of skills and avoid some of the worst presentation habits:

1. *Don't read your presentation.* Reading from notes is the single most common bad habit presenters develop. This one habit can literally destroy your ability to be naturally effective in your delivery. Minimize your use of notes by practicing your presentation

Facial expressions and eye contact are key components of effective delivery.

Cultural Note

ALTERNATIVES TO THE WESTERN PERSPECTIVE ON RHETORIC

Our preliminary discussion of the Five Canons of Rhetoric and public communication is biased toward traditional Western thought. Recent scholars argue that the Western view of rhetoric is not applicable to other cultures. For example, ancient Egyptian cultures placed a high value on knowing when not to speak—a view contrary to the Western assumption that having a lot of "talk time" indicates great power and authority.[6] Other scholars suggest that rhetoric can be more "invitational" by adhering to feminist principles of equality, immanent value, and self-determination.[7] Presenters might try to enact invitational rhetoric by engaging in dialogue with audience members and avoiding the tendency to dominate interaction.

several times. Each time you practice, try to reduce the number of notes that you need. Effective presenters should be able to deliver a five- to seven-minute presentation with only one 3" × 5" card of notes; this might not be practical for your first presentation but should be an objective for which you strive.

2. *Maintain consistent eye contact with the audience.* Your eye contact, rather than your voice, is your "secret weapon" as a presenter. Maintaining consistent eye contact causes listeners to perceive you as more confident, competent, and charming. Glancing at your notes is necessary at times, but always looking down at them causes listeners to question whether you are really prepared for your presentation. During most of your presentation you should look at your audience rather than at your notes.

3. *Be natural with your nonverbal delivery.* We naturally use our hands, body, and face to communicate messages that complement our verbal statements. Although some presenters plan to use various nonverbal behaviors, most presenters are simply encouraged to follow their instincts and do what comes naturally. Unfortunately, many students develop another bad habit—one related to reading their presentation—which diminishes their ability to be natural: tying their hands to a lectern. We commonly see students clutch the lectern, their notes, or even themselves in a death grip because of the natural apprehension accompanying any type of public performance. If your teacher allows you to use a lectern, we recommend that you place your notes on it for easy reference, but that you stand slightly to the side of the lectern. By doing this, you avoid the temptation to hold on.

TRY THIS

You can improve your own skills as a presenter by carefully observing others. Watch a prominent speaker on television or check out a videotape from your library. Make notes on how the speaker uses nonverbal behaviors like eye contact, gestures, and facial expressions. What did you find effective or distracting about the speaker's delivery?

We have now introduced you to five important skills for your presentation. Both accomplished and inexperienced presenters rely on these five foundational skills—sometimes implicitly and sometimes explicitly—to prepare and deliver presentations. We will revisit these skills throughout the book, but you are now armed with enough knowledge to begin preparing your first speech.

Tips for Preparing Your First Presentation

Now that you understand some of the foundational skills used to prepare effective presentations, you should begin thinking about how to translate your knowledge into practice and start preparing your first presentation for the class. Although teachers use a variety of approaches for the first presentation, some general strategies can help you effectively prepare for any presentation.

Tips for Planning Your Presentation

1. *Gather materials.* Especially if your first presentation is prepared entirely in class, having materials to work with is important. You should obtain and bring with you a legal pad or notebook paper to use for taking notes, a couple of 3" × 5" notecards to use for your speaking outline, and two colors of pens to prepare your presentation outline on the notecards. You can use one color to indicate main points and the other to list details or subpoints. See Figure 2.2 for an example.
2. *Carefully review the assignment expectations.* Your teacher may provide you with a written assignment description or may discuss the assignment orally in class. Before you begin working on your presentation—or before you come to class if the presentation will be prepared in class—take care to review all information about the assignment. Summarizing the key expectations in writing will help you remember exactly what you need to do when you begin working.

Figure 2.2 Sample presentation notecard.

3. *Use the invention process to accumulate information.* If your teacher allows you to prepare your first presentation outside of class, you have a full array of resources from which to select during the invention process. In addition to using information from the library or Internet, think carefully about personal experiences and local sources that may be relevant to your topic.

4. *Plan to be organized.* Recall that most of your assigned presentations should have an introduction, body, and conclusion. Also remember that most presentations have two to four main points in the body. You can plan in advance by writing headings for these sections on a page in your notebook. Once you begin preparing your presentation, you will simply fill in this template.

5. *Plan to be clear.* Once you have accumulated information during the invention process, the majority of your work should center on developing a clear central idea and main points. Although you may change these points several times as you continue preparing, taking time to plan them first will help you focus your thoughts and your work will be more efficient. For now, simple wording is most effective; later, you might edit your wording to add style.

6. *When selecting details, focus on quality, not quantity.* Using a well-explained example or statistic is far more important than trying to impress your listeners with the scope of your knowledge. When selecting details to fit under each of your main points, try to select those which are memorable, vivid, and credible. Three quotations from various "dot-com" Web sites are far less effective than a statement from a scientific journal or a detailed description of your personal experience because many people view "dot-coms" with skepticism.

7. *Edit for style.* Once you have planned your message, think of ways to "dress up" your style. Can you take the simple wording of your central idea and main points and make them rich by using a metaphor, analogy, or creative wording? Remember that style also involves using clear language. Don't overuse style to the extent that your message is obscured.

8. *If possible, practice, practice, practice.* Some teachers require that the first presentation be prepared and delivered during class, and in such cases, practice is difficult. But you can still practice preparing a speech and delivering it to a roommate or friend. Even if it is on a different topic than you deliver in class, you can still rehearse the process. If you are allowed more time to prepare your presentation, plan to practice your talk aloud a minimum of three times.

9. *Plan for effective delivery.* In advance of your presentation, you should carefully visualize what you are going to do when your turn arrives. Remember to minimize your presentation notes and to stand beside the lectern if one is present. As you are delivering your presentation, shift your focus and your eye contact among a handful of people scattered around the room. This practice will help you draw all listeners to your message. Remember that your audience does not expect perfect delivery, especially if your delivery seems natural.

10. *Enjoy the opportunity!* One of the most exciting aspects of a course in public communication is the guaranteed opportunity to talk with peers about topics of interest to you. Such experiences can be exhilarating and even give some students a "rush." If you open your mind to the possibility, we think you can experience a similar feeling. Remember that you are not trying to be a professional public speaker; you are simply trying to meaningfully connect with your listeners. Have fun with the experience!

E-Note

PRACTICING FOR IMPROMPTU PRESENTATIONS

The *Architects of Peace* project celebrates 70 women and men from around the world who devoted their lives to community activism and issues of social justice. Using the various suggestions within this section of the textbook, select a person profiled on the *Architects of Peace* Web site (**http://scu.edu/ethics/architects**) and prepare either a short impromptu speech or speech of introduction for that person.

Teachers often use the first classroom presentation to accomplish two primary objectives. First, they usually want you to become familiar with the process of preparing and delivering a classroom presentation. In particular, the first presentation creates an opportunity for you and your classmates to learn more about each other—this knowledge is important because such information will better enable you to adapt future classroom presentations to the specific interests and needs of your audience. Second, teachers typically want you to begin practicing several of the skills necessary for developing and presenting effective presentations. With these two general objectives as a starting point, teachers select from a variety of presentation formats for the first classroom presentation. We provide suggestions for four of the most common types of first presentation assignments: the impromptu presentation, presenting yourself, presenting a classmate, and the demonstration presentation.

Common Types of First Presentations

Impromptu Presentations

An **impromptu presentation** is *one that does not allow for substantial planning and practice before the presentation is given.* Although you typically are required to develop an introduction, body (with at least two main points), and conclusion, you probably will not be expected to integrate supporting materials such as detailed statistics, quotations, or multiple sources. Teachers typically use this type of assignment to provide you with the experience of presenting ideas to your classmates and to practice thinking on your feet. Impromptu presentations can take many forms. Most of the time you will have about five minutes to prepare a rough presentation outline.

Regardless of the type of impromptu your teacher selects, your objective should be to focus on two general skill areas: organization and delivery. To organize in advance of your presentation, you should use one color of pen to write the key parts of the presentation outline on one of your notecards. When you select your topic, you will typically be given a few minutes to prepare in the hallway. Using your second color of pen, write down ideas on the rough presentation outline that you created in advance (see Figure 2.2). To practice effective delivery, take care to maintain eye contact with the audience and be natural in your delivery style.

Presenting Yourself

Teachers often use the first presentation as an opportunity to have you introduce yourself to the class. Typically, your task in this type of speech is to prepare a presentation in which you describe your background and other meaningful things about yourself like significant experiences, hobbies, or interests. Because you will typically have at least one evening to prepare this presentation, your teacher might expect more in terms of supporting examples and explanations than for an impromptu presentation.

- *Develop structure.* As you prepare your presentation outline, use your legal pad to develop main points. Your main points should organize information so that audience members can easily follow your train of thought. For example, you might organize your main points chronologically, beginning with early memories and working up to recent ones, or you might arrange them topically, with one point about your family and another about your hobbies and interests.
- *Focus on small details.* Because you have time to prepare, you should carefully consider ways that you can use style to improve your creative language use.
- *Be thoughtful.* When selecting stories to tell about yourself, carefully consider which stories will teach the listeners about who you are and persuade them that you are a "credible student." Carefully selecting such examples will allow you to make friends more quickly in class and will tell your teacher that you are serious about doing well in the course.
- *Make content meaningful to the audience.* Although a presentation about you will be naturally interesting, an even better one will find ways to relate your life experiences to those of your listeners. What can they learn from your stories?

Because this assignment focuses on themselves, some students assume that the presentation can easily be planned just before class. Taking time to carefully develop and organize ideas, paying attention to small details like style, and practicing your presentation can determine whether your presentation is "excellent" or merely "average."

Presenting a Classmate

Some teachers prefer that you present information about a classmate rather than about yourself. The advantage of this approach is that the process more closely follows that which you will use in other presentations, that is, you must consult external sources during the invention process. For this presentation, you are typically asked to interview a classmate and plan a presentation about that person. In many respects, the same suggestions we provided for the self-introduction presentation apply equally well to the peer presentation. Perhaps the one additional skill necessary for this assignment is the need for effective interviewing techniques to use during the invention process.

To gather information, you must interview your classmate. A thorough analysis of interviewing skills is unnecessary for this assignment; however, the following suggestions should help you gain enough information to plan a successful presentation.

- *Plan interview questions.* The most effective strategy for conducting an interview is to preplan some questions, while remaining flexible enough to ask follow-up questions.
- *Record answers.* Effective interviewers will either tape-record or take detailed notes of answers to interview questions. A detailed recording (whether audio or written) will better enable you to select accurate information when preparing your presentation.
- *Start with the basics.* Although basic information such as a person's hometown, major, year in school, and age are potentially the least interesting facts to learn, such information is expected. Begin your interview by learning these basics.

When interviewing the person, try to discover stories which you can effectively relate to experiences or situations faced by your other classmates.

- *Ask questions about more than the basics.* One widely supported concept in communication is that each of us has layers of information that we disclose to others. Our outer layer contains basic information and is commonly revealed to others without much forethought. Subsequent layers include information about our personal beliefs, our personal values, our goals and desires, and our self-concept. This layer of information is revealed naturally as a relationship progresses. For your presentation, you might ask your partner about some of these more personal issues so that you can do a more thorough job of introducing the individual to your class.
- *Look for the novel and unique.* Each of us has characteristics and experiences that make us unique. Although we may find our hobbies or preferences familiar or routine, others may not. Ask questions to learn details that your interview partner may find ordinary, but that you think would be interesting to your classmates.
- *Be ethical.* Your short interview with your classmate could be the beginning of a solid friendship. Recognize that some information might come up during the interview that should not be divulged to the class. Moreover, your introduction of your class colleague should be done with respect and consideration.

Effective interviewing skills are valuable for careers in sales, management, health, and even teaching. Our own experience suggests that interviewing and introducing a fellow classmate is one of the more enjoyable presentation experiences you can have in class.

Demonstration Presentations

Another typical first presentation is a more formal informative speech that demonstrates something. A **demonstration presentation** *teaches audience members*

To see an example of a demonstration presentation, watch the clip titled "How to Play Drums" on the accompanying CD-ROM.

how something works or how to perform some task. Students usually pick a topic with which they have ample experience. At universities in the Midwest, "country students" commonly teach "city students" how things are done "on the farm" in presentations about many rural activities, from bull riding to raising organic vegetables. Students more oriented toward the sciences might illustrate a scientific principle. Kim, for example, used a balloon and tinfoil to demonstrate how black holes develop in space. Yet other students discuss hobbies ranging from making homemade beer to competing in waterboarding competitions.

Demonstration presentations can come across as either interesting or trivial. To prepare an effective demonstration presentation, carefully analyze how you can make your topic relevant to audience members. For example, why would listeners care to learn about waterboarding competitions when most will never engage in the activity? Here are a couple other suggestions for preparing an effective demonstration presentation:

- *Organize logically.* Because even simple processes like recycling can require several steps, it can be challenging to find clear main points for a demonstration presentation. Your main points should divide and organize multiple steps into a few logical categories. To talk about recycling, for instance, you might cover the following main points:

  I. Recycling plastic.
  II. Recycling metal.
  III. Recycling electronics.

- *Use visual aids.* One of the most effective ways to increase listeners' interest in your topic is to show them what you are talking about. Displaying diagrams and pictures often does wonders to clarify your explanation of complex or unfamiliar things. Of course, visual aids are also one of the biggest pitfalls for new presenters. In a later chapter, you will learn to effectively plan, create, and integrate visual resources into your presentation. For now, make sure that your visual resources are clear and easily seen, and that you carefully plan when to use them during your presentation.

This chapter has examined several key skills and concepts that will serve as a foundation for your presentation experiences in this class, other classes, and your life beyond college. Armed with just the basic information in this chapter, you already know more about public communication than most people. As you prepare your first presentation, be confident in the knowledge that following even a few of these suggestions will result in a very positive experience.

Sample Speech for Review and Analysis

In this presentation, Lance LeClair has the task of introducing Megan Fugelberg, one of his classmates, prior to her presenting a talk to the class. Lance had the opportunity to talk with Megan to prepare for his peer introduction presentation. As you read the text of his presentation, notice how he effectively uses ornamental language to increase the vividness and creative energy of his speech. Lance italicized his ornamental language in his speaking notes, and we have kept the italics in this reproduction of his presentation.

Chapter Two   Preparing Your First Presentation   41

Introduction of Megan Fugelberg

by

Lance LeClair

Everybody has stories about different trips they've been on, but who actually can say they've experienced a life-threatening situation on the trip? The student I'm going to introduce to you today had an *electrifying* experience she'll never forget.

Hi, my name is Lance LeClair. Last week, Megan and I sat down and got to know each other a little better. Megan is a small-town woman who grew up near Mayville. Her father, Steve, works on the farm and her mother, Maggie, works at Mayville State University. Megan also has a brother, Ross, and a boyfriend, Craig, who earned a marketing degree at Mayville State. Currently, Megan works at Wells Fargo Bank as a teller and I was *stunned* to hear that her bank pays for many of her college courses. Anyway, when we sat down we exchanged some life stories, and let me tell you, I was really *lit up* about one in particular. Well, don't let me keep you waiting, here's Megan Fugelberg to tell you about her literally *shocking* experience in Spain.

Notice how Lance makes reference back to the topic of "electrifying" and "shocking" experiences during his introduction of Megan. Besides adding stylistic language to his presentation, Lance is also foreshadowing Megan's story about a scare with electricity on her trip. Because Lance's presentation introduced a much longer talk from Megan, he did not divide his presentation into clear main points. He did, however, have a distinctive introduction and conclusion for his presentation. If he were presenting a longer talk about Megan, he would likely have created main points and added additional details and examples.

Resources for Review and Discussion

SUMMARY

In this chapter you have learned the following:

▶ The Five Canons of Rhetoric provide a useful framework for understanding key skills related to successful presentations.
  • Invention is the art of finding information and involves everything from selecting a topic to finding examples, statistics, quotations, and other forms of supporting material. A key skill during the invention process is the ability to discover new and unique angles from which to approach your topic.
  • Disposition/arrangement describes the arrangements and structure of a presentation. All presentations should have a clear introduction, body, and conclusion.
  • Style is the clear and ornamental use of language.
  • Memory is a key skill for extemporaneous delivery. Although extemporaneous presentations allow the presenter to prepare ideas beforehand, presentation notes are often minimal and the presenter must remember some details and descriptions.
  • Effective delivery does not require perfection, but does stem from being natural when presenting information to listeners.

▶ Well-developed presentations accomplish different objectives with the introduction, body, and conclusion.
  • The introduction should introduce listeners to the topic of the presentation, provide a central idea, and preview points covered during the talk.
  • The body of the presentation should expand on two to four main points and include appropriate supporting materials.
  • The conclusion of the presentation should summarize the content of the presentation and end with impact.

▶ Clarity and ornamentation are two stylistic elements that increase the effectiveness of any presentation.
  • You increase language clarity when you avoid technical language (or carefully define terms) and take care to arrange words effectively.
  • You increase language ornamentation by using analogies, metaphors, and creatively wording certain parts of your presentation.

▶ Nonverbal delivery improves when presenters avoid overusing written notes, maintain eye contact with listeners, and use natural nonverbal behaviors including gestures, movement, and facial expressions.

▶ Presenters should strategically plan ahead when embarking on any of the four most commonly assigned first presentations.
  • The impromptu presentation does not allow for substantial preparation and practice and is typically completed during class. Effective impromptu presentations should be organized clearly, and the presenter should utilize effective delivery behaviors.
  • The self-introduction presentation allows you to talk about yourself for a few minutes in front of the class. When preparing this presentation, organize carefully and find ways to make your stories meaningful for listeners.
  • The peer introduction presentation asks you to introduce one of your classmates. More successful peer introduction presentations typically stem from interviews that get beyond superficial personal information.
  • A demonstration presentation teaches listeners how something works or how to perform some task. More effective demonstrations will present topics with which you have had some experience. Make the presentation relevant for your listeners, and use visual aids when possible.

KEY TERMS

  Use the *Public Speaking* CD-ROM and the Online Learning Center at www.mhhe.com/nelson to practice your understanding of the following terminology.

Concept maps	Extemporaneous delivery	Memory
Delivery	Five Canons of Rhetoric	Ornamentation
Demonstration presentation	Impromptu presentation	Style
Disposition/Arrangement	Invention	

REFERENCES

[1] Kienpointner, Manfred (1997). On the art of finding arguments: What ancient and modern masters of invention have to tell us about the "ars inveniendi." *Argumentation, 11.2,* 225–37.

[2] Rowan, Katherine E. (1995). A new pedagogy for explanatory public speaking: Why arrangement should not substitute for invention. *Communication Education, 44.3,* 236–50.

[3] Keesey, Ray E. (1953). John Lawson's lectures concerning oratory. *Speech Monographs, 20.1,* 49.

[4] Hirst, Russel (2003). Scientific jargon, good and bad. *Journal of Technical Writing & Communication, 33.3,* 201–29.

[5] Haskins, Ekaterina V. (2001). Rhetoric between orality and literacy: Culture memory and performance in Isocrates and Aristotle. *Quarterly Journal of Speech, 87,* 158–79.

[6] Hutto, David (2002). Ancient Egyptian rhetoric in the old and middle kingdoms. *Rhetorica, 20.3,* 213.

[7] Foss, Sonja K., & Griffin, Cindy L. (1995). Beyond persuasion: A proposal for an invitational rhetoric. *Communication Monographs, 62.1,* 2–19.

APPLICATION EXERCISES

  Go to the self-quizzes on the *Public Speaking* CD-ROM and the Online Learning Center at www.mhhe.com/nelson to test your knowledge of the chapter concepts.

1. Practice your impromptu speaking skills by preparing short presentations for each of the three quotations below. The presentation notes you prepare for each quote should have a thesis statement and two main points. The thesis and main points should develop an explanation demonstrating that the quotation says something about who you are as a person.
   a. "... friendship ... is essential to intellectuals. You can date the evolving life of a mind, like the age of a tree, by the rings of friendship formed by the expanding central trunk." —Mary McCarthy
   b. "You don't need proof when you have instinct." —"Joe" in the movie *Reservoir Dogs*
   c. "Like a boxer in a title fight, you have to walk in that ring alone." —Billy Joel
2. Develop an interview outline to gather information from one of your classmates. List 7–10 questions that introduce new topics to the interview. In addition to gaining basic information like "What is your major?" and "What is your hometown?" you should also think of more interesting, unique, and out-of-the-ordinary questions to ask.

CHAPTER THREE

The reason most people never reach their goals is that they don't define them, or ever seriously consider them as believable or achievable.

DENIS WAITLEY,
THE WAITLEY INSTITUTE

Looking up gives light, although at first it makes you dizzy.

MEVLANA RUMI,
13TH CENTURY SUFI POET

Selecting a Topic and Purpose

What will you learn?

When you have read and thought about this chapter, you will be able to:

1. Search for and select a public speaking topic.
2. Evaluate a public speaking topic.
3. Identify three general purposes of public speaking.
4. Write a specific purpose for a public presentation.
5. Develop a thesis statement for a public presentation.

One of the first steps in preparing a presentation is choosing a topic. You may choose to talk about a topic that is familiar to you, or you may use this opportunity to research an unfamiliar topic about which you are curious. In either case, the choice is yours. In this chapter, we will consider selecting a topic and purpose.

Cultural Note

FREE SPEECH VS. CULTURAL RESPECT

Which is more important? Respect for cultural sensitivity or free speech? Most of us would agree that both are important. What happens if a speaker uses the word "oriental" when referring to people of Asian descent? When called on it, the speaker insists that freedom of speech allows this usage. How would you respond? Would your response depend on the ethnic makeup of your audience? Why or why not?

Maria Vega was worried about her speech topic. Having grown up in San Jose del Cabo, Maria had met many Americans who visited the Mexican city. Her family owned a jewelry store in downtown San Jose, and she had worked at the store while she was in high school. Maria had learned English as a child and had had many opportunities to practice with English-speaking customers in her family's store. She spoke with only the slightest accent. She began college in Mexico City, but she had transferred in her second year to a state university in the United States. Her sister had gone to the school before her and encouraged Maria to join her.

Maria had mixed feelings about the tourists she met in San Jose and the Americans she met at college. She certainly appreciated the economic boost that tourists provided in Mexico, but she worried about the future of her town. The old church on town square was no longer held in deep reverence as it once had been. Instead, the winter months found people eating ice cream cones and sipping tall drinks while sitting on the church steps.

The Americans she met in class were friendly, but she wondered about their values. Those who had visited the Cabo area seemed only to appreciate the bars and restaurants and not the history or the culture of the Baja Mexican area.

Maria registered for a public speaking course in her first term. She was excited about the class, but now she was facing her first speech assignment. Her instructor had scheduled Maria's presentation for the first day of the assignment. Maria had thought a great deal about the assignment, but she did not yet have a topic. What could she share with the class? What did she know that they did not know? What would her classmates like to know? How could she determine what her goal should be? Maria thought about the presentation while she was walking to class, while she was exercising, and while she was trying to fall asleep at night. Still, she did not have a topic.

Searching for a Topic

The range of topics on which you can speak is almost limitless, but sometimes, like Maria, you might have a difficult time identifying a topic for your speech. The First Amendment to the U.S. Constitution protects the right of free expression, saying, in part, "Congress shall make no law . . . abridging the freedom of speech."

Does the First Amendment mean that nothing is off limits? No. Speakers cannot defame others with falsehoods, they cannot incite audiences to take illegal action, and they cannot threaten the president's life.

The First Amendment is often the subject of debate in contemporary society. The development of the Internet, concern for children's rights, differing views on women's rights, and incidents of hate speech by a variety of groups all fuel the sometimes fiery debate about the parameters of the First Amendment. Nonetheless, you are free to speak on almost any topic that you can identify. Check with your instructors for any particular expectations they may have. Here are some of the topics of speeches included in this book:

- Apex predators
- The digital divide
- What is "ethnic cleansing"?
- Public assistance in the 21st century
- Hate crime in your state
- The use of nanotechnology on oil spills
- Health issues in underdeveloped countries
- Public security
- "No Child Left Behind"
- The phenylketonurics among us
- The guidelines for ethical decision making
- The price of prescription drugs
- Hunger Awareness Day
- The Architects of Peace project

When your instructor assigns a speech, what do you do? If you are like Maria and many other beginning speakers, you may put off the assignment as long as possible. You may consider possible topics as you go about other daily activities. How can you jump-start the process so you have more constructive time to plan your presentation?

In this section, we will discuss five methods of searching for a topic: individual brainstorming, categorical brainstorming, conducting a personal inventory, current topic identification, and Internet searching. Some of these methods will be more interesting and useful to you than others.

Individual Brainstorming

Brainstorming occurs *when you try to think of as many topics as you can in a limited time.* Without judging them, you simply list all topics that come to mind. Groups frequently use brainstorming when members get together to propose a number of ideas. After the brainstorming process, which should be limited to a specific amount of time, say five minutes, the group discusses the ideas and selects one or more by assessing their quality. Individual brainstorming occurs when you, individually, spend a certain amount of time writing down all the possible topics you can think of. After you have completed that phase of the process, you evaluate the topics and choose two or three for further research.

Categorical Brainstorming

Categorical brainstorming is similar to individual brainstorming. The difference

Conduct a personal inventory to identify topics related to your life such as experiences, attitudes, values, beliefs, interests, and skills.

TABLE 3.1 TOPICS IDENTIFIED BY CATEGORICAL BRAINSTORMING

People	Places	Things	Events
Wonkette	Kosovo	salsa	Cinco de Mayo
Bill Gates	Australia	higher education	Halloween
Dixie Chicks	Arctic National Wildlife Refuge	social justice	spring break
Lance Armstrong	Hollywood	tsunamis	Earth Day
Madonna	Lake Mille Lacs	business improvement district	birthday
Vince Chase	Napa Valley	neuroscience	Chinese New Year
Maya Lin	Bangkok, Thailand	geography	wedding
Barack Obama	South Central L.A.	blogs	funeral
Coldplay	Tibet	fishing gear	graduation
Jennifer Lopez	Miami	coffee	Race for the Cure®
Nelson Mandela	Mount Rushmore	diversity	election day
Beyoncé	Central Park	red beans and rice	Boxing Day
Chris Rock	Nepal	conventional wisdom	concerts

is that *you begin with categories that prompt you to think of topics.* For example, you might think about people, places, things, and events. Begin by writing these four categories on a sheet of paper and making four columns. Then brainstorm topics that fit in any of the four columns. Table 3.1 provides an example.

Conducting a Personal Inventory

Another strategy that might be helpful is conducting a **personal inventory.** *Consider features of your life such as experiences, attitudes, values, beliefs, interests, and skills.* Write down anything that describes you. Don't worry if your words don't sound like a topic for a presentation. No idea should be discarded at this stage. Later you will cull through this list and identify two or three topics that might work for your presentation. Here are some topics that students identified using personal inventories.

  Studying abroad
  Interning in the White House
  Service learning with listening-impaired children
  Laser surgery for better sight
  The symbols in a powwow
  Being a Muslim in the United States
  Rugby as exercise
  Free speech in Mexico
  Health care for veterans
  Private versus public education

Growing up below the poverty line

Preparing for a job interview

Managing a life-threatening disease

Pilates

Maria, who was searching for a speech topic at the beginning of this chapter, used a personal inventory to create her speech topic: San Jose del Cabo—A Vacationer's Paradise. Maria knew that she could talk about the history and culture of the city as well as the current venues for a relaxing and enjoyable vacation.

Current Topic Identification

Another way to approach searching for a topic is to consider topics of interest today. **Current topics** are *items that you find in the news, on the media, and on the minds of people in your audience.* Among the best sources of ideas on current topics are newspapers, magazines, TV news/discussions/documentaries, radio talk shows, and the Internet. Specialized magazines of political opinion and editorials from major newspapers are especially good at inspiring ideas for speeches. Student speech topics that originated in current topics include:

The case for war in Iraq	Organic farming
Are professional athletes overpaid?	Identity theft
Rising health-care costs	Weight control
Binge drinking	Anabolic steroids
Genetically modified produce	Hate crime
Investments for students	Hybrid cars
AIDS in the 21st century	Executive compensation
Nursing shortages	Same-sex marriage
Ethical issues in business	Suicide bombing
Stem cells and research	Internet privacy

Internet Searching

Today you have another tool that was not available to students of previous generations. Your access to the World Wide Web through the Internet is an invaluable resource as you search for a topic. You can use a subject-based search engine such as the Librarians' Index to the Internet, Dogpile, Google, or AltaVista. You can also use a metasearch engine such as Mamma.com for an even larger database. Many search engines provide a list of major categories of subjects that they index. For example, if you go to Google and click on "More" and then "Directory" from the Google Services menu, you will find the list of broad categories shown in Figure 3.1. These categories are then further subdivided into subdirectories. For example, clicking on the "Arts" subdirectory will take you to the specific categories of Arts shown in Figure 3.2.

You can get increasingly more detailed information as you follow individual links in these directories. For example, if you are interested in Theater and Street Performance, you will find coverage such as that shown in Figure 3.3.

While we provide an in-depth example of Google here, other sources on the Internet may be far more valuable to you. Two sources that many students use are Lexis/Nexis or EBSCOhost. These sources provide dozens of journals, magazines,

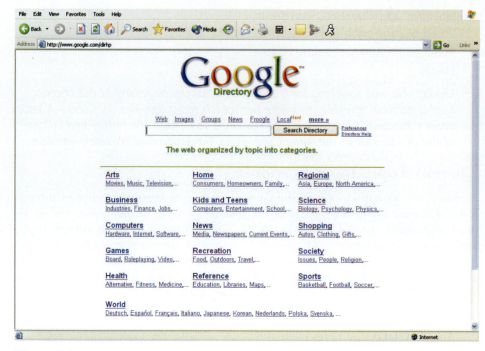

Figure 3.1 The Google directory.

Figure 3.2 Google subdirectory to Arts.

Figure 3.3 Google subdirectory to Performing Arts.

and other references. You will be able to search within them using single words or multiple words as you expand your search. However, you will need to determine if these sources are available to you on your school's library Web site or elsewhere.

Keep in mind that regardless of the search engines or indices that you use, plagiarism becomes very easy. You can cut and paste sections of text and forget to give credit to the source. You can minimally paraphrase information, which is also an infraction of the rules. The Internet is a bountiful source of information. Be careful not to take the words of others without giving credit.

Most important in searching for a topic is getting started. Journals that public speaking students completed in beginning courses revealed that students spent some time thinking about topics but did not engage in searching for a topic immediately after the assignment was given. The best strategy is to begin one or more of these searching techniques as soon as you know the speech assignment. Students who earn high grades in public speaking courses engage in this process early. You, too, can prepare an impressive presentation if you begin the process quickly.

Selecting a Topic

Now that you have identified several topics for a presentation, you will need to comb through them and select one. How can you best succeed in choosing? Here are some general guidelines for topic selection used successfully by public speaking students:

- *Speak about topics you already know.* What subjects do you know about—Web design, culinary arts, or national parks? You will save much time by choosing a familiar topic.

- *Speak about a topic that interests you.* What subjects arouse your interest—politics, social justice, or fitness? What do you like to read about? What elective courses do you choose? Selecting a topic that interests you will make the research process enjoyable.
- *Speak about topics that are uniquely your own.* If you have done a personal inventory or an individual brainstorm, examine the list for topics that might not be shared by others in the class. Consider unusual jobs or travel experiences. Consider your unique background for ideas to share with the audience.
- *Speak about a topic that is important to your local community.* Have you heard the expression "Think globally; act locally"? How can you relate international and national issues and trends to your hometown or present community?
- *Speak about topics that your audience finds interesting*—reality television, Internet dating, or interviewing do's and don'ts. What do people in your class enjoy talking and hearing about? Which of their favorite topics could you discuss with some authority? If people tend to talk about certain topics before or after class, consider those ideas for a speech topic.
- *Speak about a topic that the audience embraces, but you do not.* Do some members of your class hold ideas that they accept without question, but which you think could be challenged? For example, people in your class might have differing views on political candidates, cohabiting, or how much alcohol they should and do drink. Try to convince members of the audience to consider your thinking on the topic.

Evaluating Topics

After you have identified a general topic, the next step is evaluating it. You must determine if the topic meets standards of appropriateness for the speaker, audience, ethics, and occasion.

Appropriate for You

While you should always keep your attention on the audience, you also need to determine whether a topic is of interest to you. A speech is appropriate for you as a speaker if you can generate interest in the topic. If you are interested, you can be enthusiastic, and the audience is likely to share your feelings. If you are not, the audience will probably sense it.

Research is every speaker's obligation. You should know something about your topic, but you should also have a sincere interest in learning more about the subject. A topic is appropriate for you if you know—or can learn—more about it than most of the people in the audience. Most of us possess only

When you select a topic that is appropriate for you, you communicate your enthusiasm.

superficial knowledge of most topics. A speaker can generally learn more about a specific subject than is generally known to an audience. When you have such knowledge, you are said to have subject matter competence.

Appropriate for the Audience

A speech is appropriate for audience members if the content is both interesting and worthwhile to them. The speaker is responsible for generating audience interest. Suppose you are very interested in genetic engineering, but you realize that practically nobody else in the class holds this interest. One way to arouse audience interest might be to show how controversial genetic engineering can be. For example, consider the issue of genetically modified foods.

On several occasions when he has spoken in front of audiences composed largely of African Americans, Bill Cosby has been critical of the behavior of young African Americans. Do you believe his topic was appropriate for the audience?

Also consider whether your topic is worthwhile for the audience. If the audience is already familiar with the topic, be careful about the information you are presenting. Try to present new information about familiar topics; do not repeat what the audience is already likely to know. A presentation about a topic too familiar to the audience, for example, reality television, would probably be uninformative. A presentation about a topic that is too trivial, for instance your summer vacation at the lake, will not be worth the audience's time. A proper analysis of your audience should reveal both how interesting and how worthwhile your topic would be. In the next chapter, we thoroughly discuss audience analysis.

Maria, the beginning speech student in our opening story, decided that her audience would be more interested in considering San Jose del Cabo as a current vacation spot rather than understanding the complete history, social issues, and economic realities of the city. Maria thus limited her topic as she considered her audience and their interest in it. She was somewhat disheartened, but she accurately assessed the audience's interest.

Appropriate for the Occasion

Finally, consider the topic's appropriateness for the occasion: Is the subject significant, timely, and tailored? A speech topic is *significant* if the content meets the audience's expectation of what should occur on that occasion. In a classroom presentation, for example, a common expectation is that the speech should be on a topic of importance to the class, the campus, the community, or the world. Your breakfast preferences, your date Saturday night, or your most recent argument with your roommate probably do not warrant publicity; that is, a presentation about them would seem insignificant.

A speech is *timely* if it can be linked to the audience's current concerns. A student who gave a presentation about a revolution in Liberia did a fine job on the speech, but the revolution had occurred several years before and the student

1. Do you, as the speaker, have *involvement* with the topic?

2. Do you, as the speaker, have *competence* in the topic area?

3. Based on audience analysis, does this topic hold *interest* for your audience?

4. Based on audience analysis, is the topic *worthwhile* to your audience?

5. Is the topic *significant* in terms of the speech occasion?

6. Is the topic *timely* or *appropriate* for the speech occasion?

7. Have you appropriately *narrowed* and *limited* the topic for the occasion?

Figure 3.4 **Guidelines for topic appropriateness.**

failed to demonstrate how the topic related to the present. Ancient history can be timely if the speaker can show how that history speaks to the present.

A speech is *tailored* if the topic is narrowed to fit the time allotted for the presentation. To cover the rise and fall of the Roman Empire in a five-minute speech is impossible, but to talk about three ways to avoid obesity through diet and exercise is possible. Most speakers err in selecting too large rather than too small a topic. A narrow topic allows you to use research time more effectively; researching too large a topic will require cutting much of the material to meet the time limits of the speech.

Refer to the criteria in Figure 3.4 as guidelines for evaluating your topic for appropriateness.

TRY THIS

After you have identified a number of topics using one or more of the methods in the section on searching for a topic, pair up with a classmate. Share your lists. Have your classmate identify topics in which she or he would be interested, that are appropriate for the occasion, and that meet ethical standards. Reverse roles and identify appropriate topics from your classmate's list. What does this exercise illustrate? Are either of you surprised by the other's reaction to the topics?

Purposes of Speeches

Without a map, you do not know how to get to your destination. In public speaking, without a purpose, you do not know what you should say. In this section of the chapter, we consider *purposes* of speeches and the *thesis statement*, which is a kind of short summary of your speech. Speeches have both general purposes and specific purposes. We consider both purposes here.

General Purposes

In the broadest sense, the *general purpose* of many speeches is either *to inform, to persuade or to highlight a special occasion.* In class, your teacher may determine the general purpose of your speech. When you are invited to give a presentation to a

Chapter Three   Selecting a Topic and Purpose   55

particular group, the person who invites you may suggest a purpose. If you are not given a general purpose, you should consider the speech, the occasion, the audience, and your own motivations as you determine the general purpose of your speech.

The general purposes of speaking can sometimes overlap. You often must inform your audience before you can persuade them. Most speeches, however, can be distinguished as mainly informative, mainly persuasive, or mainly special occasion.

The Speech to Inform

The **speech to inform** *seeks to increase the audience's level of understanding or knowledge about a topic.* Generally, the speaker provides new information or shows how existing information can be applied in new ways. The speaker does not attempt to persuade or convince the audience to change attitudes or behaviors. The informative speech should be devoid of persuasive tactics. The speaker is essentially a teacher. How would the following topics lend themselves to a speech to inform?

What does it mean to be Muslim?	The Federal Marriage Amendment
After Enron: The Sarbanes Oxley Act	Early childhood literacy
Wind energy	Recognizing bias in language
Interviewing: Best practices	Purchasing a PDA
Tips for improving your grades	Wetlands ecology

Keep in mind that the main idea behind the informative speech is to increase the audience's knowledge about a topic.

William B. Harrison, Jr., chief executive officer of J. P. Morgan Chase and Company, delivered a talk to the Peterson Business Award Dinner at the Greenwich Library in Greenwich, Connecticut, on March 7, 2002. Harrison began his informative talk by stating,

> Tonight I will look at how two institutions—banks and libraries—have evolved through three great revolutions in information technology. This will be a quick, even lighthearted look.

Similarly, Dr. Two Bears, a member of the American Society of Plastic Surgeons, began her talk,

> While statistics vary on the frequency of procedures performed, an increasing number of teenagers are seeking plastic surgery.

These two speakers give dozens of speeches each year. They demonstrate their ability to state their purpose clearly and cleverly. Professional speakers can serve as good role models for beginning speakers.

The Speech to Persuade

The **speech to persuade** *seeks to influence, reinforce, or modify the audience members' feelings, attitudes, beliefs, values, or behaviors.* Persuasive speeches may seek change or they may argue that the status quo should be upheld. Persuasive speakers attempt to add to what the audience members already know, but they also strive to alter how the audience feels about what they know and ultimately how they behave. The speaker, in this instance, is an advocate. How would the following topics lend themselves to a speech to persuade?

Binge drinking should be reduced on college campuses	Why families are in crisis
	Serve the community
Young adults need to worry about heart disease	Why schools should lower tuition
	How to improve your family relationships
Medicine, ethics, and compassion	
CEOs must take responsibility	Trust must be restored in America
People must become involved with politics	Ten commandments of community
	A just AND peaceful world?
Improving American education	Ethics: One day at a time
Minorities in business	
Globalization and business development	

Daniel Ramirez, a student, began his persuasive presentation,

> Maybe you have never thought about the safety of your automobile, but after hearing my presentation today, I hope you will. Two months ago, my wife asked me to run some errands in her new car. This automobile purchase was the result of careful research and numerous consultations with *Consumer Reports* magazine. As I sped to pick up a few groceries and two items from the drugstore, nothing was further from my mind than all the investigative work she had done prior to buying the car. But when an oncoming car hit me head on, both air bags deployed exactly as they were designed to do. The engine absorbed the impact of the collision and was driven downward rather than toward the front seat. Amazingly, I walked away without a scratch.

View the video clip on the CD-ROM entitled "Conveying the Central Idea." Why should the central idea be clear? What happens if it is ambiguous?

No one in the audience could have doubted that the purpose of his speech was to be persuasive.

The Special Occasion Speech

The **special occasion speech** *is a presentation that highlights a special event.* Special occasion speeches are quite common, but they differ in many ways from the speech to inform or the speech to persuade. Special occasion speeches include presentations that have as their purpose to welcome, to pay tribute, to introduce, to nominate, to dedicate, to commemorate, and to entertain. The following topics would lend themselves to a special occasion speech.

Honoring the leader of the Boy Scouts of America	An anniversary tribute
	A nomination speech
A eulogy for an old friend	Dedication of the new library
Celebrating Campus Compact	An after-dinner "dessert"
The governor of New Mexico: A friendly roast	Words that make us laugh
	Some presidential remarks
A toast to the bride and groom	
On my retirement	

An excerpt from a special occasion speech follows:

Happy Birthday Mom!
This day means a lot to us, and I thought I'd take a few minutes today to tell you why.
The most obvious explanation, of course, is that we all like an excuse for a party!
But there's a more important reason.
We all want you to know how much we appreciate everything you've done for us.
And we all want you to know that we think you have a lot to celebrate.
For starters, you've been a great provider.
You've been the kind of mother who puts her family first, and does whatever it takes to make . . .

Specific Purposes

The general purpose involves nothing more than stating that your goal is to inform or to persuade. The *specific purpose* goes a step further. Here *you identify your purpose more precisely as an outcome or behavioral objective. You also include the audience* in your specific purpose. For example, a specific purpose statement might be, "My audience will be able to list the five signs of skin cancer." A specific purpose statement thus includes your general purpose, your intended audience, and your precise goal. Some additional examples of specific purpose statements might be the following.

My audience will be able to explain why violence and bullying in elementary schools are on the rise.

My audience will be able to define and identify hate crime.

My audience will state the benefits of walking.

My audience will identify three reasons to help register persons without homes to vote.

My audience will be able to identify helpful herbs.

My audience will be able to describe ways to close the digital divide.

My audience will stop drinking alcoholic beverages in excess.

My audience will identify three reasons to become a nurse.

Statements of specific purpose guide the entire presentation like a map or blueprint. When developing your specific purpose, consider the following four characteristics of good purpose statements.

1. They are declarative statements rather than imperative statements (expressing a command, request, or plea) or interrogative statements (asking a question). They make a statement; they do not command behavior nor do they ask a question.
   GOOD: My audience will be able to state some reasons for failing to graduate within four years.
   POOR: Why do students flunk out of college?
2. Strong specific purpose statements are complete statements; they are not titles, phrases, clauses, or fragments of ideas.
   GOOD: My audience will be able to defend our institution's policy on liquor on campus.
   POOR: The importance of liquor policies
3. They are descriptive and specific, rather than figurative and vague or general.
   GOOD: My audience will learn how to create a playlist on iTunes.
   POOR: My goal will be to demonstrate all the many things you can do with an iPod.

E-Note

GENERAL AND SPECIFIC PURPOSE

Find a passionate speech, such as the short message that President Ronald Reagan provided on January 22, 1981, as he spoke to the American hostages freed from Iran (at **http://www.reagan.utexas.edu/resource/speeches/1981/12281d.htm**). Or examine President Bill Clinton's farewell speech to the nation (available at **http://www.americanrhetoric.com/speeches/clintonfarewell.htm**). Or consider a famous historical speech such as Patrick Henry's "Give Me Liberty, or Give Me Death," which you can access at **http://theamericanrevolution.org/ipeople/phenry.asp**. Another well-known historical speech is Elizabeth Cady Stanton's "Declaration of Sentiments and Resolutions," available at **http://gos.sbc.edu/byyears/old.html**. Can you determine the general purpose and the specific purpose of the speech you have selected?

4. They focus on one idea rather than on a combination of ideas.
   GOOD: My audience will be able to distinguish between legal and illegal drugs.
   POOR: I want my classmates to avoid illegal drugs and possibly getting arrested; I also want them to know about legal drugs that may be useful to them as they become increasingly fit.

If your statement of purpose meets these standards, then you are ready to begin creating a thesis statement for your presentation. Maria determined her statement of purpose: My audience will be able to identify at least three attractions in the San Jose del Cabo, Mexico, area.

Thesis Statement

You may decide the general kind of presentation you will give and the specific goal you have before you conduct your research. However, unless you have a personal involvement with your topic, you will probably not be able to develop the thesis statement until you become more informed.

The **thesis statement** is *a summary of the speech* that typically is established early in the presentation. It is similar to the topic sentence or central idea of a written composition: a complete sentence that reveals the content of your presentation. Some examples of thesis statements follow:

- U.S. businesses need to restore trust with the public.
- Puerto Rico's Caribbean National Forest is a national treasure.
- Drug use by NCAA athletes decreased from 1985 to 2005.
- Diversity is America's good fortune.

San Jose del Cabo offers many attractions for discerning travelers.

Chapter Three   Selecting a Topic and Purpose   59

- Community service is essential for any successful democracy.
- Hispanics have become the largest minority group in the United States.
- Intercultural communication knowledge is essential for successful globalization.
- Over 1.2 million young people in Los Angeles are "at risk" and are in jeopardy of not reaching adulthood.
- Eco-terrorism has become routine.
- Moral truth is not the same in every culture.

What are some qualities of a good thesis statement? (1) The thesis statement should be a complete statement rather than a fragment or grouping of a few words. (2) The thesis statement should be a declarative sentence rather than a question, explanation, or command. (3) The thesis statement should avoid figurative language and strive for literal meanings. (4) Finally, the thesis statement should not be vague or ambiguous.

Let us examine some examples of poorly written thesis statements:

Implementing a job shadowing program

The immune system is fantastic!

Are you getting enough sleep?

Television destroys lives.

The right to vote

What is wrong with these thesis statements? The first and fifth are not complete sentences. The second is an exclamation while the third is a question. The second uses language ("fantastic") that can be defined in multiple ways, while the fourth uses exaggeration to make a point. Some of these topics may also be viewed as trivial. How could we rewrite these ideas into appropriate thesis statements?

A job shadowing program should be implemented on our campus.

The human immune system is important for homeostasis.

The human need for sleep varies with age and activity.

Excessive television viewing may lead to violent behavior.

Voting is an important element of a democratic society.

Purposes of speeches are thus general and specific. Although the general purpose is often to inform or to persuade, the specific purpose goes further. The specific purpose includes the goal of your speech as a precise outcome or behavioral objective. The specific purpose reflects considerations of your audience. The thesis statement is a one-sentence summary of the speech and should be a complete and unambiguous statement.

Let us finish this chapter by visualizing the three elements that will form the foundation of your presentation. Regardless of the purpose of your speech, all presentations usually require a topic that is appropriate for the speaker and the audience, a purpose

From Topic Selection to Thesis Statement: A Three-Step Process

TABLE 3.2 FROM TOPIC TO PURPOSE TO THESIS STATEMENT			
	INFORMATIVE PRESENTATION	PERSUASIVE PRESENTATION	SPECIAL OCCASION PRESENTATION
STEP ONE TOPIC	Wetlands ecology	The ethics of publicly held companies	An anniversary tribute
	↓	↓	↓
STEP TWO PURPOSE	To increase the audience's knowledge of wetland ecology	To convince the audience that publicly held businesses have community responsibility	To honor the couple on their tenth anniversary
	↓	↓	↓
STEP THREE THESIS STATEMENT	Puerto Rico's Caribbean National Forest is a national treasure.	U.S. businesses need to restore trust with the public.	Congratulations to Ann and Mark on a decade of love and happiness.

that is consistent with the assignment of expectations of the occasion, and a thesis statement that clearly reveals the content of your presentation. Table 3.2 illustrates the three-step process for the three general purposes of speaking: informative, persuasive, and special occasion.

Resources for Review and Discussion

SUMMARY

In this chapter you have learned the following:

▶ To search for a public speaking topic, you can use at least five different approaches:
- Individual brainstorming.
- Categorical brainstorming.
- Conducting a personal inventory.
- Current topic identification.
- Internet searching.

▶ To select a public speaking topic,
- Speak about topics you already know.
- Speak about a topic that interests you.
- Speak about a topic that is important to your local community.
- Speak about topics that are uniquely your own.
- Speak about topics that your audience finds interesting.
- Speak about a topic that the audience embraces but you do not.

▶ To evaluate a public speaking topic, determine whether the topic meets the standards of
- Appropriateness for the speaker.
- Appropriateness for the audience.
- Appropriateness for the occasion.

▶ The three general purposes of public speaking are
- To inform.
- To persuade.
- To highlight a special occasion.

▶ The specific purpose for a public speech includes considerations of
- Your general purpose.
- Your intended audience.
- Your precise goal.

▶ To develop a thesis statement for a public speech,
- You will prepare a one-sentence summary of the speech.
- You will need to be informed on your topic.

KEY TERMS

  Use the *Public Speaking* CD-ROM and the Online Learning Center at www.mhhe.com/nelson to further your understanding of the following terminology.

Brainstorming	Personal inventory	Speech to persuade
Categorical brainstorming	Special occasion speech	Thesis statement
Current topics	Speech to inform	

APPLICATION EXERCISES

  Go to the self-quizzes on the *Public Speaking* CD-ROM and the Online Learning Center at www.mhhe.com/nelson to test your knowledge of the chapter concepts.

1. Examine the following specific purpose statements. Identify those that are good examples and explain why the others are bad examples.
   a. The beauty of the Grand Teton National Park.
   b. My audience will be able to explain the current Homeland Security strategies.
   c. What do men want in their personal relationships?
   d. My audience will be able to identify five kinds of love.
   e. To persuade the audience to live and let live.
   f. To inform my audience about STDs.
   g. To identify the primary causes of cancer.
   h. My audience will be able to distinguish between moderate and binge drinking.
   i. To explain early baldness in men.
   j. My audience will go to graduate school or professional school.
   k. To inform my audience about weekend trips in the region.

l. To inform my audience about the pleasures of flying one's own plane.
m. To inform my audience about the steps to earning the Eagle Scout Award.
n. A passion for cooking.

2. Divide a piece of paper into four columns. Write one of the following general topics at the top of each of the four columns.
   a. Job experiences I have had.
   b. Places I have traveled.
   c. City, state, or area I am from.
   d. People who make me angry.
   e. Happy experiences I have had.
   f. Unusual experiences I have had.
   g. Personal experiences I have had with crime.
   h. My involvement in marriage, divorce, or other family matters.
   i. My experiences with members of other groups—the old, the young, ethnic groups.
   j. The effect of the drug culture on my life.
   k. My relationship to local, state, or federal government.
   l. My background in painting, music, sculpture, theater, dance, or other fine arts.
   m. My feelings about grades, a college education, sororities and fraternities, college requirements, student government, or alternatives to a college education.
   n. My reactions to current radio, television, or film practices, policies, or programming.
   o. Recent Supreme Court decisions that affect me.
   p. My personal and career goals.

Now, write down specific topics under each of the four general topic areas you chose. Spend no more than five minutes on this exercise brainstorming. Next, underline one topic in each of the four columns that is particularly interesting to you. From these four topics, select the one about which you have the most information or the best access to information. Can you adapt the topic to your specific audience?

CHAPTER FOUR

It is simplicity that makes the uneducated more effective than the educated when addressing popular audiences.
ARISTOTLE (384–322 B.C.), *RHETORIC*

The power of illustrative anecdotes often lies not in how well they present reality, but in how well they reflect the core beliefs of their audience.
BARBARA MIKKELSON, SNOPES.COM

Analyzing the Audience

What will you learn?

When you have read and thought about this chapter, you will be able to:

1. Explain why a speaker should analyze the audience.
2. Determine how audience characteristics affect your presentation.
3. Identify some of the demographic features of the audience that you should consider in your audience analysis.
4. Explain how worldview might affect your topic selection and the treatment of your topic.
5. Describe five methods of audience analysis.
6. Justify why you should consider the context in which you will speak.
7. Depict your classmates as a unique audience.
8. Clarify how a speaker adapts to an audience.
9. Describe the role of listening in public speaking.
10. Name the moral choices related to audience analysis.

Effective presenters try to learn as much about the members of their audience as they can before they try to communicate with them. As beginning speakers, we too often focus on our own concerns and interests. We speak on our favorite topics without considering what the audience might want or need to hear. We use language that we understand without considering that the audience might not understand it. Perhaps the individualistic culture of the United States invites more attention to self and less to audience than might be the case in more collectivist cultures, such as those represented by many Arab, African, Asian, and Latin American countries.[1]

Alexandra Sophronia was born in Greece, but she came to the United States as a baby. She visited her grandparents and other relatives in Greece at least once a year. She laughed about the accuracies and inaccuracies in *My Big Fat Greek Wedding. Because of the popularity of the film and Greek culture in general, she decided she would talk about some of the myths and misunderstandings about Greek culture.*

Alexandra knew that the topic was right for her because of her knowledge about Greece. She also knew that the topic met ethical standards for public speaking. Alexandra was concerned, however, that her classmates might not feel that the subject was interesting or worthwhile. What did they already know about Greece? Had any of them traveled to Greece? Might any of them have plans to visit the country? Did the other students travel at all? Had the students in the public speaking class already taken courses on Greek culture? How much did they already know?

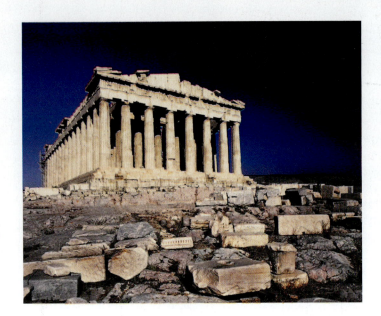

Audience Analysis

What is audience analysis? **Audience analysis** is *discovering as much as possible about an audience for the purpose of improving communication with them.* Audience analysis occurs before, during, and after a presentation. Why should a speaker analyze an audience? Think of public speaking as another version of the kind of speaking you do every day. Nearly always, when you meet a stranger, you size up that person before you disclose your message. Similarly, public speaking requires that you meet and know the members of your audience so you are able to create a message for them. Public speaking is not talking to oneself in front of a group; instead, it is effective message transmission from one person to many people in a setting in which speaker and audience influence each other.

Let us consider the wide variety of audiences you might face in your lifetime:

Your classmates	A political group
Fellow workers	A board of directors
Members of a union	A group of children
A civic organization	Community members
A religious group	A school board
Retired people	A committee of professors
A group of friends	A social club

E-Note

PRESIDENTIAL ADDRESSES

A unique audience exists for the inaugural addresses of U.S. presidents. To explore historical and contemporary events, and to acquire a better understanding of how democracy operates, examine the inaugural addresses of Woodrow Wilson, Franklin Roosevelt, John Kennedy, and Ronald Reagan. Attempt to characterize the members of each audience. Consider how the four presidents treated their audiences differently. From the perspective of audience analysis, what made each speech exceptional? Why might inaugural addresses be more alike than different? As of the printing of this textbook, a great Web resource for inaugural addresses is www.americanrhetoric.com.

Would you talk to all these audiences about the same topic or in the same way? Of course not. Your choice of topic and your approach to that topic are both strongly influenced by the nature of your audience. We focus on the audience in a presentation by learning the nature of that audience.

When we talk to individuals, we are relatively careful about what we say and how we say it. We speak differently to strangers than to intimates, differently to people we respect than to people we do not respect, and differently to children than to adults. Similarly, we need to be aware of audience characteristics when we choose a topic and when we decide how we are going to present that topic to the audience.

Imagine that you are about to speak to a new audience. How would you learn about the people in your audience? First, you could rely on "conventional wisdom." Second, you could consider a demographic analysis of the characteristics of the people, such as their gender, age, and ethnicity. Let's examine each of these general ways of learning more about an audience.

Conventional Wisdom

Conventional wisdom is *the popular opinions of the time about issues, styles, topics, trends, and social mores, the customary set of understandings of what is true or right.* Conventional wisdom includes what most people are said to think. *Newsweek* magazine devotes a few column inches each week to conventional wisdom about people and issues. Sometimes the president of the United States gets an arrow up (positive sign) one week and an arrow down (negative sign) the next week—on the same issue. Let's look at how conventional wisdom relates to audience analysis.

Conventional wisdom is a gross oversimplification, sometimes based more on the whim of the moment than on deep-seated convictions. To gain an idea of how conventional wisdom changes, consider the United States' interest in safety and security over the past decade. Before September 11, 2001, U.S.-Americans were relatively lax about these matters. Immediately afterward, U.S.-Americans were willing to subject themselves to searches and to stand in long airport lines to ensure their safety. By 2005, some people were becoming impatient with these security measures taken at airports.

Were U.S.-Americans less safe between September 11, 2001, and 2005 than they were before or after that time? Probably not. However, the events of September 11 put real fear in the residents of the United States. The salience of that fear dissipated as days went by with no further terror. The "conventional wisdom" was that Americans were in danger, but that threat lessened over time.

Conventional wisdom reflects broad patterns of thinking that may affect our behavior. Understanding it at any given point in time comes from keeping up with events, knowing what is going on in our society and in our world. Conventional wisdom also suggests topics that cry out for analysis and discussion. Suppose, for example, people in your region are very conservative and largely believe in self-rule and traditional family structures. You might give a presentation about how communication and transportation systems have created a world that is much more connected than it was just twenty years ago. You might consider the diversity of beliefs and values, such as alternative family forms, different political ideologies, and broader educational opportunities. In this way, you could initiate a critical examination of "conventional wisdom." Thus, conventional wisdom can be a starting point for further consideration of an appropriate speech topic for your audience.

Before we leave this discussion of conventional wisdom, we should mention psychological audience analysis. This form of analysis includes considerations of attitudes, beliefs, and values of the audience members. In many ways, psychological analysis is parallel to the demographic analysis, which is detailed below. Psychological analysis is beyond the scope of this text, but we encourage advanced students to investigate this more sophisticated method of audience analysis.

Demographics

What are some aspects of an audience that can affect how they interpret your message? The **demographics** (which literally means "characteristics of the people") of an audience *include gender composition, age, ethnicity, economic status, occupation, and education.*

Gender Composition

Why would a speaker care whether the audience is composed of men, women, or a mixture of the two? With some topics, the gender composition of the audience may make no difference at all. With other topics, gender representation may make all the difference in the world.

You may need to consider whether your topic is gender-linked or gender-neutral, and modify your treatment of the subject when speaking before generally male, generally female, or mixed-gender audiences. Consider the factors that may cause women and men to react differently to certain topics. Be aware that some women and some men feel that women have been victims of discrimination. They will be watchful for signs of discrimination from speakers.

In addition, you will need to take other factors into account as you consider the influence of the audience's gender composition on your topic. Analyzing an audience on the basis of gender is not an easy matter, however. Take the issue of occupation, for instance. While the average woman may earn less money than her male counterpart, many individual women make more money than the average man. A particular woman may be an executive, and a specific man may be a stay-at-home dad. Try to avoid relying on stereotypes to help you determine an audience's needs based solely on gender.

Age

The United States has a population of over 293 million people, including well over 70 million under age 18, and over 34 million age 65 or older. The "oldest old"

E-Note

GENDER INEQUALITY

Throughout history, women have been viewed as "less than men." While circumstances are better in some instances for women today, you should keep in mind that women and men are still not treated equally in most arenas. The Web site available at http://womensissues.about.com/library/blwomeneducationstats.htm provides some interesting comparisons.

According to the U.S. Department of Education, the rates of women who plan to attend college and/or enroll in college have increased and now surpass those of men (http://www.ed.gov/index.jhtml). Women have outnumbered men on college campuses since 1979 and on graduate school campuses since 1984. More U.S. women than men have received bachelor's degrees every year since 1982. Undergraduate levels rose from 41 percent to 56 percent between 1969 and 2000, according to the U.S. Census Bureau (http://www.census.gov). This same Web site, nonetheless, reports that men with professional degrees may expect to cumulatively earn almost $2 million more than their female counterparts over their work lives.

(those 80 years of age and older) are the fastest-growing group. The number of seniors in the population will grow rapidly as the Baby Boomers (those born between 1946 and 1964) begin to turn 65 starting in 2011. People who are 65 and older are projected to be 20 percent of the population in 2050 compared with 13 percent currently. A great Web site for facts and figures related to the U.S. population is www.census.gov.

Maturity changes people's preferences. Whereas many small children, and even younger adults, seem to love loud noise, fast action, and a relatively high level of confusion and messiness, some older people may be bothered by these same characteristics. Activities and events that are relevant change over one's lifetime. Look at these topics and decide which are more appropriate for young adults, middle-aged people, or the elderly. The age of your audience members will affect the topic you choose and how you treat a particular topic. Be wary of stereotyping as you consider the list.

Placing your kids in college	Plastic surgery	Competitive sports
Selecting a career	Body piercing	Choosing a major
Managing your time	Enlisting in military service	Animal rights
Saving dollars from taxes	Voting	Health care in hostels
Choosing a college or university	Selecting a tattoo	Domestic violence
Investment opportunities	Cell phones	Downsizing
Social Security reform	Selecting software	Dating issues
	Traveling in Europe	Day care facilities
		Community service

You might speak about selecting a career to a younger audience but reserve the topic of cashing in your annuities for an older audience. On the other hand, you might discuss affordable housing with either younger people or older people. However, your approach will be different if you know that your audience consists

E-Note

FOREIGN-BORN PEOPLE IN THE UNITED STATES

The number of people in the United States who are foreign born increases each year. In 2002, 32.5 million foreign-born people lived in the United States, which was roughly 11.5 percent of the country's population (for more information see http://www.census.gov/prod/2003pubs/p20-539.pdf). More than one-third of the foreign-born people are from Mexico or a Central American country. Just over one-quarter are from Asia. The foreign born are more likely to live in the West than in other regions of the United States, and they are more likely to live in central cities.

of 19-year-old undergraduates or members of the American Association of Retired Persons who are in their 60s and 70s.

The age of your audience will also partly determine what the audience knows from its own experience. Some people will know firsthand about the Vietnam War, the Beatles, and the civil rights struggles. Others will know about the first Gulf War, Seattle's grunge music culture, and the Million Man March. Young adults today will know the names of the latest bands, the most recent information technology developments, and the newest trends in clothing. The language describing these trends and developments may mystify older adults. Considering age is part of audience focus, a primary ingredient in audience analysis.

Ethnicity

Knowing the ethnic makeup and identity of your audience members can make an important difference in your effectiveness. **Ethnicity** identifies *people who are united through "language, historical origins, nation-state, or cultural system."*[2] Ethnic groups preserve communication traditions that affect the way their members speak and listen; some are only partially shared with other groups.

People exhibit and prefer different conversational patterns and expectations because of their ethnic identity. For instance, African Americans and European Americans, while sharing aspects of U.S. culture, each have unique styles of communicating. Sometimes dialects differ, sometimes conversational rules and expectations differ, and sometimes interactional styles such as use of argument and discussion differ between the two groups. A course in public speaking was difficult for members of the Blackfeet Indian Nation in Montana.[3] The Blackfeet value public speaking skills but see them as reserved for those in leadership positions (mainly the tribal elders). Blackfeet see *silence* as a primary mode of expressing interconnectedness with a listener or active receiver, so a public speaking student from the Blackfeet Nation would feel presumptuous speaking in front of a group of strangers and uncomfortable about communicating primarily with words. Understanding ethnic identity is a significant part of audience analysis. Understanding and appreciating the ethnic makeup of your audience is an essential factor in topic selection and approach.

As speakers, we need to be sure that we do not accidentally or needlessly injure or insult audience members with ethnic backgrounds different from our own. Members of the dominant culture of the United States have had tumultuous relationships with members of smaller **co-cultures,** or *groups that are similar to the larger culture but are distinguished by background, beliefs, and behaviors.* For example, Cuban Americans, native Hawaiians, Puerto Ricans, Vietnamese, and Appalachians are just a few of the groups that have been excluded from many of the privileges members of the dominant culture enjoy. Members of various ethnic groups are sensitive to the discrimination that has limited their people.

Sensitivity to members of co-cultures is essential for the contemporary speaker.

Sometimes even experienced public presenters make errors that are outrageous to members of ethnic co-cultures. Well-meaning people can accidentally use metaphors, figures of speech, language, or examples that members of co-cultures find offensive. You can learn to be more sensitive to other groups by practicing your presentation with friends who have backgrounds different from your own or by interviewing and observing other people to determine the kind of language they avoid and the types of examples, analogies, and metaphors they employ.

Economic Status

According to the Census Bureau report in September 2003, the median family income in the United States was $42,409 in 2002, which represented a decrease from 2001. This decrease was the second consecutive annual decline in median household income. Caucasians averaged $44,964 in 2002; African Americans averaged $29,177; Asians averaged $52,283; and Hispanics averaged $33,103. (For more information, see http://www.census.gov/prod/2003pubs/p60-221.pdf.)

What is the economic status of your audience? Are they primarily wealthy individuals or are they from lower economic groups? People who are wealthier tend to be more conservative, are often older, may have more education, and have probably traveled more than less wealthy people. Wealthy people may be less open to new ideas because they are accustomed to being treated deferentially, with courteous submission to their wishes or judgments. They may be more difficult to persuade because they feel that they have already made good choices. On the other hand, less wealthy people may be more liberal, younger, and may be less educated because of their age. Less wealthy people may be more open to new ideas and may be more easily persuaded because they have less to lose.

Some topics are appropriate for more affluent audiences, while other topics are right for less financially successful people. Consider the possible economic differences in your classroom. Are some students from affluent families that pay their tuition and expenses? Do other students depend entirely on their own income from one or more jobs?

Management attempts at persuasion will be more successful if they consider the average world of the employee.

Occupation

If you are speaking to a group of employed individuals, you will want to know what occupations are represented. Recently, one of the authors spoke to several hundred women in public service in Ohio. The audience included people in the governor's cabinet, state senators and representatives, mayors of many Ohio cities, and other women in elected office. The audience also included women in clerical, secretarial, and support staffs. The topic of the presentation was the role of gender in the workplace. Because so many occupations were represented, the task of audience analysis was difficult. Examples and illustrations had to be generic rather than specific. If an anecdote about a successful professional woman was used, the story had to be balanced with an anecdote about the difficulties of minimum-wage jobs to include all audience members.

If your audience is made up of pre-med and other health science majors, you might not want to talk about increased health-care costs. If you are speaking to business majors, you might want to avoid discussing corporate "welfare." Some teachers and professors like to hear about labor unions, but their supervisors and educational administrators are less fond of the topic. Of course, you can present controversial topics if your purpose is to persuade or provoke discussion, but then you must be very well prepared and know that your audience may be initially skeptical.

The language you use in your presentation is similarly affected by the audience members' occupations. You should avoid jargon that is unfamiliar to your audience, but it can be effective to use a few words that are unique to them in their work. Do your audience members come from professions in which people use concrete, specific language, or are they more likely to appreciate metaphors and comparisons?

Can you think of illustrations that come from the field of work or other experiences represented by the people in your audience? Can you draw comparisons between your topic and what the audience members spend the majority of their day doing? Do you know some of the individuals whom they hold as expert or trustworthy? Try to incorporate some of these illustrations, comparisons, and individuals in your presentation.

Education

More than one-quarter (27 percent) of adults age 25 and older had at least a bachelor's degree in 2002. Education does make a difference in earning power. In 2001, adults who were age 18 and over with a bachelor's degree earned an average of $50,623, while those with a high school diploma earned $26,795 and those without a high school diploma averaged $18,793. Advanced degree–holders (those with doctoral or masters degrees) made an average of $72,869 in 2001.

Chapter Four   Analyzing the Audience

Educational level also differed based on ethnicity and area of the country. Asians and Pacific Islanders had the highest proportion of college graduates (47 percent), followed by non-Hispanic whites (29 percent), African Americans (17 percent), and Hispanics (11 percent). The Northeast region had the highest proportion of college graduates (29 percent), followed by the West (28 percent), the Midwest (26 percent), and the South (25 percent). Even though these percentages seem quite close, the large numbers from which they are derived make them statistically different. (For more information, see www.census.gov/.)

Educational attainment is frequently related to economic status and occupation. A person's level of education may tell you very little about his or her intelligence, ambition, or sophistication. However, people with more education tend to read and write more, are usually better acquainted with the news, are more likely to have traveled, and are more likely to have higher incomes. What are some of the implications of educational level for the way you approach your audience?

- People who read and write regularly tend to have more advanced vocabularies, so adjust your language choices to the educational level of your audience.

- People who are receptive to new information need less background and explanation on current issues than those who are not.

- People who have seen more of the world tend to be more sophisticated about differences between people and cultures.

Most important of all, you need to take into account how much your audience already knows about your topic. Knowledge is not necessarily the same as education in analyzing an audience. For example, an auto mechanic might not have a degree from a university, but he clearly would have knowledge about repairing a car, and thus terms relating to auto mechanics would not have to be defined. The opposite, of course, would be true in the case of an educated audience with no background in auto mechanics, for whom all technical terms would require definition.

In addition, is the audience likely to have a position on your issue? If so, how might their knowledge level affect your attempt to increase what they know or to change their minds on the issue? For example, if you are talking to a group of older individuals, they may have established positions on Medicare, Social Security, and the inflated costs of drugs. A younger group of people might not have strong opinions on these matters.

Alexandra, the student at the beginning of the chapter who wanted to talk about the myths and misunderstandings related to Greece used conventional wisdom to determine that Greece is viewed as a safe and interesting tourist spot. She knew that 55 percent of her class was female and that the students ranged in age from 18 to 44. Most students were in the 18–21 year age range. Her classmates were primarily European American, but three students were African American. Of the two who had been born in Mexico, one was now a U.S. citizen. Another international student was from China, a second was from Uzbekistan, and a third was from Mauritania. The students were somewhat active in campus organizations. Two were in the Young Republicans and one was in the College Democrats. Two had been in the student senate, and others helped with other campus activities. Nearly all the students had participated in service learning because their campus was an "engaged institution." The students were generally able-bodied. One student was in a wheelchair, one had two hearing aids, and about one-third of them wore glasses. Most of the students were from middle-class families, and half the students worked at part-time jobs. Most were seeking an undergraduate degree, while two women were co-workers and were taking the course for career advancement. Many of the students had been raised in Protestant churches but did not attend church regularly now. Four students were Catholic, three were Jewish, two students declared themselves atheists, one was a Mormon, and one was a Muslim. This demographic information was helpful as Alexandra adapted her presentation to the audience.

Worldview

Worldview means *the common concept of reality shared by a particular group of people.* People relate to each other based on their similarity in worldview. Traditionally, in North Dakota, people lived in predominantly agricultural and rural communities. They were relatively poor and recognized their dependence on weather conditions. Consequently, they did not spend money on unnecessary items and they were relatively calm when disaster struck. Even today, many older North Dakotans are reluctant to buy expensive brewed coffee, to have manicures and pedicures, to drive luxury automobiles, or to wear designer clothing. And, as Garrison Keillor notes, they are apt to consider terrible conditions and conclude, "It could be worse."

Contrast this worldview with that of a young person who grew up in an affluent Washington, DC, suburb during the 1990s. She graduated from a good state school in the East. She has multiple tattoos, a bolt in her tongue, and has her hair colored and treated at an expensive salon. She has regular manicures, pedicures, and other spa treatments. She drives a new Toyota that was a college graduation gift from her parents and spends time at her family's summer home in Maine. At least twice a day, she buys a latte from her favorite coffeehouse. While preparing to attend graduate school, she volunteers at a shelter for families without homes on a flexible schedule so she can avoid rush hour. She becomes very annoyed with traffic, crowding, and any impediment to her routine activities. She is impatient with people who do not "move at her speed."

Imagine how difficult it would be for people from these two backgrounds to have a conversation or to create a shared reality. The older, rural upper midwesterner would not understand the young woman from Washington. Indeed, she may see her as wasteful and "flashy." The woman from Washington would see the older midwesterner as lacking in style and imagination.

What are the implications of worldview for your classroom speech? If you are attending a regional university or a community college where most of the other students are from the same part of the country as you are, you probably have some good ideas about their worldview since you share it. If, however, your

When Barack Obama addressed the 2004 Democratic National convention, he knew a great deal about the worldview of the audience.

Cultural Note

CULTURAL DIVERSITY AND CHANGE

Read the following statement written on behalf of the United Nations by Diana Ayton-Shenker, professor of international human rights law:

> The end of the cold war has created a series of tentative attempts to define 'a new world order.' So far, the only certainty is that the international community has entered a period of tremendous global transition that, at least for the time being, has created more social problems than solutions.
>
> The end of super-power rivalry, and the growing North/South disparity in wealth and access to resources, coincide with an alarming increase in violence, poverty and unemployment, homelessness, displaced persons and the erosion of environmental stability. The world has also witnessed one of the most severe global economic recessions since the Great Depression of the 1930s.
>
> At the same time, previously isolated peoples are being brought together voluntarily and involuntarily by the increasing integration of markets, the emergence of new regional political alliances, and remarkable advances in telecommunications, biotechnology and transportation that have prompted unprecedented demographic shifts.
>
> The resulting confluence of peoples and cultures is an increasingly global, multicultural world brimming with tension, confusion and conflict in the process of its adjustment to pluralism. There is an understandable urge to return to old conventions, traditional cultures, fundamental values, and the familiar, seemingly secure, sense of one's identity. Without a secure sense of identity amidst the turmoil of transition, people may resort to isolationism, ethnocentricism and intolerance.

Consider Ayton-Shenker's statement in light of your class and the diverse people who constitute your audience. How does the diversity of your class affect the development of a speech? How can you be sensitive to your multiple and diverse audience members?

class consists of people from various nearby neighborhoods, from other parts of the country, and even other parts of the world, you may have a more difficult task in understanding their worldview. Consider the class in which Alexandra found herself. Though primarily European American in background, the class included eight people who were not. The students from Uzbekistan, China, and Mauritania were truly a mystery to Alexandra as she tried to learn more about their countries, customs, and beliefs. Even though Alexandra had traveled to Mexico, she was not sure she understood the two students from that country. Considering the audience members' worldviews moves you from a demographic analysis to more precise and useful information.

Physical Characteristics

Physical characteristics include height, weight, style, fitness, gender display, and obvious disabilities. Imagine that you were going to speak to an audience of the American Federation of the Blind, to a group of individuals in wheelchairs, or to people who had another specific physical disability. How would you adjust your presentation? Most of us would do a poor job of adapting to these situations. Although members of such audiences generally ask that they be treated like those without disabilities, we tend to speak louder, perhaps unnecessarily, enunciate

76   Part One   Preparing Your Presentations

more clearly, or make other changes. We need to guard against language usage that disparages specific people, and we should be sensitive to negative stereotypes that we unintentionally may use. Even if your audience does not include people with physical disabilities, ridding yourself of negative stereotyping is important. People do negative categorizing so routinely that they do not even realize they are guilty of perpetuating myths about individuals with disabilities. For example, in his presentation "Language and the Future of the Blind," Marc Maurer, president of the National Federation of the Blind, discussed one of the stereotypes that he found particularly offensive: the idea that people who are not sighted are incompetent.

> Recently an advertisement appeared from the Carrollton Corporation, a manufacturer of mobile homes. Apparently the Carrollton Corporation was facing fierce competition from other mobile home builders, who were selling their products at a lower price. Consequently, the Carrollton Corporation wanted to show that its higher priced units were superior. In an attempt to convey this impression, the company depicted the blind as sloppy and incompetent. Its advertisement said in part: "Some manufacturers put out low-end products. But they are either as ugly as three miles of bad road, or they have so many defects—crumpled metal, dangling moldings, damaged carpet—that they look like they were built at some school for the blind." What a description! . . . It is not a portrayal calculated to inspire confidence or likely to assist blind people to find employment.[4]

Clearly, you must adjust your language to any perceived physical characteristics of your audience, but going beyond that, rid your presentation of all negative, offensive stereotyping.

Methods of Audience Analysis

Some speakers seem to be able to analyze an audience intuitively, but most of us have to rely on formal and informal means of gathering such information. Individuals in advertising, marketing, and public relations have developed complex technological means of collecting information from audiences before, during, and after their message.[5] However, most of us usually collect information about audiences through observation, informants, interviews, and questionnaires.

Observation

Observation, or *watching and listening,* reveals the most about the audience before and during the presentation. Looking at audience members might reveal their age, ethnic origin, and gender. More careful observation may reveal marital status by the presence or absence of rings; materialism by conspicuous brand names and trendy jewelry; and even religious affiliation by such symbols as a cross, skullcap, or headscarf. Many people in an audience advertise their membership in a group by exhibiting its symbols.

In the classroom, you have the added advantage of listening to everyone in your audience. Your classmates' speeches, their topics, issues, arguments, and evidence, all reveal more about them than you could learn in a complex questionnaire. Your eyes and ears become the most important tools of audience analysis that you have.

Informants

When you are invited to give a presentation outside the classroom, your best source of information about the audience may be the person who invites you. This person can be your *inside informant,* who can tell you the following:

1. What topics are appropriate?
2. What does the organization believe or do?
3. How many people are likely to attend?
4. What will the setting or occasion be?
5. How long should you speak?
6. What are the characteristics of the audience?

A key question to ask is why you were invited to speak, since that information will help establish credibility in your introduction. If they want you because of your expertise on hospice care, auto mechanics, or animal rescue, then you will want to stress that in your presentation. If they invited you because of your accomplishments or contributions to the community, then emphasize that area of your life. In any case, your informant should be able to help analyze your audience to avoid surprises.

Within the classroom, all of your classmates serve as informants. Listen to their speeches. What do they value or believe? What topics interest them? With what groups or organizations are they affiliated? What other courses are they taking? Do they volunteer on campus or serve in the community? Your classmates' presentations can provide you with valuable information about the classroom audience that will listen to your own speeches.

Interviews

Discover information about your audience by interviewing a few members of the group. These **interviews**—*inquiries about your audience directed at an audience member—*should typically occur far in advance of the speech. However, many professional speakers gain some of their most relevant material during the reception or the dinner before the presentation. The competent speaker takes advantage of this time with the audience to learn more about them, their needs, and their interests. Whether it takes place well in advance of the presentation or just before the time you will speak, an interview for information on the audience should focus on the same questions listed in the preceding section on informants.

When you are conducting an audience analysis for a classroom presentation, you can talk to a few people from class. Try to discover their opinions of your topic, how they think the class will respond to it, and any helpful suggestions for best communicating the topic. Interviews take time, but they are a great way to learn more about your audience.

Questionnaires

Whereas interviews take more time to execute than to plan, **questionnaires**—*surveys of audience opinions*—take more time to plan than to execute. The key to writing a good questionnaire is to be brief. Respondents tend to register their distaste for long questionnaires by not filling them out completely or by not participating at all.

78   Part One   Preparing Your Presentations

What should you include in your brief questionnaire? That depends on what you wish to know. Usually you will be trying to discover what an audience knows about a topic and their attitude about it. You can ask open-ended questions, yes-or-no questions, degree questions, or a mixture of all three—as long as you do not ask too many questions.

Open-ended questions are *like those on an essay test that invite an explanation and discourage a yes or no response.* Examples include:

What do you think should be done about teenage pregnancies?

What do you know about alternative energy sources?

What punishments would be appropriate for plagiarism?

Closed or **closed-ended questions** *force a decision by inviting only a yes or no response or a brief answer.* Examples include:

Should all public schools offer art and music education?
_____ Yes _____ No

Should a man be allowed paternity leave from his job when his child is born or adopted?
_____ Yes _____ No

Degree questions *ask to what extent a respondent agrees or disagrees with a statement:*

I believe that all people deserve housing.

Strongly agree   Agree   Neutral   Disagree   Strongly disagree

---

Questionnaire: Same-Sex Marriage

1. I think that same-sex couples should be allowed to marry.
   _____ Yes _____ No

2. I think that same-sex couples should be permitted to have legal connections, but should not be allowed to marry.
   _____ Yes _____ No

3. At what point should same-sex couples be allowed to marry?
   _____ Whenever they choose   _____ After cohabiting for six months
   _____ After cohabiting for a year   _____ Never

4. Our society actively punishes gays, lesbians, and same-sex couples.
   Strongly agree   Agree   Neutral   Disagree   Strongly disagree

5. What social support, if any, do you feel should be extended to gay and lesbian individuals? _____
   _____
   _____
   _____

Figure 4.1   **Sample questionnaire.**

Or degree questions may present a continuum of possible answers from which the respondent can choose:

Which of the following would be an appropriate punishment for an embezzlement of $5,000?

| $5,000 fine | $4,000 fine | $3,000 fine | $2,000 fine | $1,000 fine |
| 1 year jail | 2 years jail | 3 years jail | 4 years jail | 5 years jail |

How much paternity leave from the workplace do you think men should receive?

None   One week   Two weeks   One month   Two months   Six months

These three kinds of questions can be used in a questionnaire to determine audience attitudes about an issue. A questionnaire, such as the one in Figure 4.1, administered before your presentation, can provide you with useful information about your audience's feelings and positions on the issue you plan to discuss. All you have to do is keep the survey brief, pertinent, and clear.

Analysis of the Situation

Five factors are important in analyzing the situation you face as a speaker: the size of the audience, the environment, the occasion, the time, and the importance of the situation.

Size of Audience

The *size of the audience* is an important situational factor because *the number of listeners* can determine your level of formality, the amount of interaction you have with the audience, your need for amplification systems, and your need for special visual aids. Larger audiences usually call for formality in tone and language; smaller audiences allow for a more casual approach, a less formal tone, and informal language. Very large audiences reduce the speaker's ability to observe and respond to subtle cues, such as facial expressions, and they invite audience members to be more passive than they might be in a smaller group. Large audiences often require microphones and podiums that can limit the speaker's movement, and they may require slides or large posters for visual aids.

Speakers need to be flexible enough to adapt to audience size. One of the authors was to give a presentation on leadership to an audience of over 100 students in an auditorium that held 250 people. Only 25 students appeared. Instead of a formal presentation to a large group, the author faced a relatively small group in one corner of a large auditorium. Two hours later, the author was to speak to a small group of 12 or 15 that turned out to be 50. Do not depend on the planners to be correct about the size of your audience. Instead, be ready to adapt to the size of the audience that actually appears.

The Environment

You also must be prepared to adapt to environmental factors. Your location may be plagued by visual obstructions such as pillars and posts, an unfortunate sound system, poor lighting, a room that is too warm or too cool, the absence of a podium or lectern, a microphone that is not movable, or lack of audiovisual equipment. If you have specific audio, visual, or environmental needs, you should make your requests well in advance to the individual who has invited you to speak. At the very least, you will want to inquire about the room in which you are to speak.

Occasion

The *occasion* is another situational factor that makes a difference in how a speaker adapts to an audience. The speaker is expected to be upbeat and even funny at an after-dinner speech, sober and serious at a ribbon cutting, full of energy and enthusiasm at a pep rally, and prudent and factual in a court of law. Even in the classroom, a number of unstated assumptions about the occasion exist. You are expected to follow the assignment; not break laws or regulations of the campus, state, or nation; maintain eye contact; keep to the time limit; and dress appropriately for the occasion.

Outside the classroom, the confident presenter learns about the expectations for the occasion. Consider for a moment the unstated assumptions about these public presentation occasions:

- A high school commencement address.
- A persuasive message at a town meeting.
- A talk with the team before a big game.
- A demonstration of how to accurately read blood pressure.
- A motivational talk to your salespeople.
- An informative presentation on groundwater quality issues.
- An announcement of layoffs at the plant.

Each of these occasions calls for quite a different kind of presentation, the parameters of which are not clearly stated but are widely understood. Our society seems to dictate that you should not exhibit levity at funerals, nor should you be too verbose when you introduce another person. The best way to discover information about the occasion and expectations for it is to question the individual or the organization inviting you to speak.

Time

A further aspect of any speaking situation that makes a difference to a speaker is when and for how long the presentation is given—the *time*. Time can include the time of day, the time that you speak during the occasion, and the amount of time you are expected to fill. Early morning speeches find an audience fresh but not quite ready for serious topics. After-lunch or after-dinner speeches invite the audience to sleep unless the speaker is particularly stimulating. The optimal time to speak is when the audience has come only to hear the speaker and nothing else.

The time you give the presentation during an occasion can make a big difference in audience receptivity. You will probably find that people are genuinely relieved when a presentation is shorter than expected, because so many speeches are longer than anyone wants. To overestimate our knowledge and

Chapter Four   Analyzing the Audience

charm and how excited an audience is to hear from us is easy. Audiences will be insulted if you give a presentation that is far short of expectations—5 minutes instead of 30—but they will often appreciate a 45-minute presentation when they have expected an hour.

Importance

The final situational factor is the *importance* of the occasion, the significance attached to the situation that dictates the speaker's seriousness, content, and approach. Some occasions are relatively low in importance, although generally the presence of a speaker signals that an event is not at all routine. An occasion of lesser importance must not be treated like one of great importance, and an occasion of greater importance should not be treated lightly.

We usually perceive rituals and ceremonial events as high in importance. We see the speaker at a university commencement exercise, the speaker at the opening of a new plant, and the speaker at a lecture as important players in a major event. Speakers at informal gatherings or local routine events are somewhat further down the scale. Nonetheless, a speaker must carefully gauge the importance of an event so the audience is not insulted by his or her frivolous treatment of what the audience regards as serious business.

The Uniqueness of the Classroom Audience

Students sometimes think of the speeches they deliver in public speaking class as a mere classroom exercise, not a real speech. Perhaps this is partly because they know that they have a grade riding on their speech. They may therefore be more concerned with the grade than with communicating their message effectively to the class.

Viewing the classroom speech as a mere exercise is an error. Classroom speeches are delivered to people who are influenced by what they see and hear. In fact, your classmates as an audience might be even more susceptible to your influence because of their *uniqueness* as an audience. Table 4.1 illustrates some of the unique characteristics of classroom audiences.

The classmates who make up your audience might have their own knowledge about and positions on issues, but they are capable of changing, too, as they listen and learn. Next we will look at how you can adapt to this unique audience.

TRY THIS

Think of how you should look and act when you speak to your class. Would you look and act the same if you were going to make a presentation to (a) friends in a residence hall; (b) a group of schoolchildren; (c) administrators at your institution; (d) your parents and parents of others in your neighborhood; or (e) small business owners who live and work near your campus? Describe the differences.

TABLE 4.1 UNIQUENESS OF THE CLASSROOM AUDIENCE

CHARACTERISTICS OF THE CLASSROOM AUDIENCE	IMPLICATIONS FOR THE COMMUNICATOR
1. The classroom audience, because of the educational setting in which the presentation occurs, is exposed to messages it might otherwise avoid: the audience is "captive."	May add interactivity to increase interest and engagement.
2. The size of the audience tends to be relatively small (usually 20 to 25 students) and constant.	You can use more personal information and you can avoid microphones and other amplifying devices.
3. Classroom audiences include one person—the professor—who is responsible for evaluating and grading each presentation.	You might need to analyze the professor more carefully as an audience member than you do other members of the audience.
4. Classroom speeches tend to be short.	You must consider topics that can be managed in a brief period of time.
5. The classroom speech is nearly always one of a series of speeches in each class period.	You might keep in mind that visual aids, a dynamic delivery, and stylistic language are even more important than in other situations.
6. The speaker has an opportunity to listen to every member of the audience.	You can learn a great deal about your classmates' opinions, beliefs, and values and do a highly skillful audience analysis.
7. The classroom audience may be invited to provide written and/or oral feedback on the speech.	You can increase your skill as a communicator by carefully heeding any advice or criticism you are given.
8. The classroom speaker has more than one opportunity to influence or inform the audience.	You can show improvement over time.

Adapting to Your Audience

This chapter has characterized several tools—observation, informants, interviews, and questionnaires—to use in analyzing your audiences. These tools of analysis and audience demographics will not be beneficial, however, unless you use them for the purpose of audience adaptation. **Audience adaptation** means *making the message appropriate for the particular audience by using analysis and applying its results to message creation.*

In the case of an informative presentation, adapting to the audience means *translating ideas.* Just as a translator at the United Nations explains an idea expressed in English to the representative from Brazil in Portuguese, a speaker who knows about baud rates, kilobytes, and megabytes must be able to translate

Chapter Four   Analyzing the Audience   83

those terms for an audience unfamiliar with them. Perhaps you have already met some apparently intelligent professors who know their subject matter well but are unable to translate it for students who do not. An important part of adapting an informative speech to an audience is the skill of *translating* ideas.

Your instructors—from kindergarten through college—are essentially informative speakers. You have heard people communicate informative material for 13 years or more. Consider some of your best instructors. Why were they effective in the classroom? They probably took the time to illustrate their points, instead of simply presenting information as an endless list of facts. This is translation.

Now consider those instructors you would deem poor teachers. What did they do that invites you to rate them lower? Did they talk "over your head" and use sentence structure and language that you did not understand at the time? They may have used examples from events that occurred years before you were born and provided no context for them. They might have used a great deal of jargon that confused you and seemed unapproachable.

In the case of persuasive presentations, adaptation means *adjusting your message both to the knowledge level of the listeners and to their present position on the issue*. Use the tools introduced in this chapter and the audience characteristics you discover to help you decide where you should position your message for maximum effect. Too often speakers believe that the audience will simply adopt their point of view on an issue if they explain how they feel about the topic. Actually, the audience's position on the issue makes a greater difference than the speaker's does, so the speaker has to start by recognizing the audience's view. For example, if you believe the audience agrees with you, you can place your message early. If you believe they are in disagreement, you may need to proceed more cautiously.

Two students in a public speaking class provided excellent examples of what happens when the speaker does and does not adapt to the audience. Both speakers selected topics that seemed to have little appeal for the audience because both appeared to be expensive hobbies. One of the students spoke about raising an exotic breed of dog that only the rich could afford. The entire presentation was difficult for the listeners since they could not see themselves in a position of raising dogs for the wealthy.

The other student spoke about raising hackney ponies, an equally exclusive business. However, this student started by explaining that he grew up in a poor section of New Haven, Connecticut. His father was an immigrant who never earned much money, even though he spoke six languages. This student came from a large family, and he and his brothers pooled their earnings for many years before they had enough money to buy good breeding stock. They later earned money by selling colts and winning prize money in contests. By first explaining to the audience that he was an unlikely breeder of expensive horses, the speaker improved the chances that the audience could identify with him and his hobby. He adapted his message to the unique audience.

What kinds of messages influence you? Consider the variety of persuasive speakers you have heard—ministers, priests, rabbis, and other clergy; salespeople; teachers and parents; politicians and elected officials of our own and other countries; people lobbying for a special interest group; and people trying to convince you to change your long-distance telephone service or to make some other kind of purchase.

What kinds of appeals work for you—emotional appeals or logical ones? Do you need to believe in the ethical standards of the speaker before you will listen to what he or she has to say? Do you like to hear the most important arguments first or last? Do you tend to believe authorities, statistics, or other kinds of sources? If you use your own experiences and thoughtfully reflect on them, you may be able to understand better how others might respond favorably to you as a per-suasive speaker and adapt your message to them.

Audience adaptation occurs before, during, and after a presentation. Central to your ability to adapt to your audience are your listening skills. In the classroom, listening to other speakers reveals information that will be valuable as you pre-pare your own presentations.

Listening and Public Speaking

The Importance of Listening

Both speaking and listening are essential com-ponents of public speaking. In the past, public speaking focused more on speakers and the creation and transmission of messages than on listeners and their active participation in the process. The role of the listener in communication has gained more importance. Indeed, current experts believe that listening is essential to the development of citizenship and a civil society.[6]

You learn more by listening than by talking. Every speech you hear and every question asked and answered provides information about the people who will become your audience. Your serving as an audience member during your classmates' speeches provides you with an opportunity to analyze their choice of topics, the way they think, and the approaches they use. In short, being an audience member invites you to analyze your audience throughout the course.

You may not have thought of this fact when you enrolled in a public speak-ing class, but you will listen to many speeches for every speech you deliver. Over the course of the school term, you will likely hear between 100 and 200 speeches in your public speaking course. You will learn ways to evaluate speeches and ways to improve your own speeches. And you will learn methods of argument that you can employ.

Becoming a Better Listener

How can you improve your listening skills? Consider the many situations in which you listen: when you attend class and listen to an instructor, when you learn how to read to children from the director of the volunteer literacy program, or when you attend a lecture and listen to a visiting speaker. Your purpose is to understand the information the speaker is presenting. You may try to understand relevant information about the speaker and factors that led to the speech, as well as the central idea of the speech itself. Listening requires a high level of involvement in the communication process. Here are some suggestions, which should help you become a more effective listener.

Suspend judgments about the speaker. Suspend your premature judgments about the speaker so you can listen for information. Wait until you have heard a speaker before you conclude that he or she is, or is not, worthy of your attention. If you make decisions about people because of their membership in a particular group, you risk serious error. For example, gays or lesbians could be against same-sex marriage, members of fraternities may not be conformists, and artists are often disciplined.

Focus on the speaker as a source of information. You can dismiss people when you categorize them. When you focus on a speaker as a valuable human resource who can share information, ideas, thoughts, and feelings, you are better able to listen with interest and respect. Every speaker you hear is likely to have some information you do not already know. Try to focus on these opportunities to learn something new. Resist categorizing the speaker and dismissing his or her message as a consequence.

Concentrate your attention on the speaker. If you find yourself dismissing many of the speeches you hear as boring, consider whether you are overly egocentric. Perhaps your inclination to find your classmates' speeches boring is due to your inability to focus on other people. Egocentrism is a trait that is difficult to overcome. The wisest suggestion, in this case, is to keep in mind one of the direct benefits of concentrating your attention on the speaker: if you focus on the other person while she is speaking, she will probably focus on you when you are speaking. Even more important, you will come across better as a speaker if others perceive you to be a careful listener. Nothing else you can do—including dieting, using makeup, wearing new clothing, or making other improvements—will make you as attractive to others as learning to listen to them.

Listen to the entire message. Do not tune out a speech after you have heard the topic. More than likely, the speaker will add new information, insights, or experiences that will shed light on the subject. One professor teaches an upper-division argumentation course to twenty students each quarter. Four speeches are assigned, but every speech is given on the same topic. In a ten-week period, students hear eighty speeches on the same topic, but every speech contains some new information. The class would be dismal if the students dismissed the speeches after hearing they would all cover the same topic. Instead of considering the speeches boring, students find them interesting, exciting, and highly creative.

Focus on the values or experiences you share with the speaker. If you find you are responding emotionally to a speaker's position on a topic and you directly oppose what he or she is recommending, try to concentrate your attention on the attitudes, beliefs, or values you have in common. Try to identify with statements the speaker is making. The speaker might seem to be attacking one of your own beliefs or attitudes, but, if you listen carefully, you may find that the speaker is actually defending it from a different perspective. Maximizing our shared ideas and minimizing our differences result in improved listening and better communication.

Focus on the main ideas the speaker is presenting. Keep in mind that you do not have to memorize the facts a speaker presents. Rarely will you be given an objective examination on the material in a student speech. If you want to learn more about the information being presented, ask the speaker after class for a copy of the outline, a bibliography, or other pertinent documentation. Asking the speaker for further information is flattering; however, stating in class that you can recall the figures cited but have no idea of the speaker's purpose may seem offensive.

Recall the arbitrary nature of words. If you find that you sometimes react emotionally to four-letter words or to specific usage of some words, you may be forgetting that words are simply arbitrary symbols people have chosen to represent certain things. Words do not have inherent, intrinsic, "real" meanings. When a speaker uses a word in an unusual way, or when you are unfamiliar with a certain word, do not hesitate to ask how the word is being used. Asking for such information makes the speaker feel good because you are showing interest in the speech, and the inquiry will contribute to your own knowledge. If you cannot overcome a negative reaction to the speaker's choice of words, recognize that the emotional reaction is yours and not necessarily a feeling shared by the rest of the class or the speaker. Listeners need to be open-minded; speakers need to show responsibility in word choice.

Focus on the intent as well as the content of the message. Use the time between your listening to the speech and the speaker's delivery of the words to increase your understanding of the speech. Instead of embarking on mental excursions about other topics, focus on all aspects of the topic the speaker has selected. Consider the speaker's background and his or her motivation for selecting a particular topic. Try to relate the major points the speaker has made to his or her stated intentions. By refusing to consider other, unrelated matters, you will greatly increase your understanding of the speaker and the speech.

Be aware of your listening intensity. You listen with varying degrees of intensity. Sometimes when a parent or roommate gives you information, you barely listen. However, when your supervisor calls you in for an unexpected conference, your listening is very intense. Occasionally we trick ourselves into listening less intensely than we should. Everyone knows to take notes when the professor says, "This will be on the test," but only an intense listener captures the important content in an apparently boring lecture. You need to become a good judge of how intensely to listen and to learn ways to alter your listening intensity. Sitting on the front of the chair, acting very interested, and nodding affirmatively when you agree are some methods that people use to listen with appropriate intensity.

Remove or ignore physical distractions. Frequently you can deal with physical distractions, such as an unusual odor, bright lights, or a distracting noise, by moving the stimulus or yourself. In other words, do not choose a seat near the doorway that allows you to observe people passing by in the hall, do not sit so that the sunlight is in your eyes, and do not sit so far away from the speaker that maintenance noises in the building drown out her voice. If you cannot avoid the distraction by changing your seat or removing the distracting object, try to ignore it. You probably can study with the radio or television on, sleep without having complete darkness, and eat while other people are milling around you. Similarly, you can focus your attention on the speaker when other physical stimuli are in your environment.

Consider whether you would be able to concentrate on the speech if it were, instead, a movie you have been wanting to see, a musical group you enjoy, or a play that has received a rave review. One man said that when he had difficulty staying up late to study in graduate school, he considered whether he would have the same difficulty if he were on a date. If the answer was no, he could then convince himself that the fatigue he felt was a function of the task, not of his sleepiness. The same principle can work for you. Consider whether the distractions are merely an excuse for your lack of desire to listen to the speaker. Generally you will find you can ignore the other physical stimuli in your environment if you wish to do so.

Chapter Four   Analyzing the Audience

Ethics and the Audience

As you prepare to speak to a particular audience, remember ethical considerations, those moral choices you make as a speaker. Audiences expect different levels of truthfulness in different situations. A comedian is expected to exaggerate, distort, and even fabricate stories. A salesperson is expected to highlight the virtues of a product and think less of the competition. A priest, a judge, and a professor are expected to tell the truth. In the classroom, the audience expects the speaker to inform with honesty and to persuade with reason.

Most speakers have a position on an issue. The priest tries to articulate the church's position, the judge follows a body of precedents, and the professor tries to reveal what is known from her discipline's point of view. You, too, have reasons for your beliefs, your positions on issues, and the values you espouse. The general guideline in your relationship with your audience is that you should have the audience's best interests in mind.

Next Steps in Audience Analysis

In this chapter, we talked about audience analysis and audience adaptation. Keep in mind that this process continues as you prepare your presentation. You will apply what you learn about the audience to the research you conduct, the kinds of supporting materials you choose, and the arguments you make. In the next chapter, you will learn about why you will benefit from conducting research for your speech. Armed with the information on audience analysis and adaptation in this chapter, you will be ready to make ethical and informed decisions on using your own experiences, the Internet, and the library for conducting research.

Resources for Review and Discussion

SUMMARY

In this chapter you have learned the following:

▶ Why a speaker should analyze the audience.
▶ How audience characteristics affect a presentation.
▶ The demographic features of an audience include
  - Gender
  - Age
  - Ethnicity
  - Economic status
  - Occupation
  - Education
▶ Four methods of audience analysis that a speaker can use are
  - Observation
  - Informants
  - Interviews
  - Questionnaires
▶ Situational analysis includes
  - The size of the audience
  - The environment
  - The occasion
  - The time
  - The importance of the situation
▶ The classroom audience is unique and useful to you.
▶ Audience adaptation is the goal of audience analysis.
▶ Speakers need to apply ethical principles to their audience analysis and adaptation.
▶ The importance of listening
  - Essential to citizenship and civil society
  - Essential to success in your public speaking course
▶ Becoming a better listener
  - Suspend judgments
  - Regard the speaker as a source of valuable information
  - Concentrate on the speaker
  - Listen to the entire message
  - Focus on shared values and experiences
  - Focus on the main ideas
  - Focus on the intent of the message
  - Remove or ignore physical distractions

KEY TERMS

  Use the *Public Speaking* CD-ROM and the Online Learning Center at www.mhhe.com/nelson to further your understanding of the following terminology.

Audience adaptation	Conventional wisdom	Observation
Audience analysis	Degree questions	Open-ended questions
Closed or closed-ended questions	Demographics	Questionnaires
Co-cultures	Ethnicity	Worldview
	Interviews	

REFERENCES

[1]Samovar, Larry A., & Porter, Richard E. (2003). *Communication between cultures* (5th ed.). Belmont, CA: Wadsworth Publishing Co.

[2]Lustig, Myron W., & Koester, J. (2003). *Interpersonal competence: Interpersonal communication across cultures.* Boston: Allyn & Bacon.

[3]Carbaugh, Donal A. (1998). 'I can't do that' but 'I can actually see around corners': American Indian students and the study of public communication. In Martin, Judith N., Nakayama, Thomas K., & Flores, Lisa A. (Eds.), *Readings in cultural contexts*. Mountain View, CA: Mayfield.

[4]Maurer, Marc. (1989). Language and the future of the blind: Independence and freedom. *Vital Speeches of the Day, 56(1),* 16–22. A speech delivered at the banquet of the annual convention, Denver, Colorado, July 8, 1989.

[5]Behnke, R. R., O'Hair, D., & Hardman, A. (1990). Audience analysis systems in advertising and marketing. In O'Hair, Dan, & Kreps, Gary L. (1990). *Applied communication theory and research.* Hillsdale, NJ: Laurence Erlbaum Associates, pp. 203–21.

[6]Welton, M. (2002). Listening, conflict, and citizenship: Towards a pedagogy of civil society. *International Journal of Lifelong Education, 21,* 197–208.

APPLICATION EXERCISES

 Go to the self-quizzes on the *Public Speaking* CD-ROM and the Online Learning Center at www.mhhe.com/nelson to test your knowledge of the chapter concepts.

1. Given the observations listed below, what do you think would be the audience's probable response to a presentation on Social Security issues, world hunger, the erosion of the environment, or changing sexual mores? For each statement about the audience, state how you believe they would generally feel about the topic.
    a. The audience responded favorably to an earlier informative speech on race relations.
    b. The audience consists mainly of urban people from ethnic neighborhoods.
    c. The audience consists of many married persons with families.
    d. The audience members attend night school on earnings from daytime jobs in factories and retail businesses.
    e. The audience members come from large families.
    f. The audience includes many people from developing countries.
    g. The audience consists of people from age 18 to 29.

2. Determine answers to the following questions for your class:
    a. What is the age range of the members of the class audience?
    b. What are the economic backgrounds of the class?
    c. Describe classmates with any obvious disabilities.
    d. What styles of clothes do the audience members wear?
    e. Describe other features of the students' appearance such as style, gender-display, and fitness.
    f. How much do class members interact before and after class?
    g. Do the students read the school newspaper, other newspapers, or magazines?
    h. What interests or hobbies do the students discuss?
    i. Describe other behavior, both verbal and nonverbal, of the class members.
    j. Are various ethnic groups or co-cultures represented?

    What are the implications you might draw from these observations? How should you adapt your speech based on these observations?

3. The audiences you face today may not be identical to the audiences you will face in the future. Review the list of audiences on page 66, and add to this list three audiences to whom you foresee yourself presenting in the next ten years.

4. Listen to a speech in the classroom, on the Internet, or elsewhere on campus. Using a scale of 1–5 (1 = poor; 5 = excellent), rate your ability to listen on the following dimensions:
    _____ a. suspending judgments
    _____ b. regarding the speaker as a source of valuable information
    _____ c. concentrating on the speaker
    _____ d. listening to the entire message
    _____ e. focusing on shared values and experiences
    _____ f. focusing on the main ideas
    _____ g. focusing on the intent of the message
    _____ h. removing or ignoring physical distractions

CHAPTER FIVE

Knowledge is the only instrument of production that is not subject to diminishing returns.
J. M. CLARK (1884–1963), AMERICAN ECONOMIST

Research is the process of going up alleys to see if they are blind.
MARSTON BATES (1906–1974), AMERICAN ZOOLOGIST

Finding Information and Supporting Your Ideas

What will you learn?

When you have read and thought about this chapter, you will be able to:

1. Use research to improve all aspects of your presentation, including preparation, organization, and delivery.
2. Use personal experiences, interviews, library resources, and the Internet to locate information for your speech.
3. Cite information correctly in your speech outline and your oral presentation.
4. Critically evaluate the World Wide Web and other sources.
5. Distinguish between seven forms of supporting material appropriate for your speech.
6. Meet ethical obligations associated with the use of sources and supporting material.

This chapter will help you find information you need for your presentations. We discuss how you can use various strategies—including personal experience, interviews, and your computer—to find information. You'll also learn about evaluating sources of information and about different types of supporting material found in presentations.

92   Part Two   Selecting and Arranging Content

Richard was planning a persuasive presentation on the dangers of cell phone use. He had nearly a week before he had to speak, but he wanted to start his research quickly so that he could get it done. Richard got on the Internet and typed "cell phones and health" into a search engine. The search engine returned links to several hundred Web pages related to his topic—just what he needed.

As Richard explored various Web sites, he found one in particular that contained several articles discussing the connection between cell phone use and brain illnesses—including cancer. Richard believed he had indeed found the mother lode of information about his topic. He carefully read the materials and prepared an outline discussing key reasons why people should stop using cell phones.

After preparing his outline, Richard decided to use the remaining days before his presentation to get preliminary feedback from his teacher and to practice the presentation. When Richard met with his teacher, he learned from her that his efforts to research the presentation were not sufficient. His teacher pointed out that the Web site that he had consulted was a for-profit "dot-com" site trying to sell a device that "reduces the risk from cell phone radiation." Although the sources on the Web site looked credible, they were clearly from biased groups seeking profit. Fortunately, Richard's teacher gave him some great ideas for finding unbiased sources to use in his presentation—all was not lost!

Richard's experience is typical of the way many students start the research process for their presentations. Modern technology—including the Internet and personal computers—has made searching for information so easy that we often get into the bad habit of taking shortcuts and not checking things out. This chapter emphasizes the interrelationships between critical thinking, information literacy, and research.

Why You'll Benefit from Research

Conducting research is a key part of the speech preparation process. Not all research sources tell you the same thing. For any given speech topic—take global warming as an example—you can obtain information from various types of sources—personal experience, visual and written sources, the Internet, and even personal interviews. Each will yield different sorts of information. Personal experience might tell you how you contribute to global warming by driving your car or even by using electricity; magazine and newspaper articles might give general background defining global warming; scientific journals might provide detailed statistics on how much Earth is heating up; and Web pages might describe the activities of groups committed to understanding global warming. Effective speakers consult all types of sources as they progress through the research process.

Effectively planning your research process will improve all aspects of your presentation. The information in Table 5.1 illustrates how research helps you at each step in preparing your presentation. As you can see, research is not just one step in the speechmaking process; it is a common thread tying all steps of the process together.

Chapter Five   Finding Information and Supporting Your Ideas   93

TABLE 5.1 RESEARCH AND THE PRESENTATION PREPARATION PROCESS	
PREPARATION STEP	BENEFIT OF RESEARCH
1. Topic selection	Research helps you discover and narrow topics.
2. Organizing ideas	Research helps you identify main and subordinate points.
3. Supporting ideas	Research provides facts, examples, and definitions to give substance to your points.
4. Preparing introduction and conclusion	Research may reveal interesting examples, stories, or quotes.
5. Practice and delivery	Because your speech is well researched, you will feel more confident and will seem more credible.

One of our former students was very frustrated with her presentation when she stopped by the office. Although she had the required number of sources, Holly felt the sources she had found were of poor quality and provided little useful information. After a half-hour of help on how to use an electronic database and 10 sources later, she was much more confident that she could prepare an effective presentation. She was right. Knowing why research is important should provide you with the motivation to seek high-quality sources. The following section discusses various techniques you can use to find those good sources.

Finding Sources of Information

Effective speakers achieve success through well-crafted presentations that contain compelling evidence and support. Advances in technology, in particular the Internet and online databases, help smart researchers find high-quality information very quickly. Not all research, however, requires a mouse and keyboard. In Chapter 2, we introduced the invention process—the art of knowing when and how to use various types of sources to locate the best supporting material for your presentation.

Personal Experience

Your **personal experience,** *your own life as a source of information,* is something about which you can speak with considerable authority. One student had been a "head-hunter," a person who finds applicants for companies willing to pay a premium for specific kinds of employees. This student gave a presentation from his personal experience of what employers particularly value in employees. Another student had a brother who was autistic. In her informative presentation, she explained what autism is and how autistic children can grow up to be self-reliant and successful in careers. Your special causes, your job, and your family can provide you with firsthand information that you can use in your presentation.

Before basing your presentation on personal experience, however, you should ask yourself critical questions about the usefulness of this information. Some of your experiences may be too personal or too intimate to share with strangers or

94 Part Two Selecting and Arranging Content

even classmates. Other experiences may be interesting but irrelevant to the topic of your speech. You can evaluate your personal experience as **evidence,** *data on which proof may be based,* by considering the following questions:

1. Was your experience typical of what other people experience?
2. Was your experience *so typical* that it will bore the audience?
3. Was your experience *so atypical* that it was a chance occurrence?
4. Was your experience so personal and revealing that the audience may feel uncomfortable?
5. Was your experience one that this audience will appreciate or from which this audience can learn a lesson?
6. Does your experience really provide proof of anything?

It is also important to consider the ethics of using your personal experience in a speech. Will it harm others? Is the experience firsthand (your own), or is it someone else's experience? Retelling the experiences of a friend or even family member is questionable because secondhand information is easily distorted. Unless the experience is your own, you may find yourself passing along incorrect information. Also, personal experience is different from personal opinion. Using additional research to clarify personal experience might be necessary.

Interviews with Others

A second important source of ideas and information for your speech is other people. With its faculty, staff, and numerous students, your campus has many experts on particular subjects. Your community, likewise, is populated with people who have expertise on many issues: government workers on politics; clergy on religion; physicians, psychologists, and nurses on health care; engineers on highways and buildings; and owners and managers on industry and business. The following story illustrates how a well-crafted interview can greatly improve your presentation.

After leaving his professor's office, Richard had a new game plan for his presentation about the dangers of cell phones—actually, his topic was a little different now. Richard took his professor's advice, stopped by the library, and asked for Renee, the reference librarian his teacher knew. Richard was easily able to schedule an interview for the next day.

That evening, Richard conducted research on his new topic in preparation for the interview with Renee. The next day, Richard arrived at the library with a tape recorder and two pages' worth of questions to ask the librarian. She was full of excellent information—he actually felt excited to tackle the next stage of his research.

You may not be as lucky as Richard, who found so much information in a single interview, but you will discover that interviewing is an efficient way to gather information on your topic. The person you interview can furnish ideas, quotations, and valuable leads to other sources. First, however, learn when and how to prepare for the interview, conduct the interview, and use the results.

Preparing for the Interview

Most students are surprised that important people at their university or in their community are more than willing to talk with them about their presentation. Because the person is doing you an important favor, you have a responsibility to

Chapter Five   Finding Information and Supporting Your Ideas   95

carefully prepare for the interview. Following the suggestions below will help ensure that your interview is productive:

- *Start early.* Professionals have calendars that, believe it or not, are even more packed than most college students' calendars. You should contact potential interviewees at least one week in advance so that the two of you can find a mutually agreeable time for the interview.

- *Determine the purpose for the interview.* Using your source to find out information easily obtained from other sources like the library or the Internet is a waste of time. Use your interview to gather important analysis, clever quotations, and personally relevant stories.

- *Do your homework.* You must have some understanding of the topic to know the right questions to ask. Taking time to carefully research your topic before the interview will enable you to ask good questions.

- *Plan questions in advance.* Effective interviewers take time to plan primary questions—questions that introduce new areas of discussion—in advance of the interview.

- *Gather equipment.* The best strategy for interviewing another person is to record the interview so that you can play it back later. You cannot write fast enough to take detailed notes, and interviewees will likely get frustrated if you keep asking them to repeat their statements. Of course, you should get the person's permission to record the interview beforehand.

Conducting the Interview

Once you have scheduled and prepared for the interview, your next task is to conduct it professionally. You will find this task to be fun and engaging. Besides dressing professionally and being on time, keep in mind the following:

- *Be polite and respectful.* Interviews rarely start with the first question. Instead, expect the interviewee to express curiosity about you and your project. Be perfectly frank about your purpose, the assignment, and the audience. The interviewee is doing the verbal equivalent of a handshake with the questioning.

- *Be careful about the tone of your questions and comments.* You are not in the role of an investigative reporter performing an interrogation. Instead, you are seeking information and cooperation from someone who can help you. Your tone should be friendly and your comments constructive.

- *Be flexible.* Even though you have prepared questions, you may find that one response may answer several of your planned questions, or that your preplanned order is not working as well as you expected. Relax. Check off questions as you ask them or as they are answered. Take a minute at the conclusion of the interview to see whether you have covered all of your questions.

- *Practice active listening.* Show an interest in the person's answers. If you are recording the interview, you should provide nonverbal feedback and concentrate on generating follow-up questions to gain even more valuable information. Be alert to nonverbal cues revealed by the interviewee, including those indicating that it is time to conclude the session.

- *Remember to get the basics.* Make sure that you have the accurate *citation information,* your interviewee's name, title, the name of the company, agency, or department, and so on. You will be citing this person's words and using oral footnotes to credit them, so you need correct source information.

- *Finally, remember to depart.* Give your interviewee an opportunity to stop the interview at the designated time. The interviewee—not you—should extend the interview beyond that, if anyone does. The interviewee will appreciate your gracious good-bye and gratitude for granting the interview. As a parting gesture of good will, thank the secretary, or anyone else who has helped you, as well.

Using the Interview

After you have conducted the interview, you should immediately take time to listen to the interview tape and jot down quotations and ideas from the interview onto notecards so that you can arrange those ideas with other supporting materials you find. Don't let your memory of the interview grow cold. The longer you wait, the more likely you are to forget how you wanted to use information from the interview.

Library Resources

A third source of information is all the resources that are available at your school's library—magazines, journals, newspapers, books, videotapes, and government documents. Be sure to check with a **reference librarian,** *a librarian specifically trained to help find sources of information,* if you are unfamiliar with resources available at your library. The reference department in your library has many useful sources. In addition to specialized encyclopedias, there are specialized dictionaries, yearbooks, books of quotations, biographical sketches of prominent individuals, and atlases. A reference librarian can quickly help you determine whether these specialized reference resources are helpful for your presentation topic.

Most libraries offer a number of indexes and catalogs with the help of which you can locate sources of information. Indeed, modern libraries offer so many options for finding information, the most difficult task is often knowing where to begin. Library Web sites typically offer two general options for locating information: the electronic card catalog and electronic periodical indexes. You might need to consult with a librarian or with other students to learn how to access them.

The Electronic Card Catalog

Most libraries today have an **electronic catalog**—*a database containing information about books, journals, and other resources in the library.* The computer catalog is similar to the old card catalog because it has call numbers and entries arranged by author, subject, and title. When you search for your topic, the computer helps you narrow your search—something a card catalog cannot do. You begin by typing a word or phrase, such as "business ethics." The computer will then display a list of all the subtopics related to business ethics. When you select a subtopic from those displayed, a list of resources related to that specific topic will appear. From this, you can learn not only the title of the books and where they are located but also whether or not they are checked out and, if out, when they are due back. Sometimes a brief summary about the book is included. Figure 5.1 shows an example results page from an electronic catalog.

Electronic catalogs are not just for locating books. Most libraries allow patrons to search for titles of periodicals and other resources as well. Although the

Chapter Five   Finding Information and Supporting Your Ideas   97

Call #	HF5387 .T734 2004
Author	Treviño, Linda Klebe
Title	**Managing business ethics : straight talk about how to do it right /**
	Linda K. Treviño, Katherine A. Nelson
Edition	3rd ed
Imprint	Hoboken, NJ : Wiley, c2004

Click on the following to:		
Publisher description		
Table of contents		
LOCATION	**CALL #**	**STATUS**
Zane General Stacks	HF5387 .T734 2004Z	AVAILABLE

Descript.	xxii, 362 p. : ill. ; 23 cm.
Bibliog.	Includes bibliographical references and index
Note	E0 OHH
Subject	**Business ethics**
	Business ethics — Case studies
Alt author	Nelson, Katherine A., 1948–
OCLS #	52079623
ISBN	0471230645 (pbk. : alk. paper)
	0471222933 (USA)

Figure 5.1   **Bibliographic information from an electronic catalog.**

electronic catalog will not allow you to search for specific articles in a magazine or technical journal, you can use the catalog to physically locate the source. In some cases, the catalog will provide a link to an electronic full-text version of the periodical so that you can browse for articles.

Periodical Indexes

Periodicals are *sources of information that are published at regular intervals.* Magazines, newspapers, and academic journals are all examples of periodicals found in your library. Periodicals are a different kind of resource than books because you are often interested in specific stories or articles in them rather than the entire issue or edition as with a book. For that reason, you must use specialized databases to locate specific articles on your topic. Table 5.2 lists several of the most common databases and describes the types of information for which they are useful.

Although the indexes listed in Table 5.2 provide access to hundreds of thousands of citations, you may wish to consult even more specialized databases to which your library subscribes. If your topic is very specialized, consultation with a reference librarian could point you in the direction of valuable resources. Periodical indexes work like most search engines on the Internet. Effective researchers often use more than one periodical index to find information. For example, if your presentation deals with a medical topic like obesity, starting with a general index like Academic Search Premiere or Lexis-Nexis and then moving to a specialized index like Medline is an effective approach. Also, not every library has all these databases—a reference librarian can help you find alternatives if your library does not subscribe to a particular database.

TABLE 5.2 COMMON PERIODICAL INDEXES	
INDEX NAME	**INDEX DESCRIPTION**
Academic Search Premiere	Excellent for basic research on various topics, the Academic Search Premiere provides citations and full-text articles for more than 7,000 scholarly publications ranging from arts and literature to the sciences.
Communication and Mass Media Complete	This database provides citations and some full-text articles on topics related to communication and mass media issues.
ERIC	ERIC indexes over 900 scholarly sources covering topics generally related to education.
Humanities Abstracts	Humanities Abstracts cites articles from over 500 periodicals relevant to various humanities topics like the arts and literature.
Lexis-Nexis	This substantial database provides full-text articles from newspapers and magazines as well as transcripts of news broadcasts, legal cases, and testimony before Congress.
Medline	A premiere index for medical issues, this database offers citations and some full-text articles.
Reader's Guide	This source indexes articles from 1901 to the present. Most are from popular U.S.-American magazines.
Social Sciences Index	With citations and some full-text articles, this index covers a broad range of social-scientific topics including politics, social psychology, and crime.

The Internet

Many students now use the Internet to find information for their presentations. The Internet is an appealing research tool because information is easy to locate, many types of information from articles to multimedia files and pictures are available, and, since Web pages are mostly written for mass consumption, information on the Internet is generally easier to understand than technical academic articles are. Unfortunately, the Web can be difficult to navigate. University of Georgia professor Joseph Dominick[1] says, "Some have described using the Internet as trying to find your way across a big city without a map. You'll see lots of interesting stuff but you may never get to where you're going" (346). Becoming sidetracked and feeling somewhat overwhelmed when you're searching for information on the Web is easy, but you can make your search more effective.

If you are an experienced user of the Web, you are likely to have your own techniques for finding information. If you are less experienced, following a few basic procedures for locating material on the Web will help.

1. Begin by using a **search engine,** which is *a Web site on the Internet that is specially designed to help you search for information.* Although search engines will locate thousands of Web sites that contain the word or phrase you are searching

TABLE 5.3 WEB SEARCH RESOURCES

META-SEARCH ENGINES

Google: www.google.com

Dogpile: www.dogpile.com

Metacrawler: www.metacrawler.com

Surfwax: www.surfwax.com/

COMMON SEARCH ENGINES

Yahoo!: www.yahoo.com

AltaVista: www.altavista.digital.com

Encyclopedia Britannica Internet Guide: www.ebig.com

Excite: www.excite.com

Lycos: www.lycos.com

HotBot: www.hotbot.com

VIRTUAL LIBRARIES

The WWW Virtual Library: lib.org

Galaxy: galaxy.com

Yahoo! Libraries: dir.yahoo.com/Reference/Libraries/

---

for, one criticism of search engines is that they return hundreds of irrelevant Web sites. An alternative to using a search engine is to use a **virtual library,** which *provides links to Web sites that have been reviewed for relevance and usability.* Table 5.3 provides Web addresses for several popular search engines and virtual libraries. Meta-search engines are useful because they combine the results of individual search engines like Yahoo! and Excite.

2. Many search engines give you two options for accessing information. One option is to click on one of the several topical categories displayed on the home page of the search engine site. By following progressively more specific subcategories you can locate Web sources on a relatively specific concept, person, object, hobby, and so forth.

The other option is to conduct a keyword/Boolean search. If you are still in the initial stages of selecting and narrowing a topic, you might want to use the first option—the organized list of categories might help you in that process. You should use the second keyword/Boolean search option once you have identified and narrowed a topic.

Figure 5.2 shows you what the directory page of Google looks like—notice the topical categories listed. By clicking on the categories, you will find information that is more specific. If you click on the "biology" link under the "science" category, you can then select from a number of subtopics related to biology. Figure 5.3 shows the list of topics related to "genetics," which was a subcategory of biology. Using the search feature to look for Web pages on genetics will return a greater variety of sites,

Figure 5.2 **The Google directory page.** Notice that each topic area is a hyperlink where you can "drill down" for more detailed information.

Figure 5.3 List of Web links for the topic of genetics on Google.

Chapter Five   Finding Information and Supporting Your Ideas

some of which may not be relevant to your speech. Table 5.4 provides recommendations on how to more effectively narrow your searches.

3. Carefully *evaluate all sources of information* you find on the Internet, especially when you locate the sources through a public domain search engine rather than your university library's home page. Suggestions for evaluating Web sources and other types of information are provided in subsequent sections of this chapter.

4. Print and bookmark good sources so that you can easily reference them while planning your presentation. By bookmarking the Web page, you can easily access the site later without having to retrace the steps of your search.

5. In addition to printing and bookmarking your sources, you can subscribe to an RSS (Really Simple Syndication) feed, which will allow you to receive and save up-to-date information from that site. You can add RSS feeds to your home page or other XML-capable personal Web pages.

TABLE 5.4 TOOLS FOR NARROWING YOUR WEB SEARCH

WORD STEMMING

By default, browsers identify any Web page containing the word you entered in the search box. For example, if you want to search for the speech acronym "inform," the search engine would return sites with the words informative, information, informal, informing, and so forth. To prevent this result, type your search term with a single quote at the end.

Example: inform'

PHRASE SEARCH

If you are looking for a phrase, put the phrase in quotation marks. For example, simply typing in *homeless youth* would return all sites that contain the two words "homeless" and "youth" anywhere on the site. Placing the phrase in quote marks will return only sites using the phrase "homeless youth."

Example: "homeless youth"

BOOLEAN OPERATORS

Boolean operators allow you to specify logical arguments for what you want returned in a list of matching Web sites. When multiple terms are typed in a search box (e.g., "tobacco addiction"), the default Boolean operator is to place "AND" between the terms. Returned Web sites will contain both tobacco AND addiction somewhere on the page. Other Boolean operators include NOT (e.g., "PowerPoint NOT Microsoft"), which will return Web sites with the term before the operator but not sites with the term after the operator. You can also use the operator OR to find sites with one of two possible terms (e.g., "Gauguin OR van Gogh").

PARENTHESES

Using parentheses allows you to nest Boolean search arguments. In the following example, the search argument will look for Web sites containing the terms "media" and "violence" but not television.

Example: (media AND violence) NOT television

102 Part Two   Selecting and Arranging Content

TRY THIS

Use Yahoo! to find information about an issue relevant to your community. Be careful—not all Web sites come from credible or reliable sources. What did you learn from this exercise that could be used to narrow speech topics for your classroom speeches?

One of the problems with using the Internet for information is that this medium is unregulated. The information may be biased, or just plain wrong, because no authority monitors the content of the sites. How do you determine what information is accurate and credible? Ultimately, *you* will have to make that decision. Ask yourself whether someone would have reason to present biased information. If at all possible, verify the information through other sources, such as newspaper or magazine articles. If the source is a scholarly article, check for a list of references, and if a list of references is provided, try to determine whether the list is credible by verifying some of the sources. Finally, credible sources often provide the credentials of the individual(s) who wrote the article. If no source is provided, be cautious. Moreover, Web sources should be evaluated like any other source.

One additional point to remember is that people have different motives for creating Web pages. Some Web sites intend to provide information, others intend to persuade, and others are profit-driven. Some Web sites try to conceal their true motives—a Web site might look informative but is actually telling only part of a story to persuade you to purchase a service or product. One way to understand the motive of a Web site is to pay attention to the server extension. Table 5.5 explains the parts of a Web address and the characteristics of Web addresses with different types of server extensions. No single type of Web address—based on the server extension—is always better than another. Although knowledge of different types of Web addresses can be valuable, all Web resources deserve scrutiny.

Other Resources on the Web

In addition to search engines, several reference and primary resources are available. Although this list could change daily, the following sources may be helpful depending on your presentation topic:

- *Firstgov* (http://www.firstgov.gov). A portal to all public Web resources from the U.S. Government.
- *Fedstats* (http://www.fedstats.gov/). A government Web site providing access to statistical information from over 100 federal agencies.
- *SearchGov* (www.searchgov.com). This search engine provides access to federal, state, and local government Web sites. The site also provides links to commonly accessed Web sites and the ability to search military Web sites.
- *The CIA World Factbook* (www.cia.gov/cia/publications/factbook/). You do not have to be a secret agent to access the resources of CIA headquarters in Langley, VA. The CIA World Factbook contains detailed information about every country in the world as well as "global" statistics like the total

E-Note

EVALUATING WEB SOURCES

The University of California library has an excellent online exercise illustrating the importance of carefully evaluating Web sources. The address of the exercise is: http://www.lib.berkeley.edu/TeachingLib/Guides/Internet/Evaluate.html.

Individually, in a group, or as a class, evaluate the various Web sites listed in the UC exercise. If you click on the "tips and tricks" links, the UC Berkeley librarians provide their own analyses of how effective the various sites are.

Among the criteria that they recommend using are: (*a*) does the site explain who is responsible for the information; (*b*) is the information on the site able to be independently verified; (*c*) does the site present information in an objective, bias-free manner; and (*d*) has the site been updated recently?

TABLE 5.5 BREAKING DOWN WEB ADDRESSES

ELEMENTS OF A WEB ADDRESS

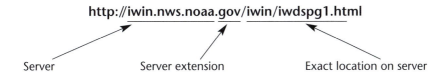

COMMON SERVER EXTENSIONS

EXTENSION	DESCRIPTION	EXAMPLE
.edu	Primarily college and university Web sites	www.ohio.edu Web site for Ohio University
.com	Primarily commercial or for-profit Web sites	www.mhhe.com Web site for McGraw-Hill Publishing Company
.gov	Government Web sites	www.ed.gov Web site for the U.S. Department of Education
.net	Primarily Internet service provider public sites; sometimes used as an alternative when a ".com" name has already been taken	www.maui.net Web site for island of Maui
.org	Primarily not-for-profit organizations	billofrightsinstitute.org Web site sponsored by the public charity, Bill of Rights Institute www.helping.org A resource site for volunteerism and nonprofit organizations

landmass in the world, the global economy, and the current estimated population of Earth.

- *Reference Resources at Yahoo!* (http://dir.yahoo.com/Reference/). If you need a dictionary, a thesaurus, almanac, quotations, or other reference resources, Yahoo! has an excellent set of links to browse.

103

104   Part Two   Selecting and Arranging Content

Even for specialized topics such as multiculturalism, co-culture, or ethnicity, the Web is an excellent resource. If you need to research various cultural issues, try these sources:

- *Yahoo! Regional* (http://dir.yahoo.com/Regional). This Yahoo! directory provides links to information on various countries and regions of the United States.
- *The WWW Library—Native Americans* (www.hanksville.org/NAresources). This site provides links to information about Native Americans on the Web.
- *Black History Quest* (http://blackquest.com). Resources on African American history and culture.
- *Latino-American Network Information Center* (http://lanic.utexas.edu/). Information on Latino history and culture in the United States.
- *Asian-Nation* (www.asian-nation.org). This Web portal provides links to resources addressing Asian American history and culture.

Evaluating and Using Sources of Information

Locating sources of information is the first step in the research process. After you find high-quality sources, the next step is to carefully evaluate those sources and then to integrate them into your preparation outline.

Criteria for Evaluating Sources

Just finding sources does not ensure that you have effectively researched your presentation. You must carefully evaluate each source for its credibility and usefulness. *The Style Manual for Communication Studies*[2] recommends that you use the following criteria when evaluating sources:

1. *Is the supporting material clear?* Sources should help you add clarity to your ideas rather than confusing the issue with jargon and overly technical explanations.
2. *Is the supporting material verifiable?* Listeners and readers should be able to verify the accuracy of your sources. Although verifying information in a book is easy—the book can be checked out and read—information obtained from a personal interview with the uncle of your sister's roommate is not.
3. *Is the source of the supporting material competent?* For each source you should be able to determine qualifications. If your source is a person, what expertise does the person have with the topic? If your source is an organization, what relationship does the organization have with the issue?
4. *Is the source objective?* All sources—even news reports—have some bias. The National Rifle Association has a bias in favor of gun ownership; Greenpeace has a bias in favor of environmental protection; TV news programs have a bias toward vivid visual imagery. What biases does your source have, and how might those biases affect the way these organizations or people frame information?
5. *Is the supporting material relevant?* Loading your speech with irrelevant sources might make the speech seem well researched; however, critical listeners will see through this tactic. Include only sources that directly address the key points you want to make.

Chapter Five   Finding Information and Supporting Your Ideas   105

These criteria are not "yes or no" questions. Sources will meet some criteria well and fail others miserably. Your job as the speaker is to weigh the benefits and problems with each source and determine whether to include the source in your speech. Indeed, you have a key ethical responsibility to carefully evaluate sources. Moreover, these criteria assume that you will take time to find out information about each source that you are using. Understanding who the author or sponsoring organization is, whether the site bases claims on supporting material or on opinion, and how recently the site has been updated are all important factors to consider.

TRY THIS

Find a Web site on a potential topic for your presentation and use the five questions for evaluating sources above to analyze the quality of the Web site as a source of information. Based on your analysis, would you use the Web site in a speech?

Source evaluation is one of the most valuable skills you can learn. Because the Internet has dramatically increased the quantity of information available to researchers, your ability to sift through multiple sources and pick out the very best is critical. Consider the example of Richard's presentation on cell phone dangers with which we began the chapter. He assumed that the initial articles that he had found on the Internet were appropriate; however, after speaking with his instructor, he learned that he was incorrect.

After meeting with Renee, the reference librarian, Richard carefully integrated information from the interview with other sources he found on the university library's Web site. In his presentation, he also used the initial sources that he found on cell phone dangers to persuade his audience that to be skeptical of information found on the Web is important. The goal of Richard's presentation was to convince audience members that seemingly good sources of Web information can actually be deceptive and biased. By using sources found through Medline, a periodical database, Richard was able to show that credible scientific studies contradicted the unsupported claims found on the Web about cell phones. And, by using the interview with Renee, Richard was able to tell audience members how they should critically evaluate Web information.

Citing Sources of Information Correctly

Once you find source material, you must provide references for the source both on your outline and in your speech. **Bibliographic references** are *complete citations that appear in the "references" or "works cited" section of your speech outline (or term paper).* Your outline should also contain **internal references,** which are *brief notations of which bibliographic reference contains the details you are using in your speech.* Internal and bibliographic references help readers understand what sources were used to find specific details like statistics, quotations, and examples. Most teachers require students to use a specific style guide for formatting bibliographic and internal references. The two most common types of style guides are the American Psychological Association (APA) and the Modern Language Association (MLA). Figure 5.4 provides sample citations for five types of sources following APA and MLA styles.

Part Two Selecting and Arranging Content

APA

Newspaper Article
Cox, J. (2004, 15 June). Financially ailing companies point to Iraq war. *USA Today*, p. 10b.

Academic Journal
Mathews, J. (1996, March). Lusting after black gold. *National Wildlife, 34,* 15.

Book
Magill, G. (Ed.). (2004). *Genetics and ethics: An interdisciplinary study* (1st ed.). Saint Louis: Saint Louis University Press.

Web Page
Hallman, L. (2004, 29 June). Red Cross movement responds to crisis in Sudan. Retrieved June 30, 2004, from http://redcross.org.

Personal Interview
(D. Craig, J. L. Kyle & L. Borich, personal communication, September 1, 2005)

MLA

Newspaper Article
Cox, James. "Financially Ailing Companies Point to Iraq War." USA Today 15 June 2004: 10b.

Academic Journal
Mathews, Jessica. "Lusting after Black Gold." National Wildlife March 1996: 15.

Book
Magill, Gerard, ed. Genetics and Ethics: An Interdisciplinary Study. 1st ed. Saint Louis: Saint Louis University Press, 2004.

Web Page
Hallman, Leslie. "Red Cross Movement Responds to Crisis in Sudan," 29 June. 2004. American Red Cross. 30 June <http://redcross.org>.

Personal Interview
Craig, Deborah, Jerri Lynn Kyle, and Lynn Borich. Personal Interview. 1 Sept. 2005.

Figure 5.4 **Five sources following APA and MLA styles.**

In addition to citing sources in your outline, you must also provide verbal citations during your presentation. Unlike the readers of a paper or presentation outline, audience members are less concerned with page numbers and titles of articles. Rather, an **oral citation** tells listeners *who the source is, how recent the information is, and the source's qualifications.* The examples listed in Table 5.6 illustrate how to orally cite different types of sources. Of these types of sources, students have the most difficulty with Web pages. Remember that the Web address is only that—an address. The Web address should be listed in the references or works cited page of your outline, but usually you do not say the address during your presentation. An exception might occur if you wanted your audience to visit that particular Web site.

Identifying Appropriate Supporting Materials

Now that you know how to look for, evaluate, and use sources, the next step is locating **supporting materials,** *information you can use to substantiate your arguments and to clarify your position.* In this

TABLE 5.6 EXAMPLES OF ORAL CITATIONS

Type of Source	Example
Newspaper article	"According to Kelly DiNardo, a reporter for *USA Today*, 2004 showed a big jump in the number of Internet fraud cases."
Research study	"Elizabeth Graham, a communication researcher, found in a 2003 study that relationships go through several contradictory trends after a divorce."
Web page	"The American Red Cross Web site, which I visited on June 30, 2004, stated that over 23,000 meals were served to Nebraska tornado victims."

section you will learn about examples, surveys, testimonial evidence, numbers and statistics, analogies, and definitions.

Examples

Examples, *specific instances used to illustrate your point,* are among the most common supporting materials found in presentations of all types. Sometimes a single example helps convince an audience; at other times, a relatively large number of examples may be necessary to achieve your purpose. For instance, the argument that communities need to do more to stop environmental pollution could be supported by citing several examples of hazardous waste sites in your community or state.

Be careful when using examples. Sometimes an example is so unusual that an audience will not accept the story as evidence of anything. A student who refers to his own difficulty in landing a job as an example of problems with the economy is unconvincing if more general statistics do not support his claim. A good example must be plausible, typical, and related to the main points of the presentation.

Two types of examples are factual and hypothetical. A *factual* example is just that—a fact. It can be verified. A *hypothetical* example cannot be verified. It is speculative, imaginative, fictional. The example can be brief or extended. The following is an example of a brief factual example:

> According to the August 5, 2005, issue of *The Chronicle of Higher Education,* the time students spent volunteering in 2004 was worth almost $4.5 billion.

Here is an extended hypothetical example:

> *An example of how nanotechnology could be used is in the case of oil spills. Suppose that billions of tiny robots, smaller in diameter than a human hair, were released at the site of an oil spill. These robots are programmed to seek out and digest oil molecules into pieces of silt that fall harmlessly to the bottom of the ocean. In less than one day, all evidence of the oil spill has been magically gobbled up by these minuscule workers. Two days later, the robots run out of energy and join the digested oil molecules on the ocean floor. In their short life span these nano-machines saved countless creatures from an ugly death and prevented millions of dollars in destruction.*

The brief factual example is *verifiable,* meaning the example can be supported by a source that the audience can check. The extended hypothetical example is

Watch the clip titled "Using an Example" on the accompanying CD-ROM.

Cultural Note

ORAL VS. WRITTEN CULTURES AND THE USE OF EVIDENCE

Walter J. Ong, formerly a professor of rhetoric at St. Louis University, suggests that important differences exist between literary and oral cultures.[3] Literary, or writing-based, cultures tend to develop ideas in a much more linear fashion than do oral cultures. According to Ong, some cultures are primary oral cultures because they have not yet developed a written language. Aboriginal cultures throughout the world represent the last known primary oral cultures. In America, we clearly have the capacity to be a written culture; however, technology like cell phones and television causes our culture to behave as if it were an oral culture. Ong calls these types of cultures secondary oral cultures. These differences between types of cultures are important. Evidence in a written culture would look very different from evidence in an oral culture. While written cultures might prefer carefully worded and thoughtfully analyzed quotations, oral cultures might prefer examples, narratives, and stories as forms of evidence.

not verifiable and is actually a "what if" scenario. Explaining to the audience that an example is hypothetical is important. Presenting a hypothetical example as a *real* example is unethical, and your credibility will be questioned if the audience learns that they were misled.

Surveys

Another type of supporting material commonly used during presentations is a **survey,** *a study in which a limited number of questions are answered by a sample of the population to discover opinions on issues.* You will most often find surveys quoted in magazines or journals. Audiences usually see these surveys as more credible than an example or one person's experience because they synthesize the experience of hundreds or thousands of people. Public opinion polls fall into this category. One person's experience with alcohol can have an impact on an audience, but a survey indicating that one-third of all Americans abstain, or one-third drink occasionally, or a certain percentage of college students binge drink supports your argument better. As with personal experience, you should ask some important questions about the evidence found in surveys:

1. *How reliable is the source?* A report of a survey in a professional journal of sociology, psychology, or communication is likely to be more thorough and more valid than one found in a local newspaper.
2. *How broad was the sample used in the survey?* Was it a survey of the entire nation, the region, the state, the city, the campus, or the class?
3. *Who was included in the survey?* Did everyone in the sample have an equally good chance of being selected, or were volunteers asked to respond to the questions, making the survey pool self-selected?
4. *How representative was the survey sample?* For example, readers of *The New Yorker* magazine may not be typical of the population in your state.
5. *Who performed the survey?* Was the survey conducted by a nationally recognized survey firm, such as Lou Harris or Gallup, or was it the local

newspaper editor? Was it performed by professionals such as professors, researchers, or management consultants?
6. *Why was the survey done?* Was it performed for any self-serving purpose—for example, to attract more readers—or did the government conduct the survey to help establish policy or legislation? Finding out who sponsored the survey is important.

Testimony

Testimonial evidence, a third kind of supporting material, is *written or oral statements of others' experience used by a speaker to substantiate or clarify a point*. Testimonial evidence shows the audience that you are not alone in your beliefs, ideas, and arguments. Other people also support you, and their statements should help the audience accept your point of view. The three kinds of testimonial evidence you can use in your speeches are lay, expert, and celebrity.

Lay testimony is *statements made by an ordinary person that substantiate or support what you say*. In advertising, this kind of testimony shows ordinary people using or buying products and stating the fine qualities of those products. In a speech, lay testimony might be the words of your relatives, neighbors, or friends concerning an issue. Such testimony shows the audience that you and other ordinary people feel the same way about an issue. Other examples of lay testimony are parents speaking about curriculum changes at a school board meeting or alumni attesting to the positive qualities of their college at a recruiting session.

Expert testimony is *statements made by someone who has special knowledge or expertise about an issue or idea*. In your speech, you might quote Senator John McCain about the war in Iraq, the Surgeon General about health care, or the president of the Sierra Club about the environment. The idea is to demonstrate that people with specialized experience or education support the positions you advocate in your speech.

Celebrity testimony is *statements made by a public figure who is known to the audience*. Celebrity testimony occurs in advertising when someone famous endorses a particular product. In your presentation, you might point out that a famous politician, a syndicated columnist, or a well-known entertainer endorses the position you advocate.

Although testimonial evidence may encourage your audience to adopt your ideas, you need to use such evidence with caution. An idea may have little credence even though many laypeople believe in it; an expert may be quoted on topics well outside his or her area of expertise; and a celebrity is often paid for endorsing a product. To protect yourself and your audience, you should ask yourself the following questions before using testimonial evidence in your speeches:

- Is the person you quote an expert whose opinions or conclusions are worthier than most other people's opinions?
- Is the quotation about a subject in the person's area of expertise?
- Is the person's statement based on extensive personal experience, professional study or research, or another form of firsthand proof?
- Will your audience find the statement more believable because you got the quotation from this outside source?

Watch the clip titled "Using Testimony" on the accompanying CD-ROM.

> **TRY THIS**
>
> *Go to the Web site http://www.quotationspage.com and search for quotations on a topic of interest. Were any of the quotations you found effective quotations for a speech? Do you think that this method of finding quotations and testimony is an effective technique for researching in preparation for your presentation?*

Numbers and Statistics

Watch the clip titled "Using Statistics" on the accompanying CD-ROM.

Numbers and statistics are a fourth kind of useful supporting material. **Numbers** *describe something in terms of quantities or amounts.* Because numbers are easier to understand and digest when they appear in print, presenters must simplify, explain, and translate their meaning. For example, instead of saying, "There were 323,462 high school graduates," say, "There were over 300,000 graduates." Other ways to simplify a number like 323,462 are to write the number on a chalkboard or poster or to use a comparison, such as "Three hundred thousand high school graduates are equivalent to the entire population of Lancaster."

Statistics are numbers such as totals, differences, percentages, and averages that *summarize data or provide scientific evidence of relationships between two or more things.* Social scientists use statistics to show how things are related. Communication researchers, for instance, know that a correlation—a statistically verified relationship between two variables—exists between communication competence and satisfaction with interpersonal relationships.

Statistics can be tough for students to decipher. For example, an audience might find this statement difficult to interpret: "Between 1991 and 2000, minority college enrollment was up 52 percent. That is the largest increase in enrollment for any demographic group during that time period." To help the audience understand the meaning of the figures, you could also provide actual minority enrollments between 1991 and 2000 and for the previous period that was studied. Or, rather than stating, "a correlation exists between college grades and fear of communicating," you could use a line graph to show that, generally speaking, students with more communication apprehension tend to achieve slightly lower grades in college and students with lower communication apprehension tend to score slightly higher grades.[4]

You can help your audience by both saying your figures and showing them using visual aids, such as pie charts, line graphs, and bar graphs. You can also use visual imagery. For example, "That amount of money is greater than all the money in all our local banks," or "That many discarded tires would cover our entire city six feet deep in a single year." Think of creative ways to help your audience simplify numbers and statistics, place them in a context, and translate them into their language. Your responsibility as a speaker is to help the audience understand your figures.

Analogies

Watch the clip titled "Using an Analogy" on the accompanying CD-ROM.

Another kind of supporting material is the analogy. An **analogy** is *a comparison of things in some respects, especially in position or function, that are otherwise dissimilar.* For instance,

Sometimes, when I'm wearing jeans on campus, I feel like a chameleon. Not because I blend in with the scenery, trees, limbs, rocks, or foliage, but because I do blend in with other people—everybody wears jeans.[5]

While providing clarification, an analogy is not a proof, because the comparison inevitably breaks down. Therefore, a speaker who argues that American society will fail just as Roman society did can carry the comparison only so far because the form of government, the time in history, and the institutions in the two societies are quite different. Likewise, you can question the chameleon–human analogy by pointing out the vast differences between the two species. Nonetheless, analogies can be quite successful as a way of illustrating or clarifying.

Definitions

Some of the most contentious arguments in our society center on **definitions,** or *determinations of meaning through description, simplification, examples, analysis, comparison, explanation, or illustration.* Experts and ordinary citizens have argued for years about definitions. For instance, when does art become pornography? Is withdrawal of life support systems euthanasia or humanitarian concern? How you define a concept can make a considerable difference in helping audience members understand your points.

Definitions in a presentation are supposed to enlighten the audience by revealing what a term means. Sometimes you can use definitions that appear in standard reference works, such as dictionaries and encyclopedias, but explaining the word in language the audience will understand is most effective. For example, say you use the term *subcutaneous hematoma* in your speech. *Subcutaneous hematoma* is jargon used by physicians to explain a blotch on the skin, but you could explain it in this way: "*Subcutaneous* means 'under the skin,' and *hematoma* means 'swelled with blood,' so the words mean 'blood swelling under the skin,' or what most of us call a 'bruise.'"

The Ethical Use of Supporting Material

Throughout this book we emphasize various ethical requirements for communication that stem from the National Communication Association (NCA) Credo on Ethics. Let's end this chapter by summarizing the ethical obligations faced by speakers when they use supporting materials:

1. *Speakers have an ethical obligation to find the best possible sources of information.* The Internet and full-text databases certainly provide us with easy research options; however, these tools do not necessarily improve the quality of our research. Yet, your audience depends on you to present the best and most accurate information possible. The best sources of information are sometimes not available online or in full-text form. Selecting a variety of sources including print sources, Internet sources, and possibly even interviews can thus help improve the overall quality of the materials on which you base your presentation.

2. *Speakers have an ethical obligation to cite their sources of information.* Of course, one reason to cite sources of information is to avoid **plagiarism,** which is

the intentional use of information from another source without crediting the source. All universities have specific codes of conduct that identify sanctions levied against those who are caught plagiarizing. Although outright plagiarism is uncommon, students mistakenly—and often—commit **incremental plagiarism,** which is *the intentional or unintentional use of information from one or more sources without fully divulging how much information is directly quoted.* Many students use large chunks of information from Web pages and other sources, sometimes directly copying and pasting. Failing to clearly identify what is directly quoted, even accidentally, is a serious form of plagiarism. Moreover, your teacher will likely evaluate your speech more favorably if you interpret the meaning of short quotations for the audience rather than relying on long quotations.

3. *Speakers have an ethical obligation to fairly and accurately represent sources.* How often have you heard politicians and other public figures complain that the media take their comments "out of context"? To avoid making unfair and inaccurate representations of sources, whether they are newspaper articles, Web pages, books, or even interviews, you must ensure that you fully understand the points being made by the source. Remember, for example, that two-sided arguments are often used to present a point. In a **two-sided argument** *a source advocating one position will present an argument from the opposite viewpoint and then go on to refute that argument.* To take an excerpt from a source where the opposing argument is being presented for refutation and imply that the source was advocating the opposing argument is unethical. As a speaker, you have liberty to disagree with points made by the sources you consult; you do not have the liberty to misrepresent those same sources.

To see an example of a well-researched presentation, watch the clip titled "Stem Cell Research" on the accompanying CD-ROM.

In conclusion, locating, understanding, and incorporating supporting material is one of the most important tasks you will undertake as a presenter of information and argument. Good research affects literally every step in the process of preparing and delivering a presentation. Taking care to effectively and ethically use your information will make you a better speaker and will earn the respect of your peers and teachers.

Resources for Review and Discussion

SUMMARY

In this chapter you have learned the following:

▶ The research process is a common thread tying together all aspects of the speech preparation process.
  - An effective research strategy means finding multiple types of sources because different books, journals, and peoples' experiences provide you with different types of supporting materials.
  - Research helps you find and narrow speech topics, identify main points, support your ideas, develop effective introductions and conclusions, and deliver your speech with confidence.

▶ Students typically use four common types of sources in their speeches: personal experience, interviews, library resources, and the Internet.
  - Personal experiences can provide useful examples but should be carefully evaluated to determine whether they are useful evidence.
  - Interviewing others can provide useful details, examples, and quotations. However, preparing for and carrying out successful interviews takes time and careful planning.
  - Library resources includes books, journals, newspapers, magazines, and government documents. Most libraries have specialized electronic databases that will enable you to find information.
  - The Internet provides easy access to large quantities of information; such sources must be carefully evaluated.

▶ Once you have found sources, you must carefully consider how you will use and cite the information.
  - To evaluate sources you should ask the following questions: Is the supporting material clear? Is the supporting material verifiable? Is the source of the supporting material competent? Is the source objective? Is the supporting material relevant?
  - Preparation outlines should include bibliographic references, which are complete lists of sources in a "references" or "works cited" section. Your outline should also include internal references, which are brief notations in the text of the outline indicating which bibliographic reference contains specific information.
  - In your presentation, you should provide oral citations of sources so listeners will know where information came from.

▶ You use supporting material as evidence for ideas and arguments in your speech.
  - Examples are specific instances or stories that illustrate your points.
  - Surveys report answers to questions designed to discover popular opinions on topics.
  - Testimony involves quotations that explain something or provide evidence that others agree with your points.
  - Numbers and statistics quantify ideas or show statistical relationships.
  - Analogies provide comparisons between things to illustrate or clarify ideas.
  - Definitions help audiences understand the meaning of specific terms used during a presentation.

▶ Presenters are obligated to follow ethical principles when selecting and using supporting material in their presentations.
  - Speakers have an ethical obligation to find the best possible sources of information.
  - Speakers must cite their sources of information.
  - Speakers are required to present fair and accurate representations of their sources of information.

KEY TERMS

 Use the *Public Speaking* CD-ROM and the Online Learning Center at www.mhhe.com/nelson to practice your understanding of the following terminology.

Analogy	Celebrity testimony	Electronic catalog
Bibliographic references	Definitions	Evidence

Examples
Expert testimony
Incremental plagiarism
Internal references
Lay testimony
Numbers
Periodicals

Personal experience
Plagiarism
Reference librarian
Search engine
Statistics
Supporting materials
Survey

Testimonial evidence
Two-sided argument
Oral citation
Virtual library

REFERENCES

[1] Dominick, J. R. (1996). *The dynamics of mass communication* (5th ed.). New York: McGraw-Hill.

[2] Bourhis, John, et al. (2002). *A style manual for communication studies.* New York: McGraw-Hill.

[3] Ong, Walter J. (2004). *Orality and literacy: The technologizing of the word* (1st ed.). St. Louis: Saint Louis University Press.

[4] Bourhis, J., & Allen, M. (1992). Meta-analysis of the relationship between communication apprehension and cognitive performance. *Communication Education, 41.1,* 68–76.

[5] Polnac, L., Grant, L., & Cameron, T. (1999). *Common sense.* New Jersey: Prentice-Hall.

APPLICATION EXERCISES

 Go to the self-quizzes on the *Public Speaking* CD-ROM and the Online Learning Center at www.mhhe.com/nelson to test your knowledge of the chapter concepts.

1. Following the example of Richard, introduced at the start of the chapter, conduct a Web search for sites discussing "dangers of cell phones." After locating a Web site on the topic, do the same search in Academic Search Premiere or some other general database. Compare the conclusions of the Web site and the articles you find. Do the articles provide independent verification of the conclusions stated in the Web site? Which sources appear most credible? Why?

2. For each of the topics listed below, identify at least three databases that you would use to locate information sources at your library. Briefly explain why you selected each database.
   Global warming
   AIDS
   The war in Iraq
   Harry Potter

3. Below is information about a magazine article and a book on the topic of student motivation. For each source, correctly write the citation in both APA and MLA styles.

MAGAZINE ARTICLE

AUTHOR: SANDY JOHNSTON, PHD

MAGAZINE: PHI DELTA KAPPAN

ARTICLE TITLE: MAKING LEARNING FUN FOR STUDENTS

YEAR: 2005

DATE: JUNE

PAGES: 34–38

BOOK

AUTHOR: KENNETH KIEWRA

TITLE: ENHANCING STUDENT MOTIVATION

EDITION: 2ND

YEAR: 2004

PUBLISHER: UNIVERSITY PRESS

PUBLISHER LOCATION: OMAHA, NE

CHAPTER SIX

Order and simplification are the first steps toward mastery of a subject.
THOMAS MANN (1875–1955),
1929 NOBEL LAUREATE, LITERATURE

Any plan formulated in a hurry is foolish.
RASHI (1040–1105),
RELIGIOUS SCHOLAR

Organizing and Outlining Your Presentation

What will you learn?

When you have read and thought about this chapter, you will be able to:

1. State why good organization helps audiences to understand.
2. Compose your presentation with a limited number of main points of equal importance in parallel form.
3. Understand when to use the time-sequence, spatial relations, cause-effect, topical sequence, problem-solution, and Monroe's Motivated Sequence patterns of organization.
4. Use transitions, signposts, internal previews, and internal reviews.
5. Apply the principles of outlining: subordination, division, and parallelism.
6. Draft a preparation outline, a key word outline, and a formal sentence outline.
7. Introduce your presentation.
8. Conclude your presentation.

Good organization heightens a speaker's credibility and helps listeners better understand a presentation. This chapter shows you the principles underlying organization, the application of those principles in practical outlines, and the choices you need to make in adapting your message to an audience through organization. This chapter also helps you introduce and conclude your presentation.

Part Two Selecting and Arranging Content

Nagora Wynkoop had a topic for his public speaking class. He knew one subject better than most other people, and that was emergency medicine. Nagora had worked for more than 20 years as a paramedic on an ambulance. Because his unit was located near some major highway systems, he and the ambulance driver spent most of their time transporting accident victims to the hospital.

Nagora knew much about first responder medicine. What he did not know was how to organize 20 years' worth of information about emergency first aid. Which of the many areas should he cover? What information should come first? How many things should he try to talk about?

Why Organize?

You have already found information about your topic; now you need to arrange your message. Research on organizing speeches indicates that speakers who give well-organized presentations enjoy several advantages over those who do not. First, audience members understand the organized presentations better.[1] Second, organized presenters appeared more competent and trustworthy than speakers who delivered disorganized presentations.[2] Clearly, audiences appreciate well-organized messages.

Speakers themselves also benefit from taking the time to carefully organize their presentations. First, they do not just *appear* more confident when their messages are better organized, they actually *are* more confident.[3] Second, they believe they deliver their presentations more smoothly.[4] Third, researchers found that the more students can learn and master the ability to organize ideas, the better analytical thinkers they become.[5] And good organizational skills you learn in public speaking apply equally well in your other endeavors.

How to Organize the Body of the Presentation

The introduction, body, and conclusion are the three main components of most formal presentations. In this chapter, we first consider the organization of the *body*, the main message. Usually, we create and organize the body of the presentation before tackling the introduction and conclusion. We do that because you need to know what your main message is before you can properly introduce or conclude that message.

Emphasize Main Points

The first task in organizing the body of the presentation is to identify your main points. Examine the ideas and arguments you have gathered, and consider the key issues you want to address. If you have written down your specific purpose, you may be able to identify your main points easily. For example, Stacey Tischer, a second-year doctoral pharmacy student, gave a presentation on breast cancer[6] with these three main points:

I. 1,500 men each year contract breast cancer.
II. Black women who are diagnosed die of the disease more often than white women who are diagnosed.
III. Self-examination, clinical examination, and even partner examination can help detect the problem.

By dividing your topic into main ideas you can better explain and discuss it further. The main points, as we see here, provide the skeleton for the body of the speech. They will be backed up with supporting materials, examples, evidence, and further divisions of subpoints and sub-subpoints. Section III above could be further explained with subpoints like these:

A. Looking and feeling are two parts to breast examination.
B. Detecting the difference between cancerous and noncancerous irregularities is very important.

As you are considering your topic, your specific purpose, and the main points that you will develop, remember this practical advice:

- Choose two or three main points.
- Word your main points in a parallel manner.
- Make sure your main ideas are approximately equal in importance.

Let us consider each of these suggestions in more depth.

Limit Your Main Points to Two to Three Points

Most messages have two to three main points, reflecting what an audience can easily remember. For some topics, you may come up with only two main points. On the other hand, you may find that some topics are more easily divisible into a greater number of points. For instance, if you are talking about a complex process like preparing for an audit, you could divide your talk into the five main steps of the process.

Remember Nagora, the emergency medical person in the opening story? He knew too much about health for a five-minute presentation. He could, however, address what happens in the first minutes with three main points in a presentation entitled "First Acts of the First Responder."

I. *Make sure the victim's heart is beating or immediately provide cardiopulmonary therapy.*
II. *Make sure external blood flow is stopped with pressure or tourniquets.*
III. *Make sure the victim is breathing or immediately provide oxygen.*

Express Your Main Points in a Parallel Manner

In speaking and writing, "parallelism" increases clarity, sounds more engaging, and lingers longer in memory. **Parallel construction** means that *you repeat words and phrases and use the same parts of speech for each item.*

An example of parallelism is this portion of a speech on organic farming:

I. The organic farmer must monitor pests.
II. The organic farmer must use direct seeding.
III. The organic farmer must transplant crops.

Parallelism incorporates some or similar words repeatedly to create a kind of rhythm in the speech. Although the parallel wording may seem subtle, the wording will affect the way you develop subsequent subpoints and sub-subpoints. In general, using parallel construction in your main points encourages more logical development of supporting ideas. When your main points are organized similarly, the audience is more likely to follow them and remember them.

Ensure That Your Main Points Are Nearly Equal in Importance

One way that you can check that your main points are of equal weight is to consider how much you subdivide each main point. If one main point has several subdivisions, but the others have none, then the point with many subdivisions must be more important than the others. Merge main points or reduce subdivisions to achieve nearly equal weight. Maybe one of the subpoints is really a main point.

Similarly, when you practice your presentation later on, you may find that you do not spend equal time on each main point. Each main point need not be granted *exactly* the same amount of time, but the time you spend discussing each point should be more or less similar. If you have three main points, you should spend about 30 percent of your time on each.

Determine the Order of the Main Points

Sometimes the order of your main points seems obvious. At other times, the organizational pattern is less clear. Your purpose and topic determine your choice of organizational pattern. In this section we provide you with some alternatives you can consider for the organization of your main points.

The general purpose of your presentation will suggest potential organizational patterns. Among the possible organizational patterns, which we will discuss below, are:

1. The time-sequence and spatial relations patterns found often in informative presentations.
2. The cause-effect and topical sequence patterns found in both informative and persuasive presentations.
3. The problem-solution and Monroe's Motivated Sequence patterns found often in persuasive presentations.

T R Y THIS

As you work your way through the six patterns of organization below, see if you can think of one example for each that is not provided in the text. For example, for the first one, think of one topic that would be treated best in the time-sequence organization.

Chapter Six   Organizing and Outlining Your Presentation   **121**

The Stages of Muscular Dystrophy*

Introduction:

I have a little brother with muscular dystrophy. Perhaps you too have family members with health issues. I hope that my presentation today will inform you about a specific disease that affects thousands of Americans, and I hope that those of you who are lucky enough not to have health problems in the family will understand better what we go through when a valued member of the family has an illness that affects us all.

Body:

I. The discovery that your child faces a lifetime with a progressive, incurable, debilitating disease happens first.

    A. The family's first response is disbelief and denial: It cannot be happening to our little boy.

    B. Among the first unmistakable symptoms are the back curve and the toe walking (the presenter shows photos).

II. The middle stage of the disease has the person requiring continuous assistance to move.

    A. An early hurdle in the middle stage is securing a wheelchair through insurance.

    B. Transporting a wheelchair requires a large vehicle, patience, and strength.

III. The late stages of the disease leave the person relatively helpless.

    A. My brother needed an expensive wheelchair with elaborate controls.

    B. Often the victim of muscular dystrophy requires surgery.

    C. Muscular dystrophy brings scoliosis (curvature of the spine).

Conclusion:

Now you know the early, middle, and late stages of muscular dystrophy. You know what the disease does to the person who has it and to the family who cares for the person with the disease. You should not feel sorry for my brother or his family. We love him, and his problems have brought our family closer together. He helps all of us to value our good health as you should value yours.

Figure 6.1   **Presentation outline using time-sequence pattern of organization.**

*Based on an outline submitted by Lynnette Sedgeman in Communication 114, Human Communication at North Dakota State University, Fall Semester, 2003.

Time-Sequence Pattern

The **time-sequence pattern** *states the order of events as they actually occur.* Use this pattern when your primary purpose is to tell your audience how something came about over a period of time. The steps in reducing water pollution, the evolution of sexual harassment policies, and the development of PDA (personal digital assistant) technology are examples of topics based on time. This pattern is also commonly used in "how to do it" and in "either/or" presentations because the audience will be unable to "do it" unless steps are followed in the correct order. A presentation outline using the time-sequence pattern is shown in Figure 6.1.

Spatial Relations Pattern

The **spatial relations pattern** *demonstrates how items are related in space.* Examples of presentations that could be organized using a spatial relations pattern would include using a map to show historic conservation sites over a period of time,

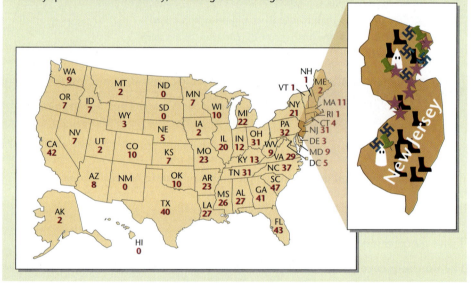

Figure 6.2 Presentation outline using spatial relations pattern of organization.

using a grid to demonstrate the arrangement of lighting for an outdoor photography shoot, or using an architectural model to explain effective kitchen design for people who use wheelchairs. An example of the spatial relations pattern in Figure 6.2 shows how a student used two related maps in his presentation.

Cause-Effect Pattern

The **cause-effect pattern** of organization *describes or explains causes and consequences.* Actually, the pattern of organization can move from cause to effect or from effect

Chapter Six   Organizing and Outlining Your Presentation

Gridlock in Paradise*

Introduction:

I'm a woman from California, a place that many Americans think is as close to Paradise as you can get. But those of us who live in Southern California have a different opinion about one thing: traffic. Los Angeles, my home town, has two of the top ten biggest gridlocked intersections in America. Let's examine this problem of traffic congestion, a problem that seems to plague every metropolitan area. Let us look first at the causes and then at the effects.

Body:

I. Practically every day the people of Los Angeles have to drive at a snail's pace because of all the people and all the cars on the road at the same time.

    A. California has more people than any other state.

    B. Los Angeles is the largest city in California.

    C. Californians love their cars, so they have many.

II. Another cause is that people in Los Angeles all seem to be on the road at once—alone.

    A. Drivers are not good about carpooling, so more cars are on the road.

    B. People are not good about using mass transit, so more cars are on the road.

    C. Everyone seems to go to work and return from work during the same time periods, making many hours of the day into rush hours.

    D. "Rush hours" is a misnomer because those hours are the slowest times to get anywhere.

III. People in Los Angeles spend more time gridlocked in their cars than anyone else in our nation.

    A. Los Angeles drivers have the longest commuting times in the United States.

    B. The city of Los Angeles has more congested highways than any other city in America.

Conclusion:

What causes highway congestion? Too many people, too many cars, too few carpoolers, too many single-drivers, too many people on the same schedule. What is the result? Slow commuting times, traffic congestion, irritated drivers, and wasted fuel. So, even though California is generally sunny and bright, the daily cloud on the horizon is the daily commute: Gridlock in Paradise.

Figure 6.3   **Cause-effect organizational pattern.**

*Based on an outline submitted by Erin Troup in Communication 114, Human Communication, at North Dakota State University, Fall Semester, 2003.

to cause. An example of effect to cause are the various spinoffs from *Law and Order*, such as *Criminal Intent* or *SVU*, stories in which the narrative begins with the murder (effect) and proceeds to the cause (conviction of the murderer). In a presentation you might use such a pattern by starting with someone almost miraculously free of pain (effect) and move toward the new drug (cause) that made the person pain-free. Two examples of cause to effect might be how increased exposure to sunshine, medicine, and even lights can defeat SAD (Seasonal Affect Disorder) or how taking a daily vitamin can increase your body's immunity to disease. Figure 6.3 illustrates a cause-effect pattern.

Part Two Selecting and Arranging Content

Topical Sequence Pattern

The **topical sequence pattern,** a highly versatile organizational pattern, *simply divides up a topic into related parts.* Be careful not to treat the topical sequence pattern as a dumper into which you can throw anything. The main points in a topical sequence have to be related to a central idea and the main points need to be related to each other: three reasons to volunteer at the food bank, two types of hybrid vehicles, and the advantages and disadvantages of jury trials. Figure 6.4 shows an example of the topical sequence pattern.

Problem-Solution Pattern

The **problem-solution pattern,** *depicting an issue and a solution,* tends to be used more often in persuasive than in informative presentations. The statement of the

---

Adopt a Healthy Lifestyle*

Introduction:

Americans are the fattest people in the world. Watch this thirty-second video clip from a *20/20* report, "Obesity in America" (Kelsi shows the video). Our kids spend more time watching TV than working in the classroom. They eat more fast food than anyone in the world. Today, my purpose is to inform you about the growing problem of obesity and reveal how you can conquer fat through diet and exercise.

Body:

I.   Obesity is on the rise in America, the nation with the fattest people on earth.

    A. Eating healthy home-cooked meals has been replaced by eating fast, fatty foods outside the home.

    B. We no longer walk to the refrigerator (exercise); we drive to the nearest fast food outlet.

    C. We no longer exercise; we just watch TV.

II. You can defeat obesity with a balanced diet.

    A. Very few Americans eat enough fruits and vegetables.

    B. Very few Americans eat too few carbohydrates.

    C. Very few Americans eat portions that are small.

III. You can defeat obesity with exercise.

    A. You can reduce weight by working out four or five times per week.

    B. You can reduce weight with strength training as part of a total body workout.

Conclusion:

Obesity is a serious health problem for Americans, including many of us in this room. How can we defeat the problem? The most effective method is controlling your diet and exercising your body. Sure, you have been told that story many times in your life, but perhaps this time you will start today to defeat a problem that could someday ruin your life.

Figure 6.4 **A topical sequence pattern of organization.**
Notice that the main heads have a logical relationship with each other. Also, this presentation both informs the audience about obesity and persuades them to take specific actions to solve the problem.

*Based on an outline submitted by Kelsi Joyce in Communication 114, Human Communication, at North Dakota State University, Fall Semester, 2003.

Chapter Six   Organizing and Outlining Your Presentation   **125**

Architecture Students Take a Hit*

I. Architecture students are being required to pay $700 extra in Spring Semester for airfare and lodging for a class trip to San Francisco. (The Problem)

II. About the only solution for students is additional indebtedness in the form of student loans or increased financial aid.   (The Solution)

Figure 6.5 **The problem-solution organization.**

*Based on an outline by Abbie Gibbs in Communication 114, Human Communication, at North Dakota State University, in Fall Semester, 2003.

problem is difficult without framing the issue in some way that indicates your own perspective, a perspective that you want the audience to adopt. For example, let us say you describe the environmental issue of establishing game preserves. Your position on the issue—that the state should pay farmers to set aside land for wildlife and natural habitat—is the perspective you urge on the audience. An example of a problem-solution pattern appears in Figure 6.5.

Your solution is even more likely to be perceived as persuasive because you will advocate some policy or action that you want your audience to embrace.

The problem-solution pattern raises three serious questions for the speaker: how much should you say about the problem, how much about the solution, and how ethical is the solution? Usually you can work out a proper ratio based on what the audience knows about the issue. If the listeners are unaware that a problem exists, you may have to spend more time telling them about the problem. On the other hand, if the problem is well known to all, you can spend most of your time on the solution. This pattern lends itself nicely to outlining, with the problem being one main point and the solution the other.

Monroe's Motivated Sequence

Monroe's Motivated Sequence[7] was developed by Alan Monroe, who applied John Dewey's work on reflective thinking to persuasion. This organizational pattern *includes five specific components: attention, need, satisfaction, visualization, and action.*

- First, capture the *attention* of your audience. You want your audience to decide that to listen to you is important.

- Second, establish the *need* for your proposal. You want to describe a problem or show why some need exists. You want your audience to believe that something must be done.

- Third, present the solution to the problem or show how the need can be satisfied. You want your audience to understand how your proposal will achieve *satisfaction.*

- Fourth, go beyond simply presenting the solution by *visualizing* the solution for the audience. You want the audience to envision enjoying the benefits of your proposal.

A Law Against Smoking in Public*

Introduction:

Like you, I walk through a cloud of cigarette smoke outside Bentley Hall every day to get to this class, a cloud of smoke from students who must smoke before class. We know now that you do not have to be a smoker to die from inhaling cigarette smoke: Secondhand smoke kills.

Ingrid Wickelgren's article in *Current Science* reported that over 400,000 people die every year from cigarette smoke. Why do I care about this subject? I lived for most of my life with smokers and asthma sufferers. I am so interested that I have been locked on the Internet for a week studying smoking. Today, I will address the issue of smoking in public places, present a solution, and describe life in a smoke-free environment.

Body:

I. **Need:** According to *Business Week* 40 million Americans smoke.

    A. The poisons in their secondhand smoke are just outside each campus building, in every bar, and even in many restaurants.

    B. When smokers smoke in public, they jeopardize everyone with their secondhand smoke.

II. **Satisfaction:** My solution is to forbid cigarette smoking in public.

    A. Smokers could smoke at home but not in public.

    B. My proposal would decrease the number of asthma victims, purify the air, and reduce deaths from smoking.

III. **Visualization:** Imagine what our lives would be like in a smoke-free environment.

    A. Unsuspecting victims of secondhand smoke would no longer perish.

    B. Everyone could breathe air in public places without fear.

Conclusion:

Action: Do not be afraid to take action yourself in this fight for clean air. Be bold enough to ask smokers to put out their cigarettes so neither of us becomes a statistic. If you are a smoker yourself, then remember: Smoking is a colorful habit: your teeth turn yellow and your lungs turn black.

Figure 6.6 **Monroe's Motivated Sequence.**
This outline in the form of a Monroe Motivated Sequence has within it the elements of a problem-solution presentation (problem: secondhand smoke; solution: no smoking in public places).

*From an outline by John R. Reindel in Public Speaking at Ohio University, 1998.

- Fifth and last, state the behavior that you expect of your audience. In this step, you request *action* or approval. You want your audience to respond by saying that they will do what you have asked. Your presentation should have a strong conclusion that asks for specific, but reasonable, action.

John Reindel, upset by the secondhand smoke that he was forced to breathe each day, followed the steps of Monroe's Motivated Sequence. See Figure 6.6.

Table 6.1 shows that each of the organizational patterns fulfills certain purposes. The time-sequence and spatial relations patterns work well in informative presentations. The problem-solution pattern and Monroe's Motivated Sequence work well in persuasive presentations. And cause-effect and topical sequence patterns work well in both informative and persuasive presentations.

Cultural Note

CULTURAL DIFFERENCES IN ORGANIZATION

Most North Americans are linear. That is, they like to arrange their thoughts in a line from most important to least important, from biggest to smallest, from tallest to shortest. Other cultures use different organizational schemes. Some East Asian cultures, for example, sound to North Americans as if they are "talking around" a subject instead of getting right to the subject because they expect a rather long "warm-up" of socializing before getting down to business. Also, they may be indirect by suggesting rather than saying something directly.

TABLE 6.1 PATTERNS OF ORGANIZATION LINKED TO GENERAL PURPOSES

Usually Informative	Either Informative or Persuasive	Usually Persuasive
Time-sequence	Cause-effect	Problem-solution
Spatial relations	Topical sequence	Monroe's Motivated Sequence

Incorporate Supporting Materials

The main points create only the skeleton of the body of the presentation. The presenter must flesh out this skeleton with subpoints and sub-subpoints. You need to decide what information to keep and what to discard. You need also to determine where and what kind of visual resources will help your audience understand your message. Refer to Chapter Five to review how to flesh out the skeleton with supporting materials in the form of examples, narrative, statistics, and evidence.

Now you know organizational patterns from which you can choose to make your presentation effective. You also know that any kind of outline is just the bones of the speech that you have to "beef up" with supporting materials and visual resources.

What Holds the Presentation Together?

Your methods of moving from one point to another, of telling the audience where you are in the overall presentation, where you are going next, and where you have been is the "glue" that holds your presentation together. Audience members cannot "reread" a speech as they can reread an essay if they get lost in a disorganized maze. Transitions, signposts, internal previews, and internal reviews are the mortar between the bricks. Together they allow the audience easy access to the information you are presenting.

Transitions are *statements or words that bridge previous parts of the presentation to the next part. Transitions can be signposts, internal previews, or internal reviews.* They almost always appear between main parts of the presentation (introduction, body,

128 Part Two Selecting and Arranging Content

and conclusion), when turning to a visual aid, or when moving from an argument to evidence. For instance, transitions might look like this:

Having explained positive purpose as the first reason for choosing a career as a nurse's aide, let us turn to the second: service to those who are in need. (Review of past point and preview of the next.)

Now that you have heard an overview of Washington, D.C.'s scenic Mall with its reflecting ponds, let me show you a map of the many museums that are free and open to the public. (Move from main point to visual aid.)

Signposts, *like road signs on a highway, reveal where the speaker is going.* Signposts are brief transitions that do not have to point backward and forward; they have only to tell the listener where the presenter is in the message. Some examples include the following:

My first point is that . . .

Another reason you should . . .

One of the best examples is . . .

To illustrate this point, I will . . .

Let us look at this picture . . .

A second, and even more convincing, argument is . . .

One last illustration will show . . .

Skillful use of signposts and transitions will clarify your organization and help you become a confident presenter.

Internal previews *inform listeners of your next point or points and are more detailed than transitions.* They are similar to the statements a presenter makes in the introduction of his or her presentation, although internal previews occur within the body of the presentation. Examples of internal previews include the following:

My next point is that education correlates highly with income.

I now will explain how to build community support for improving our middle schools.

Internal reviews *remind listeners of your last point or points and are more detailed than transitions.* They occur within the body of the presentation. Examples of internal reviews include the following:

Now that we have covered the symptoms of this disease, let's move to the tests used to diagnose it.

At this point, we have established that most students are honest when taking tests and writing papers.

Let's turn now to the second major topic of this chapter: outlining the presentation.

Principles of Outlining

The organization of a presentation is generally shown in outline form. Outlining is relatively easy to learn. Three principles of outlining govern the writing of an outline: *subordination, division,* and *parallelism.*

Subordination

The **principle of subordination** allows you to *indicate which material is more important and which is less important through indentation and symbols.* The principle of subordination is based not only on the symbols (numbers and letters) and indentations, but also on the content of the statements. The subpoints are subordinate to the main points, the sub-subpoints are subordinate to the subpoints, and so on. Evaluate the content of each statement to determine whether it is broader or narrower, more important or less important, than the statements above and below. Figure 6.7 presents an example of subordination, which will make the idea easy to grasp.

More important materials usually consist of generalizations, arguments, or conclusions. Less important materials consist of the supporting evidence for your generalizations, arguments, or conclusions. By less important, we of course do not mean that your supporting evidence is not vital to your presentation—just that it is more specific and detailed, and farther down in your outline. In the outline, Roman numerals indicate the main points, capital letters indicate the subpoints under the Roman numeral statements, and Arabic numbers indicate sub-subpoints under the subpoints. Figure 6.7 shows a typical outline format. Notice, too, that the less important the material, the greater the indentation from the left-hand margin.

Division

The second principle of outlining is the **principle of division,** which states that, *if a point is to be divided, it must have at least two subpoints.* For example, the outline illustrated in Figure 6.7 contains two main points (I, II), two subpoints (A, B) under main point I, and two sub-subpoints (1, 2) under subpoint B. With rare exceptions, such as for a single example or clarification, items will be either undivided or divided into two or more parts.

Parallelism

The third principle of outlining is the **principle of parallelism,** which states that *main points, subpoints, and sub-subpoints must use the same grammatical and syntactical forms.* That means that in a sentence outline you would use all sentences, not a mixture of sentences, dependent clauses, and phrases. The sentences would tend to appear the same in structure, with subject followed by verb followed by object, for instance. See the explanation of parallelism earlier in this chapter.

Margins and Symbols Indicating Subordination

  I. A generalization, conclusion, or argument is a main point.
      A. The first subpoint consists of illustration, evidence, or other supporting material.
      B. The second subpoint consists of similar supporting material for the main point.
          1. The first sub-subpoint provides additional support for B.
          2. The second sub-subpoint also supports B.
  II. A second generalization, conclusion, or argument is another main point.

Figure 6.7 **Margins and symbols indicating subordination.**

Part Two Selecting and Arranging Content

Subordination	Division	Parallelism

I. _____
  A. _____
  B. _____
      1. _____
      2. _____
        a. _____
        b. _____
II. _____
	Every "I" must have a "II."
	Every "A" must have at least a "B."
	
	Every "1" must have a "2."
	
	Every "a" must have at least a "b."
		Each entry must be a complete sentence, a phrase, or word; entries may not be a mix of sentences, phrases, and words.

Figure 6.8 **Outlining principles of subordination, division, and parallelism.**

An outline can use parallel construction without consisting entirely of sentences. For example, a key word outline on note cards might consist of single words used to remind you of the content as you deliver your speech. To review the information on the principles of outlining, you should examine Figure 6.8, which briefly explains each of the three principles.

Types of Outlines

In the preparation outline and delivery of a speech, you generally compose three different but related kinds of outlines. In your course, your teacher will likely instruct you about which of these outlines will be required. It also is possible that your instructor might require another type of outline that is not covered in this text. First, you might create a preparation, or working, outline. Next, you will probably develop a formal outline. Finally, you might want to create a key word outline on note cards or paper, which you can use when you deliver your presentation.

The Preparation Outline

After you have selected the topic, given it a title, developed a specific purpose, written a thesis statement, and have gathered information for your presentation, you will begin to sketch out the basic ideas you wish to convey to your audience. The **preparation outline** is *your initial or tentative conception of your presentation.*

For example, imagine that you want to speak on service learning opportunities in your community. You might start by thinking of some main point for which you can provide examples:

    I. What service learning opportunities exist in our community?
      A. Working for the local food bank
      B. Serving as a hospice volunteer
      C. Volunteering to read to immigrant children at the grade school
      D. Leading a tour of a museum

As you learn more about opportunities you can refine your list, create more main points, and delete those you deem less important. The preparation outline usually

Chapter Six   Organizing and Outlining Your Presentation   **131**

is an informal draft, a tentative plan for the points in your presentation. This type of outline is called a "working outline" because it mainly helps you sort out your initial ideas in an orderly fashion.

The Formal Sentence Outline

A **formal sentence outline** is *a final outline in complete sentence form*. The formal outline includes the following elements:

1. The title.
2. The specific purpose.
3. The thesis statement.
4. The introduction of the presentation, which may be outlined or written out in full.
5. The body of the presentation in outline form.
6. The conclusion of the presentation, which may be outlined or written out in full.
7. A bibliography of sources and references consulted.

Since you have already covered parts one, two, and three in Chapter Three, let's briefly consider parts four through seven. At the end of this chapter, we will cover the functions and techniques of introductions and conclusions.

Introduction   The introduction of a presentation should take about 15 percent of the total time and should fulfill four functions: (1) gaining and maintaining attention, (2) relating the topic to the audience, (3) relating the speaker to the topic, and (4) previewing the message by stating the purpose and forecasting the organization of the presentation. Many presenters write out their introductions so they feel secure about beginning their talk. Others outline their introductions and deliver them extemporaneously.

Body   The body of the presentation is the main part of your message. This main portion generally consists of up to three points that account for about 75 to 80 percent of the entire talk. The body should be outlined using the principles of subordination, division, and parallelism that we discussed above.

Conclusion   The conclusion should be even shorter than the introduction. If the introduction to the presentation is about 15 percent of the entire presentation, then the conclusion should be about 5 percent of the presentation and certainly no longer than 10 percent. The functions of the conclusion include: (1) forewarning the audience of the end of the presentation, (2) reminding your audience of the main points, and (3) specifying what the audience should do as a result of the presentation.

Bibliography or References   The formal outline includes a **bibliography,** or *a list of the sources consulted and the sources actually used in the presentation.* Your instructor will tell you whether you should include all of your sources or only those you actually cite. In any case, you will want to provide them in correct bibliographic form. To help you, you can purchase a Modern Language Association (MLA) or an American Psychological Association (APA) style manual or *A Style Manual for Communication Majors* by Bourhis, Adams, and Titsworth.[8] In Figure 6.9 you will find a sentence outline with everything from title to references.

Part Two Selecting and Arranging Content

Title: Social Insecurity: A Problem for Americans of All Ages

Specific Purpose: You will hear about issues that will affect you with every paycheck and every month of retirement and about how you can help shape the legislation by encouraging fellow students to voice their concerns to Congress and organized groups.

Thesis Statement: A new, revised Social Security system will affect every American regardless of age. Because of its costs, its risks, and its benefits, my audience should influence its effects on them.

Introduction: Probably few of you are worried about proposed changes to the Social Security system because you are not near retirement. But today you are going to learn that the proposed changes affect younger people the most because everyone under 55 would be under a new system that includes a mix of private investments and government collections from your paycheck.

Body:

I. The costs of the proposed alternative Social Security system will affect everyone.

  A. People 55 and older will proceed under the old system of FICA (Social Security) deductions from their paychecks and a "guaranteed" pension.

  B. People 54 and younger will be expected to contribute to specified private investments, making them less dependent and more independent of the government collection system.

  C. Everyone will be subject to the two trillion dollar transition costs (taxpayer money) necessary to launch the new system.

II. According to Richard Freeman in the *Executive Intelligence Review,* the risks are linked to the private investment accounts, which are not guaranteed to yield retirement income.

  A. Historically stocks yield 6.5% above inflation, enough to guarantee a reasonable retirement benefit at retirement.

  B. High yield on stocks depends on low interest rates, low inflation, and a relatively stable global economy.

  C. Wars, natural disasters, and economic upheavals can lower yields.

III. The benefits of the proposed alternative system are less dependence on the government, more personal choice, and a retirement that belongs to the investor.

  A. According to the Cato Institute Project the private investment plan would yield money that belongs to you.

  B. Under the proposed system you could choose from among some government-approved private investment plans that are low risk.

  C. Your private investment fund would be yours even though you could not collect on it until retirement age.

Conclusion: Because the proposed alternative to Social Security will impact every American, you should learn as much as you can about how the plan will affect you. Your senator and your representative are going to shape the president's plan for you. Now is when your opinion and your voice can make a difference. Tell them what you think, either personally or through your political party or your union. You get to help mold a plan that will either give you social security or social insecurity. The choice is yours.   *(continued)*

Figure 6.9 **A sentence outline in topical pattern with title, dual purpose, and thesis. References are in APA style.**

> **References**
>
> About the project on Social Security choice. (2005, February 18). *Cato Institute Project* [On-line]. Available: http://www.socialsecurity.org/about.html [2005, February 20].
>
> Freeman, R. (2005, February 25). Wall Street's eyes on Social Security loot. *Executive Intelligence Review* [On-line]. Available: http://www.larouchepub.com/other/2005/site_packages//ss_privatization/3208wall_st_memo.html [2005, February 28].
>
> Kessler, G. (2005, February 14-20). Questions and answers. *The Washington Post Weekly Edition*, p. 18.
>
> Morin, R., & Russakoff, D. (2005, February 14-20). Is Social Security in crisis? *The Washington Post National Weekly Edition*, p. 19.
>
> Weisman, J., & White, B. (2005, February 14-20). Crunching the numbers. *The Washington Post National Weekly Edition*, p. 19.

The Key Word Outline

The purpose of a key word outline is to reduce your full-sentence outline to a manageable set of cues that mainly remind you of what you are going to say and when you are going to say it. A key word outline encourages conversational delivery instead of an oral reading of your words.

You might want to make a key word outline on note cards or on a sheet of paper, whichever your instructor prefers. The **key word outline** is a *brief outline with cue words that you can use during the delivery of your presentation*. The outline may include words that will prompt your memory, sources that you will cite within the presentation, or even the complete quotations of material you will repeat. The key word outline may look sketchy to someone other than the speaker. Figure 6.10 is an example of a key word outline.

Figure 6.10 An example of the body of a key word outline.

Now we will move from "behind the scenes" outlining to actually speaking before an audience. In the next section you will learn the critical functions of introducing your presentation.

How Do You Introduce Your Presentation?

Whether you introduce yourself or another speaker introduces you, an **introduction,** *the beginning portion of your presentation,* serves four functions.

1. Gains and maintains favorable attention.
2. Relates your topic to your audience.
3. Relates you to the topic.
4. Previews the message by stating the purpose and forecasting the organization of the presentation.

View "Relating a Story," "Citing a Quotation," and "Arousing Curiosity" as actual examples of what you can do in the introduction of your presentation.

Gaining and Maintaining Favorable Attention

The first function of an introduction is gaining and maintaining attention. Even if they appear attentive, your audience members may not be completely focused on you or your message when you begin. You need to direct their attention.

Here are 10 possible ways to gain and maintain your audience's attention:

1. *Present a person or object.* A presenter brought a very muscular person to demonstrate safe weight lifting moves during the presentation, while another student speaking on health food gave everyone a whole-grain granola bar to eat after the presentation.

2. *Invite audience participation.* If you invite **audience participation,** *you make your audience active participants in your presentation.* One student who was speaking about some of the problems of poverty asked his audience to sit crowded elbow-to-elbow during his presentation to illustrate lack of living space. Or you can ask your audience a question and expect and acknowledge a reply.

3. *Imagine a situation.* You might have the audience imagine that they are standing on a ski slope, flying through the air, or burrowing underground.

4. *Use audio and video.* A deputy sheriff showed a videotape of a drunken driver being arrested in a presentation on driving while intoxicated. Be sure not to let your audio or visual resource dominate your time.

5. *Arouse audience suspense.* A student began her presentation by saying, "My friend Sally died last year. Today you will learn what happened to her and what could happen to you."

6. *Use slides, film, video, or PowerPoint.* A student who was studying big-city slums began with a rapid series of 12 PowerPoint slides showing trash heaps, crowded rooms, run-down buildings, and rats.

7. *Read a quotation.* One student who was delivering a presentation on some of the delights of being middle-aged quoted President Reagan's speech to the Washington Press Club dinner when he turned seventy: "Middle age is when you're faced with two temptations and you choose the one that will get you home at 9 o'clock."

8. *State striking facts or figures.* Facts and figures can bore your audience to tears or rouse them out of a stupor. A student speaking about higher education cited statistics from *The Chronicle of Higher Education*[9]:

> . . . Texas colleges have had little success in getting Hispanic students to enroll. Only 9 percent of Hispanics ages 15 to 34 in the state attended college in 2002, compared with 13 percent of blacks and 17 percent of whites in that age bracket.

9. *Tell a story.* Telling a story to gain the audience's attention is one of the oldest and most commonly used methods. Your story can be actual (factual) or created (hypothetical), as long as you tell your audience which it is. A well-honed hypothetical story must be realistic and detailed.

10. *Use humor.* Although often overused, jokes or humor to gain and maintain attention can be effective, but only if the humor is related to the topic. Too often jokes are told for their own sake, whether they have anything to do with the subject of the speech or not. Another word of caution: if you are not good at telling jokes, then you ought to practice your humor before your speech in front of the class. If the joke is offensive, you will likely lose your audience altogether.

Relating the Topic to the Audience

The second function of an introduction is relating the topic to the audience. This introductory move assures the audience of a reason for their attention, because *there is a connection between them and the topic.* A student presenting on the ethics of changing grades related the topic to her student audience by pointing out that their own university registrar has changed thousands of grades at the request of professors—nearly always raising them. The audience listened to the presentation with more interest because the presenter took pains to relate the topic to both the men and the women in class.

Relating the Topic to the Presenter

The third function of an introduction is relating the topic to the presenter. Here are two strategies:

- *Dress for the topic and occasion.* Wear clothing that will signal your credibility on a topic and that shows your relationship to the topic and the occasion.
- *Use self-disclosure* about why or how you have knowledge about the topic. Sometimes self-disclosure, revealing something about yourself that others cannot see, is confessional: "I successfully overcame drug addiction," "I have been a relationship counselor for ten years," and "I have benefited from affirmative action programs."

Previewing the Message

Often the last part of an introduction is a revelation. The presenter reveals the purpose as well as the organization and development of her presentation. **Forecasting** *tells the audience how*

Tiger Woods talks to audiences about what he knows most—golf, a subject with which he is identified and that engages his listeners.

you are going to cover the topic. This thesis statement is an example that clearly indicates both the specific purpose and the organization:

> Today I am going to provide three reasons why you should request generic prescription drugs instead of well-advertised, name-brand prescription drugs.

The type of presentation is persuasive. The specific purpose is clear, and the organization ("three reasons") is apparent.

What Are the Functions of a Conclusion?

Just like the introduction, the conclusion of a presentation fulfills certain functions: (1) to forewarn the audience that you are about to stop; (2) to remind the audience of your central idea or the main points in your message; and (3) to specify what the audience should think or do in response to your presentation. Let us examine each of the functions of a conclusion in greater detail.

The **brake light function** *warns the audience that you are about to stop*. The most blatant, though trite, method of signaling the end of a speech is to say, "In conclusion . . ." or "To summarize . . ." or "In review . . .". Another way is to physically move back from the lectern. Also, you can change your tone of voice to have the sound of finality. There are a variety of ways to say, "I'm coming to the end." For instance, you have indicated an impending conclusion as soon as you say, "Now let us take my four main arguments and bring them together into one strong statement: You should learn about the candidates before you vote."

The second function of a conclusion—*to remind the audience of the thesis of your message*—is the **instant-replay function.** You could synthesize a number of major arguments or ideas into a single memorable statement. You could simply repeat the main steps or points in the speech. For instance, a student who spoke on the Heimlich maneuver for saving a choking person concluded his speech by repeating and demonstrating the moves for saving a person's life.

The third function of a conclusion is to clearly *state the response you seek from the audience*, the **action ending function.** If your speech was informative, what do you want the audience to remember? Tell them. If your presentation was persuasive, how can the audience show its acceptance? A student who delivered a presentation on periodontal disease concluded by letting her classmates turn in their candy for a package of sugarless gum.

View some examples of concluding a presentation: "Providing an Illustration," "Relating the Presentation to the Listener's Self-Interest," or "Citing a Quotation."

Tips for Concluding

Below are some ideas for ending your presentation. Of course you can think of others that are equally effective. What works for *you* will be best.

- *End with a quotation.* Quotations provide an effective end to your talk. Confine yourself to a brief quotation or two.
- *Ask a question.* Presenters can use questions to invite listeners into their topics; they also can use questions to close their talks, encouraging the audience to learn more about the topic or to take action.

Chapter Six   Organizing and Outlining Your Presentation   **137**

- *Tell a story.* Audience members enjoy hearing stories. Stories are especially apt in a conclusion when they serve to remind the audience of the purpose of a presentation.

- *Close with a striking statement.* In a presentation on using seat belts, the speaker ended by saying: "In an accident, it is not who is right that really counts; it's who is left."

- *Review central idea and main points.* Remind the audience what you told them.

- *Forewarn the audience that you are nearly done.* Avoid abrupt endings that leave the audience hanging.

- *Tell the audience what you expect.* What do you want them to think or do as a result of your presentation?

- *Refer back to the introduction.* Closing by reminding them how you began is a good strategy. For example, your introduction can be part of a story that ends in your conclusion.

- *End strongly in a memorable way.* You want your audience to remember what you said. Often they remember what you said last best of all.

These tips are just a few of the many ways you can draw your presentation to a close. They are provided here just to jump-start your own creativity in finding ways to end your presentation.

Resources for Review and Discussion

SUMMARY

In this chapter you have learned the following:

▶ Why is organization important?
- Audiences perceive organized presenters as more competent.
- Audiences find organized messages more memorable and give them higher marks.

▶ How should you organize the body of your presentation?
- You should first divide the body into two or three main points.
- These main points should be worded in a parallel manner.
- These main points should be approximately equal in importance.
- You need to determine the order in which you will present the main points.
- Some typical ways to order or pattern your speech are the time-sequence, spatial relations, problem-solution, cause-effect, and topical sequence patterns, and Monroe's Motivated Sequence.
- You need to incorporate the supporting material for your main points.
- The effective and ethical presenter also considers the connections between ideas.
- Among the connecting devices available are transitions, brief linkages in the speech.
- Signposts tell the audience briefly where the speaker is within the speech.
- Internal previews forewarn the audience of that which is to come.
- Internal reviews remind the audience of what has already been covered.

▶ Outlining includes three important principles.
- The principle of subordination means that the symbols and indentation of your outline should show which material is more important and which material is less important.
- The principle of division states that when points are divided, they must have at least two subpoints.
- The principle of parallelism states that main points, subpoints, and sub-subpoints should use the same grammatical and syntactical forms.

▶ You will probably create three types of outlines.
- The preparation outline is your initial or tentative conception of your presentation.
- A formal outline is a final outline in complete sentence form including the title, specific purpose, thesis statement, introduction of the speech, body of the speech, conclusion of the presentation, and a bibliography of sources consulted.
- The key word outline is a brief outline—often on note cards—created for you to use during the delivery of your presentation.

▶ You learned the functions of an introduction.
- The introduction usually announces the topic, relates that topic to the audience, gains the audience's attention, and forecasts the organization or development of the topic.
- Whether or not you have been introduced by someone else, the introduction builds your credibility on the subject being presented.

▶ You learned the functions of a conclusion.
- The brakelight function forewarns the audience of the impending ending.
- The instant-replay function reviews the main points.
- The action ending is your clear statement of what you expect the audience to do or remember.

KEY TERMS

 Use the *Public Speaking* CD-ROM and the Online Learning Center at www.mhhe.com/nelson to practice your understanding of the following terminology.

Action ending function	Cause-effect pattern	Internal previews
Audience participation	Forecasting	Internal reviews
Bibliography	Formal sentence outline	Introduction
Brake light function	Instant-replay function	Key word outline

Monroe's Motivated Sequence
Parallel construction
Preparation outline
Principle of division

Principle of parallelism
Principle of subordination
Problem-solution pattern
Signposts

Spatial relations pattern
Time-sequence pattern
Topical sequence pattern
Transitions

REFERENCES

[1] Thompson, Ernest C. (1990). An experimental investigation of the relative effectiveness of organizational structure in oral communication. *Southern Speech Journal, 26,* 59–69.

[2] Sharp, H., Jr., & McClung, T. (1966). Effect of organization on the speaker's ethos. *Speech Monographs, 33,* 182–83.

[3] Greene, J. O. (1984). Speech preparation processes and verbal fluency. *Human Communication Research, 11,* 61–84.

[4] *Ibid.*

[5] Fritz, Paul A. & Weaver, Richard L., II. (1986). Teaching critical thinking skills in the basic speaking course: A liberal arts perspective. *Communication Education, 35,* 177–82.

[6] Tischer, Stacey. (2004, October). Presentation, North Dakota State University.

[7] Gronbeck, Bruce E., German, Kathy, Ehninger, Douglas, & Monroe, Alan. (1997). *Principles of speech communication*. New York: Addison-Wesley.

[8] Bourhis, John, Adams, Carey, & Titsworth, Scott (1999). *A Style manual for communication majors*. New York: McGraw-Hill.

[9] Arnone, M. (2003). A Texas-size challenge. *The Chronicle of Higher Education,* November 28, 2003. http://chronicle.com/prm/weekly/v50/i14/14201301.htm

APPLICATION EXERCISES

  Go to the self-quizzes on the *Public Speaking* CD-ROM and the Online Learning Center at www.mhhe.com/nelson to test your knowledge of the chapter concepts.

1. Think of a topic not mentioned in this chapter that would be best organized into each of the following patterns. Write the topic next to the appropriate pattern.

   ORGANIZATION PATTERN   TOPIC

   TIME-SEQUENCE:

   SPATIAL RELATIONS:

   PROBLEM-SOLUTION:

   CAUSE-EFFECT:

   TOPICAL SEQUENCE:

   MONROE'S MOTIVATED
   SEQUENCE:

   Can you explain why each pattern is most appropriate for each topic?

2. Go to the library and find the publication *Vital Speeches of the Day,* which is a collection of current speeches. Make a copy of a presentation and highlight the transitions, signposts, internal previews, and internal reviews.

3. Take any chapter in this book and construct an outline from the various levels of headings.

CHAPTER SEVEN

> You have to have confidence in your ability, and then be tough enough to follow through.
> **ROSALYNN CARTER (B. 1927),**
> **FIRST LADY OF THE**
> **UNITED STATES 1977–1981**

> Courage is resistance to fear, mastery of fear—not absence of fear.
> **MARK TWAIN (1835–1910),**
> **AMERICAN AUTHOR**

Delivering Speeches

What will you learn?

When you have read and thought about this chapter, you will be able to:

1. Identify the qualities of "effective delivery."
2. Choose when to use each of the four modes of delivery.
3. Relate how context or situation influences the type of delivery you should choose.
4. Identify the function of vocal aspects of delivery in presentations.
5. Clarify how the nonverbal aspects of delivery function in presentations.
6. Take steps to improve your delivery.

Have you observed how skilled presenters seem to know their topic and their audience? The best presenters make delivery look easy. They do so by practicing their presentations until they feel confident, look poised, and sound conversational.

142   Part Two   Selecting and Arranging Content

Sigrid Larson was cool and confident when she went to the front of the room to deliver her speech. She had practiced her speech three times in front of a full-length mirror and twice in front of two friends. Her speech was on note cards, but in her first rehearsal in front of the mirror she had found herself looking at the cards too much. Also, her voice sounded boring. During a later rehearsal, Sigrid's friends suggested some minor changes and encouraged her to put down the note cards so she could move and gesture. Her delivery was noticeably better. When the actual presentation began, for a few seconds she felt a little nervous, but once she started her introduction she was so focused on her audience and their reactions that her anxiety disappeared. She was surprised to discover that time seemed to fly as she delivered her speech. When she sat down after her presentation, she felt elated.

In this chapter you will learn some of the secrets that Sigrid Larson knows. You will learn what makes delivery effective, when to use the various modes of delivery, how to use movement and gesture effectively, how to use your voice correctly, and how to improve your delivery. You will also learn what to do about the natural apprehension accompanying public communication. Good speech delivery is not as difficult as you might think. It is easier to achieve with practice and experience.

Most politicians, preachers, and teachers make delivery look effortless because they know their subject matter well, they know their audience well, and they get considerable practice repeatedly giving the same or similar messages. You, too, can learn to deliver your presentation smoothly if you understand what your audience needs or wants, if you familiarize yourself with your subject matter before you give the speech, and if you practice your presentation to gain poise and confidence. The classroom is an ideal place to learn delivery because your teacher and classmates can give you suggestions and encouragement to improve with every speech. The difference between a merely competent presenter and a really good presenter is the difference between a hamburger at McDonald's and filet mignon at an elegant restaurant: both will provide you with a meal, but only the latter will make a memorable impression on you.[1] Your goal is to use this chapter to learn effective delivery and how to make a memorable impression.

What Is Effective Delivery?

Effective delivery is a way of presenting a speech that does not call attention to itself. Ray Grigg writes, "Too loud and we are not heard. Too bright and we are not seen. Too fancy and we are hidden. Too much and we are obscured."[2] His advice is well taken for the public presenter. If your audience is watching your gestures and your body movements and listening to your pronunciation rather than the content of your speech, you should reconsider what you are doing. Delivery should enhance the message, not distract your audience from the message.

Effective delivery appears conversational, natural, and spontaneous. Your delivery should be comfortable for you and your audience. When you speak in this manner, your audience will believe that you are speaking with them, not at them.

How can you focus on your ideas rather than on your delivery? How can you draw your audience's attention to your message rather than to your delivery? How can you sound conversational and natural? The answer to all these questions is the same. Develop your message first, and then revise your words for delivery.

To keep the focus on your message, select a topic about which you have keen interest or deep convictions. If you are committed to the ideas you present, your delivery will come naturally. If a student is upset about tuition increases, she may need no notes. The delivery naturally follows from the message. On the other hand, her emotions may interfere with effective delivery.

To begin practicing your speech, concentrate only on the basics—speaking intelligibly, maintaining eye contact, and avoiding mannerisms that will distract listeners. Be sure you are pronouncing words correctly. Avoid nervous habits such as playing with a strand of your hair, rubbing your face, tapping a pencil, or pulling on an article of your clothing. If you are practicing in front of friends, use their feedback to help you discover problems, and correct them in subsequent performances.

As you continue to grow in experience and knowledge as a public presenter, you should observe how highly experienced public presenters deliver their messages. How do they appear conversational and yet inviting to their audiences through voice inflection and body movements? What do they do to enhance the impact of their ideas? Which of these techniques can you adopt in your own speeches? Which aspect of other people's speaking styles do you want to avoid? Both positive and negative examples will help you become more effective.

What Are The Four Modes of Delivery?

The four modes of delivering a presentation are (1) extemporaneous, (2) memorized, (3) manuscript, and (4) impromptu. While each mode is appropriate for different topics, audiences, speakers, and situations, your instructor will identify which mode is suitable for your assignments.

Extemporaneous Mode

In the **extemporaneous mode** *a presenter often delivers a presentation from a key word outline or from brief notes.* This mode of delivery is most commonly taught in the public speaking classroom. Its advantages far outweigh the disadvantages for the beginning public presenter. Indeed, for most presenters, this mode is the top choice.

Extemporaneous speaking sounds conversational, looks spontaneous, and appears effortless. However, extemporaneous speaking requires considerable effort. A presenter selects a topic appropriate for the audience, completes research on the topic, organizes the main points and supporting materials, practices the presentation with a working or key word outline, and finally delivers the presentation with maximum eye contact, appropriate gestures, and motivated movement. The presenter may occasionally glance at notes, but the emphasis is on communicating a message to an audience.

You may have experienced extemporaneous speaking without realizing it. Have you ever read the assignment for a class, caught the drift of the professor's questions, jotted a few words on your notes, and then given an answer in class? Your "speech" was extemporaneous because it included your background preparation, an organization of your ideas, brief reminders, and a conversational delivery.

An extemporaneous presentation is not practiced to the point of memorization. In fact, the presenter rarely repeats the message in exactly the same words, even in practice. The idea is to keep the content flexible enough to adapt to the audience. If the audience appears puzzled by something you say, you can add a definition, a description, or an example to clarify your position. Audience members like to be talked with, not lectured at, read to, or talked down to.

What are the *advantages* of the extemporaneous mode of delivery?

1. This mode is the most versatile: The presenter, using only brief notes, can engage in excellent eye contact. This eye contact allows careful audience analysis and immediate audience adaptation. The presenter can add or delete information based on the audience's responses.
2. Extemporaneous speaking demands attention to all aspects of public speaking preparation. The presenter has an opportunity to consider the important dimensions of selecting a topic, determining a purpose, doing careful research, identifying supporting materials, organizing the presentation appropriately, and using language in a spoken style that best communicates the message. In short, the extemporaneous presentation allows high-quality communication.
3. Extemporaneous speaking invites bodily movement, gestures, and rapid nonverbal response to audience feedback.
4. The extemporaneous presentation sounds conversational because the presenter is not reciting scripted words. The presenter is talking with the audience, not at the audience.
5. An outline is easier to use as a quick reference or guide than is a manuscript of a speech.

What are the *disadvantages* of the extemporaneous speech? If the presenter must be careful with every word, if every phrase needs to be exact, the presenter might more appropriately use another mode of speaking. Under most circumstances, however, the extemporaneous mode is the presentation method of choice.

Can you think of a current presenter who uses the extemporaneous mode of delivery effectively? The speaker who uses the extemporaneous mode of delivery can move away from the podium and walk among the audience as she speaks. Frequently, this type of speaker is given high marks for confidence.

Memorized Mode

The **memorized mode** of delivery is *one in which a presenter has committed a presentation to memory*. This mode entails more than just knowing all the words; the presenter also rehearses gestures, eye contact, and movement, practicing a presentation over and over in much the same way that an actor masters a dramatic script.

Oratory contests, the lecture circuit, and banquet speeches are common places to find

Elizabeth Dole, U.S. senator for North Carolina, exhibits strong content in her speeches and is a model for effective delivery.

the memorized mode. Ceremonial occasions, where little audience or topic adaptation is expected or needed, invite memorization. Politicians usually have a stock presentation they have delivered so many times that they have every word memorized. Some presenters have delivered the same presentation so many times that they even know when and how long the audience is going to applaud, laugh, or respond. In other words, memorization is best when performance to the audience is more important than communication with the audience.

What are the *advantages* of the memorized method of presenting a speech? The main advantage is that this mode permits maximum use of delivery skills: every variation in the voice can be mastered, every oral paragraph stated in correct cadence, every word correctly pronounced at the right volume. With a memorized speech, you have continuous eye contact. Because no notes are used, bodily movements and gestures are freer. While the memorized method does not eliminate the search for the next word, you are simply searching your memory instead of your notes or manuscript.

However, the memorized mode has three *disadvantages*.

1. Memorization permits little or no adaptation during delivery. The presenter is likely to focus more on the internalized manuscript than on the listeners. If the audience appears to have missed a point, the presenter has difficulty explaining the point in greater detail.
2. Recovery is more difficult if you make a mistake. If you forget a line, you have to search for the exact place where you dropped your line.
3. Especially for beginning speakers, the presentation sometimes *sounds* memorized: the wording is too smooth, the pacing too contrived, and the presentation is too much of a performance instead of a communicative experience.

The beginning presenter is more likely to be disadvantaged than advantaged by using the memorized method. However, some formal situations, such as commencement addresses, routine political campaign speeches, and repeated rituals and ceremonies call for little adaptation, making memorization a good choice.

Manuscript Mode

The **manuscript mode** of delivering a presentation is *when a presenter writes out the complete presentation in advance and then uses that manuscript to deliver the speech but without memorizing it.* It is most useful when a presenter has to be precise, must avoid error, and must defend every word. A president who delivers a foreign policy presentation in which the slip of a word could start a war, a minister who carefully documents a sermon with biblical quotations, and a politician who releases information to the press are examples of presenters who might adopt this mode.

Some professors lecture from a manuscript. At some point they probably have written out their lecture. As a student it is likely that you have seen many manuscript speeches.

What are the *advantages* of the manuscript speech? Generally, the complete manuscript prevents slips of the tongue, poor wording, and distortion. Manuscripts often boost the confidence of beginning presenters who need the security of their manuscript.

E-Note

MANUSCRIPT SPEECHES

Senator Elizabeth Dole has made several powerful speeches. Examples include her June 3, 2004, speech entitled, "Third Annual Hunger Awareness Day," and her May 7, 2004, talk entitled, "Statement at the Senate Armed Services Committee Hearing on Mistreatment of Iraqi Prisoners." These speeches are most likely manuscript speeches. Visit Senator Dole's Web site to access both of these. Do you think Dole is effective with a manuscript speech? (As of the publication of this text, the Web site address was http://dole.senate.gov. Select "News Archives.")

The *disadvantages* outweigh the advantages, however. While using a manuscript might make the beginning presenter feel more confident, the delivery often suffers. Among the problems engendered by manuscripts are these:

1. Manuscripts frequently reduce eye contact because the presenter is reading the script rather than observing the audience.
2. The manuscript method also hinders audience adaptation. The presenter is not watching the audience; to observe and respond to audience feedback is difficult.
3. The presenter may also use fewer gestures. Being bonded to the podium and the script prevents the presenter from gesturing to emphasize or illustrate points.
4. Vocal variety may be lacking as well, because much of the presentation is being read.
5. The pacing of the presentation may be too rapid or too slow for the audience. The presenter will sound inappropriate because written style is markedly different from spoken style. Instead of sounding conversational, the presentation will sound like an essay being read.

TRY THIS

Who is a current figure who presents successfully from a manuscript? Consider actors and actresses who make presentations at awards ceremonies. How effective are they as presenters? Are they more effective when they ad-lib or add unplanned comments?

Impromptu Mode

The **impromptu mode** entails *giving a presentation without advance preparation.* Unlike the extemporaneous mode, the impromptu method uses minimal planning and preparation, and usually no practice. You may be ready for an impromptu presentation because of your knowledge, experience, and background, but you do not have any other aids to help you know what to say. The key to effective impromptu speaking is to take a moment to compose your thoughts and to identify important points instead of figuring out what you are going to say as you speak.

You have already delivered impromptu speeches. When your teacher calls on you to answer a question, your answer—if you have one—is impromptu. You were ready because you had read the assignment or had prepared for class, but you probably had not written out an answer or certain key words. When someone asks you to introduce yourself, explain something at a meeting, reveal what you know about a particular subject, or give directions, you are delivering your answer in an impromptu fashion.

What are the *advantages* of the impromptu method? This mode reveals your skill in unplanned circumstances. In a job interview, you might be asked to answer some questions for which you had not specifically prepared. Your impromptu answers may tell a potential employer more about you than if you were given the questions ahead of time and had prepared your answers. Similarly the student who can give an accurate, complete answer to a difficult question in class shows a mastery of the subject matter that is, in some ways, more impressive than in an exam or another situation in which the student may give partially planned answers.

Another advantage of the impromptu mode is that it provides you with opportunities to think on your feet, to be spontaneous. As you engage in impromptu speaking situations, you learn how to quickly identify the important points in the information you wish to share or the major arguments in your persuasive appeals you offer. Students might give impromptu speeches when volunteering at events or places such as blood drives or senior centers, while meeting with a student club, or while working.

The impromptu presentation also has *disadvantages*. Spontaneity discourages audience analysis, planned research, and detailed preparation. Most people who are seeking to gain employment, trying to sell a product, or aspiring to academic honors should not risk delivering an impromptu speech. Such circumstances require greater preparation. An impromptu presentation can mean a poor answer as easily as a good one. The lack of planning makes the outcome of the impromptu method of speaking uncertain.

Your mode of delivery must be appropriate for you, your topic, the audience, and the situation. Memorizing five pages of print may not be your style. A manuscript presentation is out of place in a dormitory meeting, a discussion among class members, or any informal gathering. Ultimately the method of delivery is not the crucial feature of your speech. In a study to determine whether the extemporaneous or the manuscript method is more effective, two researchers concluded that the presenter's ability is more important. Some presenters are more effective with extemporaneous speeches than with manuscript speeches, but others use both methods with equal effectiveness.[3]

See Figures 7.1.a and 7.1.b for a summary of the four modes of delivery.

Mode of Delivery	Need for Notes	Amount of Preparation	Best Use of Mode
Extemporaneous	Low	High	If every word does not need to be exact.
Memorized	None	Very high	Formal situations that call for little, or no, adaptation.
Manuscript	High	High	When every word must be precise.
Impromptu	None	None	When little planning, preparation, or practice is possible.

Figure 7.1.a **Four modes of delivery: Need for notes, amount of preparation, and best use.**

	Advantages	Disadvantages
Extemporaneous	Sounds conversational Looks spontaneous Appears effortless Most versatile Allows high-quality communication Invites bodily movement, gestures, and rapid nonverbal response Key word outline is easier to use as a quick reference or guide	Requires lots of practice and effort Could change the meaning because of different word choices
Memorized	Maximum use of delivery skills	Permits little or no adaptation Recovery is more difficult if you make mistakes Can sound memorized
Manuscript	Prevents slips of the tongue and poor wording	Reduces eye contact Hinders audience adaptation Might cause less frequent use of gestures Might affect vocal variety Might cause pacing to become too rapid or too slow
Impromptu	Minimal planning and practice Allows spontaneity Reveals your skill in unplanned circumstances	Discourages audience adaptation Discourages planned research Discourages detailed preparation Outcome is uncertain

Figure 7.1.b **Four modes of delivery: Advantages and disadvantages of each.**

How Can You Use Your Voice Effectively?

Effective public presenters learn to speak in front of an audience as if they are having a conversation. Their voice and movements are a natural accompaniment for their words. In fact, some teachers believe that the best way to improve delivery is not to emphasize it directly. Instead, they encourage students to let effective delivery flow from the message, the audience, and the situation.

As you study delivery, remember that delivery and the message comprise an organic whole. If what you say is important to you and to your audience, the way you say it will not be a problem for you. Like Sigrid Larson in the introduction to this chapter, you will be so busy trying to communicate your message that you will gesture, move, look, and sound like a very competent presenter.

View the video speech conclusion "Citing a quotation." How did the speaker enhance the poetry written by T. E. Lawrence? Was the speaker effective in delivering these lines?

Let's look at eight vocal aspects of delivery.

Adjust Your Rate to Content, Audience, and Situation

Rate, the first vocal characteristic of delivery, is *the speed of delivery.* Normally American speakers speak at a rate between 125 and 190 words per minute, but audiences can comprehend spoken language that is much faster. Rapid speech rate improves the speaker's credibility and rapid speech improves persuasion.[4] In another study, students shortened their pauses and increased their speaking rates from 126 to 172 words per minute. The increased rate affected neither the audience's comprehension nor evaluation of the speakers' delivery.[5] Thus, faster speaking, up to a limit, can mean better speaking.

Beginning presenters frequently vent their anxiety by speaking too quickly. A nervous presenter makes the audience nervous as well. On the other hand, fluency comes from confidence. A presenter who is accustomed to audiences and knows the subject matter well may speak at a brisk rate without appearing to be nervous.

The essential point, not revealed by the studies, is that speaking rate needs to be adapted to the speaker, audience, situation, and content of the speech. First, become comfortable with your rate of speaking. If you normally speak rather slowly, you might feel awkward talking like a competitive debater. If you normally speak at a rapid pace, you might feel uncomfortable speaking more slowly. As you learn presentational skills, you will probably find a rate that is appropriate for you.

Second, adapt your rate to the audience and situation. A grade-school teacher does not rip through a fairy tale; the audience is just learning how to comprehend words. A public presenter addressing a large audience without a microphone might speak more distinctly and cautiously to make sure the audience comprehends her words. A story to illustrate a point can be understood at a faster rate than can a string of statistics or a complicated argument. Martin Luther King, Jr., in his famous "I have a dream" speech, began his address at a slow rate under 100 words per minute, but as he became more passionately involved in his topic and as his audience responded, he took on a much more rapid pace. The rate should depend on the effect you seek.

Use Pause for Effect

A second vocal characteristic is the **pause**—*a brief silence for effect.* You might begin a presentation with a question or questions: "Have you had a cigarette today? (Pause) Have you had two or three? Ten or eleven? (Pause) Do you know what your habit is costing you a year? (Brief pause) A decade? (Brief pause) A lifetime? (Longer pause)" The pause allows each member of the audience to answer the question in his or her own mind.

Another kind of pause—the **vocalized pause**—is really not silent at all. Instead, it is *a way of delaying with sound.* The "ahhhs," "nows," and "you knows" and "whatevers" of a novice presenter are annoying and distracting to most audiences. Unfortunately, even some highly experienced presenters have the habit of filling silences with vocalized pauses. Do not be afraid of silence; most audiences would prefer a little silence to a vocalized pause.

Use Duration for Attention

Duration is *how long something lasts;* in a speech, it can mean how long the sounds last or how long various parts of the presentation last. An anchorperson who says, "Tonight, I am speaking to you from London," is likely to say this sentence by caressing every word but might deliver other parts of the newscast in rapid-fire fashion. Dwelling on the sound of your words can have dramatic impact; the duration gives the words a sense of importance.

Similarly, duration can refer to the parts of a speech: how long you spend on the introduction, the main points, the examples, and the presentational aids. As noted earlier, the duration of most introductions is usually relatively short, the body relatively longer, and the conclusion shortest of all.

Use Rhythm to Establish Tempo

Rhythm refers to *the tempo of a speech*. All the linear arts seem to have this characteristic. A novel or play starts slowly as the author introduces the characters, establishes the plot, and describes the scene. Then the emphasis shifts to the development of the plot and typically accelerates toward a climax, which brings the novel to a close. A musical piece also has some of these characteristics, though music could be said to consist entirely of rhythm.

In a speech, the rhythm usually starts off slowly as the presenter gives clues about who she is and what she is going to speak about. During the body of the speech, the tempo accelerates, with verbal punctuation indicating what is most important. The conclusion typically slows in review as the presentation draws to a close.

We also hear the rhythm of a presentation in words, sentences, and paragraphs. **Alliteration** is *the repetition of the initial sounds of words*. For instance, it is more memorable to say "color, clarity, and carets characterize a good diamond" than to say "brightness, transparency, and weight give a diamond value." Another example of rhythm occurs in sentences when initial words are repeated: "I served my country because I am a patriot; I served my country because I saw it as my duty; and I served my country because its protection is my first concern." Similarly you can achieve rhythm with rhetorical devices, such as antithesis: "Not because I loved Octavius less, but because I loved Rome more."

Use Pitch for Expression

Pitch is *the highness or lowness of a speaker's voice, its upward and downward inflection, the melody produced by the voice*. Pitch makes the difference between the "Ohhh" from earning a poor grade on an exam and the "Ohhh" you say when you see someone really attractive. Avoid the lack of pitch changes that result in a monotone and the repetitious pitch changes that result in a singsong delivery. The best public presenters use the full range of their normal pitch. They know when to purr and when to roar, and when to vary their pitch between.

You learn pitch control by constant practice like an actor does. A public speaker rehearses a presentation in front of a sympathetic audience to receive feedback on whether the words are being understood as she intends them. You may not be the best judge of how you sound to others. Therefore, trust other people's evaluations of how you sound. At the same time, speakers should recognize and develop the individual strengths they already have. For example, when you focus on your message, your pitch will support or match what you say. Compare the pitch in your voice when you tell a friend about something amazing to the pitch when you recite the pledge of allegiance.

Use Volume for Emphasis

A sixth vocal characteristic of delivery is **volume,** *the relative loudness or softness of your voice.* **Projection** means *adjusting your volume appropriately for the subject, the audience, and the situation.* Variations in volume can convey emotion, importance, suspense, and subtle nuances of meaning. You whisper a secret in conversation, and you stage whisper in front of an audience to signal conspiratorial intent. You speak loudly and strongly on important points and let your voice carry your conviction.

Use Enunciation for Clarity

Enunciation, the seventh vocal aspect of delivery, is *the pronunciation and articulation of words.* **Pronunciation** is *the production of the sounds of a word.* **Articulation** is *the physiological process of creating the sounds.* Because your reading vocabulary is larger than your speaking vocabulary, you may use words in your speeches that you have never heard spoken before. To deliver unfamiliar words is risky. Rather than erring in public, first check pronunciation in a dictionary. Every dictionary, on- and off-line, has a pronunciation key. For instance, the entry for the word *deification* in *Webster's New World Dictionary of the American Language* follows:

> **de·i·fi·ca·tion** (dē-ə-fə-ˈkā-shən) 1. a deifying. 2. deified person or embodiment.

The entry indicates that the word has five syllables that carry distinct sounds. The pronunciation key says that the e should be pronounced like the e in even, the i's like the a in ago, and the a like the a in ape. The accent mark indicates which syllable should receive heaviest emphasis. You should learn how to use the pronunciation key in a dictionary, but you can also hear a word pronounced correctly on several online sources. For example, the Bartleby.com Web site gives you the option of typing in the word and then clicking on the "Speaker" option.

Another way to improve your enunciation is to prolong syllables. Such prolonging makes your pronunciation easier to understand, especially if you are addressing a large audience assembled outside or in an auditorium with no microphone. The drawing out of syllables can be overdone, however. Some radio and TV news announcers hang onto the final syllable in a sentence so long that the device is disconcertingly noticeable.

See Figure 7.2 for some common articulation problems. Articulation errors are so common that humorous stories are often based on them. Many **malapropisms,** or *mistaking one word for another,* are based on articulation errors.

A newspaper article on malapropisms mentioned these:

"Making an obstacle of themselves" for "Making a spectacle of themselves"

"Go for the juggler" for "Go for the jugular"

"He took milk of amnesia" for "He took milk of magnesia."[6]

E-Note

BILL CLINTON

William Jefferson Clinton was considered an excellent orator during his presidency. His physical stature, and his use of gestures, bodily movement, eye contact, and vocal variety were used to his advantage. Go to **http://www.lib.berkeley.edu/MRC/audiofiles.html#clinton** and view his address at the University of California at Berkeley on January 29, 2001. What can you learn from Bill Clinton's speech "A World without Walls," and from other well-known celebrity speakers such as Bono, Angelina Jolie, and Dr. Phil concerning delivery?

Addition occurs *when an extra sound is added.* For example, a person says "pic-a-nic" instead of "picnic," "ath-a-lete" instead of "athlete," "real-ah-toor" instead of "realtor."

Deletion occurs *when a sound is dropped or left out of a word.* Examples of deletion are "rassberry" for "raspberry," or "liberry" for "library." Deletion also commonly occurs when people drop the final sounds of words such as "reveren'" for "reverend," "goin'" for "going," or "comin'" for "coming." Finally, deletion occurs when individuals drop the initial sounds of words such as "'possum" for "opossum."

Substitution occurs *when one sound is replaced with another.* For instance, when speakers use the word "git" for "get," "ruff" for "roof," or "tomata" for "tomato," they are making substitution errors.

Transposition occurs *when two sounds are reversed.* College students who call their teachers "perfessor" instead of "professor" or persons who say one "hunderd" instead of one "hundred" are making an error of transposition.

Figure 7.2 Four common articulation problems.

Use Fluency for Fluidity

The eighth vocal characteristic of delivery is **fluency**—*the smoothness of delivery, the flow of the words, and the absence of vocalized pauses.* Fluency cannot be achieved by looking up words in a dictionary or by any other simple solution. It is not necessarily very noticeable, except by its absence. Listeners are more likely to notice errors than to notice the seemingly effortless flow of words and intentional pauses in a well-delivered speech. Fluency can be improved and is related to effective communication.[7]

To achieve fluency, you must be confident in the content of your speech. If you know what you are going to say, and if you have practiced the words, then disruptive repetition and vocalized pauses are unlikely to occur.

How Can You Use Your Body to Communicate Effectively?

Eye contact, facial expression, gestures, movement, and physical appearance are five bodily aspects of speech delivery—nonverbal indicators of meaning—that are important to the public speaker. When you observe two people busily

Cultural Note

EYE CONTACT IN PRESENTATIONS

During the past two decades, a number of people from the rural mountain areas of Laos have come to the United States. Known as the Hmong, they group themselves on the basis of the same paternal ancestry. Each group has a leader who oversees most activities as well as a shaman, or medicine person, who deals with spiritual and physical problems. Because Hmong education is oral, many Americans mislabel them as illiterate.

Hmongs do not feel comfortable with direct eye contact and do not like to be touched on their heads. This aversion is linked to their religion and is not a sign of disrespect. Let's say that one of your classmates is Hmong. From the perspectives of fairness and practicality, how should you evaluate her if she does not use direct eye contact during her speech?

engaged in conversation, you can judge their interest in the conversation without hearing their words. Similarly, in public speaking, the nonverbal aspects of delivery reinforce what the speaker is saying. Researchers have found that audiences who can see the speaker, and his or her behavior, comprehend more of the presentation than audiences (such as those listening by radio or audiotape) who cannot.[8]

Use Eye Contact to Hold Audience Attention

Eye contact is *the way a presenter observes the audience while speaking*. With experience, individuals become more capable of using eye contact.[9] Audiences prefer the maintenance of good eye contact,[10] and it improves the credibility of the presenter.[11] Eye contact is one way you indicate to others how you feel about them. You may be wary of a person who will not look at you in conversation. Similarly, if you rarely or never look at audience members, they may be resentful of your seeming lack of interest. If you look over the heads of your audience or scan them so quickly that you do not really look at anyone, you may appear to be afraid. The proper relationship between you and your audience should be one of purposeful communication. You signal that sense of purpose by treating the audience members as individuals to whom you wish to communicate a message and by looking at them for responses to your message.

Eye contact—the frequency and duration of looking at the person to whom you are speaking—varies with gender, personality, and culture.[12] Americans of European descent tend to use more eye contact than do Americans of African descent when each is speaking to a predominantly European American audience. Such differences in behavior can lead to misunderstanding. The African American's averted eyes can lead the European American to interpret lack of interest. The European American's more intent eye contact could be perceived by an African American as staring or as aggressiveness. Some cultural groups such as some Latin Americans, Southern Europeans, and Arabs tend to stand close and look directly into the other person's face. Many people from India, Pakistan, and Scandinavia, on the other hand, turn their bodies toward the person to whom they are speaking but avoid steady focus on the other person's face.

How can you learn to maintain eye contact with your audience? One way is to know your presentation so well and to feel so strongly about the topic that you have to make few references to your notes. A presenter who does not know the material well tends to be manuscript-bound. You can encourage yourself to keep an eye on the audience by delivering an extemporaneous presentation from an outline or key words.

Other ways of learning eye contact include scanning or continually looking over your entire audience, addressing various sections of the audience as you progress through your speech, and concentrating on the individuals who overtly indicate whether your message is coming across or not. These individuals usually nod "yes" or "no" with their heads. You may find that you can enhance your delivery by finding the friendly faces and positive nodders who signal when the message is getting through to them.

Use Facial Expression to Communicate

Another nonverbal aspect of delivery is facial expression, using the eyes, eyebrows, forehead, and mouth for expression. Facial expression shows how we feel, and body orientation (leaning, withdrawing, turning) expresses the intensity of our emotion.[13] Children between 5 and 10 years of age learn to interpret facial expressions, and those interpretations improve with age.[14] Researchers found there were male/female differences in expressivity and self-regulation, even at six months of age, with males having more difficulty being expressive than females.[15] Some experts believe that the brain connects emotions and facial expressions and that culture determines what activates an emotion and the rules for displaying an emotion.[16] Presenters who vary their facial expression are viewed as more credible than those who do not.[17] Generally, women use more facial expressions and are more expressive than men; women smile more than men; women are more apt to return smiles; and women are more attracted to others who smile.[18]

Because facial expressions communicate, public presenters need to be aware of what they are communicating. Smiling can indicate both goodwill and submissiveness. Chimpanzees smile when they want to avoid a clash with higher-status chimpanzees. First-year students smile more than upper-class students.[19] Constant smiling may communicate submissiveness or nervousness instead of friendliness, especially if the smiling seems unrelated to the presentation's content.

You can practice in front of a mirror, videotape your practice session, or speak in front of friends who will help you. The goal is to have facial expressions consistent with your intent and your message.

The use of gestures varies across cultures.

Use Gestures to Reinforce Message

Gestures are *motions of the hands or body for emphasis or expression.* Effective use of gestures distinguishes outstanding speaking from the more mundane.[20] Although you probably are unaware of your arms and hands when you converse with someone, they may become bothersome appendages when you stand in front of an audience. You have to work to make public speaking look easy, just as skillful athletes or graceful dancers make their performances look effortless.

Angry workers sometimes appear on television to protest low prices and poor working conditions. Although they are untutored in public speaking, these impassioned people deliver their presentations with gusto and determined gestures. They have a natural delivery because they are much more concerned about their message than about when they should raise their clenched fists. You can deliver the material more naturally if your attention is focused on your message. Self-conscious attention to your own gestures may be self-defeating: the gestures look studied, rehearsed, or slightly out of sync with your message. Selecting a topic that you really care about can have the side effect of improving your gestures, especially if you concentrate on your audience and message.

Gestures differ with the size of the audience and the formality of the occasion. With a small audience in an informal setting, gestures are more like those you would use in ordinary conversation. With large audiences and in formal speaking situations, gestures are larger and more dramatic. In the classroom, the situation is often fairly formal and the audience relatively small, so gestures are ordinarily larger than they would be in casual conversation but not as exaggerated as they would be in a large auditorium.

Another way to learn appropriate gestures is to practice the material in front of friends who are willing to make constructive comments. Actresses and actors spend hours rehearsing lines and gestures so that they will look spontaneous on stage. You may have to appear before many audiences before you learn to speak and move naturally, but with practice, you will learn which natural arm, head, and hand movements seem to help.

Use Bodily Movement for Purpose

The fourth nonverbal aspect of delivery is **movement,** or *what you do with your entire body during a presentation.* Do you lean forward as you speak, demonstrating how serious you are about communicating your message? Do you move out from behind the lectern to show that you want to be closer to the audience? Do you move during transitions in your presentation to signal physically to the audience that you are moving to a new location in your presentation? These are examples of purposeful movement in a public presentation. Movement must occur with purpose. You should not move just to work off your own anxiety.

Always try to face the audience even when you are moving. For instance, even when you need to write information on the board, you can avoid turning your back by putting your notes on the board before class or by putting your visual material on posters. You can learn a lot about movement by watching your classmates and professors when they speak. Observe what works for others (and for you) through observation and practice. Avoid purposeless movement such as rocking back and forth or side to side or the "caged lion" movement in which a presenter circles the front of the room like a big cat in a zoo.

The environment in which you give your presentation helps determine which movements are appropriate. The distance between the presenter and the audience is significant. A great distance suggests presenter superiority or great respect.

View the CD-ROM video speech entitled "I'll Take the Cow Over the Chemicals." How did the speaker's delivery add or detract to the content of the speech? How could the delivery have been enhanced?

Sigrid Larson addresses students at an elementary school.

That is why pulpits in most churches loom high and away from the congregation. A presenter often has a choice about how much to move toward or away from the audience. In the classroom, a presenter who clings to the far wall may appear to be exhibiting fear. Drawing close suggests intimacy or power. Large people can appear threatening or aggressive if they approach the audience too closely, and small people behind large podiums tend to disappear from sight. You need to decide what distances make you and your listeners most comfortable and make you as a presenter most effective.

> *Sigrid Larson, the presenter featured at the beginning of this chapter, had an advantage over other students. During elementary, middle, and high school, she had competed in several pageants. When she was only 18, she competed for, and won, the state pageant and went on to compete for the Miss America crown. Although she did not emerge as Miss America, her experiences had given her great poise. Sigrid knew how to use eye contact effectively. She used varied facial expression, meaningful gestures, and effective bodily movement.*

Wear Appropriate Attire

Clothing and **physical appearance** make a difference in public speaking situations within and outside the classroom. Following are some suggestions for choosing appropriate attire for the classroom setting.

1. Wear clothing that is typical for your audience, unless you wish to wear clothing that makes some point about your presentation. An international student speaking about native dress could wear clothing unique to her country, for example.

Chapter Seven   Delivering Speeches   **157**

2. Avoid wearing clothing or jewelry that is likely to distract your audience from your message: pants that are cut too low; shirts that are too short; or too many rings in too many places.
3. Wear clothing and accessories that contribute to your credibility, not ones that lower your standing in the eyes of the audience: Avoid provocative or revealing clothing.

Public speaking outside the classroom is clearly more complicated because you have to dress for the topic, the audience, and the occasion. Violate audience expectations and they will tend to respond negatively. For example, if you were to wear provocative clothing for a presentation at an assisted-living facility, the audience would likely be distracted from the message by your outfit. When in doubt, ask the people who invited you to speak how you should dress.

Before we conclude this section, we should note that a natural style is important. No one should let public speaking immobilize them; natural instinct is important. If you use a lot of gesture in conversation, you can effectively take it up a notch in public speaking. If you use less bodily movement when you talk, but are very expressive with voice and facial expression, then that may serve you best in public speaking. The information provided in this chapter should enhance, rather than detract from, your natural style.

Question-and-Answer Sessions

Some presentations allow for a question-and-answer session. Even if your classroom speeches do not include a question-and-answer period, you may encounter this format when you speak in other settings. In this section, we offer basic guidelines for preparing for these opportunities and for handling the questions when you are presented with them.

In advance of the question-and-answer period, you should consider possible questions that others might ask. If you have friends or classmates who will listen to your speech beforehand, ask them to pose questions that occur to them. Imagine, too, what a critic might say about your presentation. Once you have determined some of the likely questions that others might ask, prepare thoughtful and thorough responses to the questions. From these answers, practice a succinct response that captures the essence of your rejoinder.

When you actually present your talk, you may be faced with questions that you did not expect. Do not panic. Instead, listen to their question carefully. If the question is not clear, ask them to repeat it or to ask again in different words. Once you believe you have accurately heard their question, repeat it back to the entire audience: "If I understand you correctly, you are asking about . . ." This approach will allow all of the members of the audience to hear the question and will also provide you with additional time to formulate an answer.

Even though a question may appear to be antagonistic, do not become defensive or angry. Keep in mind that an audience member has to exhibit a certain amount of courage to ask a question in front of everybody and therefore should be treated with respect. In addition, questions generally signal interest on the part of the audience, which is an indirect sign of a job well done on your part. Be gracious and positive as you respond to what may seem like a critical or hostile question.

158   Part Two   Selecting and Arranging Content

Be as truthful and sincere in your answer as you can. Do not be flip or sarcastic. Do not fabricate an answer if you honestly do not know the answer to the question. Be straightforward and candid in explaining that you simply do not know the precise answer to the audience member's question.

Finally, be aware that some audience members may have a particular agenda. They may have attended your speech in order to be heard, rather than to listen. If an audience member raises his or her hand to ask a question, do not be surprised if she or he launches into a long anecdote, reports contrary information, or begins to dominate the question-and-answer period. Be prepared to thank them for their comments in a congenial but clear manner, and to move the question-and-answer period to other audience members. As the speaker, you are in charge not only of the presentation but of the question-and-answer period as well.

How Can You Improve Your Delivery?

A student confessed that he had not followed instructions. Told to write a brief outline from which to deliver a speech, the student instead had written out every word. Afraid to speak in front of the class without his manuscript, he practiced by reading it word for word. After rehearsing many times, he wrote the entire speech using a tiny font so it would appear to be delivered from a brief outline on small sheets. However, as he began his speech, he found that he could not read the tiny print so he delivered the whole speech without using any written cues. All the practice had helped him; the small font manuscript had not.

To help you improve your own delivery, you might follow these helpful steps:

1. Start with a detailed working outline that includes the introduction, the body, and the conclusion. Remember to include all main points and supporting materials.
2. Distill the working outline into a speaking outline that includes only reminders of what you intend to include in your speech.
3. Practice your speech alone first, preferably in front of a mirror, so you will notice how much or how little you use your notes. Ideally, you should deliver 80 to 90 percent or more of your speech without looking at notes.
4. Practice your speech in front of your roommate, your spouse, your kids, or colleagues. Try again to maintain eye contact as much as possible. After the speech, ask your observers to explain your message—and seek their advice for improving the speech.
5. Practice your speech with minimal notes in an empty classroom or a similar place that allows you to become accustomed to its size and the situation. Focus on some of the more sophisticated aspects of delivery, such as facial expression, vocal variety, gestures, and movement.
6. Use past critiques from your instructor or classmates to provide direction for improvement on delivery.
7. If possible, watch a videotape of your own performance for feedback. If practice does not make perfect, at least the rehearsal will make you confident. You will become so familiar with the content of your speech that you will focus more on communicating your message to your audience.

Resources for Review and Discussion

SUMMARY

In this chapter you have learned the following:

▶ Effective delivery is presenting a talk by not calling attention to how you say the message.

▶ Four methods of delivery are extemporaneous, manuscript, memorized, and impromptu.
  - The method of delivery that most speech professors prefer for classroom instruction is the extemporaneous mode.
  - The extemporaneous mode allows for minimal use of notes but invites spontaneity and maximum focus on message and audience.

▶ The vocal aspects of delivery are rate, pause, duration, rhythm, pitch, volume, enunciation, and fluency.
  - You can orchestrate these vocal characteristics into a symphony of sound and movement attractive to the audience.
  - Use dramatic pause (a planned pause for effect).
  - Monotony and unintended verbal blunders, such as the dreaded vocalized pause, are the enemies of effective delivery.

▶ Nonverbal aspects of delivery are eye contact, facial expression, gestures, movement and physical appearance.
  - The keys to delivery are naturalness, sincerity, and sensitive responsiveness to the audience.

▶ Improving your delivery requires practice.
  - Starting with a script of your speech or preferably a sentence outline, move, with practice, toward fewer and fewer notes and more and more attention to your audience.
  - The key word is practice.
  - Too much practice can turn your extemporaneous speech into a memorized one, but too little can turn your well-composed speech into a comedy of errors.
  - Finding time to practice your speech may be as hard for you as finding a topic, but those who practice usually receive the best evaluations.

KEY TERMS

  Use the *Public Speaking* CD-ROM and the Online Learning Center at www.mhhe.com/nelson to practice your understanding of the following terminology.

Addition	Gestures	Projection
Alliteration	Impromptu mode	Pronunciation
Articulation	Malapropism	Rate
Deletion	Manuscript mode	Rhythm
Duration	Memorized mode	Substitution
Enunciation	Movement	Transposition
Extemporaneous mode	Pause	Vocalized pause
Eye contact	Physical appearance	Volume
Fluency	Pitch	

REFERENCES

[1] Lesly, P. (1988). Managing the human climate. *PR Reporter*. Exeter, NH: PR Publishing Co., p. 1.

[2] Grigg, Ray. (1988). *The tao of relationships*. New York: Bantam Books, p. 15.

[3] Hildebrandt, H. W., & Stevens, W. (1963). Manuscript and extemporaneous delivery in communicating information. *Speech Monographs, 30,* 369–72.

[4] Miller, N. (1976). Speed of speech and persuasion. *Journal of Personality and Social Psychology, 34,* 15–24.

[5] Diehl, C. F., White, R. C., & Burk, K. W. (1959). Rate and communication. *Speech Monographs, 26,* 229–31.

[6] Harden, M. (1999, April 18). Making the grate. *The Columbus Dispatch,* 1D.

[7] Chirumbolo, Antonio, Mannetti, Lucia, Pierro, Antonio, Areni, Alessandra, & Kruglanski, Arie W. (2005). Motivated closed-mindedness and creativity in small groups. *Small Group Research, 36.1,* 59–82. See also Nakatani, Yasuo. (2005). The effects of awareness-raising training on oral communication strategy use. *Modern Language Journal, 89.1,* 76–91.

[8] Vuilleumier, Patrik, George, Nathalie, Lister, Veronika, Armony, Jorge, & Driver, Jon. (2005). Effects of perceived mutual gaze and gender on face processing and recognition memory. *Visual Cognition, 12.1,* 85–101.

[9] Venezia, Meaghan, Messinger, Daniel S., Thorp, Danielle, & Mundy, Peter. (2004). The development of anticipatory smiling. *Infancy, 6.3,* 397–406.

[10] Napieralski, L. P., Brooks, C. I., & Droney, J. M. (1995). The effect of duration of eye contact on American college students' attributions of state, trait, and test anxiety. *Journal of Social Psychology, 135,* 273–80.

[11] Beebe, S. A. (1974). Eye contact: A nonverbal determinant of speaker credibility. *Speech Teacher, 23,* 21–25.

[12] Richmond, V. P., McCroskey, J. C., & Payne, S. K. (1987). *Nonverbal behavior in interpersonal relations.* Englewood Cliffs, NJ: Prentice-Hall.

[13] Ekman, P., & Friesen, W. V. (1967). Head and body cues in the judgment of emotion: A reformulation. *Perceptual and Motor Skills, 24,* 71–74.

[14] Gosselin, P., &. Simard, J. (1999). Children's knowledge of facial expressions of emotions: Distinguishing fear and surprise. *Journal of Genetic Psychology, 160.2,* 181–93.

[15] Weinberg, M. K., Tronick, E. Z., & Cohn, J. F. (1999). Gender differences in emotional expressivity and self-regulation during early infancy. *Developmental Psychology, 35.1,* 175–88.

[16] Ekman, P. (1969). Pan-cultural elements in facial displays of emotion. *Science, 164,* 86–88.

[17] Burgoon, J. K., Birk, T., & Pfau, M. (1990). Nonverbal behaviors, persuasion, and credibility. *Human Communication Research, 17,* 140–70.

[18] Pearson, Judy C., West, Richard L., & Turner, Lynn H. (1995). *Gender and communication.* Dubuque, IA: Wm. C. Brown Publishers.

[19] *Ibid.*

[20] Movshovitz-Hadar, Nitsa, & Hazzan, Orit. (2004). How to present it? On the rhetoric of an outstanding lecturer. *International Journal of Mathematical Education in Science & Technology, 35.6,* 813–27. See also Singer, Melissa A., & Goldin-Meadow, Susan. (2005). Children learn when their teacher's gestures and speech differ. *Psychological Science, 16.2,* 85–89.

APPLICATION EXERCISES

  Go to the self-quizzes on the *Public Speaking* CD-ROM and the Online Learning Center at www.mhhe.com/nelson to test your knowledge of the chapter concepts.

1. Examine the following topics, audiences, and situations and indicate which method of delivery would be most appropriate by placing the letter in the blank. Instead of seeking "correct answers" for these items, you should discuss them with your classmates or teacher and defend your choices based on the message, the audience, and the situation.

   A = Manuscript method
   B = Extemporaneous method
   C = Impromptu method
   D = Memorized method

   _____ You have to answer questions from the class at the conclusion of your speech.

   _____ You have to describe the student government's new statement of policy on student rights to a group of high-level administrators in the college.

   _____ You have to deliver the same speech about student life at your college three times a week for 16 weeks to incoming first-year students.

   _____ You have to give parents a "walking tour" of the campus, including information about the buildings, the history of the college, and the background of significant places on campus.

   _____ You have to go door-to-door, demonstrating and explaining a vacuum cleaner and its attachments that you are selling to individuals, couples, and even groups of roommates.

Chapter Seven   Delivering Speeches   161

2. Observe a talented public presenter—a visiting lecturer, a political presenter, a sales manager—and study that person's gestures, facial expressions, eye contact, and movement. Then answer the following questions.
   a. Do the presenter's gestures reinforce the important points in the speech?
   b. Does the presenter's facial expression reflect the message and show concern for the audience and the topic?
   c. Does the presenter maintain eye contact with the audience, respond to the audience's reactions, and keep himself or herself from becoming immersed in the manuscript, outline, or notes?
   d. Do the presenter's movements reflect the organization of the speech and the important points in it?
   e. Are the presenter's gestures, facial expressions, and movements consistent with the occasion, the personality of the presenter, and the message being communicated?
   f. Do the presenter's clothing and other adornments reinforce, rather than distract from, the message?
3. For your next speech, have a classmate, friend, or relative observe and evaluate your speech for delivery skills. Have your critic use this scale to fill in the blanks on the left.

   1 = Excellent   2 = Good   3 = Average
   4 = Fair   5 = Weak

Vocal Aspects of Delivery

_____ Pitch: highness and lowness of voice, upward and downward inflections

_____ Rate: words per minute, appropriate variation of rate for the difficulty of content

_____ Pause: intentional silence designed to aid understanding at appropriate places

_____ Volume: loud enough to hear, variation with the content

_____ Enunciation: correct pronunciation and articulation

_____ Fluency: smoothness of delivery; lack of vocalized pauses; good pacing, rhythm, and cadence without being so smooth as to sound artificial, contrived, or glib

Nonverbal Aspects of Delivery

_____ Gestures: natural movement of the head, hands, arms, and torso consistent with the presenter, topic, and situation

_____ Facial expression and smiling behavior: consistent with message, used to relate to the audience, and appropriate for audience and situation

_____ Eye contact: natural, steady without staring, includes entire audience, and is responsive to audience feedback

_____ Movement: purposeful, used to indicate organization, natural, without anxiety, use at podium and distance from audience

_____ Physical appearance: appropriate for the occasion, presenter, topic, and audience

CHAPTER EIGHT

> If all my possessions were to be taken from me with one exception, I would choose to keep the power of communication, for by it I would regain all the others.
>
> **DANIEL WEBSTER (1782–1852), AMERICAN STATESMAN**

> My use of language is part and parcel of my message.
>
> **THEO VAN GOGH (1822–1885), BROTHER OF DUTCH PAINTER VINCENT VAN GOGH**

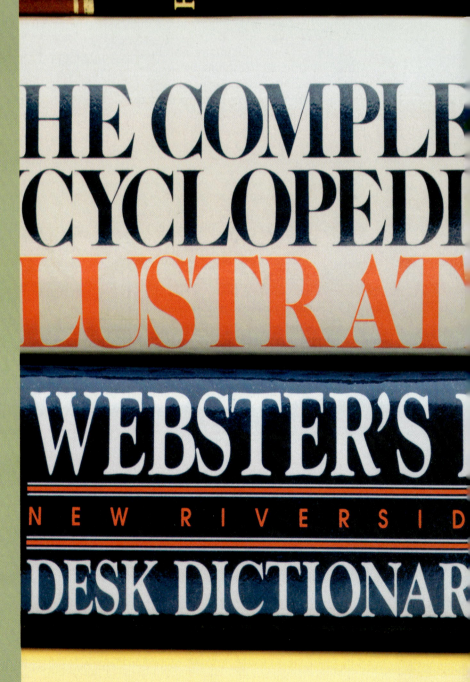

Choosing Your Words

What will you learn?

When you have read and thought about this chapter, you will be able to:

1. Distinguish between abstract and concrete language.
2. Differentiate between connotative and denotative language.
3. Provide examples of descriptive and evaluative language.
4. Use comparison and contrast to unveil meaning.
5. Use figurative language to enliven your presentation.
6. Demonstrate how written and spoken language differ.
7. Use language respectfully.
8. Choose appropriate words for public presentations.
9. Show how words can be used ethically or not.

In this chapter, you will learn how language functions in a public presentation. This chapter will help you avoid word problems, help you choose the right words, and encourage you to use words ethically.

164   Part Two   Selecting and Arranging Content

Douglas Burch appeared to be a traditional undergraduate in his 20s, but he actually was an eight-year veteran of the U.S. Army. After working at the most secret levels of the National Security Administration, he is now an engineering major and the father of an infant daughter. Here is part of a speech he delivered to his public speaking class, an audience consisting mostly of individuals 18 to 24 years old:

I want to relate a little story to you. Growing up I had this one teacher who always had to be the hardest, never made it easy, and never gave me a break. To make matters worse, she always gave me the test before she gave the lesson. How was this fair? I did learn, and I grew to love this teacher regardless of how cruel she was to me. Can you guess her name? Her name is life. She is hard and she is dirty, sometimes scary, and sometimes mean. Somehow, she is always beautiful. That is life, and we have no choice but to accept it. We do, however, have a choice to learn from it and to make the most of it. Life, you see, is comprised of a series of little tests and challenges that you learn from after the fact. When you stand back and look at life, it is one big test. When the test is complete, what will you have learned; what will you have accomplished? . . . You have to start living your dream today. You have to start making it happen today. You can't have yesterday back, and tomorrow is not guaranteed.[1]

Doug had a way with words. He turned an abstraction, life, into his teacher. His words communicated his experience with life in a vivid manner because he chose a method—**personification** or *attributing human characteristics to an abstraction.* Abstractions may be personified in any number of ways: "Death crept into the house like a stealthy thief determined to quietly take her life away" or "Her chest constricted as if a large hand had reached within her and tightened its grip on her hapless heart." Are these personifications more interesting than saying "She died" or "Her chest hurt"? Personification gives expressions new life.

Moments later in his speech, Doug Burch said to his classmates: "I wish I knew the right words to make you understand; unfortunately, your teacher is also my teacher."[2] Composing your speech always ends up being a quest to find the right words. This chapter is devoted to helping you find the right words.

Word Power

Language is a powerful symbol system used to organize and classify what our senses detect and to shape thought. We will explore the general characteristics of language to better understand its function in our presentations.

Language Is Symbolic

The 19th century U.S.-American author Nathaniel Hawthorne once said: "Words—so innocent and powerless as they are, standing in a dictionary, how potent for good and evil they become, in the hands of one who knows how to combine them."[3] Like your name, which is a representation of you, words are **symbolic** in that *they represent* *the concrete and objective reality of objects and things as well as abstract ideas.* Thus the word *computer* conjures up a CPU, monitor, and keyboard and the words *cellular phone* evoke a small handset and tiny screen.

Language Is Powerful

When words fail, wars begin. When wars finally end, we settle our disputes with words.

—Wilfred Funk[4]

Professional communicators like broadcasters, journalists, and writers know the power of words.

Diplomats, lawyers, mediators, and negotiators use words to solve the world's political issues, business problems, and legal cases. Speakers, broadcasters, PR professionals, and journalists—the world's communicators—love and depend on words. You will learn to love words too as you learn more about how words work. But first you may need to be convinced that words are powerful.

Think, for example, of the old saying, "Sticks and stones will break my bones, but words can never hurt me." Although the statement asserts that sticks and stones can be harmful but words cannot, you may remember children using it to fend off the sting of words. Actually, you might agree more that "bones heal, but wounds from words can last forever." You probably remember the words of someone who insulted you, treated you with disrespect, or commented negatively about you in front of others.

Words can cause fights, but they can mend relationships as well. Words like "I'm sorry," "You were right," "I was wrong," and "I did not mean what I said" are mending words. Words like "You did a great job," "I'd hire you any time," and "You have a fine future with this company" are words that most people would like to hear. Words can make you feel wonderful—or awful. Let us see what else words can do.

Words Organize and Classify

Words allow us to organize and classify, to group and cluster individual items into larger, more manageable units. Instead of having to identify every individual thing with a specific word, we cast them into a larger group. So we refer to cars, tables, chairs, houses, cities, states, and countries. We also use words to classify. Imagine you are trying to get your friend to locate someone in a crowd. The conversation might go something like this:

"I just saw a guy from my public speaking class."

"Which one is he?"

"The tall one."

"The blond guy with the red cap?"

"No, the one with a shaved head and sunglasses."

Cultural Note

WORD DIFFERENCES

Not all languages share words with similar meanings or even a word at all for some people or things. Until South Koreans were westernized (mostly by movies), they had no word for "kiss" and considered such behavior unhygienic. Laplanders have many words for snow, but no generic name like the English *snow*. Brazilian Guarani live among palm trees and parrots and have many words for them, but no generic name for all of them as we do in the English language.[5]

Words quickly allow you to limit your friend's search for your fellow student by gender, height, body type, hairstyle, and accessories.

Your presentations allow you to organize and classify your reality. Examine this excerpt from a talk by varsity basketball player Jason Crawford:

> My uncle Johnny grew up in a well-educated family. He moved on to college where he earned a degree in engineering, a profession he pursued to the fullest. This man was alcohol-free the first 23 years of his life. Then one day he decided to pick up a drink. Little did he know that first drink would lead to many episodes down the line.
>
> After a time he became more addicted and became an alcoholic. Johnny found himself driving home from a local bar one night and was pulled over by the police. Unable to function, Johnny decided that he was going to play a little game of cat and mouse. As the police officer approached the car, Johnny sped off. While trying to get away, he crashed into another car killing two innocent victims. Johnny was also hurt, not physically but mentally. This episode would scar Johnny for the rest of his life. Uncle Johnny is now looking at life from behind bars.[6]

Jason's presentation begins with broad organizational categories—well-educated families, alcoholics, police, and victims—and moves through classifications: an engineer, a nondrinker, a drinker, an alcoholic, an arrest resister, a killer, and a criminal. Your speeches also will use words to organize and classify.

Words Shape Thought

Have you ever thought about how words shape the way you think? We have many more words about war than about peace. D. C. Smith lists some examples: "to beat a hasty retreat," "to get off on the wrong foot," and "to mark time."[7] We have many more words describing violence than describing cooperation. Are we a more warlike culture because our vocabulary reflects more concern for conflict than cooperation?

In *Prometheus Unbound,* Percy Shelley, the English Romantic poet says of his hero, Prometheus, who gave humanity fire, culture, and science: "He gave man speech, and speech created thought, which is the measure of the Universe."[8] A similar notion comes to us from the **Sapir-Whorf hypothesis,** a theory that suggests that *our language determines to some extent how we think about and view the world.*[9]

Apparently having a large vocabulary is not only handy when you take a college entrance examination but also when you try to think of an idea and how to express it. The availability of words for a concept speeds up thought and expression, two vital processes in communication.

Levels of Abstraction

An **abstraction** is a *simplification standing for a person or thing*. The word *building* cannot capture the complexity of engineering, design, plumbing, electrical networks, glass, and steel that make up a "building."

Scholars called **semanticists,** *people who study words and meaning*, thought of a way to envision **levels of abstraction,** *the degree to which words become separated from concrete or sensed reality*. One prominent semanticist, S.I. Hayakawa[10] introduced the "ladder of abstraction" to demonstrate that words have degrees of abstractness and concreteness. The ladder of abstraction should look like a stepladder. As an example, see Figure 8.1, where the bottom of the ladder, at the most abstract level, is "living being," followed up the steps by "mammal," "omnivore," "human," "female," "teenager," and "Rebekah." Does referring to Rebekah as an "omnivore" seem the same to you as calling her by her own particular name, "Rebekah"?

While **abstract words** tend to be *general, broad, and distant from what you can perceive through your senses*, **concrete words** tend to be *specific, narrow, particular, and based on what you can sense*. At a recent class reunion, a classmate described his current occupation by saying "I'm in transportation," encouraging listeners to perceive him as anything from a pilot to a train engineer to a ship's captain—all of whom are "in transportation"—but the more specific and concrete term, *city bus driver,* turned out to be a more accurate representation.

Audiences respond more predictably to concrete than to abstract language. Consider these broad possibilities of the abstract words as opposed to the concrete words.

Abstract	Concrete
I love sports.	I'm a soccer player.
I drive a late-model vehicle.	I drive a Subaru Outback.
Some foods make me ill.	I'm allergic to milk products.
I use drugs.	I take an aspirin each day.
I'm a homemaker.	I stay at home and raise two children.

The more abstract terminology leaves much more of the meaning to chance. The concrete terms are more likely to evoke the intended meanings in the listeners.

Figure 8.1 **Hayakawa's "ladder of abstraction."**

168 Part Two   Selecting and Arranging Content

TABLE 8.1 DENOTATIVE AND CONNOTATIVE MEANINGS OF WORDS		
	DENOTATIVE MEANING	ONE CONNOTATIVE MEANING
Wolf	Wild canine in the dog family	Man who aggressively pursues women
Bigot	Someone who despises people who are different	Someone who despises people that I like
History	A record of human events	A false account of events as depicted by the winners

Denotative and Connotative Words

Public speakers need to be aware of the varied meanings evoked by their words. One means of understanding varied meanings is to distinguish between denotative and connotative meanings. **Denotative meaning** is *the direct, explicit meaning or reference of a word.* Keep in mind that dictionary meanings are really a historical listing of how words are used, not necessarily the current meanings. Our everyday use of words can be well ahead of the dictionary meanings.

The denotative meaning of the words *anorexia nervosa* might be "the pursuit of thinness through self-starvation," but to victims, their family, and friends, the term has emotional connotations as well. The **connotative meaning** of a term, *the idea suggested by a word other than its explicit meaning,* portrays "my sister who spent three years battling anorexia while she almost shriveled up and died." Compare in Table 8.1 the denotative meaning with one connotative meaning of several words to help you understand this concept. Notice that you may disagree or agree with the connotative meanings in the right-hand column—that is, words have various connotations for all of us. A practical piece of advice is that in your speeches, you need to consider not only the denotative but also the connotative power of words on your audience.

Descriptive and Evaluative Language

Communicators who are sensitive to others favor descriptive over evaluative language. **Descriptive language** *attempts to observe objectively and without judgment.* **Evaluative language** is *full of judgments about the goodness or badness of a person or situation.*

Descriptive Words	Evaluative Words
High-energy person	A person wound too tight
Expensive automobile	Overpriced, high-maintenance showmobile

You can see why evaluative words can invite trouble, and how descriptive words can help you avoid negative audience reactions. In public presentations, a speaker

Chapter Eight   Choosing Your Words   **169**

is wise not to use hot-button terms that cause a strong, negative reaction in the audience because an outraged listener might very well disrupt your entire presentation.

Comparison and Contrast

Speakers often use comparisons and contrasts to clarify their messages. Douglas Burch, whom we introduced at the start of the chapter, when asked to distinguish himself from others in an "I Am Unique" speech early in the course, first compared and then contrasted his appearance to that of others in the class:

> **Comparison:** *I then looked at my physical make-up. I am 5' 7" tall, weigh roughly 155 lbs. and have short brown hair. I think I just described 90 percent of the male population at the university.*

> **Contrast:** *I thought distinguishable marks might help separate me a little. I have over 70 stitches that have left scars, along with two scars from stab wounds. The most distinguishable mark on me is a tribal tattoo on my back which I had done in England.[11]*

A **comparison** *shows how much one thing is like another;* a **contrast** *shows how unlike one thing is from another.* You can use both for clarification for your audience.

See the video entitled "Making a Contrast."

Words of Comparison	Words of Contrast
I, like all of you, am a student.	Unlike most of you, I am from India.
I too struggle to pay for school.	I'm the third generation to attend here.
All of us love animals.	I am allergic to anything with hair, especially cats—and my boyfriend.

Using the power of language is knowing how to use comparison and contrast for clarifying your intended meaning.

Literal and Figurative Language

Language can be both literal and figurative. **Literal language** *uses words to reveal facts,* whereas **figurative language** *compares one concept to another analogous but different concept.* To say that a fighter hit his opponent 25 times in a round is literal; to say that he fought like a tiger is figurative. Literal language is what you usually find in news reports in newspapers and magazines or text-based news sources on the Internet. Figurative language is found in the lyrics of songs, in poetry, and in feature articles in magazines. The best speakers know how to use figurative language to add succulent spices to an otherwise bland broth of literal language.

Written and Spoken Language

Written and spoken language differ enormously. Table 8.2 highlights these differences. Figure 8.2 gives tips on how language can be used to increase clarity.

TABLE 8.2 COMMUNICATION DIFFERENCES AMONG SPEAKERS, LISTENERS, WRITERS, AND READERS

	SPEAKER	LISTENER	WRITER	READER
Sentence length	Uses short sentences instead of long ones	Understands short sentences better than long ones	Typically can use longer sentences than a speaker can	Can read long sentences multiple times to achieve understanding
Pace	Sets the pace	Must adjust to pace	Sets no "real-time" pace	Reads at own pace
Repetition	Reiterates ideas to optimize understanding	Needs repetition to catch meanings	Might reiterate ideas to optimize understanding	Rereads if needed for better understanding
Message transmission	Conveys verbal and nonverbal messages	Receives verbal and nonverbal messages	Conveys verbal messages	Receives verbal messages
Feedback and adaptation	Can adapt immediately to feedback	Sends and responds to feedback	Receives no feedback when writing	Sends no feedback while reading

1. Define terms in your speech so your audience will understand the *denotative* and *connotative meanings* of your words.

2. Use *descriptive language* instead of *evaluative language* to avoid misunderstanding and conflict.

3. Clarify your ideas by *comparison* and *contrast*.

4. Use *literal language* to convey facts and *figurative language* for creative expression.

5. Spoken language as opposed to written language invites shorter sentences, more repetition, and some simplification.

Figure 8.2   **Using words for clarity.**

Using Language Respectfully

An important aspect of becoming an effective public communicator is to use language respectfully. That is, you need to use words that include people, that do not establish in-group and out-group identities, and that regard people without negative judgment based on ethnicity, gender, sexual orientation, or worldview.

Use Inclusive Language

Another way to articulate this rule of artful and ethical speaking is to say that you should use **inclusive language,** *language that does not leave out groups of people.* One good principle to follow in public discourse is to call people what they themselves

Chapter Eight   Choosing Your Words   171

want others to call them. Many of our words for others come from those who dominate in a culture. Since men have dominated North American culture historically, you will find many more derogatory words for women than for men. Additionally, Native Americans did not name themselves "Indians." European explorers gave them that name when they mistakenly thought they had reached India.

You also can avoid sexist language by using inclusive language. When you consider the list below, can you add several more examples?

Sexist	Inclusive
Mankind	Humankind
Manmade	Handmade
Fireman	Firefighter
Mailman	Mail carrier
Chairman	Chair

Finally, you can increase your chances of being inclusive by avoiding slang, because this type of language often is understood by only certain groups of people. When you use slang, you risk alienating those audience members who are not part of the group that typically associates with those words and expressions.

Use Approved Names

Notice also that the principle says that you should "call people what they themselves want others to call them." Sometimes people within a co-culture call each other by names that are forbidden to people outside that co-culture. Women can call each other "girls," but they probably do not want their employer to call them by that name. Black Americans may call each other by names that would be deeply insulting if used by someone else. You are most likely to succeed as a public presenter if you use language that includes, honors, and respects others.

Stereotypes and Differences

The word *stereotype* was first used many years ago by Walter Lippman in his book *Public Opinion* in 1922. Lippman borrowed the term from the new machine at the time that printed the same sheet of print over and over, a machine called a "stereotype." Today **stereotype** has come to mean *the misjudging of an individual by assuming that he or she has the characteristics of some group—that every single individual is just exactly like the others* as in the case of the stereotype machine.

Every campus has more than its fair share of stereotypes about students who study too much, students who study too little, students who are athletes, and students who are in fraternities or sororities. We have stereotypes of professors, accountants, and engineers. But public speakers need to avoid stereotypes to avoid offense.

Similarly, you should avoid calling attention to irrelevant differences. When you describe someone as a *female* judge, a *Hispanic* professor, a *woman* doctor, or the city council member *in a wheelchair,* you are emphasizing irrelevant qualifiers about them. The implication might be that people who are female are rarely judges or doctors, that people of Hispanic origin are generally not professors, and that individuals in wheelchairs are typically not elected to city council. Or, even worse, a listener might assume that you do not believe that people from such groups ought to be in such positions.

What Words Should You Use?

You may be wondering what words you can use in your presentations. Try to use words that explain, clarify, and enlighten the audience by following the advice below.

Use Words That Simplify

You will often know more about your topic than do the people in your audience. However, you must be careful not to use language that reduces understanding. This writer, for example, is describing Senator John McCain, Republican from Arizona:

> He would see the heavens fall rather than court Iowa by supporting ethanol subsidies; who, ever an oak, never a willow, insouciantly goes his own way. . . . The media call McCain a "maverick," even though he seems to be, oxymoronically, a predictable maverick.[12]

George F. Will, a Ph.D. from Princeton, is a politically conservative commentator who, nonetheless, attacks many a Republican. His "ever an oak, never a willow" is a clever way to describe the unshakeable McCain, but many readers may have floundered on "insouciantly" and "oxymoronically," which are designed more to highlight Will's high I.Q. than to enlighten his audience. The effective public speaker tries to simplify, to render the words understandable to the audience.

Notice how Andrew Robinson, a physiology major and veteran runner, uses simple, everyday words with lots of concrete, specific detail in this health-related presentation.

George Will says Sen. John McCain is "ever an oak, never a willow," simple words to describe a complicated person.

> You and your friends decide to play a late night game of basketball. You throw on an old pair of tennis shoes and eight of you head to the recreation center. After you have been playing for forty-five minutes or so, sweat is dripping down your face and back, and you are huffing and puffing from running up and down the court. You get stuck guarding this quick kid who moves instantly from one spot to the next before you can react. He drives toward the baseline with you right on him. As he nears the bottom of the key, he crosses over to his left to get around you. You try to stop, but as you plant your left foot, you feel your ankle roll as pain shoots up your leg, and you fall to the ground.[13]

Andrew was warming up to a speech not about basketball but about selecting the correct shoes for the sport. By the time Andrew finished his speech, with more agonizing stories about painful hips, sprained ankles, and sore toes, he had convinced his audience to discard their "old pair of tennis shoes" and buy shoes dedicated to their sport. He accomplished his purpose with simple, direct words.

E-Note

SYNONYMS

A **thesaurus** is a source for synonyms; *Roget's International Thesaurus,* for example, has around a quarter of a million synonyms, including 36 for the word *thief.* The source is accessible on the Internet at http://www2.thesaurus.com/thesaurus/.

Use Substitutions and Definitions

George Will could have substituted simpler words for "insouciantly" and "oxymoronically." He could have said "indifferently" or "uncaringly" instead of "insouciantly," and he simply could have left out the word "oxymoronically," which means contradictory, or two words with opposing meanings, as in "predictable maverick." The skillful presenter chooses words that listeners will understand or defines the terms so they will understand.

Another move toward clarity is to define any language that may seem unfamiliar or potentially confusing to an audience. For example, the term "social justice" could be made clear by describing it as an effort that seeks to establish a society where basic needs are met and where all people flourish.

Use Synonyms and Antonyms

Another method of clarifying a word or concept for an audience is to use **synonyms,** *words that mean more or less the same thing,* or **antonyms,** *words that are the opposite in meaning.* Students who want an inexpensive thesaurus with around 5,000 words should try Anne Bertram's (1997) *In Other Words: Making Better Word Choices in American English.* *House* and *home, office* and *workplace,* and *film* and *movie* are sets of synonyms. Antonyms would include *beautiful* and *ugly, dry* and *humid,* and *hired* and *fired.*

Reveal the Origin of the Word

The *origin of a word* is called its **etymology.** Often a word's etymology will help an audience remember the term. For example, the word psychology means "study of the mind." Psychology comes from the Greek words *psykhe,* which means "soul," and *logia,* which means "the study of."

> **TRY THIS**
>
> *Look up the word* assassin *to see how much of the history of the word the dictionary includes. Do the same for the word* Crusades *to see when they occurred.*

Telling a more complete story about a word is more likely to make it more memorable. Every dictionary has a brief etymology of the words, but some sources tell a more complete and compelling story. Books by William Safire[14] and by

173

A. H. Soukhanov[15] reveal the stories behind the words, stories that help an audience remember the meaning and the significance of the words in your presentation. Use etymologies sparingly so you do not sound pedantic.

Use Words That Evoke Images

See the video entitled "Using a Vivid Image."

An effective speaker uses creativity to paint word pictures in the audience's minds. Many speakers have used the following illustration to help their audience understand the world population:

> If we could shrink the earth's population to a village of 100 people and maintain the existing human ratios, the village would look like this:
> 57 Asians
> 21 Europeans
> 14 from the Western Hemisphere and
> 8 Africans
> 51 females
> 70 non-white
> 70 non-Christian
> 80 living in substandard housing
> 70 illiterate
> 50 suffering from malnutrition, and
> 1 with a college education

These words create a picture in people's minds that make the concept of "world population" more concrete, specific, and easy to understand.

Doug Burch, the army veteran, had these words to say about his eight years in the armed forces. Notice how his words create images in your mind about his experience:

> I have traveled to and from different countries and have seen the most glorious sunsets. I have watched the sun rise one too many times after being up all night. I have sailed around the Spanish Isles and snorkeled among its reefs. I have shared stories and drink with dockhands along the way. I have sat in pubs and bars with strangers who do not speak English and have tried to carry on a conversation. I have learned about many cultures, and that just because ours is one of the most advanced does not mean it is the best. I am starting to feel unique because I have learned about life, and I can still smile.[16]

Colorful words create vivid images in our minds.

Use Correct Grammar

The way you talk affects your credibility with an audience. Paula LaRocque, writing for *The Quill,* says:

> Language misuse ranks high in terms of the negative reaction and irritation it can elicit from people. Most people give considerable value to their native language and their perceptions of its proper use. Thus, people who mis-utilize language are often accused of either maiming, massacring, brutalizing or butchering it. Society's inherent understanding of being civilized apparently means, in part, the ability to communicate well with grace, accuracy and without offense.[17]

Bad grammar is much like having a bit of spinach in your front teeth: Everyone sees that spinach, but nobody bothers to tell you it is there. Outside your speech class you are unlikely to encounter anyone, including your boss, who will actually say, "We are holding you back from responsible management positions because you constantly misuse the language." Nonetheless, consistent correct use of language gives a speaker credibility because other people assume the person is informed. See Figure 8.3 for some common grammatical errors.

Incorrect	Correct
He (or she) don't	He (or she) doesn't
You was	You were
I done it	I did it
Between you and I	Between you and me
I been thinking	I've been thinking
I've already took algebra	I've already taken algebra
We seen it	We saw it
Him and me went	He and I went

Figure 8.3   **Common grammatical errors.**

Adapted from *Public Speaking for College and Career,* 5th ed. by Hamilton Gregory, 1999. Used by permission of McGraw-Hill.

Use Repetition

Repetition, *repeated sounds,* has striking effects in speaking because the audience gets caught up in the cadences, or rhythms, of linguistic structure. Usually, repetition is accompanied by increased volume, increased energy, and increased forcefulness as the repeated forms build toward some climactic ending.

Observe how repetition works in this speech by Chris Meek, an engineering student and co-owner of Combat Creek Paintball:

Do you want to get involved in America's fastest growing sport?

Do you want to get involved in a sport in which size, age, and even sex make no difference?

Do you want an ultimate stress reliever in which communication and quick wits make the difference between winning and losing?

Then I have the sport for you, an adult version of capture-the-flag—paintball.[18]

Using repetition makes your speech easier to remember, makes your speech more energetic, and makes your speech more memorable.

Alluring Alliteration

Alliteration *means the repetition of an initial conso- nant.* Professional speakers use alliteration because repeated sounds make words memorable. "The Fabulous Facts about Foster Care" was Lacey Schneider's title. She began her speech by saying "Before I begin my fact-filled speech about fabu- lous foster care. . . ."[19] All those repeated "F" sounds are alliteration. Also used in advertising, repeated sounds attract attention and help listen- ers to remember.

Figure 8.4 summarizes ways that words can be used to add to the audience's experience of a pre- sentation.

- Use words that simplify.
- Use definitions and substitutions that clarify.
- Use synonyms and antonyms to compare and contrast.
- Use origins of words to promote recall.
- Use descriptive words to evoke images.
- Use correct grammar to heighten credibility.
- Use repeated words for greater understanding.
- Use alliteration to attract attention.

Figure 8.4   **Words to use in your presentation.**

Using Words Ethically

Author Aldous Huxley said, "Thanks to words, we have been able to rise above the brutes; and thanks to words, we have often sunk to the level of demons." You already know that one of the central ethical issues in the use of language in speeches is to acknowledge through oral footnotes the use of another person's words. Violating that rule can result in a failing grade for the class or even expulsion from most colleges and universities. You might be less aware that words themselves can be used unethically. Three examples here will illustrate the point: (1) exaggeration, (2) oversimplification, and (3) perspective taking.

Exaggeration and Oversimplification

Another word for exaggeration in language is **hyperbole** (hi-PURR-bull-ee), which is *a kind of overstatement or use of a word or words that exaggerates the actual situation.* To call a relatively normal fire "the biggest conflagration this city has ever seen" is an example. The ethical speaker exercises care in describing events, people, and situations. You should use vivid, concrete language as long as the words do not overstate or exaggerate. In the heat of a persuasive speech you might be tempted to state your side of the issue with exaggerated or overstated importance.

A second ethical error in language is **oversimplification,** *describing a complex issue as a simple one.* Political campaign speeches are full of examples. The candidate for the senate says, "We'll solve this crime problem with more prisons." The candidate for the state house of representatives says, "No new taxes." And the candidate for governor says "Welfare reform!" Bumper sticker slogans rarely solve problems, and neither do sound bites. The ethical speaker tries to examine issues thoroughly, states them as descriptively as possible, and provides sound reasons for why the audience should adopt a certain position on the issue without exaggeration or oversimplification.

Language and Perspective Taking

Your words reflect your **perspective,** *your point of view or perception.* The words you choose in public speaking indicate to others how you see the world, whether you intend them to or not.

Imagine you are giving a speech about taxation. If you choose to talk about "rich people," "poor people," and "middle-class people," you are using language that divides America into economic classes. That is a particular perspective. If you talk about the "struggling young people" and "the Social Security set," you are dividing Americans by age—another perspective. Talk of the "marriage penalty" and high taxes on single wage earners divides the adult population into those who are married and those who are not. No matter how you discuss the issue, you use language that indicates your perspective.

How is this concept related to ethical speaking? Consider the connotations of the words that you can use to describe individuals who earn over $100,000 annually: "top 10 percent in income," "rich people," "wealthy individuals," "fat cats," or "privileged class." Each description indicates a perspective, but some of them— like the last two—indicate a medium to strong negative connotation that may or may not be fair to high-earning individuals. In other words, the words you choose can indicate prejudice, bias, or unfairness toward individuals or groups.

Unless you are careful with your language, you can make serious errors in your depictions of people. Consider the word *Hispanic*. That word can be used to describe millions of people. Some of them are European Americans (Spanish), some of them are people of color (e.g., South Americans of African or Indian origin), some of them are Cuban Americans, some of them are Mexican Americans, and some of them are Puerto Rican. The word *Asian* is no better. The English language uses that word to cover most of the people in the world, including a good many who have little in common. Here again, the ethical speaker uses the specific description *preferred by the particular people described*. Figure 8.5 lists three ways to make sure you use words ethically.

- Avoid exaggeration.
- Avoid oversimplification.
- Recognize that your language reveals your perspective.

Figure 8.5 How to use words ethically.

TRY THIS

Given your own worldview or perspective because of who you are, you should try to think of individuals or groups that your own words tend to treat less than fairly. For example, how do you refer to a person in a wheelchair, a refugee or immigrant, or individuals from a culture other than your own? For more, go to the Wikipedia Web site, http://en.wikipedia.com/wiki/political_correctness.

Tips for Using Language in Presentations

Here are four practical suggestions for managing the words in your presentation.

1. *Choose language at a level that is appropriate for the specific audience.* Speak with a level of formality that is right for the audience and the situation. Nearly always, the language of public speaking is elevated above that which you would use on the street or in conversation with close friends. You might call it enlightened conversation.
2. *Choose language that the audience will understand.* Words the audience cannot comprehend might impress the audience with your vocabulary, but they neither inform nor persuade. If you must use words that the audience is unlikely to understand, then define, explain, or provide examples.
3. *Choose language consistent with your self, the topic, and the situation.* If you do not normally use legal or medical terms, you will feel and look uncomfortable using them in a presentation. Your language needs to fit the topic and be consistent with your level of knowledge and experience. Using overly dramatic words unwarranted by the topic constitutes exaggeration; understating complex problems indicates a lack of analysis. The situation or occasion may dictate a certain kind of language—you don't speak the same way in a mosque, synagogue, or church as you do at a football game.

See the video entitled "Using an Example."

178 Part Two Selecting and Arranging Content

4. *Choose language that meets high ethical standards.* Choose words that neither exaggerate nor oversimplify. Recognize that words reflect a perspective. Avoid language that offends others because of their race, sex, sexual orientation, or physical or mental disability. Your task is to inform, persuade, or entertain, not to offend.

Last Thoughts on Language

Richard Lederer, a Ph.D. in linguistics, taught for years in a private high school and published at least five books on language. He wrote in *The Miracle of Language* this tribute, which may aptly conclude our chapter on words.

We give thanks for language—the human essence, the skin of thought, more to the mind than light is to the eye.

May we try not only to talk, but to say something; not only to hear, but to listen; not only to write, but to communicate.

May our thoughts and aspirations become words that serve to build bridges from mind to mind and from heart to heart, creating a fellowship of those who would hold fast to that which is good.[20]

Resources for Review and Discussion

SUMMARY

In this chapter you have learned the following:

▶ Words are the most influential ingredient in your message, so you need to know that
  • Words are symbols that stand for or represent something in the world of senses or ideas.
  • Words are powerful with the potential to hurt or to mend.
  • Words organize and classify our world to help us understand it.
  • Words actually shape our thoughts.

▶ Language operates at different levels of abstraction with specific, concrete words evoking more targeted meanings.

▶ Words have denotative and connotative meaning; they describe or evaluate and make judgments.

▶ Words can compare things that are similar or contrast things that are different.

▶ Words can be literal (based on facts) or figurative (based on fancy).

▶ Spoken language and written language differ from each other.
  • Spoken language tends to use shorter sentences and simpler words, while in writing we use more complex words and sentence structure.
  • The spoken word passes by without the opportunity to look back, while anyone can go back to reread a written passage.
  • The spoken word is personal because the speaker is part of the message in a way that an unseen and unheard author is not.
  • The spoken word offers multiple ways of communicating a message through words, movement, gesture, facial expression, and voice inflection, whereas the written word looks pretty much the same on the screen and on paper.
  • The spoken word allows for immediate feedback in that the speaker sees if the audience understands and adapts if they do not—unlike the written word.
  • The receivers of the spoken word actively engage with the speaker—speaker and listener become united in the message, whereas the written word often is oblivious to reader response.

▶ Avoid problems with your words by using language respectfully, which includes calling people what they wish to be called and choosing inclusive language.

▶ Use words that simplify, use substitutions and definitions, use synonyms and antonyms, know the origins of words, use words that evoke images, use correct grammar, and use parallelism and repetition.

▶ You can use words ethically by
  • Avoiding exaggeration and oversimplification.
  • Understanding that language always emerges from a perspective.

▶ Tips for using language in a presentation:
  • Choose language at a level appropriate for the specific audience.
  • Choose language that the audience will understand.
  • Choose language consistent with your self, the topic, and the situation.
  • Choose language that meets high ethical standards.

KEY TERMS

  Use the *Public Speaking* CD-ROM and the Online Learning Center at www.mhhe.com/nelson to practice your understanding of the following terminology.

Abstraction	Concrete words	Etymology
Abstract words	Connotative meaning	Evaluative language
Alliteration	Contrast	Figurative language
Antonym	Denotative meaning	Hyperbole
Comparison	Descriptive language	Inclusive language

Levels of abstraction
Literal language
Oversimplification
Personification

Perspective
Repetition
Sapir-Whorf hypothesis
Semanticist

Stereotype
Symbolic
Synonym
Thesaurus

REFERENCES

[1] Burch, Douglas. (1999). "You can't have yesterday." Unpublished presentation delivered in Interpersonal Communication 103, Public Speaking, Ohio University, Athens, Ohio.

[2] Ibid.

[3] Lederer, Richard. (1991). *The miracle of language.* New York: Pocket Books.

[4] Ibid.

[5] Brown, Roger. (1968). *Words and things.* Glencoe, IL: The Free Press.

[6] Crawford, Jason. (1999). "Killing us one by one." An unpublished presentation delivered in Interpersonal Communication 103, Public Speaking, Ohio University, Athens, Ohio.

[7] Smith, D. C. (1997, July/August). Is the use of metaphors innocuous or cause for concern? *Peace Magazine,* http://www.peacemagazine.org. See also Lakoff, G. & Johnson, M. (1981). *Metaphors we live by.* Chicago: University of Chicago Press; and Rothstein, L. (1999). The war on speech. *Bulletin of the Atomic Scientists, 55.3,* 7.

[8] Shelley, Percy Bysshe. (1960). "Prometheus Unbound," in *John Keats and Percy Bysshe Shelley,* New York: Modern Library, p. 260.

[9] Sapir-Whorf Hypothesis Web site http://venus.va.com.au/suggestion/sapir.html.

[10] Hayakawa, Samuel I. (1978). *Language in thought and action.* Orlando, FL: Harcourt Brace Jovanovich.

[11] Burch, Douglas. (1999). "I am unique." An unpublished presentation delivered in Interpersonal Communication 103, Public Speaking, Ohio University, Athens, Ohio.

[12] Will, George F. (August 25, 1999). Giddy over McCain. *The Washington Post,* p. A17.

[13] Robinson, Andrew. (1999). "If the shoe fits." An unpublished presentation delivered in Interpersonal Communication 103, Public Speaking, Ohio University, Athens, Ohio.

[14] Safire, William. (1972). *The new language of politics.* New York: Collier Books.

[15] Soukhanov, A. H. (1995). *Word watch: The stories behind the words of our lives.* New York: Henry Holt.

[16] Burch, Douglas. (1999). "I am unique."

[17] LaRocque, P. (1999). Between you and I, misutilizing words ranks high pet-peevewise. *The Quill, 87.3,* 31.

[18] Meek, Christopher. (1999). "Aspects of paintball." An unpublished presentation delivered in Interpersonal Communication 101, Public Speaking, Ohio University, Athens, Ohio.

[19] Schneider, Lacey. (2004). "Fabulous facts about foster care." An unpublished presentation in Communication 110. Public Speaking, at North Dakota State University, Fargo, North Dakota.

[20] Lederer, Richard. (1991). *The miracle of language.* New York: Simon & Schuster, p. 243.

APPLICATION EXERCISES

 Go to the self-quizzes on the *Public Speaking* CD-ROM and the Online Learning Center at www.mhhe.com/nelson to test your knowledge of the chapter concepts.

1. Translate the abstract terms in the column on the left into more concrete terms in the blanks on the right.
   a. A recent article _____
   b. An ethnic neighborhood _____
   c. A good professor _____
   d. A big profit _____
   e. A distant land _____
   f. A tough course _____
   g. A tall building _____
   h. He departed rapidly _____
   i. She dresses poorly _____
   j. They are religious _____

Chapter Eight   Choosing Your Words   **181**

Now examine each of the words you have placed in the blanks and place a check after each one that may be a poor choice because it skews the audience's response in a negative or unduly positive direction. In other words, the word lacks honesty and accuracy.

2. Examine the words in the column on the left. Write in the blank after each word its denotative meaning and its connotative meaning. Remember that the denotative meaning is a descriptive definition; the connotative meaning is the feeling or emotion evoked by the term. In the columns to the right of letters f., g., and h., add three words and establish denotative and connotative meanings for each.

	Denotative Meaning	**Connotative Meaning**
a. Girl	_____	_____
b. Terrorist	_____	_____
c. Environmentalist	_____	_____
d. Developer	_____	_____
e. Senator	_____	_____
f.	_____	_____
g.	_____	_____
h.	_____	_____

3. Using any sources available, see if you can find the story behind the word or phrase.
   a. O.K.

   _____

   _____

   b. Trojan horse

   _____

   _____

   c. Baby boomers

   _____

   _____

   d. Eye candy

   _____

   _____

   e. Curse of the Bambino

   _____

   _____

CHAPTER NINE

A visual experience is vitalizing.
KENNETH CLARK

Nowadays people's visual imagination is so much more sophisticated, so much more developed, particularly in young people, that now you can make an image which just slightly suggests something, they can make of it what they will.
ROBERT DOISNEAU

Visual Resources and Presentation Technology

What will you learn?

When you have read and thought about this chapter, you will be able to:

1. Discuss reasons why sensory aids are important in presentations.
2. Use a computer to generate various types of visual resources.
3. Effectively integrate PowerPoint or other forms of presentation software into your presentations.
4. Plan and create graphs, tables, and charts to add clarity to supporting material and explanations.
5. Effectively use other people, objects, video and audio, slide transparencies, overhead transparencies, and handouts to illustrate points in your presentations.
6. Articulate tips for effectively and ethically using any sensory resource in your presentation.

Stimuli bombard us from the time we wake up until the serenity of sleep envelops our consciousness. Even when we are asleep, vivid—and sometimes frightening—visual imagery permeates our subconscious mind. Indeed, images captivate and inspire, all while evoking emotions ranging from fear to exuberance. In this chapter, you will learn how to create and integrate visual imagery and other sensory aids into your presentation.

184   Part Two   Selecting and Arranging Content

José Acosta was not like other students in his public communication class. First, he was a second-generation "mainlander" of Puerto Rican descent. Although he had been raised in New York, his family still clung to many traditions of their home culture. Second, José had just lost his grandfather, Salvador. José wanted to do his informative presentation on his grandfather so that he could honor his memory. Although his teacher warned José that he would "have to carefully plan his presentation to be of broad interest to his audience," José knew that he could find a way to satisfy his teacher while at the same time honoring his "papa."

After working on his presentation for several days, José was frustrated that his words just did not capture what he wanted to say. José's sister, Anita, suggested that José look through his grandfather's pictures and use those to supplement the words in his outline. With this, José struck gold. In Salvador's old chest in the basement, there were hundreds of pictures from Puerto Rico of the 1940s as well as many pictures and materials from Salvador's time with the 65th Infantry Regiment—a regiment composed entirely of soldiers from Puerto Rico. José immediately began planning how to integrate these resources into his presentation. He decided to talk about Puerto Rican culture by using his grandfather as a typical example.

José discovered what many experienced presenters already know. Visual resources and other sensory aids can make the process of preparing and presenting information much easier. Although students may at first make mistakes with such aids, presentations generally are better with them than without them. This chapter introduces you to various types of sensory aids—including computer-generated graphics and more traditional, "low-tech" resources—and discusses strategies you should use when displaying sensory aids during your presentations.

How You Can Benefit from Using Sensory Aids

Even inexperienced speakers can guess that good presentations consist of more than just the speaker talking. One way to enhance any presentation is to use **sensory aids,** which are *resources other than the speaker that stimulate listeners and help them comprehend and remember the presenter's message.* Although sensory aids can appeal to any of the five senses, the most common ones stimulate sight. These **visual aids** are *any observable resources used to enhance, explain, or supplement the presenter's message.* They include pictures, diagrams, charts, graphs, video, and even demonstrations by actual people. In fact, some might argue that presenters are always visual aids for their messages because of the nonverbal behaviors they use. Nonvisual sensory aids can include music, touchable materials with different textures, and even food—with its pleasant aroma and good taste.

There are many good reasons to use sensory aids in your presentation. First, people learn better through **dual coding,** *the use of words accompanied by other sensory stimuli.*[1] Because people learn through each of their senses—seeing, hearing, touching, tasting, and smelling—presentations that use more than one sense can open a completely different channel through which learning can occur.

Chapter Nine   Visual Resources and Presentation Technology   **185**

T R Y T H I S

Create a list of the most effective visual aids that you have seen teachers use. What do you remember about these visual aids? What made them effective in your opinion? Do you feel that you learned from them?

Second, people remember information better when sensory aids are used. Researchers have found that after listening to presentations in which visual aids are used, audience members remember approximately 85% of the content three hours later and 65% of the content after three days.[2] The same presentation without visual aids results in lower recall. Audience members remember only 70% of the information after three hours and only 10% of the information after three days. The lesson of this research is simple: Using a visual aid can have a significant impact on whether audiences remember your message.

Third, in addition to helping audience members learn and remember information from your presentation, sensory aids hold their attention and motivate them to listen.[3] Because we think much faster than someone can talk, much of our mental energy is wasted anticipating or daydreaming during presentations when the speaker talks the entire time. As a presenter, by using sensory aids you are better able to build interest and maintain audience members' attention.

Finally, effective sensory aids result in clearer messages. Using a picture or model to illustrate a complex idea can do wonders to help audience members understand your point. Moreover, by taking time to carefully locate or create your sensory aids, you will likely gain valuable knowledge that will help you explain the concept more effectively. In short, sensory aids have the potential to dramatically improve your presentation.

Types of Visual Aids and Other Sensory Resources

Because the technology has become so accessible, presenters from students to professional speakers have grown to rely on computers as a primary resource for visual and sensory aids. Of course, other options—posters, music, videos, and even handouts—still exist. This section discusses when to use each type.

Electronic and Multimedia Resources

Many classrooms are equipped with a computer and digital projector. Some classrooms even have sophisticated audio systems. If your classroom does not have this technology, mobile carts with a computer and projector might be available for use. Computers are particularly useful for presenting **multimedia materials,** which are *digital or electronic sensory resources that combine text, graphics, video, and sound into one package.* Of course, not every multimedia presentation combines all these elements. Presenters commonly use computers to show text and images to the audience; using the computer to present video and sound is less common.

Although a variety of methods can be used to present multimedia materials with a computer, we limit our discussion to the use of PowerPoint, the popular

E-Note

POWERPOINT HELP ON THE WEB

Because many students have already learned how to use PowerPoint to create basic slides, this chapter does not devote specific attention to how the program works. If you would like simple directions on how to create slides, you should visit the PowerPoint tutorial created by Act360°: **http://www.actden.com/pp/**.

presentation software from Microsoft. In particular, we examine how you can use PowerPoint to display text, tables, graphs, flowcharts, pictures, and video. The section concludes with general tips for using PowerPoint in your presentations.

Text Slides

How many times have you been in a class where the teacher shows one bullet list after another? Are those classes more exciting because of the colorful slides with text? Or not? Were you able to take notes more effectively because of them? Did the teacher seem more spontaneous or more restricted because of the slides? These questions highlight the dilemma presenters face when deciding whether or not to use a substantial number of text slides in their presentation. Simply defined, a **text slide** *relies primarily on words and phrases to show audience members information.*

Figure 9.1 shows an effective text slide created in PowerPoint. Notice how the text is organized by "bullets" and that the text is sized to fill the entire slide.

Text slides do some things well and other things not so well. Research consistently demonstrates that when written messages accompany oral information, as when text slides are used, people tend to remember the information more easily; research also suggests that written messages do little to motivate and inspire listeners.[4] Because too many text slides can actually be distracting for the listener, you should avoid using more than a few during your presentation; you are better off limiting their use to your most important or most difficult information. When using text slides, placing information into "bullet points" is often more effective than using paragraphs and complete sentences. Second, make sure that you spend enough time explaining each point on the slide. Listeners become frustrated if you spend too much time on one bullet and ignore others. Finally, avoid placing extraneous information on your slides so that audience members will not be distracted from your message.

Figure 9.1 **Text slide with bullet list.** Text slides highlight key words, phrases, and numbers.

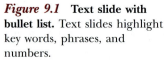

Watch the video clip titled "Presenting a PowerPoint Build" on the CD-ROM.

High-Speed Cable vs. High-Speed DSL	Cable	DSL
Cost	Modem included $50 Startup $30 per month	$150 for modem $60 startup $30 per month
Speed	2 mps downloads *Speed can slow in high-volume neighborhoods*	1.5 mps downloads *Speed drops with distance*
Problems	If cable is out, Internet is out	Must live within 3 miles of the signal source

Figure 9.2 **Table comparing high-speed Internet options.** Tables efficiently summarize, compare, and contrast information.

Tables

Tables *use text and/or numbers to efficiently summarize, compare, and contrast information.* When you insert a table into PowerPoint, you will need to know in advance the number of columns and rows that you need—including any rows or columns for headings and labels. For that reason, we recommend that you draw a rough sketch of your table so that you know the exact dimensions before you attempt to create it on the computer.

TRY THIS

Practice making a table by sketching out the rows and columns necessary to compare and contrast the right for people to assemble, speak freely, and practice their religious preferences in China, Mexico, and the United States. When creating your table, you will need to create headings for your rows and columns to clearly distinguish the topics being organized.

Both text tables and number tables can be used to compare and contrast ideas. The table in Figure 9.2 combines text and numbers to compare and contrast two high-speed Internet products. Notice how the speaker can illustrate differences between high-speed cable Internet and high-speed DSL Internet by pointing to differences between the two columns.

When using tables, practice discussing the information. As you can tell from the sample table, these types of slides contain a great deal of information, and presenters often underestimate the amount of time necessary to explain them adequately. Limiting your tables to key information and making them well organized can help you explain them more efficiently. As a rule of thumb, plan on spending about two minutes discussing tables.

Charts

A common feature of all **charts** is that they are *used to visually display quantitative or statistical information.* Because charts are intended to simplify complex numbers, taking time to carefully plan the layout and labels for a chart is important. Here is a list of the most commonly used charts in PowerPoint:

1. *Bar and column charts.* **Bar and column charts** typically *illustrate differences between categories of information.* In the example provided in Figure 9.3, the numbers of cases of theft, vandalism, and violent crime on campus are compared across three years. This *column chart* provides a quick method of comparing the occurrences of different types of crime across time. It usually doesn't matter whether you use a bar chart, which displays them horizontally, or a column chart, which displays them vertically.

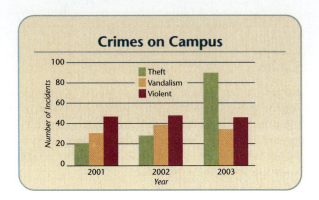

Figure 9.3 **Column chart on campus crime.** Column charts typically illustrate differences between categories (theft, vandalism, violent crime) of information (crime).

2. *Line charts.* **Line charts** *illustrate trends in quantitative data.* If you want to show how sales for a company have increased or decreased, or if you want to show trends in projected number of college graduates over the next five years, a line chart would be a perfect option. Line charts plot "dots" or markers to represent a value recorded at a point in time. Once several markers are created, a line is drawn to connect the dots and illustrate the trend. Of course, PowerPoint does all this for you. A sample line chart is provided in Figure 9.4.

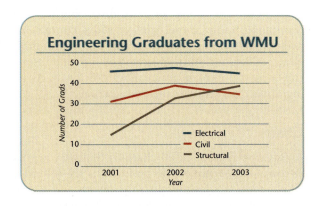

Figure 9.4 **Line chart on engineering graduates over a three-year period.** Line charts show trends, often over a period of time.

3. *Pie charts.* **Pie charts** are used to *show percentages of a whole.* If you wanted to show the percentage of students at your school who are from different ethnic groups, for instance, a pie chart would be very useful. Or, if you wanted to show the percentages of Americans who are Democrat, Republican, and Independent voters, a pie chart would usefully illustrate the numbers. Pie charts are particularly useful because the sizes of the pie pieces visually illustrate the proportion of people or items in each category. The example shown in Figure 9.5 is a pie chart showing the results of two survey questions about cancer risk among college age students. Notice how placing both pie charts on the same slide allows audience members to easily see the difference between college students' perceptions about cancer risk and their actual knowledge.

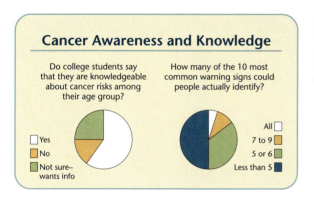

Figure 9.5 **Sample pie charts.** Pie charts show percentages of a whole.

Ohio University Health Communication students, Fall 2004.

Flowcharts

Flowcharts are *diagrams that represent a hierarchical structure or process.* Flowcharts might be used to illustrate various positions within a company or organization. For instance, the organizational flowchart in Figure 9.6 shows the leadership positions within a student club. You might also use a flowchart to represent a process, as in the example illustrating how margarine is made. This type of flowchart is illustrated in Figure 9.7.

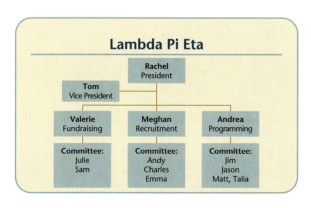

Figure 9.6 **Organizational flowchart for Lambda Pi Eta, the communication studies honor society sponsored by the National Communication Association.**

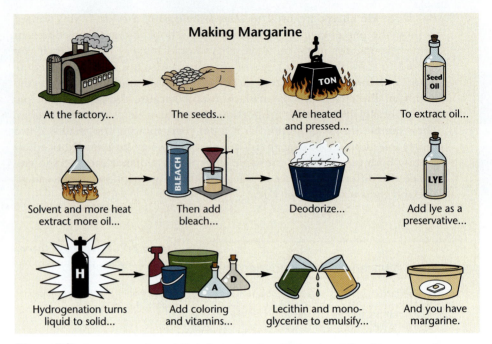

Figure 9.7 **A process-oriented flowchart showing the process of making margarine.** Flowcharts represent a hierarchy or process.

Pictures

Presentations are often enhanced by using pictures to show audience members objects, places, and even people being discussed. However, most public speaking teachers warn students that passing pictures around during a presentation is not a good idea because the activity becomes very distracting. Moreover, most pictures are so small that not everyone can see the picture if it is held up. Fortunately, PowerPoint is an easy way to display pictures so that everyone can see them.

Presenters have three basic options for using PowerPoint to display pictures. First, many pictures are available via the Internet. For instance, you can use Google.com to search for pictures related to key words associated with your topic. Remember that using a picture from the Internet is just like using a quotation—you must credit the source for the picture. Another option is to use a digital camera to take a picture. With the price of digital cameras plummeting to less than a hundred dollars, finding someone with access to one is relatively easy. Finally, if you have conventional photographs and access to a scanner, you can scan photos directly into PowerPoint. If you are unfamiliar with how to work with pictures in PowerPoint, we recommend that you ask your instructor for the location of a lab or resource person on campus. Remember that if you need to find or take pictures for use during your presentation, you will need to build extra time into your preparation process.

> *José Acosta planned to incorporate several of the pictures that he had found in his grandfather Salvador's picture chest into a PowerPoint presentation. José located the multimedia lab at his campus library and spoke to the lab*

Chapter Nine   Visual Resources and Presentation Technology   191

Figure 9.8 A picture combined with text in PowerPoint.

Figure 9.9 A picture used as a visual aid.

assistant about scanning the photos. In just a few minutes, José was able to scan several photos, maps, and other drawings that he had found in Salvador's box. Although José had never scanned a photo before, the lab assistant at the multimedia center was able to teach him how to scan photos in a matter of minutes.

Regardless of what type of picture you want to show—photos, computer generated graphics, or even drawings—the methods of inserting the pictures into PowerPoint remain the same. You can even use PowerPoint to create very basic pictures. Figures 9.8 and 9.9 show two slides used by José in his presentation about his grandfather. The first figure combines the crest of the 65th Infantry Regiment with text that briefly explains the history of the unit. The second picture shows the places his grandfather traveled to during his time in the service. These slides were used in the second part of José's presentation when he explained his grandfather's service to our country.

Video

Presenters have traditionally used videotape to present full-motion video during their presentations. Of course, this option still exists and most digital projectors can accommodate input from a VCR or even a DVD player. However, incorporating video into PowerPoint is easy, and if the clips are short (which they should be), there are advantages to using PowerPoint to display the video. Gaining access to digital video is easy if you have a digital camcorder or if you have a video converter attached to your computer. Digital camcorders are still somewhat expensive but digital video converters are typically less than $100. Many campuses have multimedia computer labs equipped to convert standard videotape to digital video.

Once you have digital video, incorporating the video into PowerPoint is no different from incorporating a picture. When you play the slide and use the mouse to click on the video, the clip will play automatically. The advantage of using PowerPoint to play the video is that you do not have to worry about switching the projector from PowerPoint (the computer) to the VCR and back again. Also, by

To see how video can be incorporated into PowerPoint, watch the speech titled "How to Play the Drums" on the accompanying CD-ROM.

Part Two Selecting and Arranging Content

creating and editing the digital video, you have complete control over how long the clip is and what the audience is able to see.

General Tips on Using PowerPoint

As a tool for public presentations, PowerPoint has begun to receive negative attention because of blunders made by poorly trained presenters.[5] Although many presenters are ineffective in the way they use PowerPoint, you should not assume that the program itself is the problem. In fact, a few simple suggestions can help you avoid the most common PowerPoint blunders.

1. *Don't overload the number of slides.* Having so many slides that you cannot possibly talk intelligently about any of them is a problem many presenters face. The ease with which we can create slides often makes including "one more" too tempting. As a general rule of thumb, you should not have more than one slide per minute. One slide every two minutes is an even better average.

2. *Don't overload any one slide.* The number of words, figures, or pictures on one slide should not exceed the amount a person can process in 30 seconds. As a practical matter, a maximum of four or five lines of text is a good rule to follow.

3. *Use a large type font.* Slides should never use less than 28-point font. Smaller type fonts are difficult to see for people sitting more than a few rows back. Also, you should stick to fonts like Times, Courier, or Arial rather than fonts based on script or handwritten typefaces, which are harder to read at a distance.

4. *Select colors with contrast.* Although PowerPoint provides many options for preset templates, take care to use coloring schemes that allow for substantial contrast between text and the background. Also take care when creating graphs and charts so that lines, bars, and pie pieces effectively contrast with the background. Also remember that dark slides shown in a darkened room can lull audience members to sleep!

5. *Avoid unnecessary images and effects.* Using too many clipart images or several fancy animation schemes can cause your presentation to appear shallow. Allowing PowerPoint slides to draw attention away from you, the presenter, is a common mistake made by inexperienced speakers. Your message, rather than the PowerPoint slides, should be the centerpiece of your presentation.

6. *Have a backup plan.* Computers fail, files get lost or corrupted, and projectors sometimes do not turn on. Most teachers will expect you to be prepared to make your presentation on the day assigned regardless of whether PowerPoint is cooperating. Taking time to print slides and copy them onto color transparencies is wise.

7. *Do not read slides to the audience.* Inexperienced presenters often forget that the audience can read. Reading text to the audience is time wasted in a presentation. Explaining points on a slide, providing conclusions that should be drawn from information on a slide, and talking about how the information on the slide bolsters your central idea and main points is a much more valuable use of time.

8. *Do not use the computer as an anchor.* Inexperienced presenters often fall into the habit of standing behind the computer while presenting. This behavior destroys your conversational delivery and takes focus away from

Cultural Note

VISUAL AID PREFERENCES AMONG CO-CULTURES

Modern presenters, probably in your class too, must be prepared to talk in front of a diverse set of people representing multiple co-cultures. A **co-culture** is *a group of people whose beliefs or behaviors distinguish it from the larger culture of which it is a part and with which it shares numerous similarities.* Little research has been done on the preferences for visual aids among different co-cultures. Vonnette Austin-Wells and Graham McDougall, researchers from the School of Nursing at the University of Texas, explored what type of visual aids work best when speaking to elderly listeners, who we may think of as forming a kind of co-culture. Austin-Wells and McDougall asked people at an independent living facility, an assisted living facility, and a senior center to watch three presentations—one using a flipchart, one using an overhead projector, and one using PowerPoint. Which do you think the older audience members liked best, the high-tech PowerPoint, the low-tech flipchart, or the tried-and-true overhead? Results of the study overwhelmingly favored PowerPoint. Across all three sites for the study, 27 of the audience members favored PowerPoint and only 7 favored the overhead—none liked the flipchart the best. During interviews with the audience members, Austin-Wells and McDougall discovered that the audience members liked the bold colors, large font, and clarity of the PowerPoint slides.

SOURCE: Vonnette Austin-Wells, Teena Zimmerman, and Graham J. McDougall, "An Optimal Delivery Format for Presentations Targeting Older Adults," *Educational Gerontology* 29.6 (2003): 493–502.

you. Asking a classmate to advance the slides based on your cues during the presentation is much more effective. Better yet, some computers are equipped with a remote mouse that allows you to advance slides while you are standing in the front of the classroom away from the computer.

9. *Use blank slides to hide your presentation.* One rule, which we discuss later, is that visual aids should not be visible when you are not referencing them. PowerPoint seemingly makes this difficult because you do not want to turn the projector on and off during the presentation. However, you can easily

Although few studies have been done related to visual aid preferences among different co-cultures, there is research that suggests that older audience members like PowerPoint.

insert blank slides between slides with content, so that a blank background is being displayed when you are not specifically referencing slides. Of course, these blank slides do not "count" toward the 1–2 slides-per-minute rule.

> ### TRY THIS
>
> *Develop a sensory/visual aid plan for your presentation. Start by listing the number of content slides you intend to use. Then, identify how many blank slides you will need so that all content slides are visible only when you are talking about them. How many slides should you create in total for your presentation?*

10. *Practice, practice, practice.* This suggestion is certainly not new, nor will this be the last time you read it. Yet, the importance of practicing your presentation takes on new urgency with the use of PowerPoint. Besides becoming used to the new technology, you will want to determine how long you will need to explain and analyze each slide that you present.

Other Visual and Sensory Resources

PowerPoint has become a very popular tool for use in presentations. Now let's look at other options available to you as a presenter for incorporating visual and sensory aids. Of course, the decision on which type of visual/sensory aid to use should be determined by your specific objective for the presentation. You should avoid using the chalkboard/dry erase board or hand-drawn posters because these types of visual aids often lack professionalism and detract from your credibility as a presenter.

Yourself as a Visual Aid

When presenting on topics with which you have significant personal experience, you are often your best visual aid. Amelia, a public communication student, was a black belt in the martial arts and used herself and a friend to demonstrate simple self-defense techniques. Because her presentation described actions and "moves," such personal demonstration was necessary. Amelia even asked for volunteers from the audience to practice several of the techniques as the presentation progressed.

Preetha, a public speaking student from India, used herself as a presentation aid when she

By using costumes and demonstrating behaviors, you can be your own visual aid.

presented an informative talk on Indian culture. Preetha dressed in traditional Indian attire for her presentation and performed a traditional Indian folk dance to illustrate folk traditions in Indian culture. You could do the same thing by performing for the audience or acting out something related to your presentation.

Objects

Any type of physical object can be used as a visual aid. When presenting a speech on percussion in rock music, David set up a drum set to show different pieces of equipment used by modern drummers. Teachers throughout the building were particularly impressed with the solo performed for his attention-getter. Other objects could include tools, historical artifacts, equipment used to play sports, devices like a hand-held computer, or water and air filters for the home.

Objects like drums can be used to enhance the sensory experience for audience members when they are appropriate to the topic.

Presenters sometimes pass objects around during their presentation. Although this approach can provide a memorable experience for audience members, you should avoid passing around valuable or breakable objects. Also, remember that objects will not reach all audience members while you are referencing them unless you have several of them. Jamie effectively used this approach during her presentation on the geology of the Flint Hills region of Kansas. She passed around several (10 or more) rocks with fossils. After showing how to identify the fossils, Jamie pointed out that the fossils provided evidence that Kansas was once a thriving seabed. Each audience member was able to see—and feel—what Jamie was talking about because she had nearly enough objects so that each audience member could look at them during her description. Be sure to check with your instructor before planning to pass around objects—some instructors discourage their use because audience members may become distracted.

Use common sense when selecting objects for use in your speech. You should never bring potentially dangerous objects like live animals or weapons. Audience members are always uncomfortable during presentations with live snakes, fencing swords, knives, and firearms. Depending on the expectations of your university, other objects might also be inappropriate. For instance, would displaying a condom be considered acceptable or unacceptable at your university or in your particular classroom? This question reinforces the importance of audience analysis—visual aids require careful forethought on your part about the audience and the situation.

Models

Sometimes bringing an actual object is not feasible. Very few classrooms can physically accommodate whales, nuclear submarines, cars, homes, cities, ancient ruins,

196 Part Two Selecting and Arranging Content

or wind farms. In such cases, a model might be a better option. **Models** are *scaled representations of an actual object or objects.* You encounter models all the time in classes. Rarely do Anatomy and Physiology students get to play *CSI* on a cadaver; however, models of the human body commonly populate these classrooms. Do you remember the tried-and-true science fair project of building a working volcano out of clay, baking soda, food coloring, and vinegar? These types of models can be both informative and interesting for audiences.

Locating or preparing a model can take a great deal of time and models may be very expensive. Taking time to plan well in advance is therefore necessary for this approach. Even the decision to make your own model (say of a city or of a rainforest ecosystem) is very time consuming. Allow at least a week to plan and prepare such visual aids.

Audio and Video

Computers and PowerPoint offer a number of options for finding and playing audio and video. If your classroom does not have a computer or if the computer cannot play your files, you must find other means. And, sometimes it is just more practical to avoid using PowerPoint. Taking time to prepare a PowerPoint presentation when all you want to do is show a 30-second clip from a TV show would be a poor use of your time. Of course, if you intend to use PowerPoint regardless, adding the clips to your PowerPoint file makes sense.

Audio and video can effectively spice up a presentation when used correctly. Joel gave an informative presentation on Led Zeppelin's influence on modern rock and effectively used short clips of songs to introduce unique aspects of Led Zeppelin's music. Joel took care to use only short clips and tried to play instrumental sections of songs so that he could still speak over the music. In her presentation on the formation of black holes, Kim used a short clip from a documentary by astrophysicist Stephen Hawking to explain how black holes are detected.

Avoid using more than a few clips throughout your presentation, and limit the clips to 20 or 30 seconds. Plan in advance how you intend to play the clips. If your classroom is equipped with a VCR, make sure you know how the unit works—classrooms are often set up differently from your home entertainment system. If you intend to use audio, make sure that you can find a way of playing the clip so that everyone can easily hear the sound.

Slide Transparencies

Although slide transparencies are becoming increasingly outdated because of computer technology, professionals in fields like the sciences, history, and theater often use slides to display pictures and photographs. Other professors might have such resources available if you do not have slides of your own. Trey, a theater major, showed slides obtained from his lighting design professor to illustrate lighting concepts used during the previous theater season at his university. You should follow many of the same suggestions we provided for using PowerPoint if you intend to use slide transparencies.

Overhead Transparencies

If your classroom is not equipped with the equipment necessary for using Power-Point, you can still take advantage of the resources offered by the program by printing PowerPoint slides on a color printer using transparency film—you can also take color printouts to a copy center for color duplication onto transparencies. Ensure that your overheads are in order and that they do not stick together before coming to class. If you fumble around with your transparencies during your presentation, you will appear unprepared. Placing sheets of white paper between the transparencies will help you stay organized and ease transitions. Also, remember to turn off the overhead projector when you are not referencing a transparency—unlike computer projectors, overhead projectors can be turned on and off multiple times during a short talk.

Handouts

Handouts helped Sally convince audience members to attend a "Race for the Cure" walk held to raise awareness about breast cancer. She provided listeners with information about the event and also gave them the Web address for the American Cancer Society. In this case, handouts helped Sally make direct appeals to the audience for their support for breast cancer prevention.

However, presenters must plan carefully when using handouts. Detailed notes and lengthy, technical information can distract listeners from the actual message. Even the act of passing materials around can be distracting for both the presenter and the listener. Hand materials out either right before or right after the presentation. Regardless of when you distribute materials, make sure that you reference them during your presentation. For instance, "The pamphlet that I passed around before identifies the location where the rally will take place," or "At the end of my presentation I will provide you with a flier identifying the Web address for the American Cancer Society" are ways to effectively reference your handout while speaking. You should also consider asking one or two members of the audience to pass out the materials so you can concentrate on your presentation.

Now that you can identify several options for using visual and sensory aids during your presentation, you should devote particular attention to using them effectively and ethically. This section provides tips and advice for integrating visual and sensory resources into your talk.

Tips on Using Visual and Sensory Aids

1. *Be audience-centered when selecting sensory aids.* When presenting a persuasive presentation on the need to eliminate "junk mail," Katherine passed around several perfume and cologne samples found in popular magazines. Several of the audience members were overwhelmed by the smells—nearly to the point of having to leave the classroom. Katherine unwittingly caused some of the annoyance that she was trying to argue persuasively against. Remember to think like an audience member when selecting sensory aids for your presentation.

TRY THIS

How might your use of visual or sensory aids differ for the following types of audiences?

- *A group of very young children*
- *A group of international visitors who speak English as a second language*
- *A group of college students*

2. *Be ethical.* Using inappropriate, dangerous, or unpleasant sensory aids can detract from your message and destroy your credibility. Indeed, presenters have an ethical responsibility not to use or display dangerous, obscene, or offensive materials. Some teachers require that you get approval for all sensory resources used during your presentation. Even if your teacher does not require formal approval, a short discussion about your plans could help you avoid problems when you give your presentation.

3. *Keep the content of your sensory aid clear and relevant.* Although you are responsible for explaining all visual and sensory aids, most should be easily understood by audience members after a few moments of reflection. Remember that irrelevant sensory aids can do more to confuse, rather than enhance, your presentation.

4. *Explain your visual aids.* The time spent carefully crafting a chart or graph is wasted if you do not explain what the graph means. Presenters often fail to explain what conclusion should be drawn from visual aids. Even pictures should be explained well enough so that audience members understand what they represent. Seeing well-done visual aids and not getting appropriate explanation is frustrating for listeners.

5. *Understand that using sensory aids takes time.* Besides the significant time involved in locating and/or creating sensory aids, such resources take time during the presentation. A 7-minute presentation can easily become a 15-minute presentation with the addition of three or four detailed visual aids. Though different types of sensory aids take different amounts of time to explain, allowing at least two minutes for the presentation and explanation of sensory aids is wise.

6. *Avoid being too simple or too complex.* Sensory aids should be professional, but they should not overwhelm the message. Hand-drawn posters, lists of ideas on the chalkboard, or hastily created PowerPoint slides cause your presentation to appear unprofessional and insincere. Likewise, trying to use every feature in PowerPoint, including animated transitions and the ever-popular "machine gun" sound for list builds, may be entertaining in your dorm room at two in the morning but will do little to impress audience members. Special effects can even be annoying if used to extreme.

7. *Strive for professionalism.* Take care to ensure that your visual aids are easy to read. If you use audio and/or video, make sure that the audio is loud enough to be heard easily and that the video is of the highest quality possible. Practicing your talk with the sensory aids is essential for giving a professional-looking presentation.

8. *Hide your visual aid when not in use.* Whether you are using an object, PowerPoint file, overhead, or even another person to help you demonstrate something, do your best to display the visual aid only when necessary. Asking your partner to step to the side of the classroom, placing the object behind the lectern, turning off the overhead projector, or using blank slides in PowerPoint are all ways you can accomplish this. Audience members might be tempted to look at the visual aid rather than at you if you do not remove the temptation.

Remember Your Purpose

Although it is an important skill, using visual and sensory aids is secondary to your main goal of communicating with audience members—such aids are simply one of many means to that end. Remember that your use of visual and sensory aids should not take the place of effective delivery, attention to organization and style, and good research. Presentation aids are just that—they supplement the message that you have already created. Your presentation is likely to be better with them than without them, but good visual aids will do little to make up for an otherwise poorly done presentation.

Resources for Review and Discussion

SUMMARY

In this chapter you have learned the following:

▶ Sensory aids improve presentations because they help listeners learn more and stay more involved with the message.
- Sensory aids are resources other than the presenter that stimulate listeners. The most common type is visual aids.
- Sensory aids improve presentations because people learn better from multiple media, they are more motivated to listen, and they perceive your message more accurately.

▶ With a computer and digital projector you can use PowerPoint to display a variety of types of visual and sensory aids.
- Text slides use words and phrases to provide audience members with information.
- Tables combine text and numbers to efficiently present information. They are particularly useful when you want to compare and contrast two or more things.
- Charts efficiently display pictures of quantitative data. Bar or column charts, line charts, and pie charts are among the most common.
- Flowcharts are diagrams that represent a hierarchical structure or process.
- By using images from the Internet, a digital camera, or a scanner, you can easily integrate pictures into your PowerPoint slides.
- Audio and video can be integrated into your PowerPoint presentation by using a digital camcorder or a digital converter attached to a computer. Audio and video clips should be short.

▶ Slides should be clear, easy to read, and simple. Have a backup plan in case your PowerPoint file cannot be used, and concentrate on preparing and delivering an effective presentation rather than relying on "PowerPoint pizzazz" to impress the audience.

▶ Other types of sensory aids can include yourself, objects, models, audio and video, slide transparencies, overhead transparencies, and handouts.

▶ Before integrating sensory aids into your presentation, you should take care to make sure that they are effective and ethical.
- Produce professional sensory aids that are audience-centered. Never use a sensory aid that could be dangerous or offensive.
- Explain your sensory aids to the audience by discussing how they directly relate to your central idea or main points.

▶ Practicing your presentation with sensory aids reveals how much time is needed to adequately explain each visual aid.

▶ Practicing good delivery techniques and hiding your sensory aids when they are not needed are ways to avoid distracting the audience from your message.

KEY TERMS

 Use the *Public Speaking* CD-ROM and the Online Learning Center at www.mhhe.com/nelson to practice your understanding of the following terminology.

Bar/column chart	Line chart	Tables
Chart	Models	Text slide
Co-culture	Multimedia materials	Visual aids
Dual coding	Pie chart	
Flowchart	Sensory aids	

REFERENCES

[1]Gellevij, Mark, et al. (2002). Multimodal versus unimodal instruction in a complex learning context. *Journal of Experimental Education, 70.3,* 215–41.

[2]Zayas-Boya, Emile P. Instructional media in the total language picture. *International Journal of Instructional Media, 5,* 145–50.

[3] Alley, Michael (2003). *The craft of scientific presentations: Critical steps to succeed and critical errors to avoid.* New York: Springer.

[4] Kiewra, K. A. (1985). Students' notetaking behaviors and the efficacy of providing the instructor's notes for review. *Contemporary Educational Psychology, 10,* 378–86.

[5] Norvig, Peter (2003). PowerPoint: Shot with its own bullets. *Lancet, 362.9381,* 343.

APPLICATION EXERCISES

 Go to the self-quizzes on the *Public Speaking* CD-ROM and the Online Learning Center at www.mhhe.com/nelson to test your knowledge of the chapter concepts.

1. Practice creating a PowerPoint presentation that integrates pictures from the Internet. Assume that your task is to create a short, 5–7 minute presentation on your university for new students. Using PowerPoint and your university Web site, locate and integrate pictures and graphics that you could use in your presentation. Remember that the source of each graphic should be identified on the slide where it is used—you can use a text box to create the reference.

2. Using the following data, create an appropriate graph or table to use during a presentation. You may have enough data to create more than one graph or table:

   A poll conducted by a nonprofit group attempted to determine differences in people's perceptions about crime depending on whether they watched more or less than 20 hours of television per week. Those who watched more than 20 hours per week were labeled as high rate viewers, and those who watched less than 20 hours per week were labeled low rate viewers. Results of the poll found that 30 percent of the low rate viewers perceived crime to be increasing whereas 81 percent of high rate viewers did. When broken down by age, high rate viewers over the age of 35 had the highest percentage, believing crime to be on the rise, with 87 percent, followed by high rate viewers under 35 with 75 percent, low rate viewers under 35 with 32 percent and low rate viewers over 35 with 28 percent. When asked to comment on their perceptions, high rate viewers typically responded something like, "Crime is everywhere—you see it every night when you turn on the news." Low rate viewers typically responded, "I feel safe in my neighborhood—I know everyone and we look out for each other."

3. A necessary skill when creating text slides is identifying key information so that the number of text slides can be limited. Create one or more text slides using the information covered in the sections "General Tips on Using PowerPoint" on page 192, and "Tips on Using Visual and Sensory Aids" on page 197.

CHAPTER TEN

We believe that an informed citizenry will act for life and not for death.

ALBERT EINSTEIN

In your thirst for knowledge, be sure not to drown in all the information.

ANTHONY J. D'ANGELO, *THE COLLEGE BLUE BOOK*

Presenting to Inform

What will you learn?

When you have read and thought about this chapter, you will be able to:

1. Explain the two principles of informative presentations.
2. Compare the four purposes of informative presentations.
3. Demonstrate the principles of learning that can be applied to informative presentations.
4. Describe how you should organize information within your informative presentation to optimize learning.
5. Explain the skills that are used in informative presentations.
6. Discuss the ethical choices you should make in informative presentations.

You know a great deal of useful information and you have a number of useful skills. As you learn more in college and in life, you may find yourself communicating your knowledge to your children, colleagues, clients, or community. The purpose of this chapter is to examine the primary means of communicating information to other people: the informative presentation.

204 Part Three Types of Presentations

Amanda Greene, a sophomore and a single mother of three young children, is older than many other students. Her day at school can best be described as hectic. On this particular morning, she has an 8:00 A.M. class, which means she must be up at 6:00 to bathe, dress, and prepare breakfast for the kids. At 7:30 she is at the day care center where she has to tell the teacher that a friend will pick up her youngest daughter at 1:30 so her child can keep an appointment with the doctor.

Amanda arrives at the classroom just five minutes before the bell. She is lucky to be a little early because she wants to ask the professor about the length of the term paper and whether or not the paper is to be double-spaced.

On her way to the next class, she sees her friend Diane, another busy student-mother, and arranges to meet her for lunch at the Oasis, a popular gathering place for nontraditional students. At noon Diane asks Amanda what she should do about her two-year-old, who cried much of the night. If it is an ear infection, she asks, does she have to go to the doctor or will an over-the-counter drug do the trick? Amanda recommends the free clinic and in turn asks Diane about where she can get information for her presentation, which is due next week.

We will follow Amanda no further through her day because the point is already well made: Amanda, like all of us, provides and receives information many times each day. The only difference between our everyday conversations and the informative presentation, the subject of this chapter, is that the presentation is longer, better organized, better researched, and delivered to more people. Amanda Greene's conversations with the others are similar in many ways to informative presentations. Let us consider some of those similarities.

1. You inform people with information they want to know, need to know, or can use when they want to know about it.
2. You adapt language that describes your knowledge to increase their understanding.
3. You define, explain, and give examples that help them apply the knowledge to their situation.

In this chapter you will discover the rhetorical principles for communicating information, the purposes of informative presentations, and the principles of learning that are especially important for communicating information to an audience. At the end of this chapter, you will find a checklist for the informative presentation. You will soon discover how important informative presenting is to our democratic ideals and to your future success.[1]

Principles of Informative Presentations

Two fundamental principles should guide your informative presentations. These are *to relate the presenter to the topic* and *to relate the topic to the audience*. Although they are important to any presentation, these principles require special emphasis in informative presentations because they focus on the relationships between the presenter and the topic and the audience and the topic. Audiences are more likely to listen to a presentation if (1) they believe the speaker is well informed and connected to the topic, and (2) the information is relevant to them.

Relate the Presenter to the Topic

The first rhetorical principle states that you, the informative presenter, must show the audience the relationship between you and your topic. What are your qualifications for speaking on the subject? How did you happen to choose this topic? Why should the audience pay particular attention to you on this issue?

Here is an example of how one student related his topic to himself:

> You heard the teacher call my name: Gary Klineschmidt. This is a German name. My grandparents came from Germany, and the small community in which I live—New Ulm—is still predominantly German with a full allotment of Klopsteins, Kindermanns, Koenigs, and Klineschmidts. Many German customs are still practiced today in my home and in my hometown. Today I want to tell you about one German custom that has been adopted by many Americans and two German customs that are practiced primarily by people of German descent.

The presenter established a relationship between himself and his topic by stating explicitly the origins of his authority to speak on German customs.

Pat Sajak, the host of *Wheel of Fortune,* gave an address at Hillsdale College in Hillsdale, Michigan, on April 4, 2002. He related the topic to himself as he noted,

> I, of course, attended Game Show University. All the great game show hosts did. I lived in the Bob Barker Dorm. I majored in vowels and consonants. It was a tough program. In the *Jeopardy* course, I had to know the questions instead of the answers. My thesis was called: "Lovely Parting Gifts: Are they really all that lovely?" Of course, the upside was that if I got stumped during finals, I was allowed to use 50/50 or phone a friend.[2]

The point is that you must relate the topic to yourself, so that the audience will respect and apply the information you communicate. Are you giving a presentation on the steps in ethical decision-making? Let the audience know about your involvement with the Boy Scouts of America. Are you giving a presentation on historic preservation? If you are a student at SUNY Plattsburgh, you might talk about your involvement with Adopt-a-Block. Are you giving a presentation on the path to U.S. citizenship? At Cal State Northridge, you might share your experience with Project S.H.I.N.E., which links college students with older immigrants and refugees who hope to learn English and become U.S. citizens.

Relate the Topic to the Audience

The second rhetorical principle of informative presentations is to relate the topic to the audience early in the presentation to ensure their interest and understanding. Again, you must be explicit: Specifically tell listeners how the topic relates to them. Remember, too, that many topics may be very difficult to justify to an audience. An informative presentation on taxes is lost on an audience that pays none. An informative presentation on the farming of genetically modified food could be lost on an urban audience. Analyze your audience to find out how interested they may be in your proposed topic.

This example demonstrates the rhetorical principle of relating the topic to the audience:

> Over half of you indicated on the audience analysis form that you participate in team sports. We have two football players, two varsity tennis players, one gymnast, three hockey players, and four persons in men's and women's basketball. Because you already possess the necessary dexterity and coordination for athletics here at San Antonio College, today you are going to learn how to apply your strength and flexibility to helping people with disabilities ride horseback.

This presenter carefully detailed the many people for whom the topic is appropriate.

Bob Wright, chair and CEO of NBC and the vice chair and executive officer of General Electric, delivered a presentation at the University of Virginia School of Law in Charlottesville, Virginia, on May 19, 2002. The title of his talk was "No Profession Is More Honorable Than the Law." Wright observed,

> Unfortunately, you young soon-to-be lawyers about to embark on exciting careers end up paying the price. You pay the price in having a public that thinks they don't want or need your services, and a public that doesn't trust your ethics or your honesty.[3]

Wright recognized the importance of relating his topic of distrust of lawyers directly to the audience of law students. When you deliver your informative presentation, remember to relate the topic to yourself and your audience.

View the three CD-ROM videos entitled "Relating a Story," "Citing a Quotation," and "Arousing Curiosity." Which of the three is most effective in fulfilling the two rhetorical principles of informative speaking? Have them explain their answers.

TRY THIS

Topics for informative speeches are all around us. Consider news stories, advertisements, or class lectures that provide unusual words for which you do not know the meaning. Most likely, your classmates are similarly in the dark about these terms. Generate at least five topics based on unknown words or ideas that come from the mass media or recent lectures you have heard. Which of these might be appropriate for a classroom speech?

How to Identify the Purpose of Your Informative Presentations

An **informative presentation** is *one that increases an audience's knowledge about a subject or that helps the audience learn more about an issue or idea.* Four purposes of informative presentations are (1) to create information hunger, (2) to help the audience understand the information, (3) to help the audience remember the information, and (4) to help the audience apply that information. How do you decide which purposes you can meet?

E-Note

RSS—REALLY SIMPLE SYNDICATION

Internet research is being improved all the time. With Google and Yahoo! potentially returning hundreds or even thousands of links in response to a single search request, subscription services such as pluck.com and Onfolio have emerged to feed subscribers a stream of relevant information from credible sources into the user's Web page that is dedicated to the subject.

Create Information Hunger

The first purpose of informative presentations is to *generate a desire for information*—to create **information hunger.** Audiences, like students, are not always receptive to new information. You have observed teachers who were skilled at inspiring your interest in poetry, advanced algebra, chemistry, or physical education. You will have an opportunity to demonstrate whether you are as skilled at communicating information to an audience of classmates.

What are some strategies for creating information hunger? Among the many possibilities are these: arouse audience curiosity, pose a puzzling question for which your presentation is an answer, and provide an explanation for an issue that has confused people.

Arousing Audience Curiosity

A useful strategy for creating information hunger is to arouse audience curiosity about your topic. Consider this speech titled "Competitive Sports: Don't Take Me Out to the Ballgame."

> It is a warm, sunny day out on the baseball field. You, playing shortstop, decide to taunt the upcoming batter with such comments as, "Easy out," "This one can't hit," "He runs like a girl," and so on. All of a sudden, there is commotion in the stands. The game is called to a halt as a fistfight in the stands ends with your father in critical condition. Seems the father of the "easy out" started calling you names, and it all spun out of control. Something like this would never happen though, would it? Unfortunately, this is becoming an all too common scenario in the area of little league and high school sports.

Speakers should use some caution in arousing curiosity. If the speaker's message is too mysterious or bizarre, the audience could lose interest or become distracted. For example, you should not wear a strange costume, behave in a weird manner, or present yourself in a way that is completely out of the ordinary.

Pose a Puzzling Question

One student, Ramona Anderson, induced information hunger this way:

> Have you read your "Mountain Dew" bottle? Your "Diet Pepsi" bottle? Your "Classic Coke" can? If you take the time to read your bottle or can, you will find an interesting message, sometimes in distinctive red print. That message says: "phenylketonurics: Contains Phenylalanine." Is this a message to aliens who dwell among us? Have you ever personally met a "phenylketonuric"? Today you are going to find out what this

208   Part Three   Types of Presentations

label means and why you should read the warning. My presentation is entitled "The Phenylketonurics among Us."[4]

The presenter posed a puzzling question about this mysterious word and its cryptic message. You can start an informative presentation by thinking of other puzzling questions that emerge in everyday life: Who are Sarbanes and Oxley? What is "smart medicine"? What common food is processed with benzene and other chemical solvents? Be sure that your question is truly puzzling and not trite or mundane.

Explain a Confusing Issue

A number of conflicts around the world today receive considerable news coverage without much explanation of the issues: lots of smoke and fire but little light. For example, how many people really understand what a stem cell is? Why is stem cell research controversial? Who supports stem cell research and who opposes it?

If you can locate controversy and confusion in issues like smokers' rights, privacy concerns, and immigration policies, you have found yourself the topic for an informative presentation. Remember, however, that you are trying to explain an issue—to bring light, not heat and smoke. Your purpose is *informative*, not persuasive.

Help the Audience Understand the Information

The second general purpose of informative presentations is to increase the ways in which the audience can respond to the world.

The kind of knowledge we possess affects our perception of the world. A poet can look at a boulevard of trees and write about her vision in a way that conveys nature's beauty to others. A botanist can determine the species of the trees, whether their leaves are pinnate or palmate, and whether the plants are healthy, rare, or unusual. A chemist can note that sulfur dioxide in the air is affecting the trees and estimate how long they can withstand the ravages of pollution. A knowledgeable person may be able to respond to the trees in all these ways. Acquiring more information provides us with a wider variety of ways to respond to the world around us.

Whether the audience is interested in the topic before you present may be less important than the interest they demonstrate after the presentation. Your audience analysis here should help you find out how much the individuals already know about a subject, so you do not bore the informed or overwhelm the ignorant. Narrow the topic so you can discuss an appropriate amount of material in the allotted time. Finally, apply your own knowledge to the task to simplify and clarify the topic.

How can you encourage the audience to understand your topic? Here are some ideas:

1. Remember that *audiences probably understand main ideas and generalizations better than specific facts and details.* Make certain that you state explicitly, or even repeat, the main ideas and generalizations in your informative presentation. Limit yourself to two to three main points.

2. Remember that *audiences are more likely to understand simple words and concrete ideas than complex words and abstract ideas.*[5] Review the content of your informative presentation to discover simpler, more concrete ways of stating the same ideas.

3. Remember that *early remarks about how the presentation will meet the audience's needs can create anticipation and increase the chances that the audience will listen and understand.*[6] In your introduction, be very explicit about how the topic is related to the audience members. Unless your presentation is related to their needs, they may choose not to listen.

4. Remember that *audience members' overt participation increases their understanding.* You can learn by listening and you can learn by doing, but you learn the most—and so will your audience—by both listening and doing.[7] Determine how to encourage your listeners' involvement in your presentation by having them raise hands, stand up, answer a question, comment in a critique, or state an opinion. Some pitfalls can occur when you involve the audience by asking them for overt participation. First, their reaction or participation might not be what you have in mind. Second, they might take more time to respond than you had intended. Third, the audience could become unruly when they are given an opportunity to talk or move around. Be aware of these potential consequences if you decide to encourage overt participation.

These four suggestions are powerful. If you observe your best teachers, you will observe that they regularly use them in their lectures.

Help the Audience Remember the Information

The third general purpose of informative presentations is to help the audience remember important points in your presentation. How can you get listeners to retain important information?

One method is to *reveal to the audience members specifically what you want them to learn from your presentation.* A presenter can tell you about the physiology of long-distance cycling and let you guess what is important until you flounder and eventually forget everything you heard. However, if the presenter announces at the outset, "I want you to remember the three measures of athletic performance: peak use of oxygen, power at peak in watts, and average power during a four- to six-hour ride," you know what to focus on as you listen. Similarly a student presenter at West Virginia University might say, "After this presentation, I will ask you to explain the two primary goals of the West Virginia Energy Express, a service program supported by AmeriCorps." Audiences tend to remember more about an informative presentation if the presenter tells them specifically at the outset what they should remember.

The announcement of the topic can occur in the introduction of the speech or soon thereafter. Some topics encourage you to announce them later. For example, if one of your classmates states, "I want to teach you how to knit," he or she might immediately lose the bulk of the audience. By luring them into the topic before telling them what they are expected to learn, the speaker might stir more audience interest. Rather than announcing the topic right away, the student could hold up some attractive products that are the finished result of knitting and ask something like, "Would you like to own this? Would you like to give it as a present to your spouse or a family member?"

Amanda Greene, the student featured at the beginning of this chapter, decided to give her informative presentation on the welfare system as viewed from a single mother's perspective. Although she regularly shared information about being a mother and had shown her classmates photos of her children, she knew that most of them did not realize that she had taken advantage of some features of public assistance in the past. She also felt that the other students probably had little experience with welfare. In order to be sure that the audience would focus on her specific purpose, she stated in her introduction, "At the end of my presentation, I want you to be able to identify three qualifications to apply for assistance."

A second method of encouraging an audience to remember (and one also closely tied to arousing audience interest) is to indicate clearly in the informative presentation which ideas are **main ideas,** *generalizations to be remembered,* and which are **subordinate ideas,** *details to support the generalizations.* In preparing for examinations many students highlight important points in their textbooks and notebooks with a highlighter pen. You can use the same method in preparing your informative presentation. Highlight the important parts and convey their importance by telling the audience, "You will want to remember this point . . . ," "My second main point is . . . ," or "The critical thing to remember in doing this is . . . ."

Using nonverbal communication such as bodily movement, gestures, and facial expressions can help your audience remember important information.

A third method that encourages an audience to retain important information includes repeating an idea two or three times during the presentation. Audiences expect important parts of the presentation to receive more than temporary attention. They expect important points to be repeated. An early study demonstrated that if you repeat important matters either infrequently (only one time) or too often (four repetitions or more), your audience will be less likely to recall your information.[8] While excessive repetition can be distracting, a second or third restatement can help the audience understand. You can and should follow the popular saying: "tell 'em what you are going to tell 'em; tell 'em; and then tell 'em what you told 'em." Research supports the idea that this is a good recipe for the introduction, body, and conclusion of a presentation. The audience usually expects a summary ending that recaps the main points.[9]

A fourth method of encouraging retention is the nonverbal practice of *pausing or using a physical gesture to indicate the importance of the information.* Just as repetition signals an audience that the thought was important, a dramatic pause or silence just before an important statement is also effective. Similarly, your own energy level signals importance, so using bodily movement, gesture, or facial expression can grab audience attention and underline a statement's importance.

Most of the research on retention has been conducted with middle-class, white audiences. If you are speaking to a more diverse audience, you may want to accept these conclusions cautiously. Some audiences appear to appreciate and learn more from several repetitions. Others may expect a great deal of enthusiasm.[10] How can you ensure that your audience will retain the information that you provide them? In the classroom, listen to your instructors' and classmates' informative presentations and try to determine what these presenters do to inspire you to remember the information. In other settings where you are likely to speak, similarly observe the successful informative presenters you encounter. Then see whether you can apply the same techniques in your own informative presentations.

Help the Audience Apply the Information

The fourth general purpose of informative presentations is to encourage the audience to use or apply the information. An effective presenter determines methods of encouraging the audience to use information quickly. Sometimes the presenter can even determine ways that the audience can use the information during the presentation.

Komiko Tanaka, who was delivering an informative presentation on community engagement, for example, had everyone in class write down where they had engaged in service learning. Another student presenter had each classmate taste foods made with chemicals. Amanda Agogino invited everyone to go online to determine how many articles they could find about accountability in corporate governance. These presenters were encouraging the audience to apply the information from their presentations to ensure that they retained the information.

Why should the informative presenter encourage the audience to use the information as quickly as possible? One reason is that *information applied immediately is remembered longer*. A second reason is that *an action tried once under supervision is more likely to be tried again later*. To think of informative presentations as simply putting an idea into people's heads, of increasing the amount they know about a topic, is easy. However, the presenter has no concrete indication that increased information has been imparted except by observing the audience's behavior.

Therefore, the informative presenter may seek a **behavioral response** from the audience, *an overt indication of understanding*. What behavioral response should the informative presenter seek? Many kinds are possible. You can provoke behavioral response by inviting the audience to talk to others about the topic, to actually apply the information, or to answer questions orally or in writing. If the audience cannot answer a question on the topic before your presentation but can do so afterward, you have effected a behavioral response in your audience.

The four general purposes of informative presentations, then, are to create a desire for information in the audience, to increase audience understanding of the topic, to encourage the audience to remember the information, and to invite the audience to apply the information as quickly as possible. Next we will examine five learning principles that relate to informative presentations.

View the CD-ROM video speech entitled "Competitive Sports." What did the speaker do to create audience hunger and to help them understand, recall, and apply the information? Provide examples.

Cultural Diversity

PRESENTING TO THE ELDERLY

Imagine that you are going to deliver a presentation to residents of an assisted care home. The people in the facility range from age 75 to 101. They are mostly women and most have graduated from college. You have been asked to deliver an informative presentation that will be of interest to them. While 140 people live in the building, you are told that about 90 to 100 will probably attend your talk. You are given 45 minutes to give your talk and to answer questions from the audience. What topics will you consider? How can you relate these topics to yourself and to your audience? How will you create information hunger? How will you help the audience understand, remember, and apply the information you provide? Can you use humor and wit? Will presentational aids be helpful? After you have made some of these decisions, talk with a family friend who is actually in assisted care or seek permission to visit an assisted care facility and chat with some of the residents. What do they think of your ideas? How well do they believe you would do with your presentation?

Principles of Learning

Informative speaking is a type of teaching. Listening to informative presentations is a type of learning. If you expect an audience to understand your informative presentation and apply the knowledge gained, you must treat the presentation as an occasion when teaching and learning both occur. Because you, as an informative presenter, are inviting the audience to learn, you can apply these five **principles of learning** to your presentation: building on the known; using humor and wit; using sensory aids; organizing your information; and rewarding your listeners.

Build on the Known

One principle of learning is that people tend to build on what they already know and to accept ideas that are consonant with what they already know. An informative presentation, by definition, is an attempt to add to what the audience already knows. If the audience is to accept the new information, it must be related to information and ideas they already hold.

Let us say that you are going to give an informative presentation on the topic of depression. What do most people in your audience know about the subject? Do they know the possible causes of depression? Do they know the difference between "feeling down" or "feeling blue" and clinical depression?[11] Do they know the symptoms of depression? Do they know the profiles of the most likely victims? Your mission is to start with audience analysis to determine what the audience knows, and then build on that knowledge with new information, presented so the material will be attractive to a variety of learning styles.

Use Humor and Wit

A second principle of learning to observe in informative speaking is to use humor and wit. **Humor** is *the ability to perceive and express that which is amusing or comical,* while **wit** is *the ability to perceive and express humorously the relationship or similarity*

212

between seemingly incongruous or disparate things. Informative presentations make the information palatable to the audience. Notice that it does not have to be funny. The principle is "Use humor and wit." Wit and humor are the clever ways you make the information attractive to the audience. Wit and humor are the packaging of the content.

One student used wit in his presentation about parenting. He was unmarried, which was well known to his classmates. The audience could hardly hide its shock when he stated in the introduction to his presentation, "I did not think anything of parenting until I had my son." His "son" turned out to be an uncooked hen's egg. He was taking a course on the family in which he was required to care for his "son," the egg, for one week. When he went out on a date, he had to find a "babysitter" to care for the egg. He had to protect the egg from breaking as he went from class to class, take the egg to meals, and tuck the egg in at night. The introduction of his "son," the egg, added wit to the wisdom of his informative presentation on parenting.

Another student began her speech "Have you ever helped someone paint a picture of the White House using only red, orange, and blue paints?" Her presentation focused on Passion Works, a community organization that promotes artistic expression and collaboration among artists with and without developmental disabilities.

Often language choices help add wit and vigor to your presentation. Darris Snelling, who was delivering a potentially boring presentation on "TV and Your Child," but enlivened his presentation with witty language, began this way:

> Within ten years almost everybody in this room will be married with a young one in the crib and another on the way. Do you want your youngster to start babbling with the words sex, violence, and crime or do you want him to say Mommy, Daddy, and pepperoni, like most normal kids?[12]

The presenter hit the audience with the unexpected. The words were witty, and they made his presentation more interesting.

Humor and wit must be used judiciously. Some topics are not appropriate for humor. In addition, simply adding a joke at the beginning of a talk is often misguided. As you can determine from the examples provided above, humor and wit must be appropriate for the topic and must be integrated into the entire message.

Use Sensory Aids

A third principle of learning is to *communicate your message in more than one way because members of the audience have different learning styles.* Verbal/linguistic individuals learn best by listening or reading, while visual/spatial individuals learn best by seeing. Effective informative presenters recognize that different people have varied learning styles. Therefore, such presenters try to communicate their messages in a variety of ways to meet diverse learning styles. In Chapter 9, we discussed sensory aids thoroughly and you may wish to review that material.

A student giving an informative presentation about diversity in higher education used a chart to explain to his audience four main indicators of diversity: college enrollment, college persistence, degrees conferred, and degrees conferred by fields. Because much of his explanation depended on the use of statistics to indicate trends in diversity, he and the audience found the chart necessary for the informative presentation.

You, too, can find a variety of methods of communicating your message to an audience that learns in diverse ways. Some material in an informative presentation is simply too detailed and complex to present orally. You might be able to get more of the message across by presenting these complex materials in a handout to the audience at the conclusion of your presentation. Other complex data may be easier to understand through a graph, a picture, an object, a model, or a person. Consider using every ethical means necessary to get your informative message to the audience.

Organize to Optimize Learning

A fourth principle of learning is to *organize your information for easier understanding.* Organization of a presentation is more than outlining. Outlining is simply creating the skeleton of a presentation. In an informative presentation, consider other organizational possibilities. How can you try to create a proper setting for learning to take place? Where in the presentation should you reveal what you expect the audience to remember? Do you place your most important information early or late in the presentation?

No hard-and-fast answers to these questions exist, but research does hint at some good suggestions:[13]

1. *When do you create a setting for learning?* The earlier you create an atmosphere for learning, the better. Make clear to audience members early in the presentation exactly what you want them to learn from your presentation.

2. *Where should important information be placed?* Audiences remember information placed early and late in the presentation, so avoid placing your most important material in the middle of your presentation. **Primacy,** or *placing the information or main point early in the presentation,* seems to work better in presentations on controversial issues, on topics that the audience cares little about, and on topics highly familiar to the audience. **Recency,** or *placing the information or main point late in your presentation,* seems to work best when audience members care about the issue, when the issue is moderately unfamiliar, and when the topic is not terribly interesting.[14]

3. *How do you indicate which parts of your presentation are main points and which are supporting?* In writing, subordination is easy to indicate by levels of

headings, but people listening to a presentation cannot necessarily visualize the structure of your presentation, which is why the effective informative presenter indicates early in the presentation what is going to be covered. This forecast sets up the audience's expectations; they will know what you are going to talk about and for approximately how long. Similarly, as you proceed through your presentation, you may wish to signal your progress by indicating where you are in your organization through transitions. Among organizational indicators are the following:

"My second point is . . ."

"Now that I have carefully explained a brief history of democracy in the United States, I will describe how democracy is viewed today."

"This story about what happened to me in the service will illustrate my point about obeying orders."

In each case, the presenter is signaling whether the next item is a main point in the presentation or supporting evidence for it.

Reward Your Listeners

A fifth principle of learning is that *audiences are more likely to respond to information that is rewarding for them.* **Reward** in this context means *a psychological or physical reinforcement to increase an audience's response to information given in a presentation.* One of the audience's concerns about an informative presentation is "What's in it for me?" The effective informative presenter answers this question not only in the introduction, where the need for the information is formally explained, but also throughout the presentation. By the time a presenter is in the middle of the presentation, the audience may have forgotten much of the earlier motivating information presented, so the presenter continually needs to remind the audience how the information meets its needs.

One student began her presentation by saying the following:

> Did you realize that, at this very moment, each and every one of you could be and probably is suffering from America's most widespread ailment? It is not a sexually transmitted disease, cancer, or heart disease, but a problem that is commonly ignored by most Americans—the problem of being overweight.

As the presenter proceeded through her information on nutrition, she kept reassuring the audience members that they could overcome the problem in part by knowing which foods to eat and which to avoid. The audience benefited by learning the names of foods that could improve or weaken health.

In this example, the reinforcement was in the form of readily usable information that the audience could apply. But rewards come in many forms. A presenter can use other, more psychological, forms of reward. "Do you want to be among the few who know what a credit card interest rate is?" The presenter who confidentially tells you about credit card debt is doing you a service because you will no longer be ignorant and you will be in the special category of those few "in the know."

Figure 10.1 reviews the five principles of learning.

1. Build on the known.
2. Use humor or wit.
3. Use sensory aids.
4. Organize your information.
5. Reward your listeners.

Figure 10.1 **Principles of learning.**

Skills for the Informative Presenter

Informative speaking employs a number of skills that help make a presentation effective. In informative speaking, those skills include defining, describing, explaining, and demonstrating. Let us explore for a moment how these skills work in an informative presentation.

Defining in an Informative Presentation

Defining is *revealing the presenter's intended meaning of a term, especially if the term is technical, scientific, controversial, or not commonly used.* Know, too, that definitions cannot substitute for other appropriate supporting materials. Presenters often forget to define the terms they use in a presentation. If a presenter has mentioned something called a "plah-see-bow" about five times without telling you what a *placebo* is, the presentation has failed to inform.

Another consideration is that the way you define a term can start a fight or establish peace. Much of the battle over end-of-life rights is centered on the medical definition of when life has ended.

Three ways to define a word are to reveal its denotation, its connotations, and its etymology. We discussed these different ways of defining a word in Chapter 8, and you may wish to review this material. For instance, the word *patois* (etymology: French word, pronounced paa-TWAA) is used for the type of language spoken by many black inhabitants of the island of Jamaica in the Caribbean. A patois is a rare language that does not extend far, in this case not even to the other Caribbean islands, and that is more of a spoken than a written tongue since its grammar and spelling are not standardized. It is an informal sort of language. That would be the word's dictionary meaning, or denotation. The connotative meanings of *patois* are more complex because few white people can speak this form of language, which has been mastered by so many black people in Jamaica. Connotatively, patois suggests a private language, such as the one limited pretty much to black people who grew up in Jamaica. It may be considered less worthy because it is informal, but because it is rich in local associations and folklore, it may also be admired by outsiders.

Actually you can define words or concepts by using methods beyond denotation, connotation, and etymology. You can compare and contrast, provide an example, or provide synonyms (similar meanings) or antonyms (opposite meanings). Whatever method you use, the important point is to remember to help your audience by defining your terms.

Describing in an Informative Presentation

Describing *evokes the meaning of a person, a place, an object, or an experience by telling about its size, weight, color, texture, smell, or your feelings about it.* Describing relies on your abilities to use precise, accurate, specific, and concrete language to make your audience vividly aware.

Mark DuPont, in a public speaking class at Iowa State University, told his classmates about his hometown of Phoenix, Arizona, using the following descriptive words:

> The heat cannot be escaped. As the sun beats mercilessly on the endless lines of automobiles, waves of shimmering heat drift from the blistering pavement, creating an atmosphere of an oven and making the minutes drag into eternity. The wide

avenues only increase the sense of oppression and crowding as lane after lane clogs with rumbling cars and trucks. Drivers who have escaped the heat of the sun in their air-conditioned cars are overwhelmed by the heat of frustration as they do battle with stoplights and autos that have expired in the August sun. Valiant pedestrians wade through the heat, pausing only to wipe from their foreheads the sweat that stings their eyes and blurs their vision. It is the afternoon rush hour at its peak, Phoenix, Arizona, at its fiercest. The crawl of automobiles seems without end as thousands of people seek out their homes in the sweltering desert city.[15]

Explaining in an Informative Presentation

Explaining in an informative presentation *reveals how something works, why something occurred, or how something should be evaluated.* You may explain a social, political, or economic issue; you may explain a historical event; you may explain a variety of theories, principles, or laws; or you may explain by offering a critical appraisal of art, literature, music, drama, film, or presentations. A wide collection of topics may be included in "explaining." You should notice that in offering your opinion, you may come very close to attempting to persuade the audience.

Do you or your classmates understand the concept of minimal tillage in organic farming, how margarine is made, the rules of NASCAR, the qualities of Chateau Malmaison Moulis wine, a shahtoosh "ring shawl," or a lyric opera? The informative presenter takes lesser known words and concepts and renders them understandable to the audience through explanation as illustrated in the excerpt from a speech provided below:

OEM & Non-OEM: Only Your Body Shop Knows for Sure

Until my daughter wrecked her Honda Civic, I had never thought about what happens at the body shop. In fact, a chance remark alerted me to the problem. When I stopped by the body shop after two weeks to see when the vehicle would be repaired, the person behind the desk said, "This one's going to take a while. Your insurer is recommending non-OEM parts." Probably he was not supposed to make the statement because the repair of that one relatively inexpensive car became a nightmare that revealed the cracks in our insurance/auto repair system.

OEM is an acronym for "original equipment manufacturer." A body shop that completely repairs a Honda with OEM parts is using Honda-made parts to replace the damaged portions of your vehicle. The body shop's other choices are to use salvage, that is, parts borrowed from wrecked vehicles or, more likely, to use non-OEM parts or imitations. The imitation parts could be as good as OEM parts, but they could also be misshapen, inferior in quality, and likely to peel and rust quickly. According to the February 1999 *Consumer Reports,* imitation door shells can be installed without the guard beams, with weak welds on guard beams, or with guard beams made with weaker steel. Similarly, knockoff hoods sometimes come without the crumple initiators that keep sheet metal from crashing straight through the windshield. Imitation bumpers can compromise your headlights, radiator, and even your airbags.

Demonstrating in an Informative Presentation

Demonstrating is *showing the audience an object, a person, or a place; showing the audience how something works; showing the audience how to do something; or showing the audience why something occurs.* For example, a student who was informing her classmates about the features of cellular phones used five cellular telephones as models. To help

View the CD-ROM video speech entitled "Mad Cow Disease." Did the speaker use defining, describing, explaining, and demonstrating? Provide examples.

218   Part Three   Types of Presentations

her classmates see the features on these relatively small objects, she used an instrument called an ELMO (electronic monitor, or document camera, or digital video projector), which magnified each phone on the screen in front of the classroom. Describing can accompany demonstrating.

Consider demonstrating those ideas, concepts, or processes that are too complex to be understood through words alone. Similarly, consider the wide variety of items and materials that can be used to demonstrate your topic that were discussed earlier in Chapter 9.

Some examples of presentations that invite a demonstration are

- The presentation by a health worker on how to inject insulin.
- A presentation by a civil engineering student on alternate transportation systems.
- A presentation by a library science major about how to find more and better information on the Internet.
- A presentation by a pharmacist showing us how to distinguish among a variety of new drugs.

Consider whether your topic would lend itself to demonstration.

Ethics and Informative Presentations

Tainted or unethical information is a common problem with people who are less than honest.

What are some guidelines for positive ethical choices in an informative presentation?

1. *Be sure of the quality of your information.*
   - Is the information accurate, verifiable, consistent, and placed in context?
   - Have you avoided implying that you have information that you lack?
   - Have you avoided making up facts or distorting information?

2. *Exercise caution when using the words of others.*
   - Have you accurately quoted the sources you have cited?
   - If you have summarized the words of others, have you paraphrased accurately?
   - Did you cite the sources of your material?
   - Have you avoided plagiarism?
   - Have you kept all quotations in proper context?

3. *Be careful not to mislead your audience.*
   - Have you told the audience of your association with groups whose work or purpose may be relevant to the topic?
   - Have you been honest?
   - Did you present all the relevant information?
   - Did you tell your audience whether your examples were hypothetical or real?
   - Have you used appropriate language to clarify words or concepts that the audience does not understand?

Chapter Ten   Presenting to Inform   219

4. *Be sure the audience needs the information.*
   - Are you providing the audience with new information?
   - Are you allowing the audience free choice to accept or reject the information you provide?
   - Can your audience make reasoned choices about the importance and accuracy of the information you are providing?

5. *Be sure that the information you are providing is in the best interests of the audience members.*
   - Are you providing information that helps rather than hurts the audience?
   - Are you providing information that advances rather than harms our culture and society?

Ethical choices affect your credibility as a source. If you are not ethical—if you bend the truth, twist the evidence, and shape information for selfish purposes—then your audience will find you less credible in the presentations that you give in future. So be careful, accurate, and honest. The checklist in Figure 10.2 will help you accomplish this.

A Checklist for the Informative Speech

_____ 1. Have you created a desire for information?

_____ 2. Have you related the topic to your audience, its modes of learning, and learning styles?

_____ 3. Have you revealed your relationship to the topic?

_____ 4. Have you used wit and humor when appropriate?

_____ 5. Have you helped your audience understand your information?

_____ 6. Have you helped your audience remember your information?

_____ 7. Can the audience apply the information?

_____ 8. Have you built new information on old information?

_____ 9. Have you used presentational aids or demonstration when needed?

_____ 10. Have you organized your message effectively and presented information ethically?

Figure 10.2

An Example of an Informative Presentation

This example is a transcription from the student speech video titled "Cell Phones: Improved Version," which was produced for this textbook. It is not a speech manuscript; it was not written before and read from during the presentation. "Cell Phones" illustrates many of the principles discussed in

220 Part Three Types of Presentations

this chapter. Notice how the presenter creates a desire for information, relates the topic to her audience, and reveals her relationship to the topic in the introduction. Has the speaker used wit and humor when appropriate? How has she helped the audience to understand the information? New information is built on old information. What might you conclude about the organization of the presentation? Finally, keep in mind that while this is a good example, it is only that—an example. You may find other ways of organizing and delivering your informative speech. As you consider the audience and the topic of your speech, you will have many valid and effective ways to organize your presentation.

Cell Phones

Relates topic to the audience

Creates a desire for information

Think fast! You are at work and you want to secretly keep track of football scores without tipping off your boss. Or, you are driving home and come across a serious accident. Even worse, as you leave the campus parking garage you notice two women being held at gunpoint. What do you do in these situations? You might decide to be an action hero and take matters into your own hands, or you might offer your best first aid to the accident victim.

Relates topic to the audience

At work, you might be able to stay close to a computer and keep up on the baseball game. Or, if you are sensible like me, you might just use your cell phone. Although a cell phone can be useful in all of these situations, we have all witnessed the dark side of cell phones. How many times have you heard a cell phone go off in class or at a movie?

Relates topic to the audience

Cell phones are increasingly popular with college students like us. In response to an informal survey, all but four of us in this class said that we own and regularly use a cell phone. We are not alone.

Statistics

According to statistics reported in the July 2004 issue of *World Watch,* just over one billion people worldwide had cell phones by the end of 2002. By the way, as you can see in the graph, this is slightly more than the number of people who had more traditional landline telephones.

Although I have owned a cell phone since my junior year in high school, I am constantly annoyed by them.

Preview of content

Because all of us should be more aware of what cell phones have to offer—both good and bad—I decided to investigate the benefits and risks of cell phones.

Purpose of the presentation

My purpose today is not to persuade you about whether to get a cell phone—most of us have already made that decision. Instead, I want to inform you about the various advantages and disadvantages of cell phones. I'll discuss the advantages first and then turn to the disadvantages.

Informative purpose in a topical sequence pattern

Signpost

We all know that the primary use of cell phones is for talking with others. In my first point, however, I will show you how cell phones are more than talk toys.

Oral citation

Any cell phone is actually a high-tech radio. According to HowItWorks.com, new cell phones provide digital connections between your phone and cell towers located throughout the country. By connecting to a tower, your cell phone is then "on-line" and able to send and receive data.

Specific example

A city the size of Normal, Illinois, for instance, could have as many as 10 cell towers serving the city and outlying areas.

Visual aid

<Gesture to screen>

Explanation

Notice in this hypothetical map of cell tower locations how the coverage of the towers overlaps slightly. The overlap of signals allows you to move throughout town without losing coverage.

Chapter Ten   Presenting to Inform   **221**

People don't just use their cell phone to talk: The digital connections allow for high-speed data transfer, which can include voice data or text data.

Informative content

Yardena Arar, writing in the June 2004 edition of *PC World,* noted that cell phones are now capable of providing mobile Web access, a wireless digital camera, or a wireless personal organizer. This picture of my cell phone shows that it has a built-in camera and color screen.

Oral citation

Visual aid

These new cell phone technologies and applications offer exciting benefits for consumers. As college students, we all know the advantage of cell phones over conventional landlines. I live with four other girls, and instead of worrying about keeping track of a combined phone bill, we each just use our cell phone.

Relates topic to the audience

Specific example

The advantages of cell phones go much beyond simplifying your life in a rental house. An August 2004 issue of *Popular Science* notes that you can use new Web-enabled cell phones to find directions using Mapquest or even high-tech GPS navigation; you can take pictures of your spring break fun; or you can even order hot dogs and beers at some baseball stadiums.

More advantages

Oral citation

Besides the everyday fun that cell phones provide, the new digital technology allows cell phones to provide important safeguards. The May 23rd, 2004, issue of *Lab Business Week* noted that cellular phones can now be used by patients to transmit information about their hearts to doctors for monitoring.

Transition

Oral citation

In the future, this technology can be expanded to help monitor patients with diabetes or to just keep in touch with elderly patients.

Although new cell phone technology has several exciting features, this technology has some important disadvantages that should be understood.

Transition from advantages to disadvantages

Specifically, cell phones pose some risk to society, cause accidents, and could potentially have negative health effects.

Specific examples

One social concern over cell phones is pollution.

A report in the magazine *Ecologist* noted that consumers in England replace over 15 million mobile phones each year—this number is higher in the U.S. Unfortunately, only about 10% of these phones are recycled. When the phones reach landfills, they pose environmental hazards because they release metals like tantalum, mercury, and lead, as well as several other toxins, into the environment.

Oral citation

Statistics

Besides harming the environment, Catherine Carroll, a writer for *Education Week,* points out that new camera phones pose potential privacy concerns for students. Because camera phones can be easily sneaked into locker rooms or even be used to cheat, many schools now ban such phones.

Oral citation

<Gesture to screen>

Visual aid

As shown in this picture, picture phone images can even be posted to the Internet. I can tell you from experience that your friends don't necessarily appreciate this.

Signpost

Although pollution and loss of privacy might seem like problems that you won't have to worry about, others are not. The May 2004 issue of *Prevention* notes that talking on the cell phone while driving dramatically increases the risk of car accidents. This risk happens when people look down to dial, become distracted, or lose their grip on the steering wheel.

Oral citation

Specific example

Even if you are not driving, your cell phone and your car can be a dangerous combination. Matthew Erhorn, a sophomore at SUNY New Paltz, received minor burns when his cell phone ignited fuel vapors while he was filling his tank.

Specific example

Even stranger accidents have been reported by cell phone users. A sixteen-year-old California girl received second degree burns on her rear end when the cell phone in her pocket inexplicably burst into flames.

Specific example

222   Part Three   Types of Presentations

Transition

Even if you are lucky enough to escape explosions or other accidents caused by your cell phone, your danger may not end there. Widespread speculation in Internet chat rooms and on unverifiable Web sites suggests that cell phones are linked to brain cancer.

Oral citation

Tamar Nordenberg, of the U.S. Food and Drug Administration, stated that concern over the cell phone cancer link stems from the low levels of radiation emitted from telephone antennas.

Evidence

Although studies do not show that there is any statistical risk of cancer from cell phone use, Nordenberg points out that there is some conflicting evidence and that additional study is warranted. If you are worried about this danger, using an external "earbud" or other type of external speaker and microphone can reduce your risk.

Transition

Now that I have told you about the benefits and potential dangers associated with cell phones, you can decide whether this new technology is generally beneficial or harmful for society.

Summary conclusion

Although cell phones do pose some very real and potentially scary dangers, new cellular technologies provide entertaining, convenient, and potentially life-saving services.

Visual aid

<Pick up phone>

Relates topic to the audience

Cell phones are just a fact of life for many of us, but the common use of such devices should not prevent us from fully understanding how they impact our lives. Cell phones pose unique challenges for all of us, but they also provide the opportunity for fun.

<Look at phone>

Humorous ending

For instance, I'm happy to report that the Cubs are currently tied with the Cards in the bottom of the 9th.

Resources for Review and Discussion

SUMMARY

In this chapter you have learned the following:

- Two principles are important in informative presentations.
  - The presenter should explicitly state the relationship between himself or herself and the topic.
  - The presenter needs to link the audience to the topic.
- The purposes of informative presentations are to generate information hunger, to help the audience understand the information, to help the audience remember the information, and to invite the audience to apply the information from the presentation.
  - Audiences comprehend generalizations and main ideas better than details.
  - Audiences comprehend simple words and concrete ideas better than big words and abstractions.
  - A sense of anticipation can encourage listening and understanding.
  - Audience participation increases comprehension.
- You learned some principles of learning you can use in informative presentations:
  - Build on the known.
  - Use humor and wit.
  - Use sensory aids.
  - Organize your information.
  - Reward your listeners.
- Methods of organizing the informative presentation include:
  - Tell your audience early what you want them to learn.
  - Place important information early and late in the presentation.
  - Use clear signals to tell your audience when a main point is coming or has just been demonstrated.
- Special skills that are useful in informative presentations include:
  - Defining explains the meaning of something.
  - Describing relies on your ability to use precise, accurate, concrete, and appropriate words to call up a sharp image for your audience.
  - Explaining reveals how something works, why it occurred, or how it should be evaluated.
  - Demonstration is using objects, processes, or procedures to be observed or participated in by the audience.

KEY TERMS

  Use the *Public Speaking* CD-ROM and the Online Learning Center at www.mhhe.com/nelson to practice your understanding of the following terminology.

Behavioral response	Humor	Principles of learning
Defining	Informative presentation	Recency
Demonstrating	Information hunger	Reward
Describing	Main ideas	Subordinate ideas
Explaining	Primacy	Wit

REFERENCES

[1] Evans, A. L., Evans, V., Lami Kanra, A. M., & Jones, O. S. L. (2004). Public speaking in a democracy. *Journal of Instructional Psychology, 31.4,* 325–29. See also Zekeri, Andrew A. (2004). College curriculum competencies and skill former students found essential to their careers. *College Student Journal, 38.3,* 412–22.

[2] Sajak, Pat (August 15, 2002). The disconnect between Hollywood and America: You possess the power. *Vital Speeches of the Day, 68:21,* 701–5.

[3] Wright, Bob (August 1, 2002). Enron: The inflexible obligations of the legal profession. *Vital Speeches of the Day, 68:20,* 635–38.

[4] Anderson, R. (1999). *The phenylketonurics among us.* An unpublished speech delivered in Interpersonal Communication 101, Public Speaking, Ohio University, Athens, Ohio.

[5] Goh, Christine C. M. (2002). Exploring listening comprehension tactics and their interactive patterns. *System, 30,* 185–206. See also Walker, I., & Hulme, C. (1999). Concrete words are easier to recall than abstract words: Evidence for a semantic contribution to short-term serial recall. *Journal of Experimental Psychology: Learning, Memory and Cognition, 25,* 1256–71.

[6] Kardash, C. M., & Noel, L. K. (2000). How organizational signals, need for cognition, and verbal ability affect text recall and recognition. *Contemporary Educational Psychology, 25,* 317–31.

[7] Springer, L., Stanne, M. E., & Donovan, S. S. (1999). Effects of small group learning on undergraduates in science, mathematics, engineering and technology: A metaanalysis. *Review of Educational Research, 69,* 21–52.

[8] Ehrensberger, R. (1945). An experimental study of the relative effectiveness of certain forms of emphasis in public speaking. *Speech Monographs, 12,* 94–111.

[9] Baird, J. E. (1974). The effects of speech summaries upon audience comprehension of expository speeches of varying quality and complexity. *Central States Speech Journal, 25,* 124–25.

[10] Perry, R. P. (1985). Instructor expressiveness: Implications for improving teaching. In J. G. Donald & A. M. Sullivan (Eds.), *Using research to improve teaching* (pp. 35–49). San Francisco: Jossey Bass.

[11] Beating the blues: Dealing with depression. (Fall, 1999). *Inova Health Source, 9.*

[12] Snelling, D. (1999). *TV and your child.* An unpublished speech delivered in Interpersonal Communication 103, Public Speaking, Ohio University, Athens, Ohio.

[13] Ehrensberger, R. (1945). An experimental study of the relative effectiveness of certain forms of emphasis in public speaking. *Speech Monographs, 12,* 94–111.

[14] Janis, I., & Feshbach, S. (1953). Effects of fear-arousing communication. *Journal of Abnormal and Social Psychology, 48,* 78–92.

[15] Dupont, Mark (Spring Semester, 1980). *Phoenix, Arizona: My hometown.* Unpublished manuscript presented in Honors Public Speaking course, Iowa State University, Ames, Iowa.

APPLICATION EXERCISES

 Go to the self-quizzes on the *Public Speaking* CD-ROM and the Online Learning Center at www.mhhe.com/nelson to test your knowledge of the chapter concepts.

1. Think of three topics about which you could give a three-minute presentation to inform. List the topics in the blanks at the left. In the blanks at the right, explain how you relate to the topic in ways that might increase your credibility with the audience.

    TOPICS   YOUR RELATIONSHIP
                          TO TOPIC
    A. _____   _____
    B. _____   _____
    C. _____   _____

2. Consider one topic that you did not use in the previous exercise and explain how you would relate that topic to an audience of your own class in an informative presentation.

3. Write down a topic for an informative presentation that you have not used in previous application exercises. Explain in the spaces provided how you could apply each of the principles of learning to that topic.

TOPIC: _____

ONE WAY THAT I COULD RELATE THIS TOPIC TO WHAT THE AUDIENCE ALREADY KNOWS IS BY _____

_____

ONE WAY THAT I COULD RELATE WIT AND HUMOR IN AN INFORMATIVE PRESENTATION ON THIS TOPIC IS BY

_____

ONE WAY THAT I COULD USE SEVERAL PRINCIPLES OF LEARNING TO GET MY MESSAGE ACROSS ON THIS TOPIC IS BY

_____

ONE WAY THAT I COULD ORGANIZE MY PRESENTATION TO HELP THE AUDIENCE LEARN MY INFORMATION IS BY

_____

ONE WAY THAT I COULD REWARD MY AUDIENCE FOR LISTENING TO MY INFORMATIVE PRESENTATION ON THIS TOPIC IS BY

_____

CHAPTER ELEVEN

We are more easily persuaded . . . by the reasons that we ourselves discover than by those which are given to us by others.

BLAISE PASCAL (1623–1662), FRENCH MATHEMATICIAN

Things do not change; we change.

HENRY DAVID THOREAU (1817–1862), U.S. PHILOSOPHER, AUTHOR, NATURALIST

Presenting Persuasive Messages

What will you learn?

When you have read and thought about this chapter, you will be able to:

1. Recognize differences between informative and persuasive purposes.
2. Explain the purpose of persuasive speaking.
3. Explain how persuasion works.
4. Apply some principles of persuasion concerning consistency, small changes, commitment levels, costs/benefits, need fulfillment, and gradual approaches.
5. Promote change using persuasion.
6. State examples of the three types of persuasive speeches: to inspire, to convince, and to act.
7. Apply critical thinking through inductive and deductive reasoning.
8. Recognize fallacies and errors in critical thinking.
9. Critically evaluate the ethical dimension of persuasive messages.

This chapter defines, analyzes, and helps you create effective persuasive messages. Much of our communication attempts to influence others. At the same time we are often the targets of persuasion. This chapter shows how to influence others through ethically responsible persuasive presentations.

228   Part Three   Types of Presentations

Gabriella Rajna had a big day ahead. Her boss, the CEO of Tidewater Supplies, Inc., had asked her to make a presentation to the company's most profitable customer. That customer, Modern Motels of America, brought in over 30 percent of Tidewater Supplies' annual earnings. Gabriella's job was to convince the CEO and six vice presidents from Modern Motels to continue using Tidewater Supplies for their linens, soap, shampoo, and cleaning supplies. The presentation would take place in their new high-rise office building in Atlanta.

Gabriella knew that at least three competitors had approached Modern Motels of America about changing accounts. She also knew that although Modern Motels was satisfied with Tidewater Supplies, like any business, Modern Motels was interested in securing the same service and supplies at a lower cost if possible. She had no way of knowing the competition's bids, but her boss had given her the authority to bargain down to a certain point. If Gabriella bargained higher than that figure and still kept Modern Motels' business, she would receive a healthy bonus. If she had to drop to the minimum, she would receive no bonus and no cheers from her boss or her colleagues because Tidewater would make little profit at that bottom-line figure. Gabriella knew that she had to give the most important persuasive presentation of her career.

The Role of Persuasion in Public Discourse

Persuasion permeates our culture so much that we may not be fully aware of its presence. In our democratic society today, we send and receive persuasive messages on crucial issues such as war and peace, taxation and representation, freedoms and restrictions, and readiness for disasters both natural and terrorist-related. These topics alone indicate how critical it is for us to understand persuasive speaking in our everyday lives, including:

- How persuasion relates to you and the main types of persuasive messages
- What social science research reveals about the audience and the message in persuasive presentations
- The strategies for acceptance of persuasive messages and how to organize your persuasive presentation
- The use of inductive and deductive reasoning, argument, and evidence—the substance of many persuasive attempts
- Some of the common fallacies that unethical persuaders try to use
- The consideration of ethics in persuasion

We begin by looking at how persuasion relates to you.

You as Target of and Sender of Persuasion

Gabriella used persuasion to make a sale, but persuasion functions just as well in civic engagement and public deliberation. Persuasive messages bombard you every day. When the phone rings, your pager goes off, or the doorbell chimes, you often are confronted with someone who sees you as a customer. Commercials punctuate television and radio programs every few minutes. Magazines and newspapers are filled with flashy ads designed to sell you products. Many Web sites are crammed with pop-ups and banner ads. The mall and the supermarket are designed to draw money out of your pocket. Political parties and charities vie for your loyalty and contributions. Today, more than ever, the traditional media, the Internet, and other people compete for your attention, your money, your time, your vote, or your membership. In doing so, they all use persuasion.

You are also the producer of persuasive messages. The persuader is often an advocate. For example, at Broward Community College in Florida, persuasive messages invite students to volunteer for Junior Achievement of South Florida. At Michigan State, the Center for Service Learning and Civic Engagement asks students to take an "alternative spring break," in which they travel and perform service for host agencies and organizations. Like students everywhere, you are as familiar with persuasion as with the air you breathe.

Your satisfaction in both private and public spheres is dependent, in great part, on your ability to be both a competent consumer and producer of persuasive messages. You do not want to be deceived by others. You want to be able to understand why you feel compelled to respond to certain messages while you disregard others. You also want to learn to be an effective and ethical persuader. Our democratic and capitalist culture thrives on persuasion. This chapter helps you to understand and to practice persuasive presentations.

What Are Persuasive Presentations?

Persuasive presentations are *messages that influence an audience's choices by changing their responses toward an idea, issue, concept, or product.* Let's compare informative and persuasive presentations. It is probably fair to say that no message is completely informative or completely persuasive. In fact, persuading and informing may work to reinforce each other, but generally we are trying to do one or the other. Figure 11.1 highlights the characteristics of the two kinds of presentations.

	Informative Presentation	Persuasive Presentation
Presenter's Intent	To increase knowledge	To change mind or action
Purpose of Message	To define, describe, explain, or demonstrate	To shape, reinforce, or change audience response
Listener's Response	To know more than before, to advance what is known	To feel or think differently, to behave or act differently, to critically evaluate the message
Audience Choice	To willingly gain new knowledge	To change behavior by choice, to be inspired or convinced by credibility, logic, or emotion

Figure 11.1 **Comparing informative and persuasive presentations.**

Types of Persuasive Presentations

The three types of persuasive speeches are the speech to inspire, the speech to convince, and the speech of action.

The **speech to inspire** is a persuasive speech, although we do not often think about inspirational messages as persuasive. *The purpose of this speech is to influence listeners' feelings or motivations.* Speeches of inspiration often occur at ceremonial events. They occur in places of worship; at graduations and rallies; and on holidays or at special events. Lacey Schneider came to class very agitated about how little she and her classmates knew about politics. Her purpose was to get her listeners to be more mindful about their own political beliefs and to then follow up by voting for a candidate who represented them. These few sentences give you the flavor of her presentation:

View "Motorcycle Club" as a speech to inspire.

> Did you know that only 31 percent of females under the age of 35 are likely to vote? I personally found this statistic to be disheartening. Now, with that figure in mind, how many women under 35 do you think know what they believe in? Unfortunately, even if they do know what they believe in, they are not expressing their beliefs by voting.[1]

You also can deliver a speech to inspire. Can you inspire your fellow students to join some cause in which you believe? Can you inspire them to be more spiritual, less materialistic, more focused on learning, or more concerned about their own community? To experience examples of inspirational speaking, watch live or televised ministers, see politicians during campaigns, or observe individuals who believe strongly in issues related to natural resources, education, gun ownership, health care, and other causes.

The **speech to convince** is *a persuasive presentation delivered with the intent of influencing listeners' beliefs or attitudes.* You may wish, for example, to convince the audience that gender equality is beneficial to both women and men, that respectful language is a reasonable goal of a multicultural society, that all people deserve housing, or that we should care more about victims of terrorism and natural disasters.

View "Stem Cell Research" and analyze the presenter's arguments using the concepts in this section of the text.

The speech to convince encourages listeners to adopt a stronger position on an issue; they are not required to act. You ask your audience only to rethink their beliefs and attitudes.

The **speech of action** is *a persuasive speech given for the purpose of influencing listeners' behaviors and actions.* The foundation of the speech of action is the changing of listeners' beliefs and attitudes, plus acting on them. You may want listeners to join an organization, to volunteer their time at local social service agencies, to eat a low-fat diet, or to vote for a particular candidate. In the speech of action, the speaker seeks an overt behavioral effect, some evidence of response consistent with the presenter's intent.

TRY THIS

Pair with another person and help each other think of instances when you have used persuasion (a) in the home, (b) at school, (c) at work, and (d) in the community.

Chapter Eleven Presenting Persuasive Messages   231

Activate your audience to vote for a new community library and recreation complex through a speech of action.

This text has attempted throughout to emphasize "vital" topics, because public discussion of important issues—civic engagement—is at the very heart of democracy. To be effective at public discourse it would be useful to learn what works and what does not. Here are some findings about audiences and messages, which relate directly to persuasive presentations.

What Communication Research Says About Persuasion

What Should You Know about Your Audience?

- One fundamental task in persuasion is **audience analysis**, *learning enough about the listeners so that you can predict their probable response to your message.*[2]
- Every persuasive appeal has a relationship dimension. If you are too pushy about achieving your purpose, your audience might resist you more and like you less.
- The **relationship** is *how the audience feels about you as the presenter before, during, and after the persuasive appeal.* You are more likely to persuade if your audience respects you, if your integrity remains intact during your presentation, and if the audience continues to believe you are credible after they have heard your presentation.
- Your classmates and people in your community will tend to respond in three different ways to a persuasive appeal: critically, defensively, or compliantly.[3]

For more information on this topic, view "Relating a Speech to the Listener's Self-Interest" on the CD-ROM.

Watch and analyze "I'll Take the Cow Over the Chemicals" to see if the presenter follows the research findings in this section.

- **A critical response** *occurs when the audience focuses on the arguments, the quality of the evidence, and the truth or accuracy of the message.* In your pitch for a state-of-the-art playground for physically challenged children, your audience may want to know how many children you are talking about.

- **A defensive response** *occurs when the audience fends off the persuader's message to protect existing beliefs, attitudes, and values.* A person proposing a tax increase for the new library may fare poorly with an audience committed to no new taxes.

- **A compliance response** *occurs when the audience does what is socially acceptable,* including pleasing the persuader or pleasing the other listeners. An audience may go along with the idea of working with Habitat for Humanity just because they do not want to appear insensitive toward their underprivileged neighbors. They comply because it is socially acceptable.

- Audiences will respond to persuasive messages depending on how motivated they are to process the message.[4]

    - Unmotivated audiences who do not take the topic seriously will respond superficially to the message. For instance, students tend to be motivated more by classes in their major than in courses they are required to complete.

    - Motivated audiences who see the topic as important to them will respond deeply by being thoughtful, analytic, and understanding. Audiences who choose to hear a presentation are more likely to respond to a message meaningfully.

    - Audiences will respond favorably to timely messages. Students about to graduate, for example, will pay more attention to a presentation on job-gaining interview skills than to a presentation on retirement possibilities. Consider whether your topic is timely.

How Can You Create an Effective Message?

Once you have a purpose to direct you and an audience to listen to you, you need to create a message that uses content most likely to gain acceptance. According to current communication research, an effective persuasive presenter will:

- Employ message production *to create, organize, and deliver a persuasive appeal.*[5]

- Use the content of a persuasive appeal *to fulfill the primary goal of influencing the listeners in a predetermined direction.* The content often consists of reasons to adopt the presenter's ideas plus supporting material to bolster those claims.

- Be **explicit,** which is *the extent to which the persuader makes his or her intentions clear in the message.*[6] Often the presenter clarifies intentions at the outset—"After this presentation you will want a new water supply for our city." But, if the audience is likely to resist the presenter's purpose, then the presenter is better off preparing the audience with reasons first and making the purpose explicit later, after the audience is more prepared—"Now I think you see the need for an expensive cleanup at the site of the old fertilizer plant."

- Use **argument,** which is *the extent to which the presenter furnishes reasons for the message claims.*[7] The skillful presenter finds the reasons, the evidence, and the proof that the audience is most likely to accept.

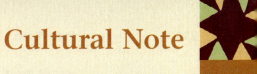

Cultural Note

IMPLICITNESS MAY BE VALUED IN COLLECTIVIST CULTURES

James Dillard and Linda Marshall, professors of communication and family studies respectively, say that U.S. students favor explicitness—communication that is direct and clear—and clarity over concern for others and avoidance of disapproval. In some cultures, implicitness—communication that is indirect and ambiguous—may be valued, especially in collectivist cultures where the group is given priority over the individual. Koreans, for example, prefer indirectness,[8] and Japanese advertising tends to make more indirect claims than does U.S. advertising.[9] Even some U.S. audiences who are high in social sensitivity may prefer an implicit approach. The goal of the persuader is to match presentation to listener preference on implicitness and explicitness.

- Use **testimonial evidence,** *the words of a cited source in support of the presenter's claims,* to produce attitude change and improve source credibility. By quoting sources whom the audience respects, the presenter will increase acceptance.
- Use **complete arguments** *including all the parts—claims and supporting material—to produce attitude change and improve source credibility.* Audiences want to know as fully as possible why they should comply.
- *Use* **specific numbers**—*percentages, actual numbers, averages, and ranges of numbers*—rather than saying "many," "most," or some other vague quantity. Being specific increases message effectiveness and improves source credibility.[10]

Now that you know more about what communication research reveals about audiences and messages, you are ready to consider particular strategies a presenter can use to influence an audience.

Fact, Value, and Policy in Persuasive Presentations

The content of persuasive presentations often revolves around three distinct kinds of questions: questions of fact, questions of value, and questions of policy.

The **question of fact** *means that the persuasive presentation seeks to uncover the truth based on fact.* That truth or fact could be anything from who did something, why something was done, to how something was done. For instance, a federal prosecutor worked for two years on a question of fact: Who leaked the name of a CIA operative, a violation of federal law? Typically you do not have two years to seek the truth, so for your persuasive presentation, you will likely choose questions of fact that take less time to uncover. Questions such as "Who is responsible for a piece of legislation concerning government-backed financial aid for college students," "What is the reasoning behind the current law concerning the disposal of electronics," or "How did specific companies receive contracts for cleaning up New Orleans after Hurricane Katrina?"

The **question of value** *raises issues about goodness and badness, right and wrong, enlightenment and ignorance.* Should all premature babies be kept alive even though some may face a lifetime of health issues? Should our society allow people to take their own lives when they suffer from chronic pain or incurable disease? Should we cut taxes at the same time that we reduce spending on social services? All of these are questions of value that get to the heart of our beliefs.

The **question of policy** *enters the realm of rules, regulations, and laws.* Should college students be prohibited from drinking alcohol on campus even though they are of legal age? Should restaurants be required to report the fat content of their products prominently on their walls or menus? Should our college require service learning as a graduation requirement? All of these questions are attempts to establish some policy that will regulate behaviors.

Organizing Your Persuasive Presentation

Now that you know how common persuasion is, what persuasive presentations are, how communication research has informed our knowledge of audiences and messages, and what types of questions persuasive speaking typically explores, you are ready to learn how to organize, structure, and design your persuasive presentation. Let us look first at how the introduction and the conclusion of a persuasive presentation can differ from those in other kinds of speeches.

Introducing the Persuasive Presentation

Your introduction may still consist of the four functions explained in Chapter 6: gaining and maintaining favorable attention, introducing the topic by relating the topic to the audience, relating the topic to the presenter, and previewing the organization and development of the speech. However, the persuasive presentation has one possible expansion and one possible exception.

The expansion relates to the part of the speech where the presenter or the person introducing the presenter reveals more about the credentials or credibility of the source than may be required in other kinds of presentations. Source credibility or *ethos* refers to the presenter's credentials, integrity, and positive relationship with the audience. In a persuasive presentation, a presenter's authority to speak is more significant, because who the speaker is may be one of the important reasons for a listener to respond to his or her persuasive message. Persuasive speakers should exercise considerable care in relating themselves to the topic.

The exception to the four functions with the persuasive presentation is that in informative speeches, presenters are most effective when they clearly reveal up front what they want the listeners to learn. However, in a persuasive presentation, if you are going to ask an audience to buy into some idea that would be repulsive to them without adequate preparation, then it probably would be better to gently ease listeners toward your purpose before revealing it explicitly. For instance, before your community accepts the idea of a new dump site in the immediate area—however badly needed—the people who will be affected would need considerable preparation in the form of reasons, needs, evidence, and even narratives or stories about how awful the current situation is without the dump.

Concluding the Persuasive Presentation

The conclusion of a persuasive presentation may need to be adapted so that the stated purpose—the last step in relating the topic to the audience—falls toward the end of the speech after much preparation has occurred.

When Gabriella presented her persuasive message to Modern Motels of America in the opening of this chapter, she used such an approach. She began talking to the Modern Motels executives about their long and satisfactory relationship with her company, Tidewater Supplies. She then told them about the quality of the sundries and cleaning supplies that her company had provided for their company over the years. She reminded them of how pleased their employees and customers had been with Tidewater products. Next she recollected how faithfully her company had serviced Modern Motels, never having failed to keep the motels supplied with high-quality products. Only after all of these preliminaries did Gabriella present the executives with a bid for her company's services.

Choosing Patterns of Organization for Persuasive Presentations

Chapter 6 covered organizational patterns in detail, but four patterns need attention here because presenters choose them most often for persuasive presentations.

Topical Sequence and Cause-Effect Patterns

These two patterns of organization work equally well for informative and persuasive presentations. When used for persuasion, the topical sequence pattern addresses advantages and disadvantages, lists reasons for accepting a proposition, and offers supporting material or a series of emotional stories to encourage acceptance of a proposition. The cause-effect pattern of organization, when used to persuade, first reveals the cause (too many housing developments displacing waterfront areas and barrier islands) and then the effect (no protection from flooding) in a speech aimed at encouraging new zoning regulations to stop wiping out protective areas.

Problem-Solution and Monroe Motivated Sequence Patterns

Presenters often use these two patterns of organization to persuade. The persuader who uses the problem-solution pattern first reveals the problem that creates the need for a solution: A lack of building code enforcement makes student rental properties unsafe. The presenter then moves to a possible solution: The city council is considering the addition of more inspectors and tougher consequences for violators—if citizens show support for the idea. The persuasive purpose is to encourage listeners to lobby the city council to solve the problem.

The Monroe Motivated Sequence is another pattern from Chapter 6 that presenters use mainly for persuasive presentations. This organizational pattern (1) begins by gaining attention so the listeners will focus on the topic, (2) establishes the need by demonstrating topic relevance, (3) reveals how the proposal will satisfy audience needs, (4) portrays the solution in a way that allows the audience to visualize themselves taking part, and, finally, (5) reveals what the listeners can do to make the visualization come true.

Once you understand the most commonly used patterns of organization in persuasive presentations, you need to consider how to shape the content of your presentation by considering some strategies for gaining compliance.

Persuasive Strategies

Consistency Persuades

The first principle of persuasion is that **consistency persuades,** meaning that *audiences are more likely to change their behavior if the suggested change is consistent with their present beliefs, attitudes, and values.* Risk takers like daring ideas. Competitive people are most likely to enter still other competitions. People who understand that "we are a nation of immigrants" are unlikely to discourage immigrants from moving into their neighborhood.

People tend to be relatively consistent. Past behavior is a good predictor of future behavior. The public speaker uses this notion of consistency by linking persuasive proposals to past consistencies. The presenter promotes change by showing how the promoted activity is consistent with the audience's past behavior.

Small, Gradual Changes Persuade

The second principle of persuasion is that **small, gradual changes persuade,** meaning that *audiences are more likely to alter their behavior if the suggested change will require small, gradual changes rather than major, abrupt changes.* A common error of beginning persuaders is that they ask for too much change too soon for too little reason. Hostile audiences especially are resistant to persuaders who ask for too much too fast. They might respond with a **boomerang effect** in which *the audience likes the presenter and the proposal even less after the presentation.*

In a presentation on energy conservation, you probably would not succeed with an appeal that bluntly says "Quit using so much electricity." However, a presenter who begins with "Shut off the lights in rooms you are not using" and moves to "turn off the hot water heater when you are gone for more than a couple of days" will more likely accomplish her goal of gaining behavioral change from the audience.

TRY THIS

By yourself but on paper write down (a) a few things that you could be persuaded to change and (b) a few things that you probably would not change for anyone or anything. Why do persuaders have to be careful what they ask for?

Benefits Persuade

The third principle of persuasion is that *audiences are more likely to change their behavior if the suggested change will benefit them more than it will cost them.* **Cost-benefit analysis,** for example, is considered every time we buy something: "Do I want this new jacket even though it means I must spend $150 plus tax? The benefits are that I will be warm and look nice. The cost is that I will not be able to replace my broken watch." The persuader frequently demonstrates to the audience that the benefits are worth the cost.

How can you use cost-benefit analysis in your classroom speech? Consider the costs to the audience of doing as you ask. What are the costs in money, time, commitment, energy, skill, or talent? Consider one of the most common requests in student speeches: communicate with your representative or senator about an issue. Many student speakers make that request without considering the probability that nobody in class has ever communicated with a senator or representative. Even if the speaker includes an e-mail address, the message writing will take a commitment of time and effort. Few students are willing to pay those costs. On the other hand, if the speaker comes to class with a letter already composed and simply asks for signatures from the class, then the cost is a few seconds of time, and the speaker is more likely to gain audience cooperation. Whenever you deliver a persuasive speech, consider the costs and how you can reduce them so the audience will feel the costs are worth the proposed benefits.

Often the goal of a persuasive appeal is to push the audience to an action like voting.

Need Fulfillment Persuades

The fourth principle of persuasion is that audiences are more likely to change their behavior if the change meets their needs. Psychology scholar Abraham Maslow created an often-cited **hierarchy of needs**,[11] *a pyramid that builds from basic physiological needs like the need for oxygen all the way up to self-actualization needs—the realization of one's highest potential* (see Figure 11.2). Maslow's pyramid makes sense.

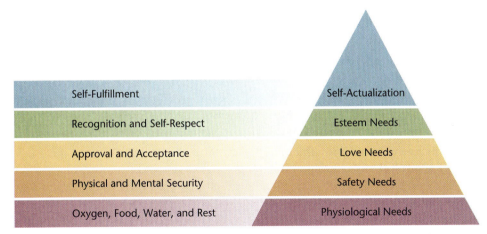

Figure 11.2 **Maslow's pyramid: A hierarchy of needs.** Audiences are more likely to change if the change meets their needs.
SOURCE: "Maslow's Hierarchy of Needs," from *Motivation and Personality*, 3rd ed., by Abraham H. Maslow, Robert D. Frager, and James Fadiman, © 1987. Adapted by permission of Pearson Education, Inc., Upper Saddle River, NJ.

As a human being, you do need all the items in the hierarchy, though many people never get very far above the second level shown in the figure, and few people think they have achieved complete self-fulfillment.

Maslow's pyramid is a useful resource for your persuasive presentations. Consider this example: At Ball State University, a civic engagement project that applies nursing care and disease prevention is looking for student workers. If you were trying to persuade students to participate in this project, you could utilize Maslow's pyramid by saying "Your family will be proud to learn that you are involved in this humanitarian concern" (Maslow's need for love, approval and acceptance), or "You will get credit and recognition for working on this project" (Maslow's need for esteem, recognition, and self-respect), or "Working to advance the health of others will make you feel great about yourself" (Maslow's need for self-actualization and self-fulfillment).

You can analyze your audience for specific needs. Do they need money? Jobs? Day care for their children or elders? Do they need help in dealing with government bureaucracies? Do they need better living conditions? Do they need to learn how to study, how to handle children, or how to live with spouses? Check out your own audience and determine what they need, because a persuasive speech that meets the audience's needs is likely to be successful.

Critical Thinking through Reasoning

A persuasive presentation can be based on ethos, pathos, or logos. Sometimes we say that others should be persuaded because an authoritative source is behind the message (ethos or source credibility): for example, the Pope, the Koran, or your boss. Sometimes we say that others should be persuaded because a touching story convinces us to take action (pathos): the homeless family, living in the city park with no blankets or food, is asking our organization for help. Still other times we argue a case for why others should be persuaded. We make a **claim,** *a conclusion of what the persuader would have the listener believe or do that invites proof or evidence.* Dillard and Marshall say that based on the research "We may assert with confidence that including evidence in a persuasive message will enhance the performance of the appeal."[12]

For more information on this topic, view video clip titled "Using Inductive Reasoning" on the CD-ROM.

Using Inductive Reasoning

The kind of reasoning in which the *persuader amasses a series of particular instances to draw an inference* is known as **inductive reasoning.** The critical thinker knows that inductive reasoning is vulnerable in several ways. One weakness is that such reasoning involves an "inferential leap" in which the presenter jumps from a series of particulars to some generalization about them, e.g., the local banks have unfair rates for students. But were those particulars typical? Were they biased in that the presenter selected them while ignoring others that did not support his claim? Inductive reasoning is like circumstantial evidence: Nobody saw the killing, but the alleged killer's fingerprints were on the gun, witnesses saw him at the scene at the time of the crime, and the killer was having an affair with the victim's estranged sister. We make an "inferential leap" to the probable notion that this particular person did the killing.

Using Deductive Reasoning

Deductive reasoning *occurs when the presenter bases her claim on some premise that is generally affirmed by the audience.* Notice that the premise does not have to be true; it just has to be widely believed by the audience. So, in some communities the major premise that "God created human beings" becomes the widely believed idea that moves easily to "Human beings inhabit Kansas" (minor premise) and "therefore, God created the people of Kansas" (conclusion). This kind of reasoning is known as deductive reasoning, an argument based on a major premise, a minor premise, and a conclusion.

For more information on this topic, view the video clip "Using Deductive Reasoning" on the CD-ROM.

Like inductive reasoning, the critical thinker can attack deductive reasoning by questioning the premises on which the persuader bases the argument. Look how significantly the argument changes if the major premise is "Evolution resulted in human beings." Whether persuaders use inductive or deductive arguments, they have plenty of generalizations and premises to argue about: Life begins at conception; Social Security should be privatized; wealthy people should receive tax cuts; retirement age should be raised; and rape victims should be told of the "morning-after" birth control pill.

Using Hard Evidence in Reasoning

Another feature of reasoned discourse is what you use as evidence or proof. From watching the various spinoffs of *Law and Order*, you know that some things are regarded as hard evidence: fingerprints, DNA, a weapon. On the other hand, other "proofs" are less likely to hold up: witness testimony, a grainy surveillance video, or a statement from an angry partner.

Similarly, in reasoned discourse we sometimes use arguments that are more convincing than others. A study in the *New England Journal of Medicine* is better proof than testimony from a drug company spokesperson. Statistics from an impartial source with a large, randomly selected sample are better than statistics from a company trying to show that its product is better than another's. Testimony from an authoritative source—a physician on your blood work or a chemistry professor on ionic compounds—is more convincing than the words of nonexperts. Anything that can demonstrate cause is convincing: Secondhand smoke causes increased lung cancer. Yet, scientific studies, statistics from carefully crafted research, testimony from experts, and arguments from cause are regarded as reliable forms of proof.

For more information on this topic, view the video clip titled "Using Statistics" on the CD-ROM.

Using Soft Evidence in Reasoning

Less convincing, but sometimes enticing, are softer proofs like analogy, quotations, and narrative. The persuader argues that "America, like Rome, will fall because of moral decline." The persuader "proves" the case by reminding us of Roman orgies and other forms of debauchery and compares that to raves, cable TV sex shows, and our many failed families. The persuader uses a quotation to "prove" that she is correct in her assessment of our national security. The persuader uses narrative to persuade by telling stories of people victimized by war, people rendered homeless by natural disasters, or middle-class people bankrupted by lapsed insurance and skyrocketing health care costs—all examples of pathos.

For more information on this topic, view the video clip "Appealing to Motivations" on the CD-ROM.

An analogy is always susceptible to rebuttal because invariably an analogy is based on comparing two things that are fundamentally unalike (e.g., Roman and American society are different in countless ways). A quotation is only as good as

For more information on this topic, view the video clip "Using an Analogy" on the CD-ROM.

240 Part Three Types of Presentations

the credibility of the person making the statement. And a narrative exhibiting pathos can be rebutted by demonstrating that the story is atypical, sensationalized, or simply beyond our ability to solve.

Using Reasoning from Cause

Determining cause can be a challenging task. For example, convincing people that smoking cigarettes is a causal factor in lung cancer took decades. For many social and political issues, the causes and effects can be complex and various. Nonetheless, we use reasoning from cause often and in two directions: Sometimes we move from cause to effect and sometimes we move from effect to cause.

Reasoning from cause means that you have to demonstrate, for example, that the leading cause of lung cancer is cigarette smoking, not air pollution, not water contamination, not genetics. Causal reasoning also means that the cause must be solidly linked to the effect; otherwise, what we are witnessing would simply be correlation, two unrelated things occurring together. Scientists can prove that smoking cigarettes and getting lung cancer are solidly linked even if every smoker does not die of cigarette use. When reasoning from cause, you must be very careful to (a) show that the cause and effect are solidly linked and (b) eliminate other possible causes. Similarly, when starting with effect, you must be careful to (a) demonstrate that effect and cause are solidly linked and (b) eliminate other possible effects.

Using Reasoning from Sign

He has a backpack and he is walking across campus; therefore, he must be a student. We reason from sign every day, but we may not be correct in doing so: The guy with the backpack turns out to be an unemployed mechanic looking for a warm building for refuge. The best way to reason from sign is to reason from multiple signs. Multiple signs ordinarily lead to a better conclusion. So, if he looks like a student, acts like a student, walks across campus like a student, and appears to know others on campus, the chances are better that he is a student. In reasoning from sign, you need a sufficient number of reliable signs that do not contradict and are not accidental or coincidental.

Using Reasoning from Generalization

This deductive form of argument depends on the acceptance of the statement. "All spiders have eight legs," for example, is a truism since arachnids are differentiated from insects (six legs) by the number of legs. Many generalizations are less sound: "Belonging to a fraternity is good." This generalization could encounter some rebuttal from those who believe that belonging to a fraternity lowers grades and increases negative behavior.

Normally a persuader argues from generalization by applying a generalization that is widely accepted or provable to a particular case: "All honors graduates are intelligent; Fred is an honors graduate; therefore, Fred is intelligent." However, many generalizations are not unquestionable truths. One could argue in rebuttal that many honors graduates are not highly intelligent; instead, they are people of ordinary intellect who just work harder and longer than others.

Now that you know more about how persuaders use reasoning in their presentations, let us look at fallacies, poor reasoning that you should strive to avoid.

Avoid Fallacies

A **fallacy** is *an error in reasoning that weakens an argument.* Fallacies come in many forms, but those described here are the ones we have found public speaking students to (mis)use the most.

Name Calling. This fallacy unfairly categorizes people by slapping a label on them. Today, calling someone a "liberal" may be perceived by many citizens as a slam, while labeling someone a "conservative" may be perceived as a compliment. As a political candidate, would you perhaps win an election by labeling your opponent "a liberal?" How can you avoid name calling in a presentation?

- Omit the label and refer instead to the person's record.
- Decide for yourself if an idea has merit without regard for the label.

Glittering Generality. The technique behind the "glittering generality" is to embrace a word that symbolizes some highly positive virtue. The glittering generality invites us to accept and approve an idea without examining any evidence. For example, "We need to bring democracy to country X" is a statement that exploits our very positive attitude about our form of democracy without analyzing its appropriateness to another nation or region. The critical questions to ask are:

- Does the idea in question (transplanting democracy) have a legitimate relationship to the virtuous word (democracy)?
- Is a misguided plan (transplanting democracy) being advanced simply by linking it to a positive name?

Bandwagon Technique. With this fallacy, the speaker encourages the listener to do something because "everyone" in the same valued group is doing it. For example, you should vote for a candidate because all of the union members are doing so. The critical questions to ask are:

- What is the evidence for adopting or rejecting this idea?
- Does this idea serve or hinder my interests regardless of who else allegedly is following this idea?

Circular Reasoning. This fallacy uses two unproven propositions to prove each other. Pit bulls should be outlawed because they are vicious animals. We know they are vicious animals because they should be outlawed.

- Avoid circular reasoning by making certain that your assumptions can be proven.

Either/Or. This fallacy assumes that everything is binary, that every issue has two opposite positions: Either you are for me or you are against me. However, someone certainly could be fairly neutral, neither for nor against. The fact is that few issues have only two opposite points of view. Most issues have multiple positions. How do you avoid this fallacy?

E-Note

THE INSTITUTE OF PROPAGANDA ANALYSIS

In 1938 the Institute of Propaganda Analysis developed seven methods used to short-circuit critical thinking. That analysis of propaganda remains so popular today that a Google search on the Institute produces around 400,000 items about propaganda. To save time, go to **www.propagandacritic.com**, where you will find a list of propaganda techniques defined and explained.

- Recognize that most issues are complicated enough to have multiple points of view.

Post Hoc Fallacy. The actual name of this fallacy is *"post hoc ergo propter hoc,"* an expression that means "after this; therefore, because of this." Fortunately, this fallacy is easier to explain than to pronounce. For instance, I no sooner bought a new battery than my transmission failed; I met her and my misfortunes began; and I walked under a ladder and almost immediately was splashed by a passing car. This fallacy attributes misfortunes to an event that occurred before the misfortune even though the event did not actually cause the misfortune. You can avoid this fallacy if you are always aware of the following.

- Just because two things occur together close in time does not mean that one caused the other.
- Realize that often things occur close in time by accident or coincidence, not because one caused the other.

Ethics and Persuasive Speaking

Persuasive presentations offer ample opportunities for positive purposes or for ethical mischief. Persuasive speaking can result in the advancement of a good cause or the purchase of a product you do not need, never wanted, and that you will never use. Distinguishing between ethical and unethical persuasive appeals is a challenging task for which the following guidelines apply:

1. *Be careful whom you trust.* The best-looking, smoothest-talking presenter can be a pathological deceiver, while an unattractive, inarticulate person can have your best interests in mind. Listeners need to watch who they trust, and presenters need to provide credentials to show they are trustworthy. They need to demonstrate their source credibility.

Michael Moore uses documentary films to persuade. Do you believe he is a successful persuader? An ethical one?

242

2. *Analyze and evaluate messages for reasonableness, truth, and benefit to you and the community.* Many vendors try to convince you to buy in a hurry because rushing limits your reasoning. They do not want you to carefully consider whether the decision really makes sense. As a critical thinker, you will want messages to meet standards of reasonableness.
3. *You and your messages will be more persuasive if you have a long, positive history* ("The thing you get to lose once is your reputation"); if your past invites others to trust you and your word; and if others tend to benefit from your messages as much or more than you do (that is, you do not seek compliance for selfish purposes). Are you building a history that will help you or harm you when you attempt to persuade others?
4. *Always be respectful of your audience.* If you treat them as you would want to be treated, you will avoid many ethical problems.
5. *Avoid fallacies.* If you always strive to use sound reason tempered by critical thinking, then you will skillfully avoid those short circuits to reasonable thought that we know as fallacies.

See Figure 11.4 for a checklist that reviews the important features of the persuasive presentation, including the ethical dimension.

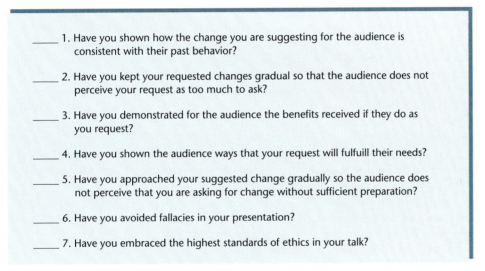

Figure 11.4 **Checklist for the persuasive presentation.** You do not have to do everything on the checklist; instead, they remind you of what you can do in your presentation.

An Example of a Persuasive Presentation

This example is a transcription from the student speech video titled "Sharks: The Misunderstood Monster,"[13] which was produced for this textbook. It is not a speech manuscript; it was not written in longhand before and read from during the presentation. "Sharks" illustrates many of the principles discussed in this chapter. Notice how the presenter begins with specific numbers to gain the attention of his audience, relates the topic to his audience, and reveals his relationship to the

244 Part Three   Types of Presentations

topic early in the presentation. Has the speaker used wit and humor when appropriate? Does he use complete arguments? What are some of the strategies he uses to persuade? What might you conclude about the organization of the presentation? Does he follow the ethical guidelines discussed in this chapter? Keep in mind that while this is a good example, it is only that—an example. As you consider the audience and the topic of your speech, you will likely have other strategies, ways of organizing and delivering your persuasive presentation that are valid and effective.

Sharks: The Misunderstood Monster

Uses specific numbers to gain attention and invite participation. [Step One Monroe's Motivated Sequence: gain attention and focus audience attention on the topic]

They are represented by over 350 different species. They appeared 200 million years before the dinosaurs and were on this earth around 399 million years before humans. They have remained virtually unchanged over those 400 million years.

And HUMANS are basically the only thing they have to fear. I am speaking of the shark. One of nature's most wonderful, yet most feared and misunderstood animals.

Sensory aid

(visual aid: SIX PHOTOS [on one slide] SHOWING DIVING SHARKS)

Relates the topic to the audience

These dates prove that sharks have a record of endurance. And so why would we need to care about their extinction?

Expert testimony

According to Stephen D. McCulloch, Division Director for the Dolphin Research and Conservation Program at Harbor Branch Oceanographic Institution, the shark is an "Apex Predator" which means it is an "indicator species which can help us to better manage irreplaceable natural resources." Sharks also play an important role in keeping other species in check and, therefore, in maintaining a critical balance within the fragile ocean environment.

Benefits persuade

[Step Two Monroe's Motivated Sequence: establish need]

Immune to most all disease, including cancer, sharks are the subject of intensive medical research that could some day benefit humans. Ultimately, their preservation will ensure ours . . . and likewise, their destruction will ensure the eventual destruction of our oceans . . . on which all mankind depends.

Relates the topic to the speaker

I have been a shark enthusiast ever since I can remember and have done extensive research on sharks over the past fifteen years. Even as a little kid, I would watch Shark Week every year on the Discovery Channel.

Preview of content
Question of fact

Sharks are an imperative part of our ocean and they need to be protected. In my speech, we will establish the truth about how dangerous sharks really are, how dangerous WE are to sharks, and what we can do to protect them.

Signpost

First of all, let's dispel some of the myths of how dangerous sharks are.

Uses analogy

[Step Three Monroe's Motivated Sequence: Satisfaction, Sharks are not the threat you thought they were.]

Sharks are not an imminent danger to humans. I would like to use an analogy to prove this. Think about what you are more afraid of, flying or driving. I would bet that many of you are more afraid of flying.

People fear flying even though their chances of being involved in an aircraft accident are about 1 in 11 million. On the other hand, your chance of being killed in an automobile accident is 1 in 5000.

Expert testimony

According to Flight Captain Ron Nielsen of fearlessflight.com, you are statistically at far greater risk driving to the airport than flying on an airplane, So why would I bring this up? Because the reason why we fear flying is the same reason that we fear being attacked by a shark: sensationalism.

Statistics

Even deaths from lightning exceed the number of attacks by sharks by more than double.

Visual aid

(visual aid: TABLE COMPARING NUMBER OF LIGHTNING FATALITIES VS. FATALITIES FROM SHARKS)

Chapter Eleven   Presenting Persuasive Messages   245

But for some reason, a lightning fatality doesn't seem to make a good news story. The fact is, shark attacks are rare, but when one happens, it is sure to become national news.

(visual aid: TABLE SHOWING NUMBER OF SHARK ATTACKS)   *Visual aid*
    Simple numbers

The U.S. Consumer Product Safety Commission reports that there were 37 known vending machine fatalities between 1978 and 1995—an average of 2.2 deaths by vending machine per year. Over the past 10 years, there were a total of six recorded shark attack fatalities in the U.S.—an average of .6 deaths per year.

So the next time you are afraid of stepping in the ocean, take a second to think about whether you bought a Pepsi that day . . . and survived.   *Humor and wit*

We believe that sharks are a threat to us, but the truth is that we are much more of a threat to sharks.   *Transition*

With the media blowing every shark attack story out of proportion, and individuals spreading shark propaganda, such as the story told by this picture—which, by the way, is completely fake—humans have created a public fear of sharks that is contributing to their demise. The truth of the matter, according to sharkattacks.com, is that compared to the 10–15 people killed by sharks each year around the world, over 100 million sharks perish at the hands of humans annually.   *Visual aid*
    Inductive reasoning
    Oral citation

And many populations may face extinction. Although sharks are killed for such things as jewelry and cosmetics, sharks are also killed for sport—or, you might say, to make men feel macho.   *Specific examples*

(visual aid: MULTI PHOTOS OF SHARKS BEING DISMEMBERED)   *Visual aid*

And as stupid as it is to kill something because it makes you feel like a bigger man, another reason for killing sharks is much worse: shark fin soup.   *Transition*

This so-called delicacy has caused millions of sharks to be hunted in an extremely brutal manner. Poachers catch a shark, cut off its fins, and then throw the shark back in the ocean—STILL ALIVE! Would anyone besides an ignorant, sadistic freak ever grab a dog, cut off its legs and throw it back into its yard?   *Hypothetical example for clarification*

Because most of the world thinks sharks are nothing more than killing machines, the brutal pursuit of "meat" for shark fin soup escapes notice. Sharks just aren't as cute as whales, dolphins, or seals. Apparently, people don't care whether they are eradicated into extinction or not.

But we need to care. We are the biggest threat to sharks, but we need to become their biggest protectors.   *Persuasive appeal*

What can we do to protect the shark? How can we help stop the needless killing and maiming of sharks?

(visual aid: TEN THINGS YOU CAN DO)   *Visual aid*
    [Step Four Monroe's Motivated Sequence: help audience visualize solutions]

Number one, do not use any products based on them and do not buy any jewelry or clothing that is obtained from sharks. And I hope it goes without saying . . . don't eat shark fin soup.   *Action step*

Just as important, spread the word. Let others know that millions of sharks are senselessly killed every year. Let them know the truth about the rate of shark attacks . . . that humans are over 1,100 times more likely to die from a bicycle accident than a shark attack.   *Statistics*

You can join organizations to help protect the shark. (visual aid: AWARE LOGOS) Project AWARE, which stands for Aquatic World Awareness, Responsibility, and Education, is a foundation that actively protects all aquatic life. Its campaign, Protect the Sharks, focuses on the problems I have described.   *Relates topic to audience*

Many organizations are campaigning to get certain species of sharks on the endangered species list.

Part Three   Types of Presentations

Oral citation
Simple numbers

According to the Web site of the Australian government, the population of the great white shark has experienced at least a 20 percent decrease in its population. And for an animal that gives birth to just a small number of pups every two or three years, this could be detrimental.

[Step Five Monroe's Motivated Sequence: call to action]

There are also organizations that raise funds for shark protection. Some collect donations via their Web sites. Two of these are sharksurvivor.com and sharktrust.org, where you can actually adopt a shark.

Handout

And if you are interested, I have several copies here of the Protect the Sharks educational brochure published by Project AWARE.

So now that you know what you can do, I leave the next step up to you: doing something about it.

Summary review

Today I have told you the facts about how dangerous sharks are to humans, and about how dangerous humans are to sharks. I also made recommendations for what we can do to protect them. With this information you now realize that sharks are a critical part of our ocean and need to be protected.

Visual aid

(visual aid: REUSE FIRST SLIDE 6 PHOTOS OF DIVING SHARKS)

Expert testimony
Ending quotation

I would like to leave you with this thought by Richard Martin, director of the ReefQuest Shark Research Program. "One can devise all manner of important-sounding ecological reasons why sharks should be protected. The truth is, we still don't fully understand the nature and extent of sharks' role in marine ecosystems. Sharks should be protected because a world with them is more interesting and diverse than one without."

Action step

Indeed, the scariest consequence of eliminating sharks from the sea is our own ignorance about what would happen. The choice is up to us.

Resources for Review and Discussion

SUMMARY

▶ You are both a sender and receiver of persuasion.
▶ Persuasive presentations change the audience.
▶ We identified three types of persuasive speeches:
  • The speech to inspire influences listeners' feelings.
  • The speech to convince influences listeners' beliefs or attitudes.
  • The speech of action influences listeners' behaviors or actions.
▶ Research in persuasion reveals useful applications to audience analysis and message production.
▶ Fact, value, and policy are three types of questions around which most persuasive presentations revolve.
▶ The organization of a persuasive speech can be similar to and different from other types of speeches.
  • The introduction and conclusion may depend on the credibility of the source and the nature of the change you are seeking from your audience.
  • We discussed four organizational patterns: topical sequence, cause and effect, problem-solution, and Monroe's Motivated Sequence.
▶ We considered four strategies of persuasion.
  • Consistency persuades.
  • Small, gradual changes persuade.
  • Benefits persuade.
  • Fulfilling needs persuades.
▶ Apply critical thinking through various kinds of reasoning.
  • Inductive reasoning uses specific instances and an inferential leap.
  • Deductive reasoning uses widely accepted premises to draw convincing conclusions.
  • Hard evidence has the most credibility.
  • Soft evidence can convince with more difficulty.
  • Reasoning from cause can be challenging because you have to show a solid link between cause and effect.
  • Reasoning from sign draws upon reliable signs that do not contradict and which are not accidental or coincidental.
  • Reasoning from generalization is used when you can count on wide acceptance or when the generalization is easily provable to a particular case.
▶ Fallacies
  • Weaken an argument.
  • Compromise ethical speaking.
▶ Ethical guidelines for persuasive presentations include:
  • Be careful whom you trust.
  • Analyze and evaluate messages for reason, truth, and benefit to you and your community.
  • Be aware of your history; it will impact the trustworthiness of your message.
  • Always be respectful of your audience.
  • Avoid fallacies.

KEY TERMS

  Use the *Public Speaking* CD-ROM and the Online Learning Center at www.mhhe.com/nelson to practice your understanding of the following terminology.

Argument
Audience analysis
Boomerang effect
Claim
Complete arguments
Compliance response
Consistency persuades
Cost-benefit analysis
Critical response

Deductive reasoning
Defensive response
Explicitness
Fallacy
Hierarchy of needs
Inductive reasoning
Persuasive presentations
Question of fact
Question of policy

Question of value
Relationship
Small, gradual changes persuade
Specific numbers
Speech of action
Speech to convince
Speech to inspire
Testimonial evidence

REFERENCES

[1] Schneider, Lacey (2004, Spring Semester). "Do you know where you stand?" An unpublished presentation delivered in Communication 110 (Honors Section), North Dakota State University, Fargo, ND.

[2] Dillard & Marshall, p. 481.

[3] Based on Chaiken S., Liberman, A., & Eagly, A. H. (1989). Heuristic and systematic processing within and beyond the persuasion context. In J. S. Uleman & J. A. Bargh (Eds.), *Unintended thought* (pp. 212–52). New York: Guilford Press.

[4] Liberman & Eagly.

[5] Dillard & Marshall, p. 481.

[6] Blum-Kulka, S. (1987). Indirectness and politeness in requests: Same or different? *Journal of Pragmatics, 11,* 131–46.

[7] Dillard, J. P., Wilson, S. R., Tusing, K. J., & Kenney, T. (1997). Politeness judgments in personal relationships. *Journal of Language and Social Psychology, 16,* 297–325.

[8] Holtgraves, T. (1997). Styles of language use: Individual and cultural variability in conversational indirectness. *Journal of Personality and Social Psychology, 73,* 624–37.

[9] Mueller, B. (1987). Reflections of culture: An analysis of Japanese and American advertising appeals. *Journal of Advertising Research, 27,* 51–59.

[10] O'Keefe, D. J. (1998). How to handle opposing arguments in persuasive messages: A meta-analytic review of the effects of one-sided and two-sided messages. In M. E. Roloff (Ed.), *Communication yearbook, 22* (pp. 209–49). Thousand Oaks, CA: Sage.

[11] Maslow, Abraham H. (1943). A theory of human motivation. *Psychological Review, 50,* 370–96.

[12] Dillard, James P. & Marshall, Linda J. (2003). Persuasion as a social skill. In John O. Greene & Brant R. Burleson (Eds.), *Handbook of communication and social interaction skills* (pp. 479–513). Mahwah, NJ: Lawrence Erlbaum.

[13] Rice, J. E. (2005). "Sharks: the misunderstood monster. An unpublished speech." North Dakota State University, Fargo, ND.

APPLICATION EXERCISES

 Go to the self-quizzes on the *Public Speaking* CD-ROM and the Online Learning Center at www.mhhe.com/nelson to test your knowledge of the chapter concepts.

1. Persuasive speeches often appeal to an audience's unmet needs. Since needs vary according to the community, college, class, and individual, you can make yourself more sensitive to audience needs by ranking the five unmet needs that you believe are important to your audience.

   a. _____

   b. _____

   c. _____

   d. _____

   e. _____

2. After reading the section on principles of persuasion, you should be able to identify cases in which they are correctly used. Examine the following cases and indicate which of the following principles is being observed:

C = *Consistency persuades*
S = *Small changes persuade*
B = *Benefits persuade*
N = *Fulfilling needs persuades*
G = *Gradual approaches persuade*

_____ a. To save my audience members considerable time and effort, I am going to provide them with a form letter that they can sign and send to the administration.

_____ b. Because I know most of my classmates are short of cash, I am going to tell them how to make some quick money with on-campus jobs.

_____ c. I plan to wait until the end of the speech to tell the audience members that the organization I want them to join will require two hours of driving per week.

Chapter Eleven   Presenting Persuasive Messages   249

_____ d. My audience of international students already believes in the value of learning public speaking, so I think the listeners will respond favorably to my recommendation for a course in voice and articulation.

_____ e. I would like my audience to cut up all their credit cards, but since they are unlikely to do so, I am instead going to ask that they try for a zero balance each month to avoid interest and fees.

Answers

a. B, b. N, c. G, d. C, e. S

CHAPTER TWELVE

Never doubt that a small group of committed individuals can change the world. Indeed, it's the only thing that ever has.
MARGARET MEAD (1901–1978), U.S. ANTHROPOLOGIST

Groups don't just get things done—they make extraordinary accomplishments in the face of overwhelming obstacles.
BUD BAUMANN, VICE PRESIDENT FOR CIGNA CORPORATION

Working and Presenting as a Group

What will you learn?

When you have read and thought about this chapter, you will be able to:

1. Explain what small groups are and why they are commonly used for public presentations.
2. Display effective leadership skills as you participate in small groups.
3. Use effective group communication skills.
4. Apply effective decision-making and problem-solving procedures.
5. Integrate individual presentations into a group presentation.
6. Evaluate individual and group productivity.

Business and professional speaking situations rarely involve just one person presenting to a large audience. Especially for many entry-level and mid-management positions, most public communication involves a team or group. Although group-based presentations have many benefits, these presentations also require greater coordination and planning. This chapter teaches you how to work in groups to prepare a high-quality presentation.

252   Part Three   Types of Presentations

Kim was assigned to work with a group of classmates—Antwan, Richard, Shelly, and Li—to prepare a persuasive presentation. Kim was pulling a "B+" in the class so far and really needed to nail the last speech to have a chance at an "A." Of course, the fact that the last presentation was group-based did not help. Kim had worked in groups before for other classes and knew that one or two slackers could ruin everything for the others. She was determined to not let that happen—she would write everyone's speeches if she had to. At the first meeting Kim came prepared with assignments for everyone and started by saying, "I have a plan that will ensure an 'A' for everyone. . . ."

Antwan, a well-liked and charismatic student, arrived at the group meeting just on time. He knew everyone from class, but had never really talked with some of the people in his group. One student, Kim, immediately started bossing people around. Antwan listened for a while and then spoke up, telling the group that they needed to slow down and actually talk about the assignment before making decisions on who was going to talk about what. He ended by saying, "The best way to get a bad grade on this is to rush things and not work together."

Li listened as Antwan and Kim talked and calmed down a little and actually started laughing about something that had happened in class earlier in the day. Now that the group had set some ground rules on how to talk with each other— most notably that no one should boss other people around—Li was ready to get to work. Li was majoring in sociology and had several good topics that they could possibly work on as a group. In fact, she and Richard were taking another course together, which required them to work at a senior center near school. Now, Li was ready to offer some suggestions for them to consider.

Compare Li's, Antwan's, and Kim's initial experiences in the group with your own when working alone on a presentation. You did most of your work by yourself and you made all the important decisions about your presentation. On the other hand, because you were in charge of your own presentation, you did not have someone like Li who could help you find a topic, nor did you have someone with Antwan's charisma to help you with delivery. Working in groups makes some things more difficult. Because groups have to negotiate about things, they often take a little longer to make decisions. But groups generally perform much more effectively than individuals on difficult tasks. This chapter teaches you how to enrich your group experiences. You will first learn about the nature of groups and why they are an increasingly common tool for public communication.

How Are Small Groups and Public Communication Connected?

What Are Small Groups?

Small group communication is *the interactions among three to nine people who are working together to achieve an interdependent goal.*[1] This definition, while to the point, invites further exploration.

First, *small* group implies that each member of the group is aware of the other members of the group and they all react to each other as individuals. Thus, *small* refers to members' mutual awareness of each other as individuals, not to absolute size. To illustrate the idea of mutual awareness, a class of 25 students may seem large on the first day of school but seem like a small group by the end of the term. Typically, small groups contain at least 3 people, but they may have as many as 15 (rarely more) members. Although the number of people in a small group has practical limits, the important characteristic is that members perceive themselves to be a collective entity. We arbitrarily eliminate the dyad (two people) from this definition because small groups are fundamentally different from dyads. For example, if one member leaves a dyad, the dyad falls apart. However, members often leave small groups, sometimes to be replaced by new members, and the group itself continues. Clearly, small groups are different from dyads.

Members of a small group *interact* in such a way that each can influence and be influenced by the others. This interaction occurs through communication, which is often face-to-face, but other channels of communication qualify, such as over a computer network. The substance that creates and binds a group together is the verbal and nonverbal communication that occurs among members. In a small group, members continually send and receive messages. The work of the group is accomplished through this communicative activity.

Finally, *interdependence* implies that one member cannot achieve the group's goal without the other members achieving the goal also. For example, for one basketball player on a team to win a game while the other members lose is impossible. They *all* win or lose together. The success of one member is dependent on the success of all the members. This principle suggests that cooperation among members must exist. Even though members may disagree, as was the case with Kim and Antwan initially, they must seek a joint outcome that will be satisfactory to all.

TRY THIS

Make a list of all the groups that you belong to. How do you think those groups illustrate the principle of interdependence?

The definition of small group communication establishes *communication* as the essential process within a small group. Communication creates a group, shapes it in unique ways, and maintains it. Like other forms of human communication, small group communication relies on verbal and nonverbal signals that are perceived, interpreted, and responded to by other people. Group members pay attention to each other and coordinate their behavior to accomplish the group's assignment. Perfect understanding between the person sending the signal and those receiving the signal is impossible; in a group, members strive to have enough understanding so that the group can achieve important objectives.

Why Are Small Groups Used for Presentations?

Small groups are increasingly used to facilitate public communication. First, important business presentations are often organized so that people with different backgrounds and skills discuss issues with which they each are familiar. So, Tate from research and development might introduce the concept for a new product, Shania from marketing might discuss how the new product compares with competitors' products, Scott from advertising might discuss initial plans for selling the product, and Emma, the project director, might discuss the timetable for rollout of the product. These types of presentations are increasingly common because many companies and organizations use **self-managed work teams,** or *groups of workers with different skills who work together to produce something or solve a problem,* to handle important issues like new product development, quality control, and human resources.

A second reason small groups are often used for public presentations is that they can make the process less stressful for everyone. Groups can help counteract many of the difficulties we face during public presentations because they satisfy our need for inclusion, affection, and control. **Inclusion** suggests that *people need to belong to, or be included in, groups with others.* As humans, we derive much of our identity, our beliefs about who we are, from the groups to which we belong. Starting with our immediate families and including such important groups as our church, mosque, or synagogue; interest groups; work teams; and social groups—all these help us define who we are. During public presentations, this need for inclusion might be particularly important because of the vulnerability that many of us feel. **Affection,** another essential need, *means that we humans need to love and be loved, to know that we are important to others who value us as unique human beings.* The emotional support from group members sharing similar experiences can build affection among group members, thus making us feel more comfortable. Finally, we have a need for **control,** or *the ability to influence our environment.* We are better able to exercise such control if we work together in groups. Preparing a good public presentation is challenging, but groups let us accomplish the task more effectively, thus satisfying our desire for control.

Although the content and format for group presentations differ, each has the following common elements:

1. *Group members share in responsibility.* Regardless of how the presentation is formatted, all group members share the task of preparing, and to some extent, presenting the presentation. Even if some group members are not responsible for the delivery of information, they might be responsible for preparing and controlling multimedia resources like PowerPoint or videos.

2. *Group members are interdependent.* As discussed at the beginning of the chapter, small groups are interdependent in the sense that all group members are essential to positive outcomes for the group. In most presentations, this interdependence is enhanced because each group member typically adds unique and necessary information about a topic. If one group member does not do his or her job, the audience will not have a complete understanding of the topic.

3. *Group presentations are more interactive.* When one presenter talks to an audience, norms and implicit rules often prevent audience members from asking questions or interrupting the speaker. Group presentations are inherently less focused on one-way transmission of information. Because multiple people speak and share ideas, a "democratic spirit" ensues and discussion in and among presenters and audience members flows more freely.

4. *Group presentations are coordinated.* Rather than having the right and responsibility of worrying about only your own message, as a member of a group you must be concerned about how your message fits within the context of other presenters' ideas. Such coordination takes careful planning.

Chapter Twelve   Working and Presenting as a Group   255

Group presentations are enjoyable, and in many cases, more productive than individual presentations.

TRY THIS

Identify three groups that you belong to: one that meets your need for inclusion, one that meets your need for control, and one that meets your need for affection.

Key Skills for Effective Group Presentations

Although group presentations differ from traditional informative and persuasive individual presentations, there are similarities. For instance, your individual component of a group presentation should be well researched, effectively organized, and delivered well. For the sake of clarity, however, here are some of the unique skills that may be required for a group presentation.

1. *Creativity.* The real benefit of working on presentations as part of a group is the chance to capitalize on the collective creativity of many people. Your ability to do good research and use a clever approach for discussing your topic will be greatly enhanced through group dialogue. This implies that groups working on a presentation should devote enough time to brainstorming and discussion of the topic(s) being addressed in the presentation.

2. *Coordination.* Group presentations should be well coordinated. For instance, there should be smooth transitions from one speaker to the next; visual aids should be coordinated as a group rather than each individual having her or his own approach (for instance, using one PowerPoint file rather than several separate files); all group members should dress professionally; and group members should have a plan for where those who are not presenting should stand or sit. In short, for group presentations every small detail should be planned in advance to demonstrate a well-coordinated effort.

3. *Identification and quick resolution of conflicts.* Because group efforts of any kind—presentations included—require that members work together, identifying and resolving conflict is essential for group success. To identify and manage conflict, group members should engage in open dialogue where they can explain and check their perceptions. If conflict is actually present, all group members should take part in talking through potential causes and solutions for the conflict. Conflicts surrounding group presentations typically stem from workload distribution, scheduling, and personality clashes among individual group members.

4. *Ability to incorporate discussion.* Group presentations typically invite more dialogue among presenters and between audience members and presenters. When planning group presentations, you and your team members should carefully discuss how and when to invite audience participation. You may want to prepare questions—perhaps in the form of a brief handout—that you want audience members to react to as the presentation progresses.

Key Skills for Effective Group Communication

Although groups are well suited to solving difficult problems, good group work does not happen without effort. Two types of skills emerge as most important: leadership skills and interaction skills.

Group Leadership Skills

A **leader** is *a person who influences the behavior and attitudes of others through communication.* For most groups you belong to for your classes, leaders will have to naturally emerge. In some cases, the teacher might assign one person to coordinate the activities of the group; in that case, the teacher is assigning a designated leader. Group leaders gain influence over group members through the use of **power,** which is *the interpersonal influence that one person has with others.*[2] According to this perspective, group leaders are likely to strategically use power depending on the type of group and relationships among people in the group. Research suggests that leaders use:[3]

- **Reward power** by *giving followers things they want and need,* including tangible items such as money, material goods, and personal favors or intangible things such as special attention, acknowledgment, and compliments.

- **Punishment power** by *withholding these same items.* For example, a leader who frowns because a member has failed to complete an assigned task is administering a form of punishment.

- **Coercion** as a form of *punishment that attempts to force compliance using hostile tactics.* Genuine leaders should not resort to coercion, because force breeds resentment.

- **Legitimate power** *by virtue of title or position.* Legitimate leaders have the right to do certain things in groups that other members may not do, such as calling meetings, preparing the agenda, checking on the work of other members, and making assignments.

- **Referent power** by *gaining the respect and admiration of group members.* When someone likes you, you have considerable influence over that person. The more people are admired and respected, the more others copy their behavior, and the greater is their power to influence the group.

- **Expert power** when *the group members value the leaders' knowledge or expertise.* For instance, if your group must conduct a panel discussion for class and you are the only one who has ever participated in a panel discussion, you have expertise the others value and, thus, can influence them because they respect your knowledge.

All members of a group have the ability to influence other members. In the opening story about Kim, Antwan, Richard, Shelly, and Li, Kim most likely tried to use reward power by enticing other group members to follow her lead to get an "A" on their presentation. Antwan, on the other hand, probably relied on his natural charisma to establish referent power. And, perhaps more subtly, Li was ready to use expert power to influence the group.

TRY THIS

People often assume that some types of leadership power are always better than other types; however, this is not necessarily the case. Come up with at least one instance when each type of power might be necessary to get the group's task accomplished.

In the case of Kim, Richard, Antwan, Shelly, and Li, we might conclude that the group has too many leaders. Actually, when groups of competent people work together, multiple leaders often emerge. In these situations, group members must recognize the need for a unique approach to group leadership. **Distributed leadership** assumes that *each member is expected to perform the communication behaviors needed to move the group toward its goal.* In fact, groups seem to be more productive when they distribute leadership functions. When groups with one leader are compared to groups whose members all engage in leadership behaviors, overall leadership activity, not the designated leader's activity alone, predicts group productivity.[4]

Some groups may not have people like Kim, Antwan, and Li who are willing and able to take on leadership roles. In those situations, you might need to take charge. Consider these suggestions[5] for effective leadership if faced with such a situation:

1. Effective leaders *are skillful communicators.* Emergent leaders speak frequently, although not necessarily the most frequently, in a group and are able to articulate their ideas clearly.
2. Effective group leaders *communicate a grasp of the task.* Their communication reveals extensive knowledge about the task, how to organize and interpret information, and what procedures will help get the job done efficiently.
3. Effective group leaders *synthesize ideas.* They are good at structuring disorganized or ambiguous information, at asking probing questions to bring out pertinent information, and at evaluating inferences and conclusions drawn from information.
4. Effective group leaders *do not control dialogue.* Group members dislike dogmatic leaders. Groups produce more and better alternatives if their leaders withhold their own opinions until later in a discussion and encourage members to consider multiple viewpoints.
5. Effective group leaders *are group-centered.* Effective leaders are not arrogant; they exhibit personal commitment to the group's goals in both word and deed, and they confront members who are more self- than group-centered.
6. Effective group leaders *respect others.* They are sensitive to nonverbal signals, and they are courteous when interacting with other group members. They also take steps to minimize or eliminate the insensitivity of others.
7. Effective group leaders *share rewards and take punishment.* Trusted leaders give credit to the group for accomplishments and work to develop the leadership competencies of all members. Leaders also avoid blaming group members for failures.

As you enact your own leadership style, be aware that you may have to display different leadership characteristics depending on the situation, time constraints, available resources, etc. *Democratic leaders* encourage members to participate in group decisions, even major ones: "What suggestions do you have for solving our

258   Part Three   Types of Presentations

problem?" This style of leadership works best in situations where there is plenty of time and relationship development is just important as task accomplishment. *Autocratic leaders* maintain strict control over their groups, including making assignments and giving orders: "Here's how we'll solve the problem. First, you will . . ." An *authoritarian leader* might be most effective in situations where there is little time, few resources, or when group members are unwilling or unable to work independently. *Laissez-faire leaders* are nonleaders who take almost no initiative for structuring a group discussion but may respond to questions: "I don't care; whatever you want to do is fine with me." Although the laissez-faire style is rarely effective, this approach might be used in situations where group members are more knowledgeable and have more expertise than the designated leader.

Group Interaction Skills

Although effective leadership is critical for groups to succeed, effective groups ultimately depend on effective communication among all group members. The roles you perform as a group member are important for helping the group establish unity, achieve agreed-upon outcomes, and resolve conflict.

Group roles comprise a set of behaviors that perform a function for the group. For formal roles, these actions are often specified in writing. For informal roles, members perform actions so regularly that others begin to expect them. For example, at the ASPCA, the other volunteers rely heavily on Jeff's timekeeping.

When you observe the roles people perform in groups, ask yourself what function they serve. The function, not the behavior itself, determines someone's role. For instance, Rich's joking would have a positive function if he joked occasionally to relieve tension during an argument. However, his constant and inappropriate joking performs the negative function of pulling the group off task. A member's actions must be interpreted in the context of what else is happening in the group.

A number of classification schemes describe typical group functions that members' actions serve. One common scheme classifies behaviors by whether they perform task, maintenance, or self-centered functions. **Task functions** are *behaviors that are directly relevant to the group's purpose and that affect the group's productivity.* Their purpose is to focus group members productively on their assignment. **Maintenance functions** are *behaviors that focus on the interpersonal relationships among members;* they are aimed at supporting cooperative and harmonious relationships. Both task and maintenance functions are considered essential to effective group communication. On the other hand, **self-centered functions** are *behaviors that serve the needs of the individual at the expense of the group.* The person performing a self-centered role implies, "I don't care what the group needs or wants. *I* want . . . " Self-centered functions manipulate other members for selfish goals that compete with group goals. Examples of statements that support task, maintenance, and self-centered functions are shown in Table 12.1. The list is not exhaustive; many more functions could be added.

Group functions performed by a member combine to create a member's informal role, which is a comprehensive, general picture of how a particular member typically acts in a group. An example of how individual functions combine to create a role is shown in Figure 12.1. As you can see, information-giving and opinion-giving behaviors primarily characterize the information specialist role. The storyteller role includes several behaviors such as dramatizing, relieving tension, supporting, summarizing, and clarifying. Combinations of behavioral functions create other informal roles.

Chapter Twelve   Working and Presenting as a Group   **259**

TABLE 12.1   CATEGORIES OF BEHAVIORAL FUNCTIONS

TASK FUNCTIONS AND STATEMENTS

Initiating and orienting	"Let's make a list of what we still need to do."
Information giving	"Last year, the committee spent $150 on publicity."
Information seeking	"Carlos, how many campus muggings were reported last year?"
Opinion giving	"I don't think the cost of parking stickers is the worst parking problem students have."
Clarifying	"Martina, are you saying that you couldn't support a proposal that increased student fees?"
Extending	"Another thing that Toby's proposal would let us do is . . . "
Evaluating	"One problem I see with Cindy's idea is . . . "
Summarizing	"So we've decided that we'll add two sections to the report, and Terrell and Candy will write them."
Coordinating	"If Rosa interviews the mayor by Monday, then Jim and I can prepare a response by Tuesday's meeting."
Consensus testing	"We seem to be agreed that we prefer the second option."
Recording	"I think we decided at our last meeting. Let me check the minutes."

MAINTENANCE (RELATIONSHIP-ORIENTED) FUNCTIONS AND STATEMENTS

Establishing norms	"It doesn't help to call each other names. Let's stick to the issues."
Gatekeeping	"Pat, you look like you want to say something about the proposal."
Supporting	"I think Tara's point is well made, and we should look at it more closely."
Harmonizing	"Jared and Sally, I think there are areas where you are in agreement, and I would like to suggest a compromise that might work for you both."
Tension relieving	"We're getting tired and cranky. Let's take a 10-minute break."
Dramatizing	"That reminds me of a story about what happened last year when . . . "
Showing solidarity	"We've really done good work here!" or "We're all in this together."

SELF-CENTERED FUNCTIONS AND STATEMENTS

Withdrawing	"Do whatever you want; I don't care," or not speaking at all.
Blocking	"I don't care if we've already voted; I want to discuss it again!"
Status and recognition seeking	"I have a lot more expertise than the rest of you, and I think we should do it the way I know works."

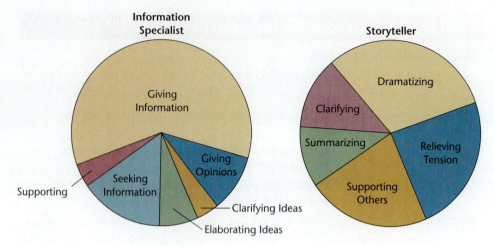

Figure 12.1
Behavioral functions combine to create roles.

SOURCE: *Communicating in Groups*, 2nd ed., by Gloria J. Galanes and John K. Brilhart, 1993. Reproduced with permission of The McGraw-Hill Companies.

Improving Your Group Communication Skills

Although the functions and roles tell us specific skills needed to communicate effectively in groups, a few additional principles help clarify strategies for effective and ethical group behavior.

1. *Relate your statements to preceding remarks.* Public speakers do not always have the opportunity to respond to remarks by others, but small group members do. Your statement should not appear irrelevant. Clarify its relevance to the topic under discussion by linking your remark to the preceding one. To make relevant comments you should do the following:

   - Briefly note the point made by the previous speaker that you want to address. We oftentimes hear people say, "I want to piggyback on Bill's comment by noting that we can meet our goal by . . ."
   - State your point clearly and concisely.
   - Summarize how your point adds to the comments made by others. For example, "So, I agree with Bill. We need to fundraise, but we can't get so caught up in raising money that we forget about our goal of volunteering."

2. *Use conventional word arrangements.* When you speak, you should use clear and more-or-less common language so people can understand you. Consider this comment: "I unequivocally recognize the meaningful contribution made by my colleague." While the language might impress some, perhaps a simple "I agree" would work just as well. Try the following to improve your verbal clarity during group discussions:

   - After connecting your idea to the discussion or previous speaker, state your point and then provide one piece of supporting information or additional explanation.
   - When done, ask whether anyone needs you to clarify your point.

3. *Speak concisely.* Do not be long winded. The main advantage of small groups is their ability to approach a problem interactively. If you monopolize talk time, that advantage of small group communication could be diminished or lost completely. To learn to speak concisely, try the following:

Chapter Twelve   Working and Presenting as a Group   261

- Write your idea down before speaking. People who are wordy during group discussions often spend much of their time trying to figure out what they want to say.

- Try to talk for no more than 30 seconds to one minute at a time. Of course, this time limit is arbitrary; however, one minute should be enough to get an idea out for the group, and you can always answer questions to clarify further.

4. *State one point at a time.* Sometimes this rule is violated appropriately, such as when a group member is presenting a report to the group. However, during give-and-take discussion, stating only one idea promotes efficiency and responsiveness. To ensure this practice, try the following strategies:

- As a group, appoint a **process observer,** *a person who is in charge of keeping the group discussion moving along and also preventing any member from bringing up more than one idea at a time.* After using the process observer a few times, these behaviors become second nature.

- If you have several ideas that vary in importance, provide some of the less important points to group members in written form for later reflection. Save discussion time for the most important ideas.

5. *Be ethical when handling conflict.* Group members must learn to manage **group conflict,** which is *an expressed struggle between two or more interdependent members of a group who perceive incompatible goals.*[6] Although some conflict can actually help groups make better decisions because ideas are debated and tested more vigorously, too much conflict may result in decreased group cohesiveness and could actually cause the group to cease functioning. To manage conflict, group members must be ethical in the way they approach disagreement and must also be willing to listen to and compromise with others. Ethical disagreement happens when you express your disagreement openly, disagree with ideas rather than people, base your disagreement on evidence and reasoning, and react to disagreement positively rather than defensively.[7]

Group Problem Solving

Kim, Antwan, and Li were faced with an **ill-defined problem,** or *a task with undefined objectives.* Of course, the group members knew they were to prepare a presentation, but its content and format were left to group members to decide. Ill-defined problems are exactly the type of problems that groups, rather than individuals, are best at solving. To tackle ill-defined problems, however, groups must be systematic in the way they discuss issues.

Groups using systematic procedures to solve problems have higher-quality discussions and are more effective at solving problems than are groups that do not use systematic procedures. Following a structured procedure often reminds discussants of something they forgot to do (such as analyze the problem thoroughly) and suggests logical priorities.[8] Effective problem solving starts with an appropriate discussion question, includes an explicit discussion of the criteria the group will use to judge potential solutions, and follows a systematic problem-solving procedure.

Wording the Discussion Question

A full analysis of the problem facing the group involves a discussion of the nature, extent, and cause of the problem. To accomplish this, problem-solving groups discuss three types of questions. *Questions of fact* deal with whether something is true or can be verified. *Questions of value* ask whether something is good or bad, better or worse. Cultural and individual values and beliefs are central to questions of value. *Questions of policy* ask what action should be taken. The key word *should* is either stated or implied in questions of policy. Examples of each type of question are presented in Table 12.2.

Sometimes, complex problems must address a combination of questions. The environment, for example, requires discussion of fact, value, and policy questions. Well-stated questions are clear, measurable, and focused on the problem rather than on a solution. First, the language and terminology should be concrete rather than abstract. If you use ambiguous terms such as *effective, good,* or *fair,* providing examples helps each group member understand as close to the same meaning as possible. Second, a well-stated discussion question helps group members know when they have achieved a solution. For example, a task force charged with "preparing a presentation by May 15 on why the number of children at risk for academic failure has increased in the community" knows exactly what to do by what deadline. Finally, a group should start its problem solving with a problem question

---

TABLE 12.2 QUESTIONS OF FACT, VALUE, AND POLICY

FACT

How has the divorce rate changed in the past 15 years?

How many Hispanic students graduate from high school each year?

What percentage of college students graduate in 4 years?

How often, on average, does a person speak each day?

What occupations earn the highest annual incomes?

VALUE

Why should people seek higher education?

How should Americans treat international students?

Does our legal system provide "justice for all?"

How should young people be educated about AIDS?

What is the value of standardized tests for college admission?

POLICY

What courses should students be required to take?

Should the state's drunk driving laws be changed?

What are the arguments for and against mandatory retirement?

Should the United States intervene in foreign disputes for humanitarian reasons?

What advantages should government provide for businesses willing to develop in high-risk areas of a city?

TABLE 12.3 PROBLEM QUESTIONS VS. SOLUTION QUESTIONS	
PROBLEM QUESTIONS	SOLUTION QUESTIONS
How much electricity is used each day on campus?	How can we motivate people to conserve electricity on campus?
Why are more people not volunteering for the regional Special Olympics?	How can we recruit more volunteers for the upcoming regional Special Olympics?
How can we make Ginny Avenue safer to cross?	How can we get the city council to reduce the speed limit on Ginny Avenue?

rather than a solution question. **Problem questions** *focus on an undesirable present state and imply that many solutions are possible.* They do not bias a group toward one particular option. **Solution questions,** on the other hand, *slant the group's discussion toward one particular option.* Solution questions may inadvertently cause a group to ignore creative or unusual options because they blind members to some alternatives. Examples of problem and solution questions appear in Table 12.3.

Typical discussion questions facing a group preparing a presentation might include:

- How much time do we have for the presentation?
- Is each person expected to perform according to explicit instructions?
- How much time are we willing to spend working as a group and individually on the presentation?
- Do group goals go beyond getting a good grade on the presentation?
- Should someone be in charge of scheduling meetings, keeping notes, and checking on the progress of individual group members?
- What topics would be good for our group to consider for the presentation?

By devoting time during the first couple of meetings to answering these questions, your group can function more efficiently and be more productive.

Discussing Criteria

Criteria are *the standards by which a group must judge potential solutions.* For example, a solution's likely effectiveness ("Will it work?"), acceptability ("Will people agree with our recommendations?"), and available resources ("Do we have enough time to tackle a topic this broad?") are common criteria. Group members should discuss and agree on criteria before adopting a solution. Because criteria are based on the values of group members, two members, each using rational tools of decision making, can arrive at different conclusions. The more similar group members are in age, gender, ethnicity, background, attitudes, values, and beliefs, the more easily they can agree on criteria.

Two kinds of criteria are common. **Absolute criteria** are *those that MUST be met; the group has no leeway.* **Important criteria** are *those that SHOULD be met, but the group has some flexibility.* Group members should give the highest priority to criteria that *must* be met. Ideas that do not meet absolute criteria should be rejected, and the rest ranked on how well they meet important criteria.

264   Part Three   Types of Presentations

TABLE 12.4 ABSOLUTE AND IMPORTANT CRITERIA FOR A GROUP PRESENTATION ASSIGNMENT	
ABSOLUTE CRITERIA (*MUST* BE MET)	IMPORTANT CRITERIA (*SHOULD* BE MET)
• Must involve all group members. • Must last between 30 and 40 minutes total. • Must include an average of three sources of information per person. • Both group and individual presentations must be organized appropriately.	• Should be easy to research. • Should emphasize visual information. • Should be rehearsed several times. • Should be interesting to all audience members on face value.

Your group presentation assignment likely will be a problem accompanied by absolute and important criteria. Notice in Table 12.4 that absolute criteria for the presentation come directly from the teacher. The group must meet those criteria to achieve a passing grade on the assignment. Important criteria established by the group are somewhat less tangible but will likely result in a higher grade for the presentation. Once these criteria are established, group members will have a logical basis for brainstorming and evaluating options for the presentation.

Identifying Alternatives

One of the most important jobs a leader has is to encourage group creativity. One *procedure that encourages creativity* is **brainstorming,** a technique that originated in the advertising industry to help develop imaginative advertising campaigns. Group brainstorming is generally enhanced when groups are highly cohesive, when leaders are chosen democratically, and when group members have substantial knowledge related to the problem being addressed.[9] Research suggests that the presence of any two of these factors allows groups to outperform individuals when brainstorming. The idea is to come up with every alternative imaginable. Critical evaluation kills creativity, so the main rule of brainstorming is "no evaluation," at least during the brainstorming process. Evaluation of the ideas takes place *after* the group has exhausted imagination.

Your group can use brainstorming in a variety of ways during your discussions about the presentation. Initially, brainstorming identifies possible topics for the presentation. Once a topic has been chosen, your group might need to brainstorm formats for how to present the information. Last, brainstorming might help individual group members to plan and present an effective message.

Evaluating Alternatives

After your group has adequately brainstormed alternatives, the final task is to evaluate alternatives. At this stage in the discussion, use the criteria you identified earlier to judge the usefulness of each possible solution. Your group should quickly eliminate solutions failing to meet absolute criteria. Once the nonviable

E-Note

GROUP PRESENTATION RESOURCES ON THE WEB

Because small group communication is becoming such a vital component of many organizations, consulting firms now offer professional workshops aimed at helping companies and organizations implement effective group practices. 3M corporation has a Web site containing several resources that can help you improve your group communication skills. The Web site also offers advice on group presentations. Visit the Web site at: **http://www.3m.com/meetingnetwork/readingroom.** While visiting the site, jot down at least two practical suggestions that your group should consider for its presentation.

---

alternatives are eliminated, group members must evaluate each alternative based on remaining important criteria. Eventually, the group must determine which alternative best meets the set of important criteria identified by the group earlier.

Shelly listened as Kim, Antwan, and now Li talked about doing this and that for the group presentation. Everyone was cool, but the discussion was going around in circles, and they were having a difficult time getting things spelled out. Shelly had read the chapter on group communication and suggested they follow the problem-solving outline discussed in the chapter. After some good-natured ribbing about her being an overachiever for reading the chapter so thoroughly, the group tentatively followed Shelly's suggestion. After about half an hour, the group had brainstormed topics, selected a topic (thanks mostly to Li's list of ideas), and developed a plan for structuring the presentation. The outcome was righteous; after four days' worth of efficient work, the group was able to practice the presentation several times. The end result was the highest grade in the class on the assignment!

Types of Group Presentations

A wide variety of group presentations exists. At the annual convention of the National Communication Association (www.natcom.org), faculty and students from around the country typically make presentations—in groups—using one of these formats: panels, discussion groups, roundtable discussions, town hall meetings, and debates. Members of a law firm trying to land a big client might use four or five representatives to carefully overview the services and expertise of the firm—following more or less a panel discussion format. At Pace University in New York City, a group of students in a computer science course might prepare and present a multimedia symposium discussing and demonstrating Web site design for nonprofit organizations in their lower Manhattan community. Let's look at several common approaches to group presentations: symposia, panel discussions, and debates.

Symposia

A **symposium** is *a type of group presentation where individual members of the group divide a large topic into smaller topics for coordinated individual presentations.* Typically, one of

265

Presenter	Time	Responsibility
Leslie	00:00–03:00	Opening Remarks • Attention getter • Listener relevance link • Preview the objectives of the symposium
David	03:00–09:00	Causes of Water Shortages • Increased Population • Increased Development • Drought
Karla	09:00–15:00	Current Policies Governing Water Shortages • Mandatory Rationing • Federal Policies • Treaties with other States
Todd	15:00–21:00	Effects of Water Shortages • Diminished Water Quality • Economic Harms • Damage to Ecosystems
Alane	21:00–27:00	Potential Solutions • Recycling Storm Runoff • Desalinization • Cloud Seeding
Leslie	27:00–40:00	Concluding Remarks and Audience Questions • Summary • Call to action • Questions (10 minutes)

Figure 12.2 **Schedule for symposium on water shortage.**

the group members acts as a moderator for the symposium and provides an introduction and conclusion for the group in addition to brief transition statements introducing each individual presenter. The moderator might also be responsible for fielding questions from the audience.

Groups preparing for a symposium presentation must initially decide on a topic and then discuss how specific aspects of the topic can be addressed by individual presenters—taking care to ensure that each presenter has a roughly equal amount of information to cover. Consider a group choosing to do a symposium on the topic of water shortage. With five people, one person will act as a moderator. The remaining four members of the group must decide who will handle specific aspects of this relatively broad topic. After doing initial research, the group can compile a list of topics and subtopics related to water shortage. Then, after preparing a working outline of those ideas, the group can divide areas of responsibility and prepare a tentative schedule for the presentation. Figure 12.2 provides a sample schedule for a 40-minute symposium.

Depending on your teacher's preference, you might be asked to do a particular type of symposium. Although each type has different content, the general format for each type is typically the same as that illustrated in Figure 12.2.

Current Issue Symposium

The water shortage symposium in Figure 12.2 is an example of a current issue group presentation. The objective of this presentation is to provide a coordinated and detailed analysis of some current event or significant issue. Much of the group's effort for this type of presentation must be devoted to brainstorming, researching, and outlining potential topics. Typically, though not always, a current issue symposium tackles topics that are somewhat broader than in an individual presentation. In addition, your teacher will probably expect you to address topics in more depth because you can draw on the research and ideas of other group members.

Multimedia Symposium

Because groups are often better at producing creative solutions to problems, some teachers assign a special type of symposium asking group members to pay particular attention to the use of multimedia resources. Angela Garcia, a sociology professor at the University of Cincinnati, asks her students to prepare multimedia symposia discussing aspects of a culture from outside the United States, including language, ethnicity, and communication.[10] Garcia requests that students incorporate music, video, art, and other multimedia resources as part of their presentations. Similar approaches could be used to examine any variety of topics.

For this type of symposium, group members should think creatively when brainstorming for multimedia resources to use and should also practice several times to coordinate all aspects of the presentation. For instance, you want to avoid playing long clips from songs or movies. Longer clips (more than 30 seconds) take attention away from the message(s) you want to relay and can actually confuse listeners. Because using multimedia resources tends to take a great deal of time, practicing the entire presentation is recommended—otherwise, one person might take substantially longer than expected and the entire time allocation plan could be destroyed. Remember that multimedia resources also take much longer to prepare than other types of presentation resources—you might need to edit video or audio, and you might need to combine your resources into a PowerPoint presentation. Finally, emphasizing creativity is important. Students often assume that showing video is the best form of multimedia. Music, art, pictures, and even people to interview (on tape) are all potential resources for a multimedia presentation.

Cultural Symposium

A third type of symposium asks each group of students to pick a unique culture or co-culture to analyze. One group of students chose to analyze the Native American co-culture for their symposium. One student in the group discussed origins of various Native American tribes, another analyzed how various bands developed unique customs, rituals, and beliefs, another traced what happened to many of the larger tribes during the 1800s when westward expansion of the white population caused many conflicts and forced evacuations, and a fourth student analyzed the current status of many of the tribes, including the issues of casino gambling on reservations and Native American mascots of sports teams. As you can see, the group analyzing Native American issues used a basic chronological arrangement to divide responsibilities among group members. Although some of the individuals used PowerPoint and other multimedia resources, others did not— but the same project could have been done as a "Multimedia Presentation," where all group members would have been required to use multimedia.

Cultural Note

GROUPS USED TO REDUCE RACIAL CONFLICT

Grant High School, one of the most ethnically diverse high schools in Los Angeles' San Fernando Valley, has 32 distinct ethnic cultures represented in the 3,300-person student body population. Although several ethnic groups are represented, the majority of students are either Latino (51%) or white (36%). Many of the white students are of Armenian descent and represent a unique co-culture in the school. Unfortunately, the potential positive aspects of substantial diversity have been short-circuited by racial tension. Each October, Latino and Armenian American students regularly engage in clashes—students have even been stabbed and shot. No one is quite sure what caused the racial tension to brew.

In efforts to build racial harmony, communication students from California State University Northridge, in partnership with the National Communication Association, the Southern Poverty Law Center, Campus Compact, and the American Association of Higher Education, have initiated a program called "Communicating Common Ground." The purpose of this program is to use small group intervention to promote racial harmony, unity, and understanding. At Grant High School, younger students from different ethnic backgrounds are placed in small groups of 12 people to brainstorm the following issues:

- Why do racial tensions exist?
- What groups experience racial tensions in the school?
- What can parents, students, and faculty do to address this racial tension?

Because the program at Grant High School is still in the early stages, the long-term effect of small group interventions on students' attitudes and behaviors is unknown. In their report to the National Communication Association, project coordinators from Grant High School and Cal State Northridge reported no violent episodes during the last academic year. In addition to the Cal State Northridge–Grant High School project, 29 other Communicating Common Ground initiatives have been carried out across the country.

SOURCE: Adapted from Hilary MacGregor, "Project Seeks Common Ground to End School's Violence," *Los Angeles Times* (October 22, 2000): B1, and the National Communication Association Web site (http://www.natcom.org/Instruction/CCG/calstate.htm).

Teaching Symposium

Groups are particularly effective at taking complex ideas and determining how to present them to audiences. For that reason, some group assignments are designed as teaching presentations. A common approach is to ask a group to choose topics from a textbook chapter or some other resource or reading assigned by the teacher and then present information from that resource to the class. The objective of the group is to teach the class important information, skills, and strategies discussed in the chapter or reading. Although the teaching symposium is similar to the other types of symposia discussed, group meetings should pay particular attention to the best ways to teach the assigned material. Group members should discuss how to combine activities, discussion questions, multimedia, and traditional lectures so that the material will engage audience members. Although you are students, you should think like a teacher for this assignment.

Presenter	Time	Responsibility
Rob	00:00–03:00	Opening remarks
Natalie	03:00–06:00	Defining student-managed farm markets
Suchita	06:00–09:00	Working with the college farm
Chris	09:00–12:00	The costs and benefits for students
Brian	12:00–15:00	How students can participate in the decision-making process
Chris	15:00–17:00	Discussion group directions– Answer the following questions: • What benefits do you see for a farm market? • What drawbacks do you see in the plan? • What would you like to see in a farm market? • Other questions
	17:00–27:00	Group discussions led by members of the panel
Rob	27:00–37:00	Group reports, audience questions, and concluding remarks

Figure 12.3 **A panel presentation over the plan for a new student-managed farm market.**

Panels

Symposia are more or less similar to other types of presentations you might prepare in your class—like an informative or persuasive presentation. Symposia differ from those presentations because a group of people must coordinate their individual presentations around a common topic. **Panels** differ from symposia because they *rely less on the transmission of information between the presenter and the audience, and focus more on interaction and dialogue in and among presenters and audience members.* A typical panel presentation begins with a moderator introducing a topic for discussion, followed by brief introductory statements by panelists, and then time for interaction between and among panelists and audience members. Figure 12.3 provides a basic outline for a panel discussion on the topic of student-managed farm markets.

As you can see, this panel format builds in time for audience members to discuss issues raised by the panelists in small groups. Then, after short group discussions, the entire class returns to a general discussion of whether to propose a student-managed farm market. Using small groups to generate audience participation is wise if the panel is presenting on a topic that is controversial or that many audience members might wish to discuss. As an alternative to using small group discussions, presenters can make longer opening statements, and some of the time devoted to small group discussions could be redirected to time for audience questions.

Panel discussions are particularly effective for topics that are controversial and/or are very relevant to most audience members. These types of presentations work less well for topics about which audience members know little. They may not have enough background to effectively discuss issues or ask questions. Consequently, groups planning for a panel presentation format should carefully consider whether this format is appropriate for the audience and topic.

The moderator is very important to a panel discussion format. Besides introducing speakers, the moderator must field audience questions and know to which member of the panel to direct questions. The best moderators are those who know a great deal about the material and who are able to think on their feet quickly. Watching Sunday morning political talk shows is an excellent way to see panel discussions in action—nearly all use this format.

TRY THIS

After watching one or more television shows based on a panel discussion format (consider a political talk show, a sports talk show, or even a daily talk show), identify skills that you think are important for the moderator to have. After listing the important moderator skills you observed, consider how you could use those skills to enhance your presentation.

Debates

In a **debate,** *members of the group divide responsibilities to prepare both "pro" and "con" presentations on a controversial issue or question.* Consider this question: "Should the city create new ordinances to enact tougher penalties for individuals who have nuisance parties in their apartment or house?" Various cities have such policies. Nuisance parties are typically defined as parties with excessive noise, underage alcohol consumption, and/or excessive public intoxication. These types of parties are most problematic in neighborhoods where "locals" and students live close together.

If your group wanted to debate the effectiveness of nuisance party ordinances, you would first need to divide group members into pro and con sides. Those individuals assigned to the "pro" side might interview local citizens, law enforcement officers, and university administrators to determine arguments in favor of such ordinances. Those on the "con" side would surely interview students, and might interview local attorneys and civil rights leaders to get opposing arguments. For many debate topics, including nuisance party laws, a great deal of information is available at the library and on the Internet.

Debate formats typically include two types of presentations: constructive presentations and rebuttal presentations. In **constructive presentations** *you initially present arguments—both for and against an idea.* In **rebuttal presentations** *presenters respond to arguments raised by the opposing side.* If you are a "con" presenter making a rebuttal, you will analyze and critique the arguments in favor of nuisance ordinances. One additional principle in debates is that the side in favor of changing the **status quo**—*the way things are currently done*—typically gets the first and last word. Figure 12.4 provides a sample format for a group debate over nuisance party laws.

Notice how each side in the debate has equal time to present its ideas. In addition, notice that the amount of time devoted to James's presentation is the

Presenter	Time	Responsibility
Doug	00:00–03:00	Introduce topic and preview format
Steve	03:00–09:00	Constructive speech in favor of nuisance ordinance
Becky	09:00–15:00	Constructive presentation against nuisance ordinance
James	15:00–19:00	Rebuttal of Becky's "con" presentation
Andi	19:00–25:00	Concluding "con" rebuttal
James	25:00–27:00	Concluding "pro" rebuttal
Doug	27:00–40:00	Summary of key arguments and time for audience questions

Figure 12.4 **Debate over nuisance party laws.**

same as everyone else's, but that his time is divided into a first rebuttal and a concluding rebuttal. This division of time allows the "pro" side to speak first—to lay out their case for change—and last in the debate. The format described in Figure 12.4 also includes a moderator and time for questions from the audience. Some teachers may require groups to build in time for members from each side to cross-examine the other side rather than having time for audience questions. Finally, some teachers may have the audience "vote" for a winner of the debate after the last presentation has been made.

Public debate is likely one of the most challenging presentations you will make. The experience is worth the effort. Students often comment that these presentations were more enjoyable in the long run than most other types. Successful debaters know much about the topic in question so they can think on their feet. In addition, debate arguments are always based on good evidence and audience adaptation.

Evaluating Group Productivity

Using groups to accomplish any task—whether the task is organizing a dance for local seniors, planning a community health fair, or raising awareness of environmental issues on campus—involves risk. The group can fail to become interdependent and work together, or one or more members can fail to accomplish their assigned duties adequately. For that reason, observation of, reflection upon, and evaluation of group behaviors is important. Some teachers even include your reflection on group activities as a component of your grade in the course.

Observing and reflecting on your group's activities requires careful evaluation of the group as a whole as well as individual members' contributions to group tasks. Figure 12.5 provides a sample progress evaluation form that your group can use to track work on your group presentation. Before adjourning each meeting, your group should discuss responses to the questions on the form. One form should be completed for each meeting.

Group Progress Form

Group Members: Sue, Jim, Andrea, Lau, and Keran

Presentation Topic: Still deciding

Meeting #1   Date: Nov 3   **Members Present:** All

Objectives for Meeting: Talk about assignment
                                        Brainstorm initial topics

Outcomes of Meeting:

We brainstormed an initial list of 12 topics. After thinking about them and combining some topics, we narrowed the list to 3 good topics: the environment, health and wellness, and seniors in our community.

Assignments for Next Meeting Scheduled for: Nov 5

Each person is supposed to find one article (or book) on each topic. At the next meeting, we will discuss the articles and select a final topic. Everyone is supposed to e-mail article citations to the rest of the group so that we do not duplicate research.

Figure 12.5 **Example of a group progress form.**

In addition to evaluating the progress of your group as a whole, you might also be asked to evaluate the individual contributions of group members. Taking time to review previous information on leadership and group communication skills will help you complete this reflective evaluation. Figure 12.6 provides an example evaluation sheet based on leadership behaviors and group communication behaviors. Notice that you rate each person, including yourself, and provide brief comments. When commenting on member performance, take care to provide descriptive feedback. Notice how Andrea provided descriptive comments about both her and Keran's behaviors during group meetings. Descriptive rather than exclusively evaluative feedback is more productive in helping people understand how others perceive their behaviors. Although the sample shows evaluations only for Andrea and Keran, your evaluation should be of each group member.

In closing, you should understand that group presentations should follow the principles and practices presented throughout this book for individual presentations. Accordingly, group presentations involve research and audience analysis. They should be organized, supported, rehearsed, and delivered effectively. The overall group presentation should also have an introduction and conclusion, which follow the guidelines provided for individual presentations. And to ensure professional delivery, groups should plan and practice how to make smooth transitions from one speaker to another and coordinate their visual aids. Group presentations do require planning and cooperation; however, the format also allows

Chapter Twelve   Working and Presenting as a Group

Group Evaluation Form

Your name: Andrea

Directions: Rate each member of your group on how well they display leadership qualities and how well they engage in group communication behaviors. Use the following scale for numeric responses and provide comments as necessary. Remember that "Self-Centered Functions and Statements" are undesirable qualities of group communicators. Consequently, a rating of "5" would indicate that the person avoids those behaviors. Write "NO" if you did not observe the person using a particular category of behaviors.

1 = Very Ineffective

2 = Ineffective

3 = Neither Effective or Ineffective

4 = Effective

5 = Very Effective

Group Member Name	Task Functions and Statements	Maintenance Functions and Statements	Self-Centered Functions and Statements	Leadership Behaviors and Qualities
Andrea (me)	4	3	3	4
	Comments: I was the person who tried to keep the group on task. I most often used opinion giving and coordinating statements during discussions. I need to work on getting along with other group members when we have disagreements—should avoid dominating discussion. I tended to use status seeking comments because I wanted to get things done.			
Keran	4	4	4	5
	Comments: Keran was the real leader of the group. She handled conflict between Lau and me when it came up. Keran took care to schedule meetings and take notes. Keran was really good at initiating discussions and harmonizing. She was an effective leader because she made sure all of us had a say in group decisions and did not try to boss people around.			

Figure 12.6   **Group member evaluation example.**

presenters to capitalize on the talents of multiple individuals. Consider the quote by U.S. anthropologist Margaret Mead that began this chapter: "Never doubt that a small group of committed individuals can change the world. Indeed, it's the only thing that ever has."

Resources for Review and Discussion

SUMMARY

In this chapter you have learned the following:

▶ Small groups contain between three and fifteen people who interact, are interdependent, and use communication to create a bond.
  • Small groups are used to facilitate public presentations because many organizations require people to specialize and, consequently, no one person can effectively know all the details necessary for a presentation.
  • Groups make the process of presenting less stressful because they help us meet our needs for affection, inclusion, and control.
▶ A leader is someone who influences the behavior of others in the group. Any member of a group can be a leader.
  • Leaders use power to influence others. Various forms of power include reward, punishment, coercion, legitimate, expert, and referent power.
  • Some groups function under a distributed leadership model where each member performs some leadership roles.
  • Effective leaders are skillful communicators who understand the task facing the group, synthesize ideas, and take steps to ensure that communication within the group is open and respectful.
▶ Effective group communication skills require that group members perform various roles for the group.
  • A role consists of a set of behaviors that perform some function for the group.
  • Various roles enable group members to accomplish one of three functions: task functions, maintenance functions, and self-centered functions. Although task and maintenance functions may help the group achieve desired outcomes, self-centered functions often come at the expense of the group.
  • Effective group communicators are concise, clear, relevant, and ethical in the way they talk with others in the group.
▶ Group decision making involves four steps: (1) wording the discussion question, (2) discussing criteria for evaluating potential solutions, (3) brainstorming alternatives, and (4) evaluating alternatives. The group leader(s) can play an important role in helping the group maintain structure and creativity throughout this process.
▶ Various formats can be used for group presentations.
  • A symposium is a group presentation where individual members of the group divide a large topic into smaller topics for coordinated individual presentations.
  • A panel is more interactive than a symposium and relies less on the transmission of information from speaker to audience.
  • A debate involves group members presenting both pro and con messages about a controversial topic or issue.
▶ When evaluating group productivity, you should reflect on how well the group met the goals established through dialogue and planning, and you should also reflect on and evaluate how well individual members contributed to group activities.

KEY TERMS

  Use the *Public Speaking* CD-ROM and the Online Learning Center at www.mhhe.com/nelson to practice your understanding of the following terminology.

Absolute criteria	Debate	Leader
Affection	Distributed leadership	Legitimate power
Brainstorming	Expert power	Maintenance functions
Coercion	Group conflict	Panel
Constructive presentations	Ill-defined problem	Power
Control	Important criteria	Problem questions
Criteria	Inclusion	Process observer

Punishment power	Self-centered functions	Status quo
Rebuttal presentations	Self-managed work teams	Symposium
Referent power	Small group communication	Task functions
Reward power	Solution questions	

REFERENCES

[1] Galanes, Gloria, Adams, Katherine, & Brilhart, John (2004). *Effective group discussion: Theory and practice.* New York: McGraw-Hill.

[2] Wilmot, William, & Hocker, Joyce (2001). *Interpersonal conflict.* New York: McGraw-Hill, p. 104.

[3] French, John R. P., & Raven, Bertram (1981). The bases of social power. In Dorwin Cartwright & Alvin Zander (Eds.), *Group dynamics: Research and theory* (p. 317). New York: McGraw-Hill,

[4] Barge, J. Kevin (1989). Leadership as medium: A leaderless group discussion model. *Communication Quarterly, 37.2,* 237-47.

[5] Adapted from Galanes, Gloria, Adams, Katherine, & Brilhart, John (2004). *Effective group discussion: Theory and practice.* New York: McGraw-Hill, p. 204.

[6] Wilmot, William, & Hocker, Joyce (2001). *Interpersonal conflict.* New York: McGraw-Hill, p. 41.

[7] Galanes, Gloria, Adams, Katherine, & Brilhart, John (2004). *Effective group discussion: Theory and practice.* New York: McGraw-Hill, p. 318.

[8] Poole, Marshall Scott (1983). Decision development in small groups II: A study of multiple sequences in decision making. *Communication Monographs, 50.3,* 227.

[9] Moore III, Robert M. (2000). Creativity of small groups and of persons working alone. *Journal of Social Psychology, 140.1,* 142-44.

[10] Garcia, Angela (2001). Group multi-media presentations in "the sociology of language and ethnicity." *Radical Pedagogy, 3.3,* NP.

APPLICATION EXERCISES

 Go to the self-quizzes on the *Public Speaking* CD-ROM and the Online Learning Center at www.mhhe.com/nelson to test your knowledge of the chapter concepts.

1. For each of the types of leadership power (reward, punishment, coercion, referent, and expert), identify an example of a leader you have encountered who uses that type of power. Briefly describe the leader, how she/he uses power, and discuss the effectiveness of the person's leadership qualities.

2. Evaluate your own behaviors as a group participant. Select a group in which you are a regular member. As you review the categories of behavioral functions listed in Table 12.1, identify your strengths as a group communicator and at least one behavior that you should improve upon or eliminate.

3. Pick a topic that is of interest to you. For that topic, generate the following types of questions:
   a. Fact
   b. Value
   c. Policy
   d. Problem

APPENDIX A

Ceremony and ritual spring from our heart of hearts: those who govern us know it well, for they would sooner deny us bread than dare alter the observance of tradition.

F. GONZALEZ-CRUSSI, 1936– , PATHOLOGIST AND PHYSICIAN, CHILDREN'S MEMORIAL HOSPITAL, CHICAGO

A society emphasizing social rituals and manners requires a kind of reverence for words to adequately express sentiment and feeling.

WILLIAM VAN O'CONNOR, 1915–1966, PROFESSOR OF ENGLISH, UNIVERSITY OF CALIFORNIA–DAVIS

Speaking on Special Occasions

What will you learn?

After reading and thinking about this chapter, you will be able to:

1. Explain how ceremonial presentations differ from other types of presentations in purpose, style, structure, and formality.
2. Describe several types of ceremonial presentations, including presentations to welcome, praise, introduce, nominate, dedicate, commemorate, honor, and entertain.
3. Prepare a ceremonial presentation appropriate to an audience, setting, and occasion.

Most of this book is devoted to planning, preparing, and delivering presentations for practical purposes—to teach audience members about a topic or persuade them to change in some way. Although many of our public presentations involve such objectives, another common type of speaking situation involves *presentations that highlight a special event.* These speeches are quite common and are generally referred to as **special occasion presentations.** This chapter teaches you about special occasion presentations by showing how they differ from other types of presentations, identifying the various types of special occasion presentations, and guiding you in developing your own special occasion speeches.

A–2   Appendix A

Kim had worked tirelessly for a month and a half to put the finishing touches on *her biology class' sustainable agriculture garden. As project manager, Kim was in charge of everything from planning the layout of the garden to helping individual teams implement sustainable agriculture techniques to maximize yield. The day before the grand opening of the garden, Dr. Lehman told Kim that he wanted her to "do a short talk" commemorating the grand opening. Kim knew much about the garden, but she was initially at a loss for how to approach the presentation. Leslie, Kim's roommate, was currently taking a public speaking class and suggested that Kim approach the presentation as a special occasion speech.*

Leslie gave Kim good advice, because Kim's presentation on the sustainable agriculture garden probably would best be approached as a speech to dedicate or commemorate. Although Kim might inform her audience about aspects of the garden, and perhaps persuade them about the importance of sustainable agriculture, her presentation probably would not work well if she prepared a traditional informative or persuasive presentation because such a presentation would likely not fit the occasion well.

Special occasion presentations are unique when compared with more traditional informative and persuasive presentations. Specifically, special occasion presentations have unique approaches in purpose, style, organization, and formality.

Unique Characteristics of Special Occasion Presentations

Purpose

Recall from previous chapters that the primary purpose of an informative speech is to teach and the primary purpose of a persuasive speech is to change behaviors or beliefs. Although special occasion presentations might try to inform or persuade, these objectives are typically secondary. Rather, the primary purpose of a special occasion presentation is to perform a **ritual,** *a ceremonial act that is characterized by qualities or procedures that are appropriate to the occasion.*

All cultures have ceremonial rituals. Weddings, funerals, grand openings, award ceremonies, and graduations are all examples of ritualized events. During such events, public presentations often punctuate important moments. At a wedding reception, for instance, the toasts to the new couple made by the "best man" and "maid of honor" are punctuating moments, as is Kim's dedication of the garden. The ritualistic nature of special occasion speeches is important. Such rituals help bring certainty and comfort to otherwise stressful events, they help attendees know what to expect, and they help attendees and audience members share in a common collective experience, such as wishing good tidings to a newly wedded couple or dedicating a new garden to a devoted teacher. Some scholars go so far as to say that ritualized presentations at special occasions help link together the past, present, and future.

Style

Special occasion speeches typically differ in style from more traditional informative and persuasive speeches. Recall from Chapter 2 that style refers to the clarity

Cultural Note

WEDDING CEREMONIES WITH A CULTURAL TOUCH

In America, wedding rituals dictate that the bride wear something old, something new, something borrowed, and something blue to be safe and happy. In her book, *Wedding as Text: Communicating Cultural Identities through Ritual*, author Wendy Leeds-Hurwitz explores the cultural traditions of wedding ceremonies. Leeds-Hurwitz suggests that all aspects of modern weddings are based on ritualistic expectations drawn from cultural scripts. Thus, speeches in tribute to the bride and groom, gifts, colors, and even the exchange of rings are culturally sanctioned traditions. As one explores wedding ceremonies for different cultures such as Indian, Asian, Latin American, and North American, the role of public speaking changes to signify unique cultural traditions.

and ornamentation used during a presentation. Whereas a typical informative or persuasive speech might selectively use stylistic devices like narratives, metaphors, similes, or analogies, special occasion speeches might emphasize such techniques. Because special occasions are highly ritualistic, they invite the use of *highly stylized*, or **ornamental language.**

TRY THIS

Assume that you are giving a special occasion presentation honoring a teacher who positively influenced you. Identify a narrative or story that you could tell to illustrate the desirable qualities of that teacher. Consider how you could use such a narrative effectively in a presentation.

Organization

When speaking to inform or persuade, you must pay particular attention to how you organize large quantities of information. Because special occasion presentations are less concerned with information dissemination and argumentation, and more concerned with setting a particular tone for the occasion, you need to handle the organization of such presentations differently than you would an informative or persuasive presentation. For instance, although special occasion presentations still should have an introduction, body, and conclusion, they typically have less obvious transitions between main points. Instead, their ornamental styling may suggest more subtle and creative ways to signal transitions between ideas. Moreover, special occasion presentations often are relatively short, and developing several main points may not be practical. In a presentation to introduce someone, for example, you should have a short introduction, provide a brief biography of the person, conclude by welcoming them, and invite applause or recognition. Taking time to "fully develop" several main points may be unnecessary and inappropriate.

Formality

Based on the previous sections, you might have guessed that special occasion speeches tend to be a bit more formal than traditional informative and persuasive presentations. Because you are taking part in a ritualized event and because you will likely try to make your style more ornamental, your special occasion speeches may appear more formal in tone.

Being formal does not mean being "stuffy." Rather, formality in this context refers more to the degree of professionalism you might use to share your ideas with your listeners. You might practice your presentation so often that you can memorize particular wordings and phrases; you might make extra efforts to use a full array of nonverbal gestures to accentuate your message; you may even, in some situations, go so far as to prepare a manuscript and practice that delivery technique. In sum, special occasion presentations are just that—special. Taking extra efforts to polish your presentation will allow you to have a more meaningful impact in setting the appropriate tone for the situation.

Types of Special Occasion Presentations

Although the potential number of different types of special occasion presentations is quite large, you will learn here about seven of the most common purposes for special occasion speaking:

- to welcome
- to pay tribute
- to introduce
- to nominate

- to dedicate
- to commemorate
- to entertain

These categories should provide some guidance for almost any special occasion at which you find yourself speaking.

Presentations to Welcome

Presentations to welcome are intended to *set a tone for a larger event by inviting all participants—including other presenters and audience members—to appropriately engage the event.* By "engage the event" we mean that events have a certain tone or feel, and the welcome speech should set that tone for the attendees. If the event is joyful, like an awards ceremony, the welcome speech should set a happy tone. If, on the other hand, the occasion is more serious, like an academic conference on your campus, the welcome speech should establish the professional tone necessary for that conference.

Welcome presentations typically are brief. Such presentations might try to accomplish two specific purposes. First, the presenter should typically welcome any honorees, important guests, or other noteworthy participants in the event. Second, the presenter should provide a brief message establishing the purpose of the event. During this latter stage, the presenter should use language, stories, or other stylistic devices to set the appropriate tone for the occasion.

Presentations to Pay Tribute

Presentations to pay tribute are designed to *offer celebration and praise of a noteworthy person, organization, or cause.* Speeches of tribute can be further subdivided into the following: eulogies, celebratory roasts, wedding toasts, retirement

Watch the "Motorcycle Club" speech on the accompanying CD-ROM for an example of a tribute presentation.

E-Note

BIOGRAPHIES ON THE WEB

Practice your skills for tribute speaking by creating a tribute presentation for a famous person. To find materials for your presentation, consult your library for published biographies in addition to consulting the online Biography Center Web site at: **http://www.biography-center.com/**. The Biography Center provides links to biographical information for over 11,000 famous and historical individuals from around the globe.

addresses, anniversary tributes, and other special events designed to celebrate the life or work of an individual or entity. For example, one of our campuses has a Campus-Community Day, established to celebrate the long heritage of the campus and community working together. Speeches at that event are tribute speeches because they honor the combined efforts of the two entities—the campus and the community.

Because tribute speeches include several different types, you should take care to fully analyze the situation to determine what focus would be most appropriate. However, nearly all tribute presentations attempt to provide some biographical sketch of the person/entity being honored. Generally speaking, tributes make extensive use of narratives to tell stories about the honoree. Such stories are effective at evoking emotion while at the same time celebrating the past. In some cases, tribute speeches might end by looking toward the future. For a retirement presentation, you might wish someone well as they take on new adventures in life; for a celebratory roast, you might encourage the honoree to "keep up the great work."

Presentations to Introduce

Speeches of introduction *are designed to tell us about the person being introduced and to help establish their ethos—in this case ethos might include credentials and/or good will.* Speeches of introduction usually precede a longer address, which will be presented by the person being introduced, and are typically brief. Speeches of introduction usually focus on biographical information about the speaker being introduced, but they also may emphasize why this particular speaker was asked to speak.

Presentations to Nominate

Speeches of nomination *introduce and honor someone you wish to place in contention for an award, elected office, or some other competitively selected position.* In clubs that you belong to, officers and other leaders in the organization may be nominated for their positions through a short speech or presentation. Nomination presentations vary in length depending on the nature of the nomination. In the United States, the Republican and Democratic Party conventions, for example, feature several lengthy speeches to nominate candidates for the national presidential election. For your clubs, a very short speech might suffice to nominate officers.

Speeches of nomination should focus on two things: the qualifications of the nominee and the reason these qualifications match the characteristics of the office, position, or award to be granted. If you are nominating someone for a

A–5

treasurer position, you would briefly describe the necessary skills for the treasurer in your particular club. After defining the skills or attributes of the position, you would then describe how the nominee exhibits those skills or attributes. Although you should try to be as specific as possible in describing the qualifications of the nominee, you should avoid providing too many details. Talking for too long or providing a lengthy list of accomplishments distracts audience members (i.e., potential voters).

Presentations to Dedicate

A **dedication presentation** *honors someone by naming an event, place, or other object after the honoree.* A dedication presentation could be as simple as a professional athlete saying that he or she dedicated his or her game to their parents, or as elaborate as the dedication of a Navy ship. These types of speeches will vary in length and focus depending on the setting, the honoree, and the event, place, or object being dedicated. Typically, the speaker in such presentations will talk about the dedication and the reasons why the honoree is a worthy namesake. Consider the example of Kim, who you read about at the beginning of this appendix:

> *After working on her presentation for several hours, Kim felt confident that she was ready to speak. As she walked to the podium beside the first sustainable garden on campus, Kim was proud that the project had come together so well. After taking a deep breath, Kim began . . .*
>
> *"Ladies and gentlemen, I am very pleased to provide the opening remarks at the grand opening of this garden. If you will permit me, however, I would like to take a moment to explain why I would like to name this garden after my advisor and professor, Dr. John C. Lehman. Dr. Lehman epitomizes the intended purpose of this garden, because his tireless efforts as a mentor have made a tough area of study 'sustainable' for numerous people like me . . ."*

Presentations to Commemorate

Commemorative addresses typically are speeches that are part of some ritualized event like a graduation, a holiday, or even a unique local occasion like First Amendment Day. **Commemorative addresses** mostly are *designed to set a tone for the event—much like a welcome speech—and also usually are considered the primary, or keynote, presentation for the event.* For example, most graduation ceremonies have a graduation speaker who is supposed to give new graduates advice for their future—such speeches set a tone for the entire graduation ceremony. Of course, the highly ritualized nature of such events means that commemorative addresses are more formal and make greater use of stylistic devices.

When planning a commemorative address, analyzing the audience and situation is very important. You must carefully determine (1) what length and tone the audience expects, and (2) how to creatively highlight specific values that capture the essence of the occasion. Commemorative addresses should use subtle transitions and supporting material. Commemorative presentations should also highlight the unique ideas and thoughts of the presenter more than other types of speeches should.

Speaking on Special Occasions   A–7

Presentations to Entertain

The final type of special occasion speech is a presentation to entertain. As the name suggests, **presentations to entertain** *are designed to make a point in a creative and oftentimes humorous way.* Entertainment speeches are sometimes called "after dinner speeches" because events often schedule these types of speeches as part of a social time or banquet.

Although the name suggests that the entertainment speech should be all about fun and laughs, presenters should also make some substantive point. In other words, stand-up comedy and speeches to entertain are different from each other. Generally speaking, speakers should plan their presentations by thinking about a more formal, perhaps even serious, message and then finding ways to make that message more humorous. If effectively prepared, the difference between the entertainment speech and more traditional informative and persuasive speeches will be less pronounced than between the other types of special occasion speeches. You should have a clear thesis statement as well as obvious main points, although these structural elements may be presented more subtly than one would expect in persuasive or informative presentations. After determining the point you want to make, you should find ways to interject humor that are appropriate to the audience and natural to the situation. Finally, pay particularly close attention to practicing delivery. Whether or not audience members perceive your presentation to be humorous depends on how you "sell" a line. Being able to "sell" a line involves a combination of delivery and timing. Working with others to develop humorous material and to refine your delivery is essential for a successful entertainment presentation.

TRY THIS

Using the central idea from your informative or persuasive presentations, plan a short, one-minute entertainment speech on the same topic. Use friends and other students to help brainstorm humorous ways to approach your topic, and practice your delivery to achieve maximum impact.

How to Prepare Special Occasion Presentations

Special occasion presentations vary widely in type, purpose, and setting. As such, no textbook or class could ever prepare you for every possible special occasion speech. At the same time, the success of special occasion presentations, as is the case with other types of presentations, typically centers on one concept: how well you analyze your message in relation to the audience and situation. Figure A.1 is a brief worksheet you can use to plan your special occasion presentations. In this figure, we use Kim's plan to dedicate the grand opening of a new sustainable agriculture garden as an example.

A–8   Appendix A

Figure A.1 Worksheet for planning a special occasion presentation.

Special Occasion Presentation Worksheet

1. Define the Occasion
Describe elements of the speaking situation that will be important to the message you intend to convey in your presentation.

a. the audience:
Approximately 10 members of my class, 5–10 faculty, and 5 or so administrators. Students from other classes could attend, but I have no way of knowing.

b. the event or setting:
To provide opening remarks for the sustainable agriculture garden. The garden will open to the public for the first time after my presentation.

c. other speakers or activities before and after presentation:
Dr. Lehman will provide some introductory remarks and welcome audience members. I will speak next and the ribbon will be cut after my presentation.

2. Define the Message
Describe the ideas, emotions, or attitudes that you want to convey. List any stylistic devices like metaphors or narratives that you want to bring into your message.

a. primary message:
I want to accomplish two purposes: (1) to talk about the process of creating the garden, and (2) to dedicate the garden in Dr. Lehman's name. This will be a surprise to everyone, but the dept. chair said that such a dedication is a great idea.

b. stylistic device ideas:
Use the metaphor of "sustainable growth" to talk about Dr. Lehman as a mentor. Tell the story about how he helped me pass Plant Biology my freshman year by meeting with me and a few other students in the arboretum every Friday.

c. main points (if applicable):
Main points should follow the two parts of the primary message. Should do the dedication last to catch Dr. Lehman by surprise.

Sample Special Occasion Presentation

The following example of a speech to pay tribute illustrates many of the principles you have learned about special occasion presentations. Notice how the speaker explicitly links the message to the occasion by talking about Rodney's love for his motorcycle while at the same time commemorating his accomplishments as a committed club citizen.

A Tribute to Rodney Freshley

Establishes connection between award recipient and audience.

Rodney Freshley is a complicated person. He is dedicated to his wife, Sally, and daughter, Samantha. He is an outdoorsman. He loves to hunt and fish.

Speaking on Special Occasions

And above all, he is fascinated by his motorcycle, the Harley-Davidson Sportster 1200 Roadster: hundreds of pounds of chrome and steel, and tons of torque. Rod is the guy who always chooses to "ride herd" on road trips. He stays in the back of the pack so he can help the group stay in formation, help anyone who has trouble, and warn the less watchful of hazards they may have overlooked.

Uses style (vivid language) to increase audience attention.

He was a pioneer in our club, one of the three founders. Now in its fifteenth year, our cycle club is the oldest and the biggest in the region. We have bikers of all ages in our club and people from many occupations, businesses, and professions. We are united in our love of the road, the wind in our face, and the adventure of the highways.

Uses past accomplishments to establish context for the recognition.

Although these accomplishments are noteworthy by themselves, Rodney deserves recognition today for a much more important reason. Each year our club sponsors a holiday toy drive for disadvantaged children. Each member of the club is responsible for obtaining at least five toys. Rodney not only met this goal, he shattered the previous record by pounding the pavement and getting over 130 toys donated. Today we celebrate Rodney's service and long-term commitment by awarding him the Outstanding Member Award.

The term "shatter" is a stylistic device (a metaphor) that helps the speaker introduce the recipient's recent accomplishment.

Resources for Review and Discussion

SUMMARY

▶ Special occasion presentations differ from informative and persuasive presentations along four dimensions.
- The purpose of special occasion presentations typically is focused on setting a tone for a ritualized event like a wedding or graduation.
- The style of a special occasion presentation is typically more formal and professional. Special occasion speakers might make greater use of ornamentation like metaphors, figurative language, or narratives.
- Although special occasion presentations should have clear organization with an introduction, body, and conclusion, they may use more subtle methods for signaling transitions between main points and subpoints.
- Special occasion presentations typically try to set a more formal, professional tone. Specific types of special occasion presentations, like the speech to entertain, may emphasize lighthearted humor.

▶ Seven common types of special occasion presentations include:
- The welcome presentation sets a tone for an event and invites all participants to share in active participation.
- Speeches of tribute offer celebratory praise for a person, organization, or cause. Eulogies, toasts, and retirement farewells are examples of tribute speeches.
- Introduction presentations welcome and introduce a primary or keynote speaker. Such speeches tend to be brief and primarily focus on biographical information.
- Nomination presentations are persuasive in intent and introduce someone you wish to place in contention for an honor, award, or elected office. Such speeches emphasize qualifications of the nominee.
- Dedication presentations honor an individual or organization, usually by dedicating or naming something (a building, an event, a scholarship, etc.) in their honor.
- Commemorative presentations include graduation addresses, holiday addresses, and other speeches at festive events.
- Entertainment presentations use humor and levity to make a somewhat serious point. Such speeches are typically more similar to informative or persuasive presentations, but they use humor to emphasize the point of the speech. Taking time to prepare and practice is essential for a successful entertainment presentation.

KEY TERMS

 Use the *Public Speaking* CD-ROM and the Online Learning Center at www.mhhe.com/nelson to practice your understanding of the following terminology.

Commemorative address	Presentation to pay tribute	Special occasion presentations
Ornamental language	Presentation to welcome	Speech of introduction
Presentation to dedicate	Ritual	Speech of nomination
Presentation to entertain		

APPLICATION EXERCISES

 Go to the self-quizzes on the *Public Speaking* CD-ROM and the Online Learning Center at www.mhhe.com/nelson to test your knowledge of the chapter concepts.

1. Special occasion presentations tend to emphasize the use of stylistic devices. Pick a person who you would consider a "mentor" for you. This person could be another professor or teacher, a family member, or some other individual who has helped you grow personally. After identifying that individual, create a metaphor describing how that person

has helped you. For example, in the opening narrative, Kim used the metaphor of "sustainable growth" to describe Dr. Lehman, her mentor.

2. To understand how special occasion speeches serve as ritualistic events, look only so far as your campus. Attend an event on campus that involves speeches. The event could be a public lecture, an awards ceremony, or even a commencement. List all of the speeches you saw at the event and analyze how the speeches "fit" into the ritual being enacted. Why do you think speeches are part of our rituals?

3. Practice presenting to nominate through the "class award" activity. Your class will manage an annual "Community Engagement Award." You should be prepared to nominate (and speak in favor of) a person from your community who you would like to place in contention for the award. The recipient of the award, who your class recommends, will be given a certificate and be invited to speak to your class.

glossary

GLOSSARY

A

absolute criteria   263
Standards for selecting alternatives that must be met, giving the group no leeway.

abstract words   167
Words that are general, broad, and distant from what you can perceive through your senses.

abstraction   167
A simplification standing for a person or thing.

action ending function   136
The third function of a conclusion, to state the response you seek from the audience.

addition   152
An articulation problem that occurs when an extra sound is added.

affection   254
Humans need to love and be loved, to know that we are important to others who value us as unique human beings.

alliteration   150, 175
The repetition of an initial consonant, a repeated sound.

analogy   110
A comparison of things in some respects, especially in position or function, that are otherwise dissimilar.

antonyms   173
A word or words that are the opposite in meaning from another word.

articulation   151
The physiological process of creating the sounds of a word.

audience adaptation   82
Making the message appropriate for the particular audience by using analysis and applying its results to message creation.

audience analysis   66, 231
(1) Discovering as much as possible about an audience to improve communication with them. (2) Learning enough about listeners to be able to predict their probable response to your message in a public speaking situation.

audience participation   134
The speaker makes the audience active participants in the presentation.

B

bar/column chart   188
A visual aid used to illustrate quantitative differences between categories of information.

behavioral response   211
An objective of a presentation to inform that is met when the audience shows an overt indication of understanding through action.

bibliographic references   105
Complete citations that appear in the "references" or "works cited" section of your speech outline.

bibliography   131
A list of the sources consulted and the sources actually used in the presentation.

boomerang effect   236
A phenomenon in which the audience likes the presenter and the proposal on the issue less after the presentation than they did before it.

brainstorming   47, 264
(1) Generating as many ideas for topics as you can in a limited period of time without pausing to evaluate them for quality. (2) A creative procedure for generating ideas and potential solutions to problems.

brake light function   136
Warns the audience that you are about to stop.

C

categorical brainstorming   47
Approaching the brainstorming process by beginning with categories that prompt you to think of topics.

cause-effect pattern   122
An organizational arrangement in which part of the speech describes or explains causes and consequences.

G

Glossary

celebrity testimony 109
Statements made by a public figure who is known to the audience.

channel 9
The means of distributing your words, whether by coaxial cable, fiber optics, microwave, radio, video, or air.

chart 187
A visual aid used to visually display quantitative or statistical information.

claim 238
A conclusion of what the persuader would have the listener believe or do that invites proof or evidence.

closed-ended questions 78
Questions that force a decision by inviting only a yes or no response or a brief answer.

co-culture 193
A group of people whose beliefs or behaviors distinguish it from the larger culture of which it is a part and with which it shares many similarities.

coercion 256
A form of punishment that attempts to force compliance with hostile tactics.

commemorative address A–6
Designed to set a tone for an event—much like a welcome speech—and usually are considered the primary, or keynote, presentation for the event.

common ground 16
Features you share with your audience.

communication 11
A transaction in which speaker and listener simultaneously send, receive, and interpret messages.

communication apprehension 18
An individual's level of fear or anxiety associated with either real or anticipated communication with another person or persons.

comparison 169
Shows how much one thing is like another by highlighting similarities.

competence 16
A thorough familiarity with your topic.

compliance response 232
The audience does what is socially acceptable based on the persuader's message.

concept maps 29
Pictures or diagrams that allow you to visualize main and subordinate ideas related to a more general topic.

concrete words 167
Words that are specific, narrow, particular, and based on what you can sense.

connotative meaning 168
The idea suggested by a word other than its explicit meaning.

consistency persuades 236
The concept that audiences are more likely to change their behavior if the suggested change is consistent with their present beliefs, attitudes, and values.

constructive presentations 270
Debate presentations where arguments for both sides of the debate are initially presented.

contrast 169
Shows how unlike one thing is from another by highlighting differences.

control 254
The ability to influence our environment.

conventional wisdom 67
The popular opinions of the time about issues, styles, topics, trends, and social mores; the customary set of understandings of what is true or right.

cost-benefit analysis 236
The idea that an audience is more likely to change their behavior if the suggested change will benefit them more than it will cost them.

criteria 263
The standards by which a group must judge potential solutions.

critical response 232
The audience focuses on the arguments, the quality of the message, and the truth or accuracy of the message.

current topics 49
Topics that are of interest today because they are in the news, in the media, and on the minds of people in your audience.

D

debate 270
Members of a group divide responsibilities and present both "pro" and "con" sides of a controversial topic.

deductive reasoning 239
The presenter bases his or her claim on some premise that is generally affirmed by the audience.

defensive response 232
The audience fends off the persuader's message to protect existing beliefs, attitudes, and values.

defining 216
Revealing the presenter's intended meaning of a term, especially if the term is technical, scientific, controversial, or not commonly used.

definitions 111
Determinations of meaning through description, simplification, examples, analysis, comparison, explanation, or illustration.

degree questions 78
Questions used in interviews and in audience analysis; questionnaires that ask to what extent a respondent agrees or disagrees with a question.

deletion 152
An articulation problem that occurs when a sound is dropped or left out of a word.

delivery 33
The verbal and nonverbal techniques used to present the message.

demographics 68
Audience characteristics such as gender, composition, age, ethnicity, economic status, occupation, and education.

demonstrating 217
Showing the audience an object, person, or place; showing the audience how something works; showing the audience how to do something; or showing the audience why something occurs.

demonstration presentation 39
A talk intended to teach audience members how something works or how to perform some task.

denotative meaning 168
The direct, explicit meaning or reference of a word.

describing 216
When the presenter evokes the meaning of a person, place, object, or experience by telling about its size, weight, color, texture, smell, or his or her feelings about it.

descriptive language 168
Attempts to observe objectively and without judgment.

disposition 30
The arrangement and structure of a presentation.

distributed leadership 257
A leadership theory explicitly acknowledging that each member is expected to perform the communication behaviors needed to move the group toward its goal.

dual coding 184
Because people tend to learn words separately from other sensory stimuli, presenters can use words as one channel, and other senses as another channel through which information can be presented.

duration 149
The amount of time devoted to the parts of a speech (e.g., introduction, evidence, main points) and the dwelling on words for effect.

dynamism 16
The energy you expend in delivering your message.

E

electronic catalog 96
A database containing information about books, journals, and other resources available in the library.

enunciation 151
A vocal aspect of delivery that involves the pronunciation and articulation of words; pronouncing correctly and producing the sounds clearly so that the language is understandable.

ethnicity 70
People who are united through "language, historical origins, nation-state, or cultural system."

etymology 173
The origin of a word.

evaluative language 168
Language that is full of judgments about the goodness or badness of a person or situation.

evidence 94
Data on which proof may be based.

examples 107
Specific instances used to illustrate your point.

expert power 256
Exists when the other members value the leaders' knowledge or expertise.

expert testimony 109
Statements made by someone who has special knowledge or expertise about an issue or idea.

explaining 217
Reveals how something works, why something occurred, or how something should be evaluated.

extemporaneous delivery 33
A mode of delivery that allows some preparation but does not require the presenter to script out or memorize a preparation.

extemporaneous mode 143
A method of speech delivery in which the presenter delivers a presentation from a key word outline or from brief notes.

eye contact 153
A nonverbal aspect of delivery that involves the speaker's looking directly at audience members to monitor their responses to the message; in public speaking, eye contact is an asset because it permits the presenter to adapt to audience responses and to assess the effects of the message.

F

fallacy 241
An error in reasoning that weakens an argument.

feedback 10
Verbal and nonverbal responses by the audience.

figurative language 169
Comparing one concept to another analogous but different concept.

Five Canons of Rhetoric 27
The essential skills associated with public dialogue and communication that Roman scholars synthesized from the teachings of Greek philosophers and teachers. The Five Canons are invention, disposition, style, memory, and delivery.

flowchart 189
A visual diagram representing hierarchical structures or sequential processes.

fluency 152
A vocal aspect of delivery that involves the smooth flow of words and the absence of vocalized pauses.

forecasting 135
Tells the audience how you are going to cover the topic.

formal sentence outline 131
A final outline in complete sentence form, which includes the title, specific purpose, thesis statement, introduction of the speech, body of the speech, conclusion of the speech, and a bibliography of sources.

G

gestures 154
A bodily aspect of delivery that involves motions of the hands or body to indicate emphasis, commitment, and other feelings about the topic, audience, and occasion.

group conflict 261
An expressed struggle between two or more interdependent members of a group who perceive there to be incompatible goals.

H

hearing 17
Receiving sound waves.

hierarchy of needs 237
A pyramid that builds from basic physiological needs like the need for oxygen all the way up to self-actualization needs—the realization of one's highest potential.

humor 212
The ability to perceive and express that which is amusing or comical.

hyperbole 176
A kind of overstatement or use of a word or words that exaggerates the actual situation.

I

ill-defined problem 261
A task facing the group that has unclear or undefined objectives.

important criteria 263
Standards for evaluating alternatives that should be met, but the group has some flexibility.

impromptu mode 146
A method of speech delivery in which the presenter has no advanced preparation.

impromptu presentation 37
A type of talk that does not allow for substantial planning and practice before the presentation is given.

inclusion 254
People need to belong to, or be included in, groups with others.

inclusive language 170
Language that does not leave out groups of people.

incremental plagiarism 112
The intentional or unintentional use of information from one or more sources without fully divulging how much information is directly quoted.

inductive reasoning 238
The persuader amasses a series of particular instances to draw an inference.

information hunger 207
The presenter generates a desire in the audience for information.

informative presentation 206
A presentation that increases an audience's knowledge about a subject or that helps the audience learn more about an issue or idea.

G–4　　Glossary

instant-replay function　136
The second function of a conclusion, to remind the audience of the thesis of your message.

internal previews　128
Statements that inform listeners of your next point or points and are more detailed than transitions.

internal references　105
Brief notations of which bibliographic reference contains the details you are using in your speech.

internal reviews　128
Statements that remind listeners of your last point or points and are more detailed than transitions.

interviews　77
Inquiries about your audience directed at an audience member.

invention　27
The art of finding information.

K

key word outline　133
A brief outline with cue words created for you to use during the delivery of your presentation.

L

lay testimony　109
Statements made by an ordinary person that substantiate or support what you say.

leader　256
A person who influences the behavior and attitudes of others through communication.

legitimate power　256
Interpersonal influence bestowed to a leader by virtue of title or position.

levels of abstraction　167
The degree to which words become separated from concrete or sensed reality.

line chart　188
A visual aid that illustrates trends in quantitative data.

listening　17
Interpreting sounds as a message.

literal language　169
Words used to reveal facts.

M

main ideas　210
Generalizations to be remembered in an informative presentation.

maintenance functions　258
Behaviors that focus on the interpersonal relationships among members.

malapropism　151
Mistaking one word for another.

manuscript mode　145
A method of speech delivery in which the presenter writes out the complete presentation in advance and then uses that manuscript to deliver the speech but without memorizing it.

memorized mode　144
A method of speech delivery in which the presenter commits the entire presentation to memory by either rote or repetition; appropriate in situations where the same speech is given over and over to different audiences.

memory　32
The "lost canon of rhetoric," this fundamental skill requires speakers to have a strong mental awareness of the messages they intend to present.

message　9
The facial expressions seen, the words heard, the visual aids illustrated, and the ideas or meanings conveyed simultaneously between source and receiver.

message production　232
Creating, organizing, and delivering a persuasive appeal.

Monroe's Motivated Sequence　125
An organizational arrangement based on reflective thinking that includes five specific steps: attention, need, satisfaction, visualization, and action.

movement　155
A nonverbal aspect of delivery that refers to a presenter's locomotion in front of an audience; can be used to signal the development and organization of the message.

multimedia materials　185
Digital or electronic sensory resources that combine text, graphics, video, and sound into one package.

N

noise　10
Interference or obstacles to communication.

nonverbal messages　9
Movements, gestures, facial expressions, and vocal variations that can reinforce or contradict the accompanying words.

numbers 110
Supporting material that describes something in terms of quantities or amounts.

observation 76
A method of audience analysis based on what you can see or hear about the audience.

open-ended questions 78
Like essay questions, questions that invite an explanation and discourage yes or no responses from the person being questioned.

oral citation 106
Tells the audience who the source is, how recent the information is, and the source's qualifications.

ornamentation 31
The creative and artful use of language.

oversimplification 176
A complex issue described as simple.

panel 269
Group presentations that utilize short introductory statements from panel members and then provide time for interaction and dialogue between the presenters and audience members.

Parallel construction 119
Repeating words and phrases and using the same parts of speech for each item.

pause 149
An intentional silence used to draw attention to the words before or after the interlude; a break in the flow of words for effect.

periodicals 97
Sources of information that are published at regular intervals.

personal experience 93
Using your own life as a source of information.

personal inventory 48
Trying to determine a topic by considering features of your life such as experiences, attitudes, values, beliefs, interests, and skills.

personification 164
Attributing human characteristics to an abstraction.

perspective 176
Your point of view; the way you perceive the world, reflected in the words you choose.

persuasive presentations 229
A message delivered to an audience by a speaker who intends to influence audience members' choices by changing their responses toward an idea, issue, concept, or product.

physical appearance 156
The way we look, including our display of material things such as clothing and accessories.

pie chart 189
A visual aid illustrating percentages or components of a whole.

pitch 150
A vocal aspect of delivery that refers to the highness or lowness of the speaker's voice, its upward and downward inflection, the melody produced by the voice.

plagiarism 14, 111
(1) A speech, outline, or manuscript from any source other than you. (2) The intentional use of information from another source without crediting the source.

power 256
The interpersonal influence that one person has with others.

preparation outline 130
The initial or tentative conception of a speech in rough outline form.

presentation to dedicate A–6
Honors someone by naming an event, place, or other object after the honoree.

presentation to entertain A–7
Designed to make a point in a creative and oftentimes humorous way.

presentation to pay tribute A–4
Designed to offer celebration and praise of a noteworthy person, organization, or cause.

presentation to welcome A–4
Intended to set a tone for a larger event by inviting all participants—including other presenters and audience members—to appropriately engage the event.

primacy 214
Placing your best argument or main point early in the presentation.

principle of division 129
An outlining principle that states that every point divided into subordinate parts must be divided into two or more parts.

Glossary

principle of parallelism 129
An outlining principle that states that all points must be stated in the same grammatical and syntactical form.

principle of subordination 129
An outlining principle that states that importance is signaled by symbols and indentation.

principles of learning 212
Principles governing audience understanding by building on the known, using humor or wit, using presentational aids, organizing information, and rewarding listeners.

problem questions 263
Group questions that focus on the undesirable present state and imply that many solutions are possible.

problem-solution pattern 124
An organizational arrangement in which part of the speech is concerned with the problem(s) and part with the solution(s) to problem(s).

process observer 261
A person assigned to keep the group on task and to keep members from dominating discussion by bringing up multiple points.

process of communication 10
The dynamic interrelationship of source, receiver, message, channel, feedback, situation, and noise.

projection 151
Adjusting your volume appropriately for the subject, the audience, and the situation.

pronunciation 151
The production of the sounds of a word.

punishment power 256
A form of interpersonal influence where the leader withholds something followers want and need.

Q

question of fact 233
The persuasive presentation seeks to uncover the truth based on fact.

question of policy 234
The persuasive presentation raises issues about goodness and badness, right and wrong, enlightenment and ignorance.

question of value 233
The persuasive presentation enters the realm of rules, regulations, and laws.

questionnaires 77
Surveys of audience opinions.

R

rate 148
A vocal aspect of delivery that refers to the speed of delivery, the number of words spoken per minute; normal rates range from 125 to 190 words per minute.

rebuttal presentations 270
Debate presentations where one side presents points in response to arguments advanced by the other side.

receiver 9
The individual or group that hears, and hopefully listens to, the message sent by the source.

recency 214
Placing your best argument or main point late in the presentation.

reference librarian 96
A librarian specifically trained to help find sources of information.

referent power 256
Interpersonal influence based on gaining the respect and admiration of group members.

relationship 231
How the audience feels about you as a presenter before, during, and after the persuasive appeal.

repetition 175
Words repeated exactly or with slight variation.

reward 215
A psychological or physical reinforcement to increase an audience's response to information given in a presentation.

reward power 256
A form of interpersonal influence where the leader gives followers the things they want and need.

rhythm 150
The tempo of a speech, which varies by part (e.g., introductions are often slower and more deliberate) and by the pacing of the words and sentences.

S

Sapir-Whorf hypothesis 166
Our language determines to some extent how we think about and view the world.

search engine 98
A Web site on the Internet that is specially designed to help you search for information.

Glossary

self-centered functions   258
Behaviors that serve the needs of the individual at the expense of the group.

self-managed work teams   254
Groups of workers with different skills and duties who work together to produce something or to solve a problem.

semanticist   167
A person who studies words and meaning.

sensory aids   184
Resources other than the speaker that stimulate listeners and help them comprehend and remember the presenter's message.

signposts   128
Direct indicators of the speaker's progress; usually an enumeration of the main points: "A second cause is . . ."

situation   10
The time, place, and occasion in which the message sending and receiving occurs.

small, gradual changes persuade   236
The principle of persuasion that says audiences are more likely to alter their behavior if the suggested change will require small, gradual changes rather than major, abrupt changes.

small group communication   252
Interaction between 3 to 9 people working together to achieve an interdependent goal.

solution questions   263
Group questions that slant the group's discussion toward one particular option.

source   8
The originator of the message; the speaker.

source credibility   16
The audience's perception of your effectiveness as a communicator.

spatial relations pattern   121
An organizational arrangement in which events or steps are presented according to how they are related in space.

special occasion speech   56
A presentation that highlights a special event.

speech of action   230
A persuasive speech given for the purpose of influencing listeners' behaviors and actions.

speech of introduction   A–5
Designed to tell us about the person being introduced and to help establish their ethos.

speech of nomination   A–5
Introduces and honors someone you wish to place in contention for an award, elected office, or some other competitively selected position.

speech to convince   230
A persuasive presentation given for the purpose of influencing listeners' beliefs or attitudes.

speech to inform   55
A speech that seeks to increase the audience's level of understanding or knowledge about a topic.

speech to inspire   230
A persuasive speech given for the purpose of influencing listeners' feelings or motivations.

speech to persuade   55
A speech that seeks to influence, reinforce, or modify the audience members' feelings, attitudes, beliefs, values, or behaviors.

statistics   110
Numbers that summarize data or provide scientific evidence of relationships between two or more things.

status quo   270
The way things are currently done.

stereotype   171
A hasty generalization about an individual based on an alleged characteristic of a group.

style   31
The use and ornamentation of language.

subordinate ideas   210
Details that support the generalizations in an informative presentation.

substitution   152
An articulation problem that occurs when one sound is replaced with another.

supporting materials   106
Information you can use to substantiate your arguments and to clarify your position.

surveys   108
Studies in which a limited number of questions are answered by a sample of the population to discover opinions on issues.

symbolic   164
Words represent the concrete and objective reality of objects and things as well as abstract ideas.

symposium   265
A group presentation where individual members divide a large topic into smaller topics for coordinated individual presentations.

synonyms 173
A word or words that mean more or less the same thing.

T

table 187
A visual aid that combines text and/or numbers to efficiently summarize, compare, and contrast information.

task functions 258
Behaviors that are directly relevant to the group's purpose and that affect the group's productivity.

testimonial evidence 109
Written or oral statements of others' experience used by a speaker to substantiate or clarify a point.

text slide 186
A visual aid that relies primarily on words and phrases to present and summarize information.

thesis statement 58
A one-sentence summary of the speech.

time-sequence pattern 121
An organizational arrangement in which events or steps are presented in the order in which they occur.

topical sequence pattern 124
An organizational arrangement in which the topic is divided into related parts, such as advantages and disadvantages, or various qualities or types.

transitions 127
Statements or words that bridge previous parts of the presentation to the next part. Transitions can be signposts, internal previews, or internal reviews.

transposition 152
An articulation problem that occurs when two sounds are reversed.

trustworthiness 16
The degree to which the audience perceives the presenter as honest and honorable.

two-sided argument 112
A source advocating one position will present an argument from the opposite viewpoint and then go on to refute that argument.

V

verbal messages 9
The words chosen for the speech.

virtual library 99
Web sites that provide links to sites that have been reviewed for relevance and usability.

visual aids 184
Any observable resources used to enhance, explain, or supplement the presenter's message.

vocalized pause 149
A nonfluency in delivery characterized by such sounds as "Uhhh," "Ahhh," or "Mmmm" or the repetitious use of such expressions as "okay," "like," or "for sure" to fill silence with sound; often used by presenters who are nervous or inarticulate.

volume 151
A vocal characteristic of delivery that refers to the loudness or softness of the voice; public presenters often project or speak louder than normal so that distant listeners can hear the message; beginning presenters frequently forget to project enough volume.

W

wit 212
The ability to perceive and express humorously the relationship or similarity between seemingly incongruous or disparate things.

worldview 74
The common concept of reality shared by a particular group of people, usually referred to as a culture or an ethnic group.

credits

CREDITS

Photos

Page 2: © AP/Wide World Photos; **4**: © Stewart Cohen/Getty Images; **7, 24**: © AP/Wide World Photos; **27**: © Luke Frazza-Pool/Getty Images; **33**: © Jon Feingersh/CORBIS; **39**: © Creatas/PictureQuest; **44**: © Jose Luis Pelaez/CORBIS; **47**: © Syracuse Newspapers/Dick Blume/The Image Works; **52**: © Bonnie Kamin/Photo Edit; **53**: © Brenda J. Turner/ZUMA/CORBIS; **58**: © Witold Skrypczak/SuperStock; **64**: © AP/Wide World Photos; **66**: © Charles O'Rear/CORBIS; **71**: © Digital Vision/Getty Images; **72**: © David Paul Morris/Getty Images; **74**: © Mike Segar/Reuters/CORBIS; **90**: © AP/Wide World Photos; **116**: © Barry Rosenthal/Getty Images; **135**: © Chris Trotman/NewSport/CORBIS; **140**: Bob Daemmrich\PhotoEdit, Inc.; **144**: © Nell Redmond/AFP/Getty Images; **154**: © Ian Waldie/Getty Images; **156**: Courtesy of the authors; **162**: © SuperStock, Inc./SuperStock; **165**: © Frederick M. Brown/Getty Images; **172**: © Reuters/CORBIS; **182**: © AP/Wide World Photos; **193**: © Journal Courier/The Image Works; **194**: © Michael S. Yamashita/CORBIS; **195**: © Justin Pumfrey/Getty Images; **202**: © PhotoDisc/Getty Images; **210**: © AP/Wide World Photos; **213**: © PhotoDisc/Getty Images; **226**: © AP/Wide World Photos; **231**: © PhotoDisc/Getty Images; **237**: © Max Whittaker/CORBIS; **242**: © AP/Wide World Photos; **250**: © Warren Morgan/CORBIS; **A**: © Tom Carter/PhotoEdit, Inc.

Text

Quote, p. 8: Peggy Noonan quote from *Simply Speaking*, New York: ReganBooks, 1998.

Figure 3.1: The Google™ directory screen capture is a trademark of Google, Inc. Reprinted by permission.

Figure 3.2: The Google™ subdirectory to Arts screen capture is a trademark of Google, Inc. Reprinted by permission.

Figure 3.3: The Google™ subdirectory to Performing Arts screen capture is a trademark of Google, Inc. Reprinted by permission.

Excerpt, p. 75: From "The Challenge of Human Rights and Cultural Diversity," United Nations, ww.un.org/rights/. Used by permission of United Nations Publications Department of Public Information.

Excerpt, p. 76: From Marc Maurer speech "Language and the future of the blind: Independence and freedom," *Vital Speeches of the Day*, 1989, 56(1), pp. 16–22. Reprinted by permission of City News Publishing Company.

Figure 5.2: The Google™ directory screen capture is a trademark of Google, Inc. Reprinted by permission.

Figure 5.3: The Google™ subdirectory to Genetics screen capture is a trademark of Google, Inc. Reprinted by permission.

CD-ROM Activity, p. 148 (Annotated Instructor's Edition): Excerpt from the introductory chapter of *Seven Pillars of Wisdom* by T. E. Lawrence. Ware, Hertfordshire: Wordsworth Editions Limited, 1997.

Credits

Excerpt, p. 174: From "Between you and I, misutilizing words ranks high pet-peevewise" by Paula LaRocque, *The Quill*, May 1999. Reprinted by permission.

Figure 8.3: "Common Grammatical Errors," adapted from *Public Speaking for College and Career*, 5th ed. by Hamilton Gregory, 1999. Used by permission of McGraw-Hill.

Excerpt, p. 178: From *The Miracle of Language* by Richard Lederer, New York: Simon & Schuster, 1991, p. 243.

Figure 9.9: Marching Orders for the 65th. Map adapted from www.sea-surveyor.co.il/atlantic.gif.

Excerpt, p. 205: From Pat Sajak speech, "The disconnect between Hollywood and America: You possess the power," *Vital Speeches of the Day*, August 15, 2002, 68(21). Reprinted by permission of City News Publishing Company.

Excerpt, p. 206: From Bob Wright speech, "Enron: The inflexible obligations of the legal profession," *Vital Speeches of the Day*, August 1, 2002, 68(20). Reprinted by permission of City News Publishing Company.

Figure 11.2: "Maslow's Hierarchy of Needs," from *Motivation and Personality*, 3rd ed., by Abraham H. Maslow, Robert D. Frager, and James Fadiman, © 1987. Adapted by permission of Pearson Education, Inc., Upper Saddle River, NJ.

Figure 12.1: "Behavioral functions combine to create roles," *Communicating in Groups*, 2nd ed., by Gloria J. Galanes and John K. Brilhart, 1993. Reproduced with permission of The McGraw-Hill Companies.

Cultural Note, p. 268: Adapted from Hilary MacGregor, "Project seeks common ground to end school's violence," *Los Angeles Times* (October 22, 2000): B1, and the National Communication Association Web site (http://www.natcom.org/Instruction/CCG/calstate.htm).

index

Note: Page numbers in *italic* type indicate illustrations, figures, or tables.

Absolute criteria, 263, *264*
Abstraction, levels of, 167
Abstract words, 167
Action, as purpose of presentation, 230
Action ending function, 136
Addition, as articulation problem, *152*
Affection, 254
Age of audience, 68–70
Alliteration, 150, 175
Alternatives, in problem solving
   evaluating, 264–265
   identifying, 264
American Association of Higher
   Education, 268
American Psychological Association
   (APA) style guide, 105, *106*, 131
Analogies, 32, 110–111, 239
Antonyms, 173
Anxiety about public speaking, 18–21
Appropriateness of topic
   for audience, 53
   guidelines, *54*
   for occasion, 53–54
   for speaker, 52–53
Approved names, 171
Architects of Peace project, *37*
Argument, 232
Aristotle, 27, 64
Arrangement; *see* Disposition
Articulation, 151, *152*
Asian-Nation, 104
Attire, 135, 156–157
Audience; *see also* Audience analysis
   adaptation to, 82–84
   appropriateness of topic, 53
   classroom, 81
   ethics, 87, 218–219
   ethnicity, 70–71
   eye contact, 153–154
   feedback, 10
   gestures, 155
   helping, to apply information, 211
   helping, to remember information,
     209–211
   helping, to understand information,
     208–209
   improving, 14
   influence on, 11
   information hunger, 207–208
   insulting, 14
   language, 177
   relating topic to, 135, 205–206

   relationship to presenter, 231
   respect from, *17*
   response to persuasive
     presentations, 232
   rewards for, 215
   role of, in communication process, 9
   size, 79
   source credibility, 16
   speaking rate and, 149
   visual/sensory aids, 195, 197
Audience adaptation, 82–84
Audience analysis, 66–76; *see also*
     Methods of audience analysis
   age, 68–70
   conventional wisdom and, 67–68
   definition of, 66
   economic status, 71
   education, 72–74
   gender, 68
   occupation, 72
   persuasive presentations, 231
   physical characteristics, 75–76
   worldview, 74–75
Audience participation, 134
Audio material, 134, 196
Austin-Wells, Vonnette, 193
Authoritarian leaders, 258
Autocratic leaders, 258
Ayton-Shenker, Diana, 75

Ball State University, 238
Bandwagon technique, 241
Bar charts, *188*, 188
Bartleby.com, 151
Bates, Marston, 90
Baumann, Bud, 250
Behavioral functions, 258, *259*, *260*
Behavioral response, 211
Benefits, persuasion through, 236–237
Bibliographic references, 105, 131
Biography Center, A-5
Blackfeet Indian Nation, 70
Black History Quest, 104
Body language, 34, 152–157; *see also*
     Nonverbal messages
   appearance, 156–157
   eye contact, *33*, 34, 153–154
   facial expression, *33*, 154
   gestures, 154–155
   important points indicated by, 210
   movement, 155–156
Body of presentation
   cohesion, 127–128
   emphasis of main points, 118–120
   function of, 30, 131

   order of main points, 120–126
   supporting materials, 127
Bono, 152
Bookmarks, Internet, 101
Boolean searching, 99, *101*
Boomerang effect, 236
Brainstorming
   categorical, 47, *48*
   group problem solving, 264
   individual, 47
Brake light function, 136
Brevity, role in public speaking, 13
Broward County Community
   College, 229
Bullet points, 186

California State University Northridge,
   205, 268
Camcorders, 191
Cameras, digital, 190
Campus Compact, 268
Career, public speaking as aid in, 6–7
Carter, Rosalynn, 140
Categorical brainstorming, 47, *48*
Cause, reasoning from, 240
Cause-effect pattern of main points,
   122–123, 235
Celebrity testimony, 109
Chalkboards, 194
Change, persuasion and, 236
Channel, in communication process, 9–10
Charts, 187–189
Choosing a topic; *see* Topic selection
The CIA World Factbook, 102
Cicero, 27
Circular reasoning, 241
Citation of information sources,
   105–106, *106*, *107*
Claim, 238
Clarity, 31, 151, *170*
Clark, J. M., 90
Clark, Kenneth, 182
Classification, language as tool for,
   165–166
Classmate, presenting, 38–41
Classroom audience, 81, *82*
Clinton, Bill, 58, 152
Closed-ended questions, 78
Clothing, 135, 156–157
Co-cultures, 71, 193
Coercion, 256
Column charts, 188
Commemorative addresses, A-6
Common ground, role in source
   credibility, 16

I–1

Communicating Common Ground
program, 268
Communication, definition of, 11
Communication apprehension (CA), 18
Communication process, 8–11, *12*
channel, 9–10
definition of, 11
feedback, 10
message, 9
noise, 10
receiver, 9
situation, 10
source, 8–9
Comparisons, 169
Competence, role in source credibility,
16, 53
Complete arguments, 233
Compliance response, 232
Concept maps, 29, *29*
Conclusion
action ending function, 136
brake light function, 136
function of, 30, 131, 136
instant-replay function, 136
persuasive presentations, 234–235
tips, 136–137
Concrete words, 167
Conflict resolution, group presentations
and, 255, 261, 268
Connotative meaning, 168
Consistency, 236
Constructive presentations, 270
Content of persuasive presentation, 232
Contrasts, 169
Control, 254
Controversial issues, 208
Conventional wisdom, 67–68
Convincing, as purpose of
presentation, 230
Coordination, group presentations and,
254, 256
Cosby, Bill, *53*
Cost-benefit analysis, 236–237
Creativity, group presentations
and, 254
Criteria, 263–264
Critical response, 232
Critical thinking
fallacies, 241–242
reasoning, 238–241
Cultural differences
audience analysis, 70–71
audience preferences, 211
change, 75
elderly audiences, 212
evidence, 108
eye contact, 153
free speech versus respect, 46
language, 166
organization of presentations, 127
presentation, 18
rhetoric, 34
visual aids, 193
weddings, A-3
Cultural symposium, 267
Curiosity, arousing, 207

Current issue symposium, 266–267
Current topics, 13, 49

D'Angelo, Anthony J., 202
Debates, 270–271
Dedication presentations, A-6
Deductive reasoning, 239
Defensive response, 232
Definitions
in informative presentations, 216
in language use, 173
as supporting material, 111
Degree questions, 78–79
Deletion, as articulation problem, *152*
Delivery, 142–158
body language, 152–157
effective, 142–143
extemporaneous mode, 143–144
as fundamental skill, 33–34
impromptu mode, 146–147
improving, 158
manuscript mode, 145–146
memorized mode, 144–145
natural, 34, 155, 157
question-and-answer sessions,
157–158
voice, 148–152
Democracy
National League for Democracy,
Burma, 2
and public speaking, 6
in a thesis statement, 59
and public discourse, 231
in groups, 257
Democracy (vital topic of), 13, 31, 37,
55, 56, 57, 59, 103, 122, 187, 215,
230, 237, 241, 262, A-6
Democratic leaders, 257–258
Demographics, 68
Demonstration presentations, 39–40,
217–218
Denotative meaning, 168
Descriptive language, 168–169, 216–217
Dewey, John, 125
Differences, 171
Digital camcorders, 191
Digital cameras, 190
Digital video converters, 191
Dillard, James P., 238
Disabilities, stereotypes involving, 76
Discussion, group presentations and, 255
Disposition, as fundamental skill,
30–31
Distributed leadership, 257
Diversity (vital topic of), 13, 55, 56, 58,
59, 70, 75, 76, 78, 93, 104, 108, 110,
122, 127, 134, 153, 174, 184, 191,
193, 204, 205, 206, 212, 213, 231,
232, 233, 234, 236, 262, 263, 267,
268, A-4
and information retention, 211
Division, principle of, 129
Doisneau, Robert, 182
Dole, Elizabeth, *144*, 146
Dominick, Joseph, 98
Dress, 135, 156–157

Dr. Phil, 152
Dry erase boards, 194
Dual coding, 184
Duration, vocal, 149–150
Dynamism, role in source credibility, 16

EBSCO-host, 49
Economic status of audience, 71
Education (vital topic of), 13, 55, 56, 57,
107, 110, 128, 134, 188, 229, 232,
234, 262
Education of audience, 72–74
Effectiveness in public speaking
listening, 17
source credibility, 15–16
Einstein, Albert, 202
Either/or fallacy, 241
Elderly audiences, 212
Electronic catalog, of library, 96–97, *97*
Emotions, of speakers, 4
Entertainment, presentations for, A-7
Environment (vital topic of), 13, 29, 31,
55, 58, 60, 92, 120, 123, 125, 133,
186, 208, 216, 218, 232, 235, 236,
240, 243–246, 263, 266, 269, 271, A-3
Enunciation, 151
Ethics (vital topic of), 13, 55, 56, 58, 59,
60, 79, 97, 106, 107, 128, 135, 206,
208, 233, 239
and the audience, 87
in use of supporting materials, 111
and language, 170–171, 176–177, 178
and sensory aids, 198
and informative presentations, 218
and persuasive presentations,
242–243
Ethnicity of audience, 70–71
ethos, 16, 234, 238
Etymology, 173–174
Evaluation of information sources,
102–105
Evaluative language, 168–169
Evidence; *see also* Supporting materials
cultural differences, 108
definition of, 94
hard, 239
personal experience as, 94
soft, 239–240
testimonial, 233
Exaggeration, 176
Examples
brief, 107
extended, 107
factual, 107
hypothetical, 107–108
as supporting material, 107–108
Expert power, 256
Expert testimony, 109
Explanation, in informative
presentations, 217
Explicitness, 232
Extemporaneous delivery, 33, 143–144
Eye contact, *33*, 34, 153

Facial expression, *33*, 154
Fact, question of, 233, 262, *262*

Index   I–3

Fallacies, 241–242
  bandwagon technique, 241
  circular reasoning, 241
  definition of, 241
  either/or, 241
  glittering generality, 241
  name calling, 241
  post hoc, 242
Fear of public speaking
  reducing, 18–21
  understanding, 18
  worst-case scenarios, 5–6
Fedstats, 102
Feedback, 10
Feminism, rhetoric and, 34
Figurative language, 169
First Amendment, U.S. Constitution,
  2, 46–47
Firstgov, 102
Five Canons of Rhetoric, 27–34
  delivery, 33–34
  disposition, 30–31
  invention, 27, 29–30
  memory, 32–33
  overview, *28*
  style, 31–32
Flowcharts, 189, *189*, *190*
Fluency, vocal, 152
Forecasting, 135–136, 215
Foreign-born people in U.S., 70
Formal sentence outline, 131, *132–133*
Franklin, Benjamin, 16
Free speech, 46–47
Funk, Wilfred, 165

Garcia, Angela, 267
Gender
  audience, 68
  facial expression, 154
  inequality, 69
  language, 171
Generalization, reasoning from, 240
Gestures, 154–155, 210
Glittering generality, 241
Gonzalez-Crussi, F., A
Grammar, 174–175, *175*
Grant High School, Los Angeles, 268
Gregory H., 175
Grigg, Ray, 142
Group conflict, 261
Group presentations
  debates, 270–271
  panels, 269–270
  symposia, 265–268
Groups, 252–273; *see also* Group
    presentations
  common elements in
    presentations, 256
  communication skills, 260–261
  evaluation, 271–273, *272*, *273*
  interaction skills, 258
  leadership skills, 255–258
  presentation skills, 254–255
  presentation types, 265–271
  problem solving, 261–265
  racial conflict addressed through, 268

resources on Web, 265
  roles, 258, *260*
  small groups, 252–255

Handouts, 197
Hard evidence, 239
Harrison, William B., Jr., 55
Hawthorne, Nathaniel, 164
Hayakawa, S. I., 167
Health (vital topic of), 13, 32, 55, 56,
    57, 58, 59, 107, 108, 118, 119, 121,
    123, 124, 126, 128, 132, 136, 188,
    189, 190, 197, 207, 208, 209, 212,
    213, 215, 218, 235, 238, 262, 271
Hearing, 17
Henry, Patrick, 58
Hierarchy of needs, *237*, 237–238
Hmong, 153
Humor, 212–213
Huxley, Aldous, 176
Hyperbole, 176

Ill-defined problem, 261
Importance
  of main points, 120
  nonverbal indication of, 210
  of occasion, 81
  of topic, 13
Important criteria, 263, *264*
Impromptu presentations, 37, 146–147
Inaugural addresses, 67
Inclusion, 254
Inclusive language, 170–171
Incremental plagiarism, 112
Individual brainstorming, 47
Inductive reasoning, 238
Influence, power of, 11
Informants, audience analysis through, 77
Information hunger, 207
Information sources
  citation, 105–106, *106*, *107*
  evaluating, 104–105
  Internet, 98–104
  interviews, 94–96
  library, 96–98
  personal experience, 93–94
Informative presentations, 55, 204–222
  building on what is known, 212
  checklist, *219*
  creating information hunger, 207–208
  definition in, 216
  definition of, 206
  demonstration in, 217–218
  description in, 216–217
  ethics, 218–219
  example of, 219–222
  explanation in, 217
  helping audience apply
    information, 211
  helping audience remember, 209–211
  helping audience understand, 208–209
  humor and wit, 212–213
  organization of material, 214–215
  persuasive versus, *229*
  principles, 204–206
  relating presenter to topic, 205

relating topic to audience, 205–206
  rewards for audience, 215
  sensory aids, 214
  translation of ideas in, 83
In Other Words (Bertram), 173
Inspiration, as purpose of
    presentation, 230
Instant-replay function, 136
Institute of Propaganda Analysis, 242
Interaction, group presentations and, 256
Interdependence, group presentations
    and, 256
Internal previews, 128
Internal references, 105
Internal reviews, 128
Internet; *see also* Internet searches
  addresses, *103*
  pictures available on, 190
  presentations taken from, 14–15
Internet searches, 98–104
  evaluating, 102, 103, 104–105
  narrowing, *101*
  plagiarism, 51
  problems, 51, 92, 98, 102
  relevant topics, 15
  resources, *99*
  RSS feeds, 101, 207
  search engines, 49–51, 98–102
  sources for, 102–104 (*see also* search
    engines)
Interviews, 94–96
  audience analysis through, 77
  conducting, 95–96
  guidelines, 39
  preparation, 94–95
  using, 96
Introduction, 134–136
  function of, 30, 131
  gaining and maintaining attention,
    134–135
  persuasive presentations, 234
  previewing message, 135–136
  relating topic to audience, 135
  relating topic to presenter, 135
Introduction, speeches of, 38–41, A-5
Invention, as fundamental skill, 27, 29–30
Invitational rhetoric, 34

Jolie, Angelina, 152
Joyner-Kersee, Jackie, 7

Keesey, Ray, 31
Keillor, Garrison, 74
Kennedy, John, 67
Key word outline, 133, 143
Keyword searching, 99
King, Martin Luther, Jr., 149
Kyl, Aung San Suu, 2

Ladder of abstraction, *167*
Laissez-faire leaders, 258
Language, 164–178
  abstraction levels, 167
  alliteration, 175
  antonyms, 173
  comparison and contrast, 169

Index

Language, *(Cont.)*
definitions, 173
descriptive versus evaluative, 168–169
ethics, 176–177
etymology, 173–174
evocative, 174
grammar, 174–175, *175*
inclusive, 170–171
literal versus figurative, 169
meaning of, 85–86, 168
names, 171
organization and classification, 165–166
power of, 165
repetition, 175
sexist, 171
simplification, 172
substitutions, 173
symbolic character of, 164–165
synonyms, 173
thought shaped by, 166–167
tips, 177–178
word choice, 172–175, *175*
written versus spoken, 169, *170*
LaRocque, Paula, 174
Larson, Sigrid, 142, 156
Latino-American Network Information Center, 104
Lay testimony, 109
Leaders
authoritarian, 258
autocratic, 258
definition of, 255
democratic, 257–258
laissez-faire, 258
Leadership skills, group, 255–258
Learning; *see* Principles of learning
Learning styles, 214
Lecterns, 34
Lederer, Richard, 178
Leeds-Hurwitz, Wendy, A-3
Legitimate power, 256
Levels of abstraction, 167
Lexis/Nexis, 49
Library resources
electronic catalog, 96–97, *97*
periodical indexes, 97, *98*
Life skills, public speaking and learning of, 6
Lincoln, Abraham, 13
Line charts, *188*, 188
Lippman, Walter, 171
Listening
role in public speaking, 17
tips, 17
and adapting to audience, 84–86
in an interview, 93
Literal language, 169
Literary cultures, 108; *see also* Written language
Logic; *see* Reasoning
logos, 16, 238

Main points
emphasis, 118–120, 210, 214–215
equal importance, 120

limiting, 119
order, 120–126
parallel construction, 119–120
supporting materials, 127, 214–215
Maintenance functions of behavior, 258, *259*
Malapropisms, 151
Mann, Thomas, 116
Manuscript mode of delivery, 145–146
Marshall, Linda J., 238
Maslow's hierarchy of needs, *237*, 237–238
Maurer, Marc, 76
McCain, John, 109, 172, *172*
McDougall, Graham, 193
McLuhan, Marshall, 10
Mead, Margaret, 250
Meaning
denotative versus connotative, 168
language and, 85–86
Memorized delivery, 144–145
Memory, as fundamental skill, 32–33
Message
in communication process, 9
nonverbal, 9
verbal, 9
Message production, 232
Metaphors, 32
Meta-search engines, 49, 99
Methods of audience analysis, 76–79
informants, 77
interviews, 77
observation, 76
questionnaires, 77–79, *78*
Michigan State University, 229
Mikkelson, Barbara, 64
The Miracle of Language (Lederer), 178
Models, as visual resource, 195–196
Moderators, 266, 269, 270
Modern Language Association (MLA) style guide, 105, *106*, 131
Modes of delivery
advantages and disadvantages, *148*
extemporaneous, 143–144
impromptu, 146–147
manuscript, 145–146
memorized, 144–145
notes, preparation, and use, *147*
Monroe, Alan, 125
Monroe's Motivated Sequence of main points, 125–126, 235
Moore, Michael, *242*
Movement, bodily, 155–156
Multimedia materials, 185
Multimedia symposium, 267

Name calling, 241
Names, approved, 171
Narratives, 32, 137, 240
National Communication Association (NCA), 111, 265, 268
Native Americans, 171
Natural delivery, 34, 155, 157
Need fulfillment, persuasion through, 237–238

Nervousness; *see* Anxiety about public speaking
Newsweek, 67
Noise, in communication process, 10
Nomination, speeches of, A-5–A-6
Nonverbal messages, 9, 34; *see also* Body language
Noonan, Peggy, 8
Notecards
for presentations, 35, 37
sample, *35*
Notes for presentation; *see also* Notecards
consulting, 34
extemporaneous delivery, 143
quantity of, 33–34
taking, 35
Numbers, as supporting materials, 110, 233

Obama, Barack, *74*
Objects, as visual resource, 195
Observation, audience analysis through, 76
Occasion of presentation
analysis of, 80
appropriateness of topic, 53–54
special occasion speeches, 56–57
Occupation of audience, 72
O'Connor, William Van, A
Onfolio, 207
Ong, Walter J., 108
Open-ended questions, 78
Oral citations, 106, *107*
Oral cultures, 108, 153; *see also* Spoken language
Organization, language as tool for, 165–166
Organization of presentations, 118–128
benefits, 118
emphasis of main points, 118–120
indicators of, 127–128
informative presentations, 214–215
as learning aid, 214–215
order of main points, 120–126
persuasive presentations, 234–235
special occasions, A-3
supporting materials, 127
Ornamentation, 31
Ortega y Gasset, José, 24
Outlines
formal sentence, 131, *132–133*
key word, 133
preparation, 130–131
Outlining presentations, 128–133
division, 129
parallelism, 129–130
subordination, 129
types of outlines, 130–133
Overhead transparencies, 197
Oversimplification, 176

Pace University, 265
Panels, 269–270
Parallelism, principle of, 119–120, 129–130
Parentheses, *101*

Pascal, Blaise, 226
pathos, 16, 238
Pauses, 149, 210
Pens, colors indicating importance of ideas, 35, 37
Periodical indexes, 97, *98*
Periodicals, 97
Personal experience, 93–94
Personal inventory, 47–48
Personification, 164
Perspective, 176–177; *see also* Worldview
Persuasive presentations, 55–56, 228–246
   action as purpose, 231
   adjustment of message, 83
   audience analysis, 231
   benefits, 236–237
   change, 236
   checklist, *243*
   conclusion, 234–235
   consistency, 236
   convincing as purpose, 231
   definition of, 229
   effective, 232–233, 236–237
   ethics, 242–243
   example of, *243*
   fallacies, 241–242
   individuals as producers and receivers of, 228–229
   informative versus, *229*
   inspiration as purpose, 230
   introduction, 234
   need fulfillment, 237–238
   organization, 234–235
   question of fact, 233
   question of policy, 234
   question of value, 233–234
   reasoning, 238–241
   responses, 232
Phrase search, *101*
Physical appearance, 135, 156–157
Physical characteristics of audience, 75–76
Pictures, 190–191, *191*
Pie charts, 189, *189*
Pitch, vocal, 150–151
Plagiarism
   detecting, 14–15
   ethical use of supporting materials, 111–112
   incremental, 112
   Internet and, 51, 112
Plato, 27
Pluck.com, 207
Policy, question of, 234, *262*, 262
Posters, 194
Post hoc fallacy, 242
Power, 255–256
PowerPoint, 185–194
   charts, 187–189
   flowcharts, 189
   pictures, 189–191
   special effects, 192, 198
   tables, 187
   text slides, 186
   tips, 192–193

tutorial, 186
video, 191–192
Practice
   basics of speaking, 143
   facial expression, 154
   gestures, 155
   importance of, 36
   multimedia symposium, 267
   pitch, 150
   PowerPoint, 194
   variations, 158
Preparation outline, 130–131
Presentations; *see also* Communication process; Group presentations; Public speaking
   cultural differences, 18
   delivery, 142–158
   demonstration, 39–40
   first, 37–40
   fundamentals (*see* Five Canons of Rhetoric)
   impromptu, 37
   organization, 118–128
   outlining, 128–133
   planning, 35–36
   presenting classmate, 38–39, 40–41
   presenting yourself, 38
   purpose, 54–59
   structure, 30
   three-step process basic to, 59–60
Presenters
   audience relationship to, 231
   relating topic to, 135, 205
   self-introduction presentations, 38
   as visual resource, 194–195
Presenting yourself, 38
Presidential addresses, 67
Primacy of information, 214
Principles of learning, 212–215
   building on what is known, 212
   humor and wit, 212–213
   organization of material, 214–215
   rewarding listeners, 215
   sensory aids, 214
Principles of outlining, 128, *130*
Problem questions, 263, *263*
Problem-solution pattern of main points, 124–125, 235
Problem solving, 261–265
   criteria, 263–264
   evaluating alternatives, 264–265
   identifying alternatives, 264
   ill-defined problems, 261
   wording the discussion question, 262–263
Process observer, 261
Process of communication; *see* Communication process
Projection, 151
Prometheus Unbound (Shelley), 166
Pronunciation, 151
Propaganda, 242
Public communication fundamentals; *see* Five Canons of Rhetoric
Public Opinion (Lippman), 171
Public opinion polls, 108

Public speaking; *see also* Presentations
   benefits, 6–7
   fear of, 5–6, 18–21
   features, 12–13
   fundamentals (*see* Five Canons of Rhetoric)
   popularity of, 7–8
   public communication versus, 26
Punishment power, 256
Purpose of presentations, 54–59
   general, 54–57
   information, 55
   persuasion, 55–56
   special occasion, 56–57
   specific, 57–58
   statements of, 57–58
   thesis statement, 58–59

Question-and-answer sessions, 157–158
Questionnaires, audience analysis through, 77–79, *78*; *see also* Surveys
Question of fact, 233, *262*, 262
Question of policy, 234, 262, *262*
Question of value, 233–234, 262, *262*
Questions, 136, 207–208
The Quill, 174
Quotations, 110, 134, 136, 239–240

Racial conflict, groups used for addressing, 268
Rashi, 116
Rate, 148–149
Reading presentation, avoidance of, 33–34
Reagan, Ronald, 13, 58, 67, 134
Reasoning, 238–242
   from cause, 240
   deductive, 239
   fallacies in, 241–242
   from generalization, 240
   hard evidence, 239
   inductive, 238
   from sign, 240
   soft evidence, 239–240
Rebuttal presentations, 270
Receiver, in communication process, 9
Recency of information, 214
Reference librarian, 96
Reference Resources at Yahoo!, 103
References, 131
Referent power, 256
Relationship, of audience to presenter, 231
Repetition, 175, 210
Research, 92–112
   benefits, 92–93
   citing information sources, 105–106
   ethical use of supporting materials, 111–112
   evaluating information sources, 104–105
   finding information sources, 94–104
   presentation preparation process, *93*
   supporting materials, 106–111
Responsibility, group presentations and, 256

Reward power, 256
Rewards, for audience, 215
Rhetoric; *see also* Five Canons of Rhetoric
  invitational, 34
Rhythm, speaking, 150
Roget's International Thesaurus, 173
Roosevelt, Franklin, 67
RSS (Really Simple Syndication) feeds, 101, 207
Rumi, Mevlana, 44

Safire, William, 173
Sajak, Pat, 205
Sample speech, 40–41
San Antonio College, 206
Sanger, Margaret, 24
Sapir-Whorf hypothesis, 166
Scanners, 190
Search engines, 49–51, 98–102, *99*
SearchGov, 102
Searching for topic; *see* Topic search
Seinfeld, Jerry, 5
Selecting a topic; *see* Topic selection
Self-assessment, positive versus negative, *20*
Self-centered functions of behavior, 258, *259*
Self-disclosure, 135
Self-introduction presentations, 38
Self-managed work teams, 254
Semanticists, 167
Sensory aids; *see also* Visual resources
  benefits, 184–185
  as learning tools, 214
  tips, 197–199
Sentence outline, 131, *132–133*
Sexist language, 171
Shelley, Percy, 166
Sign, reasoning from, 240
Significance of presentation, 53
Signposts, 128
Simplification, 13, 172
Situation, 10
  environment, 79–80
  importance, 81
  occasion, 80
  size of audience, 79
  speaking rate and, 149
  time, 81
Slang, 171
Slide transparencies, 196
Small group communication, 252
Small groups
  definition of, 252–253
  value of, 253–255
Smiling, 154
Smith, D. C., 166
Soft evidence, 239–240
Solution questions, *263*, 263
Soukhanov, A. H., 174
Source, in communication process, 8–9
Source credibility, 15–16
  common ground, 16
  competence, 16
  dynamism, 16

persuasive presentations, 234
  trustworthiness, 16
Sources of information; *see* Information sources
Southern Poverty Law Center, 268
Spatial relations pattern of main points, 121–122
Speakers; *see* Presenters
Special occasion presentations, 56–57, A-1–A-9
  commemoration, A-6
  dedication, A-6
  entertainment, A-7
  example of, A-8–A-9
  formality, A-3–A-4
  introduction, A-5
  nomination, A-5–A-6
  organization, A-3
  preparation, A-7–A-8
  purpose, A-2
  style, A-2–A-3
  tribute, A-4–A-5
  welcoming, A-4
Specific numbers, 233
Speeches; *see* Presentations
Spoken language, 169, *170*; *see also* Oral cultures
Stanton, Elizabeth Cady, 58
Statistics, as supporting materials, 110, 233
Status quo, 270
Stereotyping
  age, 69
  definition of, 171
  disabilities, 76
Stories; *see* Narratives
Style, as fundamental skill, 31–32
Style guides, 105, *106*
A Style Manual for Communication Majors (Bourhis, Adams, Titsworth), 131
Subject matter competence, 53
Subordinate ideas, 210, 214–215
Subordination, principle of, *129*, 129
Substitution, as articulation problem, *152*
SUNY Plattsburgh, 205
Supporting materials, 106–111; *see also* Evidence; Information sources
  analogies, 110–111
  definition of, 106
  definitions as, 111
  ethical use, 111–112
  examples, 107–108
  for main points, 127, 214–215
  numbers and statistics, 110
  surveys, 108–109
  testimony, 109
Surveys, as supporting material, 108–109; *see also* Questionnaires
Symbolic nature of language, 164–165
Symposia
  cultural, 267
  current issue, 266–267
  definition of, 265
  multimedia, 267
  teaching, 268
Synonyms, 173

Tables, *187*, 187
Tailoring of presentation, 54
Task functions of behavior, 258, *259*
Teaching symposium, 268
Technology (vital topic of), 13, 55, 56, 92, 94, 105, 107, 187, 217, 218, 219–222
Testimony, 109, 233
Text slides, 186, *186*
Thesaurus, 173
Thesis statement, 58–59
  characteristics of good, 59
  three-step process to, 59–60
Thoreau, Henry David, 226
Three-step process basic to presentations, 59–60
Time
  brevity best for speeches, 13
  delivery and, 148–150
  impact of, 80–81
Timeliness of presentation, 53–54
Time-sequence pattern of main points, 121
Topical sequence pattern of main points, 124, 235
Topic evaluation, 52–54
  appropriateness for audience, 53
  appropriateness for occasion, 53–54
  appropriateness for speaker, 52–53
  guidelines, *54*
  topics to avoid, 14–15
Topics; *see also* Topic evaluation; Topic search; Topic selection; Vital topics
  current, 13, 49
  important, 13
  relating audience to, 135, 205–206
  relating presenter to, 135, 205
  relevant, 15
  three-step process from, 59–60
  useful, 14
Topic search, 46–51
  brainstorming, 47
  current topic identification, 49
  getting started on, 51
  Internet searching, 15, 49–51, 92
  personal inventory, 47–48
Topic selection, guidelines for, 13–14, 51–52
Transitions, 127–128
Translation of ideas, 82–83
Transposition, as articulation problem, *152*
Tribute, presentations for, A-4–A-5
Trustworthiness, role in source credibility, 16
Twain, Mark, 140
Two-sided arguments, 112

United Nations, 75
University of Cincinnati, 267

Value, question of, 233–234, *262*, 262
Van Gogh, Theo, 162
Verbal messages, 9
Video, 191–192, 196
Video converters, 191

Index   I–7

Virtual libraries, 99
Visual aids, 184
Visual resources, 184–199
  benefits, 184–185
  charts, 187–189
  electronic, 185–186
  ethics, 198
  flowcharts, 189
  gaining audience's attention, 134
  handouts, 197
  hiding, when not in use, 193–194, 199
  language evocative of images, 174
  models, 195–196
  multimedia, 185–186
  objects, 195
  overhead transparencies, 197
  pictures, 190–191
  PowerPoint, 185–194
  presenters as, 194–195
  purpose, 199
  slide transparencies, 196
  tables, 187
  text slides, 186
  tips, 197–199
  video, 191–192

Vital topics
  definition of, 13
  on the Web, 15
  and persuasive presentations, 231
Vocalized pause, 149
Voice, 148–152
  duration, 149–150
  enunciation, 151
  fluency, 152
  pauses, 149
  pitch, 150–151
  rate, 148–149
  rhythm, 150
  volume, 151
Volume, vocal, 151

Waitley, Denis, 44
Webster, Daniel, 162
Wedding as Text (Leeds-Hurwitz), A-3
Weddings, A-3
Welcoming, presentations for, A-4
Will, George, 172
Wilson, Woodrow, 67
Wit, 212–213
Woods, Tiger, *135*

Words; *see also* Language
  abstract versus concrete, 167
  denotative versus connotative, 168
  word choice, 172–175, *175*
Word stemming, *101*
Work, public speaking as aid in, 6–7
Working outline, 131
Worldview; *see also* Perspective
  of audience, 74–75
  language as shaping, 166–167
World Wide Web; *see* Internet
Worst-case scenarios, 5–6
Wright, Bob, 206
Written language, 169, *170; see also*
  Literary cultures
The WWW Library, 104

Yahoo!, *50–51*, 99, *100*
Yahoo! Regional, 104

Zimmerman, Teena, 193